CORRECTION CHART: GRAMMAR, PUNCTUATION, MECHANICS, EFFECTIVE SENTENCES

abb	error in abbreviation (24)
ad	incorrect use of adjective or adverb (8)
agr	lack of agreement (6)
cap	incorrect capitalization (21)
case	pronoun case error (7)
cs	comma splice (4)
dm	dangling modifier (26)
frag	sentence fragment (3)
ill	illogical construction (29)
ital	incorrect use or omission of italics (22)
mp	misplaced parts (27)
nu	numeral or spelled-out number (23)
/ /	faulty parallelism (28)
punc	punctuation error
,	comma (9)
;	semicolon (10)
:	colon (11)
—	dash (12)
.	period (13)
?	question mark (14)
!	exclamation point (15)
“ ”	quotation marks (16)
’	apostrophe (17)
-	hyphen (18)
( )	parentheses (19)
[ ]	brackets (20)
ref	faulty pronoun reference (31)
ro	run-on sentence (5)
shift	shift (30)
shift/t	shift in tense (30a)
shift/m	shift in mood (30b)
shift/p	shift in person (30c)
shift/v	shift in voice (30d)
shift/d	shift in discourse (30e)
sub	subordination error or subordination needed (25)

FOURTH EDITION

RHETORIC

MADE PLAIN

FOURTH EDITION

ANTHONY C. WINKLER

JO RAY McCUEN
Glendale College

HARCOURT BRACE JOVANOVICH, PUBLISHERS

San Diego New York Chicago Atlanta Washington, D.C.
London Sydney Toronto

ISBN: 0-15-577079-9
Library of Congress Catalog Card Number: 83-81889
Printed in the United States of America

Preface

The title of this book, *Rhetoric Made Plain,* describes its authors' aim—to present the principles of rhetoric as concretely as possible, to illustrate every idea with practical examples, and to practice the art of clear writing which the book attempts to teach.

The organization of its chapters is simple: each is based on a question student writers should ask themselves during the prewriting and writing process. Each chapter then focuses on answering the question through explanation, example, and exercises. We prescribe both a step-by-step prewriting method—finding a voice, formulating a thesis, and organizing and outlining the topic; and a writing method—getting from outline to paragraphs, finding the right word, and revising the final essay.

This Fourth Edition, above all else, tries to come to grips with the *realities* of writing. Every English teacher knows that many principles of composition are more honored in the breach than the observance by professional writers. Nor has this fact escaped the notice of students, who often ask why. In this edition of *Rhetoric Made Plain* we close the gap between principles and practice in a novel way: to each of the chapters in Parts 1 and 2 we have added a subsection titled "Applications." Here we examine the difference between classroom principles and real-world practice. For example, the Application at the end of Chapter 3 deals with the explicit thesis, which student writers are forced to use, and the implicit thesis, which professional writers often use. We explain the difference between the two and offer a justification of the classroom practice. Other Application topics include "Role-playing on Paper," "Rhetorical Patterns and the Essay Exam," and "Form and Function in the Paragraph."

Even without this new section, the Fourth Edition of *Rhetoric Made Plain* would still be a substantial revision. We have completely rewritten two chapters—Chapter 1, "What Is Rhetoric?," and Chapter 2, "What Should I Sound Like?"—to make them more practical and useful. To Chapter 5, "How Do I Get from Outline to Paragraph?," we have added a full discussion of beginning and concluding paragraphs. We have also substantially revised Chapter 7, "What Is the Right Word?," and Chapter 11, "Writing about Literature."

Chapter 10, "The Research Paper," has been rewritten to conform with the latest documentation style—parenthetical references—of the Modern Language Association. This style has been voted on, accepted, and is currently in use in *PMLA*, but as of this writing has not yet been promulgated in the

MLA Handbook. Thus, three alternative styles of documentation are discussed: footnotes, endnotes, and the new parenthetical style now favored by MLA. Chapter 10 also includes a new research paper on an appealing topic—Agatha Christie's hero, Hercule Poirot.

Finally, the grammatical explanations in the Handbook have been expanded and many new examples added. In so doing, we have had the advantage of valued criticism from many of our colleagues. Especially helpful to us were reviews by Professors MariLyn Beaney, Leigh Holmes, Bette B. Lansdown, and S. A. Newell, all of Cameron University, Oklahoma, to whom we offer our thanks.

Anthony C. Winkler
Jo Ray McCuen

Contents

FOURTH EDITION

RHETORIC

MADE PLAIN

Part ONE

Prewriting

1
What is rhetoric?

Definitions of rhetoric
Audience and purpose
Writing as a process

Application: The "Fog Index" of clarity

Exercises

The mind travels faster than the pen;
consequently, writing becomes a question
of learning to make occasional wing shots,
bringing down the bird of thought
as it flashes by. A writer is a gunner,
sometimes waiting in his blind for something
to come in, sometimes roaming the
countryside hoping to scare something up.

—E. B. White

THE QUESTION FORMING THE TITLE of this chapter is seldom asked outside English classes. Millions have never even heard of the word *rhetoric*; to this number must be added the other millions who have heard it but do not know its meaning. Yet though many may be ignorant about rhetoric, few escape its influence. Advertisers use the principles of rhetoric to sell products, politicians to win votes, mothers to scold children—to name a few of the nearly limitless uses to which rhetoric is daily put. "In its most general significance," wrote the critic and educator Mortimer Adler, "rhetoric is involved in every situation in which communication takes place between men."[1]

Definitions of rhetoric

But what does "rhetoric" mean? Rhetoric is the art of putting one's case in the strongest and best possible way. All those strategies of communicating in speech and writing that we all use every day in an attempt to sway each other come under its heading, with practical effects so many and widespread that we take them for granted. When we open a popular novel we expect it to be plainly written, with ordinary words framed into speakable sentences. We do not expect it to sound like this sentence from a report by a Chicago economist:

> The unanticipated rebound in consumer spending in the third quarter of 1979, which more than regained the ground lost in the second quarter's decline, has combined with the shift in monetary policy announced in early October to change significantly the configura-

[1]Mortimer Adler, *How to Read a Book* (1939).

> tion of activity during 1980, although the full year results will not differ greatly from the forecast issued in September as part of the long range plan background material.[2]

Because of rhetoric, cookbooks are not written like legal contracts, insurance policies do not read like love letters, and love letters do not sound like State of the Union speeches. Yet there is no law that this should be so. It is merely the effect of rhetoric—a combination of audience expectation and writers' desire to please that operates like a force of nature. No doubt there are badly written cookbooks, but few are either published or read; pompous lovers have trouble multiplying, and flippant insurance companies go bankrupt. This desire of writers to please—to communicate with their audience—is the basic law of rhetoric.

But it is a law of which students are generally unaware. Most of their number regard grammar, not rhetoric, as the ruling principle of good writing. The difference between grammar and rhetoric is simple enough. Grammar tells a writer where words go, what idioms mean, how sentences should be framed. Just as drivers obey the rules of the road, writers follow the rules of grammar. They know that they should not begin a sentence with "one" and then suddenly switch to "you," as in "One must try to do well or you will be embarrassed." That is called a shift in point of view and, like most grammatical lapses, tends to muddy a writer's meaning. While grammar speaks in terms of right or wrong, rhetoric speaks in terms of better or worse. When you know the rules of grammar, it is easy to say if two passages you've written are grammatically right or wrong. But it is far harder to say whether the first version is better or worse than the second.

Yet that is exactly what you must learn to do if you wish to write well. Of course, you must write grammatically: you shouldn't dangle your participles or muddle the antecedents of your pronouns. But writing grammatically is only the first step; the next step is to write effectively. And this is where grammar ends and rhetoric begins. Now you must think rhetorically about your work. Take, for example, this student paragraph:

> During high school, my favorite English course was English literature. Literature was not only interesting, but it was also fun. Learning about writers and poets of the past was enjoyable because of the teachers I had and the activities they scheduled. Teachers made past literature interesting because they could relate the writers back into the time in which they were living. This way I not only learned about English writers but also about English history.

[2]Quoted in William E. Blundell, "Confused, Overstuffed Corporate Writing Often Costs Firms Much Time—and Money," *The Wall Street Journal*, 28 Aug. 1980.

Grammatically, this is correct; rhetorically it is empty. It cries out for examples, for supporting detail. Which writers and poets did the student find so interesting? What activities did her teacher schedule to make them seem so? Without such details, the paragraph is repetitive, shallow, and monotonous.

The fact is that the vast majority of teachers—and readers—judge writing not on its grammar, but on its effectiveness. They take the viewpoint of Cicero, the Roman orator and statesman, who declared, "People do not praise an orator for correct grammar. They only laugh at him if his grammar is bad." No rule of grammar calls for the use of supporting detail in a paragraph, but it is a central principle of rhetoric. And if you do not observe it in your writing, your papers will seem empty and dull no matter how correct your grammar.

Audience and purpose

How do you learn to think rhetorically about your writing? First, you bear in mind two truths about writing: it has an audience; it is done for a purpose. Knowing who will read your writing tells you what kind of language to use; knowing why you are writing tells you what you must do. For instance, if you were to write a letter to the deputy district attorney of your city, asking him to excuse you from testifying at a trial, you would write in concise, impersonal English. On the other hand, if you were confiding musings of loneliness to your diary, you might allow yourself to digress and to become emotional. In the former case your audience is a critical public officer and your purpose is to get a request granted. In the latter case your audience is your indulgent self and the purpose is to unload frustrations. Between these two extremes lie myriad shades of other audiences and purposes, each requiring the proper kind of writing.

Mainly, audience and purpose give a writer a useful and necessary *context* for writing. Context hints at what might work and what might flop; it warns of perils and points to possible breakthroughs. Anyone knows that a letter to a child must be written in simple words and short sentences, and that a note of sympathy to a grieving friend should not be flippant—anyone, that is, who thinks about the effect of the words being written. As the English writer W. Somerset Maugham put it, "To write good prose is an affair of good manners." For like good manners, good prose is always appropriate. It fits the audience; it suits the purpose. This fitting and suiting of one's writing to the occasion are the concerns of rhetoric.

Is any of this discussion applicable to the kind of writing freshmen do? Every bit of it is. In many ways, the burden on the freshman writer is the heaviest of all. For every word the freshman writes exposes him or her to a possible scolding. Even under the best circumstances, it is difficult for a writer to produce work to be fed directly to a critic. Yet that is exactly what student writers must do—and weekly at that. The second problem faced by student writers is with the context of their writing assignments—or rather, with the lack of one. In the real world of business or pleasure, context occurs naturally with an assignment. If you are instructed by your boss to write a memo, you are told to whom and why. But for whom do you write your essays and why? The natural context for writing enjoyed by the professional has suddenly been replaced by a manufactured one. Your writing is for your teacher; its purpose is to earn you a grade. Every word you write will be subject to judgment. This is the worst possible situation for a writer.

Yet in another sense, it is the best situation in which to learn the art of rhetoric. As a student writer, you are faced daily with an unchanging audience over the course of the term to whose tastes you must learn to adapt. The assignments are varied, requiring you to conceive of a secondary guiding purpose for them other than the larger one of getting through the course. The feedback is immediate: you immediately know what you have done right or wrong. And the opportunities for correction and improvement are many: you always have the next essay in which to sharpen your rhetorical skills.

Writing as a process

Learning to write well is a mystifying process that cannot be mastered by rote the way you might ingest facts about the anatomy of a fish or the chemistry of a nebula. It involves learning a *process*, and that is always harder to do than memorizing a set of facts. The parts of a bicycle can be memorized from a manual, but no one can learn to ride a bicycle merely by reading a book about it. *Scribendo disces scribere* says the Latin proverb—"You learn to write by writing."

Laboratory research has recently made some discoveries about the process of writing. Here are the chief ones:

1. *Composing is a laborious, back-and-forth process.* Most writers compose in a halting, lurching way. A writer will pen a few sentences, pause to go back and revise them, compose several new sentences, and then pause again to reread and edit further before continuing with the paragraph. "In their thinking and their writing," says one researcher, "writers 'go back' in order to push thought forward."[3]

[3]Faye Peitzman, "What's Wrong with Our Composition Teaching?" in *In the Trenches: Help for Newly Recruited, Shellshocked, and Battle-Fatigued Teachers of Writing* (Los Angeles: University of California, 1982).

Any professional writer will recognize the truth of this observation, but often it comes as a revelation to students who tend to worry when their own compositions emerge by similar fits and starts. Be assured that this back-and-forth movement is a healthy and normal part of composing. Researcher Sondra Perl suggests that writers who accept the halting, stumbling nature of composing actually have an easier time with this necessary process of "waiting, looking, and discovering" than those who fight against it.[4]

2. *The topic can make a difference in your writing.* Professional or amateur, few writers are entirely free to choose their own topics. Most have topics assigned to them by employers, peers, circumstances. Yet when choice does exist, the lesson from both common sense and research is that you should always pick the topic you like the best. The fact is that most people write better when they write about a subject that appeals to them.

It is no mystery why this should be so. We all try harder when we are engaged in a labor of love—whether building our dream house or writing an essay. Unfortunately, many students are content to settle for the topic that seems simplest to research or easiest to write about regardless of whether or not they find it appealing. It is a mistake to do so. Summarizing the effect of topic-enthusiasm on student writers, Faye Peitzman says that when students write for their own enjoyment, they "behave more like experienced writers" than when they are forced to write.[5]

3. *Your writing will not automatically improve with each essay.* In its application to writing improvement, the adage "Practice makes perfect" must be somewhat modified. Practice will eventually make your writing better, but not necessarily right away. You may earn an "A" on your second paper and a "C" on your fifth. Yet the lower grade is no reason to despair, for it is a mistake to assume that your writing must automatically improve with every assignment. The earlier paper may have required only a simple structure and treatment, while the later paper may have been more complex and therefore harder to do.

The point is that writing cannot be compared to an endeavor such as swimming, in which progressive improvement can be expected with every lap swum. It is more realistic to compare writing to a sport like archery. The first arrow might hit the bull's-eye while the tenth might entirely miss the target. An archer's overall accuracy will gradually improve with practice, but never to the point of absolute certainty for any one arrow. In practical terms, this simply means that you shouldn't brood if you find a later essay turning out worse than an earlier one. Your overall writing skills are bound to improve, even if the improvement isn't reflected in any single essay.

[4]Sondra Perl, "Five Writers Writing: The Composing Processes of Unskilled College Writers," Diss. New York University 1978.

[5]Peitzman, "What's Wrong with Our Composition Teaching?"

Application: The "Fog Index" of clarity

Clarity inevitably begins in the classroom. Here and now is the place to practice it in your own prose. The question is, how can you tell if your own prose is murky or clear? The answer is to measure its readability.

Experts agree that two factors more than any others affect the clarity of writing: word usage and sentence length. Long sentences are harder to read than short ones: unfamiliar words are harder to understand than familiar ones. The "Fog Index," invented by Robert Gunning, is the simplest way of measuring readability. Its score corresponds to the grade level of the writing sample. To find the fog index of a passage do the following:

1. Take a sample of about 100 words. Find the average number of words per sentence, treating independent clauses as separate sentences. (Example: "She went to the dentist; she did some shopping; she took a taxi home." Count as three sentences.)
2. Calculate the percentage of words with three or more syllables in the sample. Don't count proper names, easy combinations like "pawnbroker," or verbs that reach three syllables by the addition of *-es* or *-ed*.
3. Add the average number of words per sentence to the percentage of difficult words and multiply the total by 0.4. The score represents the sample's grade level of difficulty. For a long work, average the scores obtained from several samples.[6]

Here is an example of a Fog Index score calculated from a freshman's paper on Keats:

> The *poetry* of Keats possesses an *ethereal quality* removed from *reality* yet still *containing* questions as to the *validity* of *reality*. Keats uses poetry as a *vehicle* to convey himself away from the pain of his *existence*, to promote the ideal *qualities* of life seen in *mythology* and legend. This *fanciful chariot* of *imagery* removes him from *reality* and allows him to question his values without *undermining* his ideals.

The passage contains 69 words in three sentences, for an average of 23 words per sentence. Its percentage of difficult words is 24.6. The Fog Index is $23 + 24.6 \times 0.4$ = grade 19+—harder than the essays found in *Atlantic*, *Harper's*, *Time*, and *Newsweek*, according to Gunning's survey of popular magazines.

[6]Robert Gunning, *The Technique of Clear Writing* (New York: McGraw-Hill, 1968).

But is the sample harder because it is deep or because the writing is murky? Students often confuse the two—a murky style with deep thinking. The paradox of writing is that most of the time only clear prose can be truly deep; otherwise, what may seem like a profound idea may, in fact, be merely an obscure sentence. Most readability experts believe that even technical material need not exceed a 13th-grade level. Simplicity of style is found in the work of most major writers. J. D. Salinger's novel *Catcher in the Rye* has a fog index of 6; Somerset Maugham's biography, *The Summing Up*, an index of 10. On the other hand, the eligibility section of the food-stamp act—hardly a profound document—has an index of 26.41.

Applied to your own writing, the Fog Index can tell you if you're being clear or cloudy. The examples below—versions of a popular nursery rhyme—will give you a notion about the range of styles represented by the above numbers:

> It has come to our attention that an elderly female, whose place of residence is a leather foot covering, has dependents who are so numerous that she fails to comprehend the proper course of action she should pursue. (As a bureaucrat might write it; Fog Index: 22.6)
>
> Sources report that an old woman living in a shoe has so many offspring she can't decide about how to cope with her family. (As a newspaper might write it; Fog Index: 11.3)
>
> There was an old woman who lived in a shoe. She had so many children, she didn't know what to do. (The original; Fog Index: 4.2)[7]

Of course, the point is not to write by numbers, but to write clearly. A test such as the Fog Index is best used as a guide to revising. Occasionally, we all use a big word when a little one would do, or write a long sentence when two or three short ones would be clearer. If nothing else, the Fog Index will remind you that bigger and longer are not always better. This is a useful rule to remember when you are revising your work.

EXERCISES

1. After studying the following paragraphs, suggest the purpose of each paragraph and the audience for which it is intended. Give specific examples of language suitable to that audience.

   a. At first our Greg was a model child. Healthy, happy, unfailingly sweet-tempered, he was a total joy as a baby. When he was one year

[7]Gayle White, "Ever Wonder Why You're in a Fog?" *Atlanta Constitution*, 10 Oct. 1978.

old, he thought that everything mother and father wanted him to do was wonderful. His second birthday passed, and he remained cooperative and adorable. Aha, I thought, the "terrible twos" that everyone complains about must result from inadequate attention and discipline.

Then Greg turned 2¾ years old. Suddenly we had an obnoxious monster in the house. His favorite word was "No!" and he used it constantly. At the simplest request he would stamp his feet and cry. It took a battle to get him to put on clothing he had previously worn happily. Favorite foods were thrown on the floor. It became almost impossible to take him shopping because he would lie down in the store and refuse to move. There was constant tension in the house, and my husband and I became irritable, too. We felt as if we were living on the slopes of a volcano, and we found ourselves giving in to Greg too much in order to avoid the threatened eruptions.

b. Others will debate the controversial issues, national and international, which divide men's minds. But serene, calm, aloof, you stand as the nation's war guardians, as its lifeguards from the raging tides of international conflict, as its gladiators in the arena of battle. For a century-and-a-half you have defended, guarded, and protected its hallowed traditions of liberty and freedom, of right and justice.

Let civilian voices argue the merits or demerits of our processes of government: whether our strength is being sapped by deficit financing indulged in too long; by federal paternalism grown too mighty; by power groups grown too arrogant; by politics grown too corrupt; by crime grown too rampant; by morals grown too low; by taxes grown too high; by extremists grown too violent; whether our personal liberties are as firm and complete as they should be.

These great national problems are not for your professional participation or military solution. Your guidepost stands out like a tenfold beacon in the night: duty, honor, country.

c. To give Eleanor her due, any suspicion as to the slightest inclination on her part toward Mr. Slope was a wrong to her. She had no more idea of marrying Mr. Slope than she had of marrying the bishop, and the idea that Mr. Slope would present himself as a suitor had never occurred to her. Indeed, to give her her due again, she had never thought about suitors since her husband's death. But nevertheless it was true that she had overcome all that repugnance to the man which was so strongly felt for him by the rest of the Grantly faction. She had forgiven him his sermon. She had forgiven him his low church tendencies, his Sabbath schools, and puritanical observances. She had forgiven his pharisaical arrogance, and even his greasy face and oily vulgar manners. Having agreed to overlook such offences as these, why should she not in time be taught to regard Mr. Slope as a suitor?

d. Earthquakes are often accompanied by a roaring noise that comes from the bowels of the earth. This phenomenon was known to early geographers. Pliny wrote that earthquakes are "preceded or accompanied by a terrible sound." Vaults supporting the ground give way and it seems as though the earth heaves deep sighs. The sound was attributed to the gods and called theophany.

The eruptions of volcanoes are also accompanied by loud noises. The sound produced by Krakatoa in the East Indies, during the eruption of 1883, was so loud that it was heard as far as Japan, 3,000 miles away, the farthest distance travelled by sound recorded in modern annals.

e. I beg you to excuse a father who dares to approach you in the interests of his son.

I wish to mention first that my son is 22 years old, has studied for four years at the Zurich Polytechnic and last summer brilliantly passed his diploma examinations in mathematics and physics. Since then he has tried unsuccessfully to find a position as assistant, which would enable him to continue his education in theoretical and experimental physics. Everybody who is able to judge praises his talent, and in any case I can assure you that he is exceedingly assiduous and industrious and is attached to his science with a great love.

f. Letters written by a potential customer asking suppliers for free materials, information, or routine services are among the easiest to write. The customer will usually receive what he or she is asking for since it is to the supplier's advantage to provide it. The potential customer need only be clear and courteous. In writing routine request letters, give all the information the supplier will need in order to be really helpful, keep your request as brief as possible without omitting important details, and express your wishes courteously and tactfully.

2. Write two different one-page essays explaining the reasons why you wish to pursue a certain career. Address the first to the personnel manager of an organization that might hire you and the second to your father. Contrast the language and phrasing of each essay and explain the differences between them.

3. The following letters both refuse credit to a potential customer. How does the second differ in purpose from the first?

a. Please accept our regrets that we cannot offer you a 60-day credit for the meeting of your organization here at Pine Lodge in July of 1984. When you held your meeting here last year, we had the embarrassing experience of having to wait six months before you made full payment on your bill. I am sure that you will understand that we cannot take chances on such bad credit risks.

b. Thank you for choosing Pine Lodge again for your 1984 meeting. We consider it a pleasure to have you, although we must ask you to send us a 25% deposit and to make full settlement when you check out. This is now our standard arrangement with organizations similar to yours. If these arrangements are satisfactory, we shall do our best to make sure that your group is extended every courtesy and service during its stay.

4. A restaurant owner has sent the following memorandum to the waiters and waitresses working for him. Rewrite the memo to create a more positive tone, without destroying its purpose.

   To: All waiters and waitresses

   I've had it with you lazy clowns! This month's profits fell 20% below last year's at this same time. Now, any fool can tell that the problem is your sloppy service to the customers, your excessive breaking of china and glassware, and your horsing around instead of paying attention to such details as keeping the food warm, setting the tables properly, and getting the customer's order straight. So, I'm warning you: either start doing your job right, or you'll find yourselves fired.

5. Assuming an educated audience, label the purpose of the following passages as (1) to inspire, (2) to get action, (3) to amuse, (4) to inform.

   a. Please send us either a check within the next week or an explanation if some problem has arisen. We are eager to cooperate with you.
   b. Conscience is a sacred sanctuary where God alone may enter as judge.
   c. In great straits, and when hope is small, the boldest counsels are the safest.
   d. Men seldom make passes
      At girls who wear glasses.
   e. The more one comes to know men, the more one admires the dog.
   f. "Gavelkind" is the custom of having all of the sons of an estate holder share equally in the estate upon the death of the father. Most of the lands in England were held in gavelkind tenure prior to the Norman Conquest.
   g. Seek not the favor of the multitude; it is seldom got by honest and lawful means. But seek the testimony of few; and number not voices, but weigh them.
   h. Botticelli isn't a wine, you dunce! Botticelli is a cheese.

i. The Indus River is approximately 1,900 miles long. It rises in the Kailas range of Tibet, flows west across Kashmir, India, and then moves southwest to the Arabian Sea.
j. Flaming manifestoes and prophecies of doom are no longer much help, and a search for scapegoats can only make matters worse. The time for sensations and manifestoes is about over. Now we need rigorous analysis, united effort, and very hard work.

2

What should I sound like?

When we see a natural style,
we are quite surprised and delighted,
for we expected to see an author and find a man.

—Blaise Pascal

BE THYSELF IN THY WRITING: that is the gist of this chapter. Be yourself in a letter to your mother; be yourself in an essay for your teacher. Don't try to sound impressive or to write in a voice that is not naturally your own. Consider, for instance, this passage from a student essay:

> The teacher played a colossal and major role in my absorption of English. Through his immense knowledge, he helped in the training of my mind and conditioning to proper English and literature usage. And with his keen wit, he made the class and the subject seem replete with liveliness and enjoyment.

Asked to express this idea in his everyday language, the student said: "I enjoyed the class because my teacher knew the subject and made it lively and enjoyable." Why didn't he write that? The student replied, "Because it would have been too simple."

But what he said was better than what he wrote. It was better because it was clearer and more direct, had the simplicity of speech, and altogether lacked the pompousness of his writing. As we pointed out in Chapter 1, many gifted writers do write simply, in what has been called the plain or familiar style. It is a style of writing that, as the English essayist William Hazlitt put it, uses language "as an unvarnished medium to convey ideas." It is writing whose first aim is to say something clearly.

The dark side of freshman composition is that many students are not content to be themselves in their papers, to truly express their own opinions in their own voices. Many believe that they must write English papers in a voice other than their natural one. Most of us have laboriously acquired our voice through years of schooling and use—with minor variations—on relatives, acquaintances, friends, and teachers. We can be more formal or less, choosing to write in longer or shorter sentences or to use bigger or smaller words, but when we try to write outside our natural voice we lose our sense of proportion: we become stilted, pedantic, and literary—in the negative sense of the word.

It is so with many students. They do not use the simple word if a difficult one occurs to them. They will not make a point straightforwardly if they can find a way to make it roundabout. Why? Surely one reason is that students are trying to write in a style they think will appeal to an English teacher.

As a group, few people have been more rigidly stereotyped than English teachers. There may be a few English teachers who are obsessively prim and proper in speech and writing—who value form over content, who love big words and starchy sentences, and who are unforgiving of the slightest error of grammar—but most are very different. What most English teachers value is clear writing—writing that says what the writer wants to say without flourish or pretense. If the writer is also sensible and stylish, so much the better. But practice clarity in your writing and you will please your teacher.

What can you do to write in a clear, unpretentious voice? We have a few suggestions to offer.

Aim for an oral writing style

Try to project the simplicity and straightforwardness of speech into your prose. The point is that all of us—even the professional writer—speak more than we write. All of us learned to speak before we learned to write. Our language skills are grounded in the spoken word and sentence. When we write, we are venturing into unfamiliar territory. Peering silently at the words on the page cannot give you a true feel for the way your writing sounds. You must read it aloud. Sham and pretense are always easier to detect on the tongue than on the page.

But the style of oral language permits no pretense. It is direct and straightforward. It does not use terribly long sentences because we cannot easily speak such monsters and breathe at the same time, nor can our listener readily understand them. Oral language uses simple words because of the need to utter them. In contrast, stuffy writing is never oral. It is language utterly removed from the natural rhythms of speech. Its sentences are written without regard for breathing, its words chosen without respect for the tongue. Ernest Boyer, a former U.S. Commissioner of Education, received the following memo from a member of his department:

> This office's activities during the year were primarily continuing their primary functions of education of the people to acquaint them of their needs, problems and alternate problem solutions, in order

> that they can make wise decisions in planning and implementing a total program that will best meet the needs of the people, now and in the future.[1]

As Boyer commented, "In a million years you would never say that on the phone. The other person would say, 'He's gone mad.'"

But should you try to write exactly the way you talk? Well, not exactly. There are, after all, basic differences between speaking and writing. In speech you can use nonverbal cues to show transitions from one idea to another—you can gesture or raise your eyebrows—but in writing you cannot. Writers must use more formal transitions, mechanical links such as "moreover," "however," or "in fact." Speakers also have the advantage of feedback, which writers do not. For instance, speakers can watch for clues as to whether their audience likes and understands what they are saying, whereas writers have no such advantage. So the voice you project onto the page cannot be the voice you'd use in a casual chat with a friend. As Hazlitt said:

> To write a genuine familiar or truly English style, is to write as any one would speak in common conversation, who had a thorough command and choice of words, or who could discourse with ease, force, and perspicuity, setting aside all pedantic and oratorical flourishes.

In other words, what you should aim for is the voice you would use in a serious conversation with someone you like, admire, and respect.

Say what you really mean

In 1979, after the near disaster of the Three Mile Island nuclear plant, the National Council of Teachers of English conferred its Doublespeak Award on the nuclear industry. Publicists of the industry described fire as "rapid oxidation" and explosion as an "energetic disassembly." Plutonium did not contaminate, it "took up residence." (Doublespeak, as these examples make clear, is evasiveness in writing and speech.) "We wanted to keep our jobs," confessed a writer for the industry.

A great deal of bad writing is caused by this kind of indirectness. The motive for it is the same in nearly every case: its writers feel insecure and timid about an opinion and try to play it safe by not being committed to a particular point of view. Here is an example, taken from a student analysis of a poem:

[1] "The State of the Language, 1977," *Time*, 2 Jan. 1978.

> In conclusion, one could say that this is a very farfetched poem—but one could also say that this is a very realistic poem with a lot of depth and continuity.

This is plainly an attempt to play it safe: the writer giveth and taketh away in the same breath. But since "farfetched" and "realistic" are nearly opposites, one opinion cancels out the other. Under the illusion of having said something, the student in fact has said nothing. Rather than write with such timidity, you're better off saying what you really think. All you have to do then is support your views, which later chapters will show you how to do.

Avoid "collegese"

"Collegese" refers to student writing that is crammed with buzzwords picked up from various disciplines. The suffix *-ese* added to a noun denotes the language or dialect of a certain region or group. People from Brooklyn, for example, are said to speak "Brooklynese," and bureaucrats are accused of writing "bureaucratese." Such dialects are not easily understood by someone outside the particular group.

Stricken with collegese, the student writes about "ego needs" (from psychology), "dyadic relationships" (from sociology), or the need to "interface" or to "maximize gains" (from business courses). Here are some examples of collegese followed by translations into plain English:

Collegese: The trip provided a superior environment for the strengthening of the primary dyadic relationship in my life between Laura and me.
English: The trip brought Laura and me closer.
Collegese: I knew that I could not satisfy the ego needs of my parents unless I had high-achieving academic goals.
English: I knew that my parents wouldn't be pleased unless I did well in school.
Collegese: At this point in my life I am planning a career that will enable me to interface with other people.
English: I am planning a career that will enable me to work with people.

Use familiar words

"I never write 'metropolis' for seven cents a word because I can get the same price for 'city,'" Mark Twain observed. Even writers who are not paid by the word would do well to follow this advice. "City" is a first-degree word—meaning that it comes first to mind, is used in everyday speech, and suggests an image. "Metropolis" is a second-degree word—meaning that it is less familiar, not much used in everyday speech, and does not readily suggest an image. Where you have a choice, you should always use the first-degree word. One of the very rare exceptions to this rule is when the less familiar word has a specific, technical meaning you need.

But in most cases, the everyday word will do. What's more, you're also less likely to misuse it. The words whose meanings you truly know are those that make up your speaking vocabulary, not the ones you've lately dug up in a dictionary. One student wrote, "The first of the two poems was untitled and *cherished* two main ideas." What he meant to say was that it "had" two main ideas. Better to use the word you know than to misuse the one you don't.

Application: Role-playing on paper

Do writers role-play when they write? Some teachers think so, and they blame role-playing on paper for much bad writing. Consider this anecdote:

> Last fall I had an advanced undergraduate student, bright, energetic, well-informed, whose papers were almost unreadable. He managed to be pretentious, dull, and disorganized in his paper on *Emma*, and pretentious, dull, and disorganized on *Madame Bovary*. On *The Golden Bowl* he was all of these and obscure as well. Then one day, toward the end of the term, he cornered me after class and said, "You know, I think you were all wrong about Robbe-Grillet's *Jealousy* today." We didn't have time to discuss his objections, so I suggested that he write me a note about them. Five hours later I found in my faculty box a four-page polemic, unpretentious, stimulating, organized, convincing. Here was a man who had himself taught freshman composition for several years and who was incapable of committing any of the more obvious errors that we think of as characteristic of bad writing. Yet he could not write a decent sentence, paragraph, or paper until his rhetorical problem was solved—until, that is, he had found a definition of his audience, his argument, and his own proper tone of voice.[2]

The teller of this anecdote—a veteran English teacher and writer—believes that most students write badly because they have no *rhetorical stance*. That

[2]Wayne C. Booth, "The Rhetorical Stance," in *Now Don't Try to Reason with Me* (Chicago: University of Chicago Press, 1970).

is, they have no sense of the three elements common to most writing: the available arguments on a topic, the interests of the audience, and the voice—or implied character—of the speaker. It is the last of these that interests us here—the voice or implied character of a speaker.

What is the implied character of a speaker? It is what the speaker's words say about the speaker. When we put words on paper, we say something about something, and our words say something about us. We assume a stance, a pose, toward our material. We play a role in it. If we are writing as an expert, we may be tempted to write in a puffy and inflated style as we imagine befits our expertise. In short, the role we play may lead us to write badly. Here is an example. It illustrates what one magazine calls the "emperor syndrome" in business writing, where a sense of self-importance corrupts the writing voice of executives:

> All sales personnel are hereby instructed to abide by company policy respecting offering unauthorized discounts to a prospect in order to secure the order. Sales staff are again categorically reminded that it is a contravention of company policy to offer quantity discounts without prior approval of supervisory personnel, and that any violation of this policy will result in immediate and absolute dismissal without exception.[3]

Can you hear the voice in this? It is trumpeting "This is the boss speaking." The weight of office has clearly gone to this writer's head—and pen.

Economists, sociologists, and other scientists suffer from much the same malaise: role-playing on paper causes them to write badly. An anecdote from Malcolm Cowley, the well-known critic and poet, bears this out:

> I have a friend who started as a poet and then decided to take a post-graduate degree in sociology. For his doctoral dissertation he combined his two interests by writing on the social psychology of poets. He had visited poets by the dozen, asking each of them a graded series of questions, and his conclusions from the interviews were modest and useful, though reported in what seemed to me a barbarous jargon. After reading the dissertation I wrote and scolded him, "You have such a fine sense of the poet's craft," I said, "that you shouldn't have allowed the sociologists to seduce you into writing their professional slang—or at least that's my judgmental response to your role selection."
>
> My friend didn't write to defend himself; he waited until we met again. Then dropping his voice, he said: "I knew my dissertation was badly written, but I had to get my degree. If I had written it

[3]Quoted in "The Need for Clarity in Business Writing," *Financial Executive*, Jan. 1979.

> in English, Professor Blank"—and he mentioned a rather distinguished name—"would have rejected it. He would have said that it was merely belletristic."[4]

What is interesting about this story is that it concerns a student who could write well but felt forced to write badly. Many writers in a similar situation have pleaded the same excuse—that it is not enough to write plainly, that they feel obliged to use the voice of their calling no matter if it is fuzzy and filled with jargon. In the same article, Cowley cites this example of what he was complaining about to his friend:

> In effect, it was hypothesized that certain physical data categories including housing types and densities, land use characteristics, and ecological location constitute a scalable content area. This could be called a continuum of residential desirability.

But a determined movement has now arisen against this kind of writing because companies are discovering that it is expensive. In one case an oil company spent millions reinventing a chemical one of its scientists had discovered five years before and reported on in an unreadable memo.[5] One consultant is on record as saying that bad writers are a prime factor in the whole drop in the growth of American productivity. Another says: "Their idea of what constitutes good writing is something that is excessively pompous and stilted. They go on and on, never getting to the point."[6]

Does that sound familiar?

EXERCISES

1. The following sentences contain collegese. Rewrite them to project a natural voice.

   a. The highlight of my summer was a journey to the Metropolitan Museum of Art, where I investigated works of artistic merit.
   b. When aged parents live with their children, certain modes of living need to be observed in order to fulfill the privacy needs of all concerned.

[4]Malcolm Cowley, "Sociological Habit Patterns in Linguistic Transmogrification," *The Reporter*, 20 Sept. 1956.

[5]William E. Blundell, "Confused, Overstuffed Corporate Writing Often Costs Firms Much Time—and Money," *The Wall Street Journal*, 28 Aug. 1980.

[6]Both quotations are from "The Righting of Writing," *Time*, 19 May 1980.

c. In their lecturing activity, many university professors exhibit a tendency toward loquaciousness.
d. My overmobility while dancing indicates lack of talent as regards coordinating body movement with music.
e. Three conditions today militate against optimum marital harmony.
f. With reference to school activities, my expectations are to join one of the fraternities on campus.
g. One's enrollment in an art appreciation course serves to maximize one's sense of the liberal arts.
h. History attests to the fact that power has a corrupting influence.

2. Pretend that your best friend has asked you for advice on how to make a smooth adjustment to college. Answer this request in a brief letter. (Remember to be yourself; after all, you are writing to your best friend.)

3. Replace the unfamiliar word in italics with a familiar one that has the same meaning.

   a. Suddenly I saw a *curvature* in the road.
   b. It is his *prerogative* to sit in that seat.
   c. What an *audacious* man!
   d. The play ends when he gives her a tender *osculation*.
   e. I wish you *perpetual* health.
   f. The senator wore a *vermilion* jacket.
   g. The pyramid was *obtruncated*.
   h. He has a *monarchical* bearing.
   i. Her *bucolic* life was ideal.
   j. Without the government's *subvention*, they would starve.

4. The following sentences reveal ambiguity or lack of conviction. Rewrite each sentence to create a definite opinion.

   a. I don't believe in advocating strikes, but yet sometimes striking is the only way labor can get its way.
   b. The man was an original thinker to the point where his eccentricity landed him in a mental hospital.
   c. Sometimes parents falsely accuse their offspring of working below capacity at school.
   d. I suspect that Henry David Thoreau probably was a deep thinker, but his *Walden Pond* did not exactly strike me as fascinating.
   e. It is my considered opinion that Laura in the story "Flowering Judas" is subconsciously in love with her leader, Braggioni; on the other hand, I may be wrong.

5. In the following sentences replace the hackneyed expressions with fresh ones so that an individual voice emerges.

   a. Congress fought tooth and nail to get the new law passed.

b. Although Wagner was an egocentric man, he really burned the midnight oil and worked until the wee hours of the morning on his operas.
c. It seems that Abraham Lincoln was as honest as the day is long.
d. When Benedict first approaches Beatrice, she tells him to go peddle his wares elsewhere.
e. Charles Dickens, for all intents and purposes, might as well have been poor because he spent money as if it were going out of style.

3

What is a thesis?

Come out with your subject pointed.
Take a stand, make a judgment
of value, make a thesis.

—Sheridan Baker

THE THESIS IS A SENTENCE that summarizes what the essay is about. In it, the writer declares the purpose of the essay: to support or oppose an issue; to explain a process; to describe a scene. This declaration of purpose guides the writer's efforts and prepares the reader for the essay's content.

The thesis is composed during the prewriting process—before an outline is drawn up or a paragraph written. Prewriting refers to the initial thought and research you devote to a subject before you begin to write about it. Writers must ask themselves some basic questions during the prewriting stage: What do I want to say? How do I intend to say it? The answers to these questions will inevitably lead to the thesis.

Choosing the thesis

You have been given a writing assignment by your instructor. The wording of the assignment may or may not contain an implicit thesis. For example, the instructor may ask you to oppose or support a certain quotation or to contrast two views of an event in history. Each of these topics contains a thesis. What you must now do is find evidence and specific detail that support the thesis. However, the assignment may simply be to write an essay about a general subject, leaving it up to you to choose a specific topic and frame it into a thesis.

In this case, the first thing you should do is think about the subject. Jot down your random thoughts and questions as they occur. Initially, you are building a list of broad topics that you might want to write about. Pursue any unusual slant on the subject. Look at it from different viewpoints.

Imagine that the instructor has assigned an essay about any aspect of American life. Your session of thinking may yield a list such as this:

1. What is American life, anyway?
2. Most Americans eat more than they need.

3. Baseball is the most American of games.
4. Are there any advantages to living in America?
5. Have Americans become less patriotic in the last one hundred years?
6. Most Americans are fond of parades.
7. Being an American entails some responsibilities.
8. The American system of justice is based on trial by jury.
9. "I am not a Virginian, but an American," said Patrick Henry.

What you have now is a collection of random ideas and questions. You search among them for the one that appeals to you and choose the statement about the jury system, number 8. Recently you read an article about the composition of juries and found it very interesting.

You have reached the second step in finding a thesis—narrowing your focus to a specific topic. Now you must free associate again and try to come up with another list of ideas, this one on the jury system:

1. It is the duty of all Americans to serve on a jury when called to do so.
2. Many Americans resent jury duty.
3. Should jurors be paid more money than they currently receive?
4. American justice is usually dispensed by a jury of one's peers. Is this a good system?
5. How can any jury ever be said to contain one's peers?
6. Jurors are called in wasteful numbers.

The last idea catches your attention. You remember that your father complained recently about being called to jury duty and then never being put on a case. You pose a question to yourself: Why are so many jurors called at the same time?

This question brings you to the third and last step in your search for a thesis. You must think of answers to your question, and one of these answers—the most concise, the one that interests you the most—will be your thesis:

1. More jurors are called than are needed because the process of forming a jury is riddled with red tape.
2. Since the jury system is most likely run by a group of old fossils, more jurors are called than are ever used.
3. More jurors are called than are needed because empaneling a jury is a complex process: perhaps we should study alternate systems.
4. More jurors are called than are needed because most people called turn out to be undependable.

5. More jurors are called than are ever used in cases because of three reasons: (a) court schedules are unpredictable, (b) trials sometimes drag on, and (c) prisoners often plea-bargain to avoid a long court trial.

Of these answers, the fifth would make the best thesis because it makes a well-defined point that can be easily fleshed out with supporting details.

Each of the other sentences in the list contains a flaw. The first is too broad and technical to be developed in a short essay. The second uses an ambiguous image—"old fossils." The third pulls in two directions the writer would find hard to reconcile—the complexity of the jury system and the need for an alternate system. The fourth is not specific enough—a writer would labor hard and long to write an essay about it. The fifth is the best choice.

Key words in the thesis

The thesis of your essay is a statement in which certain key words are nested. These are the words that the essay must amplify with definitions, explanations, and examples. Sometimes a thesis contains only one key word; sometimes it contains more. The following theses contain a single key word, which is underlined:

1. Pheasant hunting is a <u>tiring</u> sport.
2. I am a <u>jealous</u> person.
3. Investing in the stock market is <u>risky.</u>

Most of the time, however, theses will contain several key words:

1. Good English is <u>clear,</u> <u>appropriate,</u> and <u>vivid</u>.
2. Studies show that as children the real achievers in our society were <u>independent</u> and <u>spirited</u>.
3. Riding a bicycle to work has <u>several advantages</u> over driving a car.
4. Soviet children are members of collectives—nurseries, schools, camps, youth programs—that emphasize <u>obedience,</u> <u>self-discipline,</u> and <u>subordination</u>.

Occasionally, the thesis will contain a proposition that is inseparable from its individual words. The essay will have to amplify the whole statement:

1. <u>Students should be advised against majoring in subjects where job prospects are limited.</u>
2. <u>If the United States is to survive, Americans will have to learn to conserve their country's resources.</u>

Characteristics of a good thesis

The precision with which you formulate your thesis helps to determine the quality of your essay. A good thesis *predicts*, *controls*, and *obligates*.

The thesis predicts

For the thesis to predict, it must assert a proposition that is discussable. Some propositions, however, such as the following, are so self-evident that they warrant no further discussion:

1. A relationship exists between excessive eating and gaining weight.
2. Rich people usually live in big houses.
3. In our country, movie stars are greatly admired.

When carefully planned, your thesis should predict the general direction in which your essay will move and should dictate what sort of explanation or evidence you must provide. But none of the above statements dictate either direction or evidence. Each is a truism that would make a bad thesis, thus leading to a dead-end essay. In contrast, the following theses contain discussable assertions and predict where the essay is likely to go:

> Interviews with Yasser Arafat sometimes take place at odd hours and in strange places.
>
> —*Time*, April 14, 1980

(The reader immediately wants to know what is meant by "odd hours and strange places.")

> The new black stereotype comes off as a sleek, sophisticated professional light-years away from the ghetto experience.
>
> —Vernon E. Jordan, Jr.

(The reader wants examples and details that clarify the new stereotype.)

> It is a truism that criminal organizations and criminal activities tend to reflect social conditions.
>
> —Lewis Yablonsky

(The reader wants to see proof that this assertion is true.)

The thesis controls

Another important function of the thesis is to control the direction of the essay. The thesis tells the writer what to do. It establishes the subtopics of the essay in the order they should be discussed. Consider this thesis:

> Today, religion is no longer the uncontested center and ruler of human life because Protestantism, science, and capitalism have brought about a secularized world.

Inherent in this thesis is the structure of the essay. Here is its implicit order of topics:

1. A description of medieval society when religion was the center of human existence.
2. An explanation of how Protestantism secularized the world.
3. An explanation of how science secularized the world.
4. An explanation of how capitalism secularized the world.

The advantage of such a structured thesis is twofold. First, it commits the writer during the prewriting stage. Before a single paragraph is written, the writer knows what kind of supporting detail is needed: information about the secularizing influences of Protestantism, science, and capitalism. Second, the thesis controls the actual development of the essay. The writer knows that there are four specific topics to cover in a specific order.

The beginning writer should write essays that are based on structured theses. Then there is no worrying about what should come next and there is little chance of digression. Here are some examples of theses that vary in the degree of control they would exert over an essay:

Loose control: The defects in the process of presidential primaries can be cured.

Tight control: There are two cures for the defects in the process of presidential primaries: (1) instituting regional rather than state primaries, and (2) reserving a bloc of seats at the convention for uncommitted delegates.

Loose control: We live in an age of change and mobility.

Tight control: Today's ambitious worker, in pursuit of a satisfying job, will relocate and change jobs several times before retirement.

In each case, the second thesis is better than the first because it exercises the greater degree of control over the essay.

The thesis obligates

When a writer strays from the thesis, the result is often vague, unfocused writing. If the thesis is *Police officers spend more time controlling traffic and providing information than they spend enforcing the law,* then you must prove this point in your essay. You should not rhapsodize about the heroism of the police or complain about police brutality. Likewise, if your thesis is *California college students are sexually more liberated than their New York counterparts*, then that is the only point you should discuss. You should not write about the disputed intellectual superiority of New York college students or weave in facts about vegetarianism in California unless these issues are somehow related to the sexual behavior of college students in California and New York.

However, it follows that in order to write a focused essay the wording of the thesis must obligate the writer to write only about a single issue. Consider this thesis, for example:

> Definitions of obscenity change as society changes, and the courts' decisions on censorship reflect the legal profession's confusion on the issue.

This thesis is pulling in two directions. The first part of it requires a discussion of how definitions of obscenity reflect changes in society, while the second part leads to a discussion of the legal profession's confusion on obscenity. An essay based on this thesis would fall into two unassimilated parts. The student should rewrite the thesis until it discusses a single issue. Here is a suggested revision of the thesis, which unifies its two parts and commits the writer to a single idea:

> Because definitions of obscenity change as society changes, the courts have handed down some contradictory decisions on censorship.

Although many students worry about making their theses too restrictive, student theses rarely suffer from this fault. If there is a common student error, it is usually making the thesis too broad. A broad thesis cannot be adequately developed within the average length of a student paper. None of the following theses is restrictive enough to be dealt with in a student essay:

1. Parachuting is unbelievable!
2. The Vietnam war was stupid.
3. Evaluating college teachers is an interesting idea.

Ambiguous key words like *unbelievable*, *stupid*, and *interesting* need to be replaced. To predict, control, and obligate the course of an essay, a thesis must be unambiguous, structured, and restrictive. Common sense also tells us that the scope of the thesis must be in proportion to the length of the essay. A broad thesis is not suited to a short essay, nor a narrow thesis to a long essay.

Here is a synopsis of the process you should use to find a thesis:

1. Think about the subject area and jot down your ideas, questions, and speculations. Choose the one idea from this list that most appeals to you.
2. Narrow the topic further by again thinking about it and writing down your ideas. From this list select the narrowed idea that you would like to write about.
3. Ask yourself a question about the narrowed topic and give several answers. The best answer to this question will be your thesis.

The statement of purpose

Some essays are purposeful without really ever developing a main idea. For instance, if you want to list the steps involved in winterizing a house or to explain how to parallel ski or to trace the issues that caused open antagonism between Japan and China in 1894–95, your paper will not open with a thesis, but with a statement of its purpose. Here are some examples of statements of purpose:

1. The purpose of this essay is to list some of the aspects of prison life that brutalize rather than reform inmates.
2. In this paper I intend to list five characteristics of the typical TV soap opera.
3. This essay will identify and evaluate the present leaders of the feminist movement.
4. My report deals with the Palestinians' major demands—what they are and which ones have been partly met.
5. By tracing the etymology of "nice," "brave," "enthrall," "idiot," "villain," and "acid," I intend to illustrate how some words in English have undergone amelioration and others pejoration.

The difference between a thesis and a statement of purpose is one of wording rather than of effect. Both control the course of the essay; both inform the reader what the paper intends to do. The thesis, however, expresses directly the idea that the essay will develop whereas the statement of purpose is worded as the intention of the author. Statements of purpose are commonly found at the beginning of scientific or technical essays.

Eight errors to avoid when composing a thesis

1. **A thesis cannot be a fragment; it must be expressed as a complete sentence.**

Poor: How life is in a racial ghetto.
Better: Residents of a racial ghetto tend to have a higher death rate, a higher infant mortality rate, and a higher unemployment rate, than do residents of the suburbs.

2. **A thesis must not be worded as a question.** (Usually the answer to the question could be the thesis.)

Poor: Do Americans really need large refrigerators?
Better: If Americans did their marketing daily, as do most Europeans, they could save energy because they could use smaller refrigerators.

3. **A thesis must not be too broad.**

Poor: The literature of mythology contains many resurrection stories.
Better: One of the oldest resurrection myths is the story of the Egyptian god Osiris.

4. **A thesis should not contain unrelated elements.**

Poor: All novelists seek the truth, and some novelists are good psychologists.
Better: In their attempt to probe human nature, many novelists become excellent psychologists.

5. **A thesis should not contain phrases like *I think* or *in my opinion* because they weaken the writer's argument.**

Poor: In my opinion public buildings should be required by law to have no-smoking zones because of the adverse effects on health of "passive smoking."
Better: Public buildings should be required by law to have no-smoking zones because of the adverse effects on health of "passive smoking."

6. **A thesis should not be expressed in vague language.**

Poor: Religion as part of the school curriculum should be avoided because it can cause trouble.
Better: Religion as part of the school curriculum should be avoided because it is a highly personal commitment.

7. **A thesis must not be expressed in muddled or incoherent language.**

Poor: Homosexuality is a status offense to the effect that the participants are willing so that the relationship is voluntary in character rather than the type described in a victim-perpetrator model.
Better: Homosexuality between consenting adults should be considered an alternate life-style rather than a crime.

8. **A thesis should not be expressed in figurative language.**

Poor: The Amazons of today are trying to purge all the stag words from the language.
Better: Today's feminists are trying to eliminate the use of sex-biased words from public documents and publications.

A final word of advice: after you have compiled a list of possible topics, do not choose the one that seems easiest to write about. If you do, you have probably chosen a platitude such as "Football is becoming too commercial," or "Marijuana should be legalized because it is no worse than alcohol." Such commonplace statements seem easy to write about but, in fact, are terribly difficult because so much has already been written about them. If you are a superb writer, you might be able to find something fresh to say about a stale topic; but if you are like the rest of us, you'll probably only repeat what everyone else has already said, making your essay dull and unoriginal.

Application: Explicit versus implicit thesis

Students must write with a thesis: that is a law of freshman composition. But is it a law observed by professional writers? Generally, no. Professional writers do not usually write with an explicit thesis. Why, you may wonder, the difference?

The answer is deceptively simple: the professional writer does not need one. The aim of a thesis is to exercise control over the flow of ideas. It is a means to an end like the leash on a dog. Without a thesis, many student writers would stray from the point or bark up the wrong tree. Their essays would not be unified and coherent. In contrast, professional writers can write in a unified and coherent way without an explicit thesis. The effect is the same, the means of achieving it different. The student needs a leash; the professional writer no longer does.

The point is this: If you can write with order and structure—if you can express yourself without drifting from your main point—you do not need a thesis. You are already using one in effect, if not in name. Implicit in your writing is your main idea—your thesis—though it is left unsaid. Here is an example, a short article in which a thesis is implied in the title and in the writer's arguments, but not explicitly stated.

AGE SNEAKS UP, LEAVES YOU WITH COMPROMISES

Michael Swift

It happens so abruptly. You go to bed in a familiar place, certain of who you are, and you wake up a stranger on the far side of the bridge of growing old. Not that you are old—not yet; it's just that you are no longer young.

You have arrived in the land of no illusions and little enthusiasm where nothing is all that crucial anymore. Once you saw purpose in making sense out of life. Now you see that the whole damn show makes no sense at all.

There's only one destination on this side of the bridge, and you won't avoid it, no matter how much you jog or play raquetball or lift weights. Though you exercise like mad trying to fend off physical deterioration, though you do 50 sit-ups and 75 push-ups every morning, the pot belly stays firmly in place; your body has thickened, coarsened, just as your soul has.

Attempting to hold onto this body, this life, as long as possible, you have tried to quit smoking. But the best you'll ever do is keep the daily intake to four or five cigarettes. You also need at least one drink or a more potent chemical to get through the day or the night. You once got naturally high on sunrises or sunsets, new songs or plans for tomorrow.

Oh, what high hopes you had back then when you were special. You were going to save the world. Now you know that humanity will never change, that life on this planet most likely will never be much different or better. Banal, predictable world—it used to shock and bewilder you so. Now you can understand anything, even child abuse or atomic warfare. You might not tolerate such things, but you understand how they can happen.

The truth will heal, they told you. Now you do nothing but fabricate. On your first day in college, the dean warned about dragging your ideals through the mud. Now you're a master of compromise, more Gertrude or Polonius than Hamlet.

College. Senior year. The last time you were completely happy. Now you wish you had been a bit more serious, spent a little more time learning and a little less drinking and having a good time in general.

They told you that anyone can grow up to become President of the United States, even you. Now it's clear that you'll never become president of anything.

Childhood and the little town you came from are so remote as to be unreal. Today you're big-city through and through, even though you didn't conquer the big city exactly as you thought you would—but that isn't such a great disappointment, after all.

Your mother is gone now. Your father, too. You're on your own. You could do anything you like—if you didn't know so much about "golden years" and perhaps having to spend them in a furnished room waiting for Social Security checks that may not come.

Once you wanted to be clever and witty and rich and famous and handsome and beautiful and daring and brave. Now you just want to be comfortable. You'd rather stay at home than venture out to try your wit and daring on some sultry beauty. You used to be obsessed with sex; now you'd rather feel close to the one you love than be intoxicated with passion. And you don't miss the high spirits in the bars. Watching TV at home is fine; the sit-coms have become as amusing as anything by Noel Coward or Moliere.

Age has its virtues, you realize. No longer are you intimidated by haughty waiters or aloof sales clerks. No longer do you worry about being *au courant*; you can wear any old thing and no one will notice.

Yes, you're more old than young; you've become a true sage, a veteran of the human condition. All that's left is an easy death on the Gold Coast of Florida or gradual oblivion somewhere in soporific Southern California. And you're really not surprised that this fate isn't the least bit troubling at all.

In the preceding essay, the writer does not drift from his point, nor lose sight of his purpose, yet he does not use an explicit thesis. To write with such structure without an explicit thesis takes skill, control—and experience. Many beginning writers cannot do it. They become seduced by side issues, stray from the point, lose their train of thought. And so the explicit thesis has become a requirement of classroom writing. It is a useful device for the inexperienced, but for the professional writer it can be too simplistic—too much of a formula. Experienced writers cannot freely explore a topic in all its complexity if they are tethered to a thesis.

Although you too may later abandon the use of a thesis, for now it is a convention of classroom writing that will help you. The thesis allows you to prethink the form of your essay. It gives you a map to follow, a promise to fulfill. But eventually, as you become a more experienced writer, you will probably outgrow its usefulness.

EXERCISES

1. Formulate a thesis for one of these topics. Use the step-by-step method outlined in the chapter.

   adolescence
   women and the draft
   obligation of parents
   the entertainment world
   spectator sports

2. Find a picture that expresses some aspect of today's society, such as violence, youthful idealism, promiscuity, or religious piety; then write a thesis that could serve as an appropriate caption.

3. Underline the key words of the following theses:

   a. Memory entails recall, recognition, and revival.
   b. An argument must present both sides of the question being debated.
   c. The Amish people resist public education because they believe that a simple farm life is best and that formal education will corrupt their young people.
   d. A good farmer cooperates with weather, soil, and seed.
   e. Laura in "Flowering Judas" by Katherine Anne Porter is tortured by doubt, guilt, and disappointment.
   f. The race tracks, the ballparks, the fight rings, and the gridirons draw crowds in increasing numbers.

4. Which of the following theses is the best? Support your choice.

   a. Forest fires are enormously destructive because they ravage the land, create problems for flood control, and destroy useful lumber.
   b. Installment buying is of great benefit to the economy, having in mind the consumer to use a product while paying for it and being like forced savings.
   c. Television is a handicap.

5. The following theses are poorly worded. Analyze their weaknesses in terms of the eight errors discussed earlier, and rewrite each to make it clear and effective.

   a. In my opinion, birth control is the most urgent need in today's world.
   b. Just how far should the law go in its tolerance of pornography?
   c. How Christian missionaries were sent to the Ivory Coast of Africa to introduce western civilization.

d. The history of psychology had its conception with Plato and came to full term with Freud.
e. Strip mining is an environmentally destructive solution to the problem of fuel shortage, and the fuel shortage is caused by our government's foreign policy.
f. In the United States, the press is the watchdog of society.
g. Three factors may be singled out as militating against the optimum adjustment that partners in the marriage relationship should experience as money, culture, and education.
h. Homemaking is the most meaningful work a woman can perform.
i. The problem with sound pollution is, How much longer can our ears bear the noise?
j. The noteworthy relaxation of language taboos both in conversation and in print today.
k. My feeling is that educationists are just as infatuated with jargon as are sociologists.
l. Retirement homes need not be depressing places which commercial activities can bring residents together in shared experiences.
m. The city of New York is in bad shape.

6. From the following pairs of theses, pick out the thesis with the discussable issue. Explain your choice.

a. (1) The Eiffel Tower is located near the center of Paris.
   (2) Three spectacular crimes have been committed near the Eiffel Tower in Paris.

b. (1) Michelangelo's "David" symbolizes the best qualities of youthful manhood.
   (2) Michelangelo's "David" is carved out of white marble from Carrara.

c. (1) The Model A Ford became popular because it was dependable and uncomplicated.
   (2) Close to a million people still own Model A Fords today.

d. (1) In Hemingway's *Farewell to Arms*, the knee injury suffered by Frederick Henry symbolizes man's wounded spirit.
   (2) In Hemingway's novel *Farewell to Arms*, Frederic Henry is shot in the knee while driving an ambulance truck.

e. (1) The Greek historian Herodotus claimed that the city of Troy was destroyed in 1250 B.C.
   (2) Troy was an important city because any fortress built on its site could control all shipping traffic through the Dardanelles.

f. (1) Good grammar is the equivalent of good manners.
   (2) According to the rules of grammar, "he don't" is a barbarism.

4

How do I organize?

Observe how system into system runs,
What other planets circle other suns.

—Alexander Pope

OUTLINING IS PLANNING YOUR ESSAY in advance of writing it. Your plan will show what topics you intend to discuss, in what sequence, and with what degree of emphasis. An outline allows you to conceptualize the essay from beginning to end and makes it easier to write an essay than to create one at random. Lapses of inspiration may not be entirely eliminated by an outline, but if you stall in mid-essay, at least you will have a guide to turn to. If your essays have been repeatedly criticized for lacking structure, you will certainly benefit from outlining before you begin to write.

The outline

The outline is simply a summary of what you plan to say in your essay. The outline tells you what you have to do, where you have to go, and when you have gotten there. If you are sidetracked habitually by details or bogged down in vast quantities of information, outlining is an indispensable means of imposing structure on your essay.

A convention has evolved for the formal outline. The title of the essay is centered at the top of the page with the thesis below it. Then the thesis is broken down into its main ideas, designated by Roman numerals I, II, III, IV, V, and so on. Subideas branching off the main ideas are designated by capital letters A, B, C, and so on. Examples of these subideas are marked by Arabic numbers. Further details supporting the examples are designated by lower-case letters a, b, c. In theory, this subdividing could go on forever; in practice, it rarely extends below the fourth level with the listing that is designated by lower-case letters. Here is the framework of the formal outline:

TITLE

Thesis

I. Main Idea
   A. Subidea
      1. Example of subidea
         a. Detail supporting example

The outline omits introductory materials, transitions, and illustrations; it lists only major ideas and subideas of the essay. Outline convention dictates that main ideas start at the left of the page and subideas are indented. As you move from left to right, you move from the more important to the less important.

Rules for outlining

Whether typed or handwritten, an outline must observe the following rules:

1. Don't make the outline too long. One page of outline usually is the basis for five pages of developed writing.
2. Don't clutter the sentences of your outline. Use as few words as possible in each entry.
3. Whenever possible, use parallel wording for subordinate entries.
4. Align your entries properly. Do not allow the second line of an entry to go further toward the left margin than the first line:

Wrong: A. Art therapy is a relatively new psychological approach in the
treatment of mental illness.

Right: A. Art therapy is a relatively new psychological approach in the
   treatment of mental illness.

5. Leave one-inch margins all around the outline.

A sample of proper outlining appears in the following section.

Creating the outline

Every workable outline is the natural outcome of questions you ask yourself when you first think about putting your ideas on paper: Which information should come first? Which notes should get major attention, which minor attention, and which should be brought in as supporting details? In answering these questions, you begin to outline.

To create an outline, begin with the thesis of your essay and divide it into smaller ideas. It is an axiom of division that nothing can be divided into fewer than two parts. From this it follows that under every main idea that has been divided, at least two subideas must appear. In other words, for every **I** there must be at least a **II;** for every **A,** at least a **B.** Consider this example:

> Thesis: Extremes in temperatures can have dangerous effects on mountain climbers.
> I. The dangerous effects of excessive heat
>   A. Heat exhaustion
>   B. Heat stroke
> II. The dangerous effects of excessive cold
>   A. Surface frostbite
>   B. Bodily numbness

The logic of division will always produce an outline characterized by symmetry. A byproduct of this symmetry is evenness in the treatment of all topics. Notice also that each entry is worded in more or less parallel language. This wording underscores the equal importance of the entries and emphasizes the major divisions in the outline.

Organizing the short essay

Short essays (about three hundred words long) are usually written in class under the pressure of a one- to two-hour time limit. A teacher may assign students to write three paragraphs about some trend in history, art, or psychology or to write an informal essay on a social custom or whether or not voting should be compulsory. Obviously, a student can't spend a great deal of time outlining such an essay. The student must rely on past research or on his or her own store of experience and general knowledge. Yet some sort of outline is necessary to prevent aimless wandering around the topic and panicky, last-minute rewriting. How can such an essay be outlined?

Outlining by paragraphs

First, of course, you must devise a thesis. Let us assume that your English instructor has asked you to write an in-class essay on the experience that has most influenced your life. Since you are a Vietnam veteran, you decide to write a brief essay on the psychological problems suffered by returning Vietnam veterans. You think about the subject for several minutes and come up with the following thesis:

> Many Vietnam veterans had terrible memories, deep feelings of guilt, and periods of depression.

One way to outline the short essay is to assume that each idea contained in the thesis will function as a topic sentence for a paragraph. You simply write out each main idea and fill in subideas as they occur to you. The formal numbering system of the outline need not be used since the outline is for your personal convenience and will not be submitted with the essay. Here is a sample paragraph outline for the thesis on Vietnam veterans, with three separate paragraphs blocked out:

VIETNAM VETERANS

Thesis: Many Vietnam veterans had terrible memories, deep feelings of guilt, and periods of depression.

Many Vietnam veterans had terrible memories.
- These terrible memories were often reinforced by agonizing flashbacks.
  - Frightening battle scenes were replayed in their minds as in a movie.
  - They actually saw artillery flashing and heard bombs exploding.

Many Vietnam veterans had deep feelings of guilt.
- They felt that their society had rejected them.
  - Some felt that friends and neighbors regarded them as murderers.
  - The public's disapproval of the war increased their feelings of guilt.

Many Vietnam veterans had periods of depression.
- They were not glorified heroes as they had expected to be.
  - They felt that their country was ashamed of them.
  - Some men felt great self-contempt, which led to depression.

With such an outline you know the general direction of your essay and you need not puzzle over what points it should cover. You can spend the rest of your time writing the essay, providing examples and details that support your thesis, and creating logical and smooth transitions between the major ideas.

Outlining by key words

The thesis on Vietnam veterans contained three main ideas that considerably simplified its outlining. But not all theses are that conveniently divisible. Consider this thesis:

Children should encourage independence in their aged parents.

No obvious divisions are apparent in this thesis. Yet this one contains key words that provide a clue to how it may be outlined. The implicit aim of the essay—found in the key words "encourage independence"—should be to explain how or why children should encourage independence in their aged parents.

> Thesis: Children should *encourage independence* in their aged parents.
>
> I. Children should encourage their aged parents to contribute to society.
>
> II. Children should encourage their aged parents to be financially independent.
>
> III. Children should encourage their aged parents to have an independent social life.

Each outline entry, supported by appropriate examples and details, can function as a separate topic sentence in a three-paragraph essay. Here, for example, is how the first entry could be developed:

> Children should encourage their aged parents to contribute to society. To be old is not necessarily synonymous with being useless. Old people, like everyone else, cannot feel independent unless they give something of themselves to their communities. All kinds of jobs are open to them. They can work as volunteers in the thrift shop of a hospital; they can function as aides in a center for handicapped children, where love and patience are invaluable qualities; or they can help out in Red Cross activities. Church welfare societies are always looking for people to wrap packages or sort clothing. Political organizations appreciate all kinds of help. Volunteer work is just one of many ways for the elderly to maintain a sense of independence.

Organizing the long essay

The long essay can be a week-end assignment or a research paper completed over the course of several weeks. Students are expected to write an essay five to ten pages long with appropriate and accurate documentation on topics such as the following: "Why the Shark Is Such a Successful Predator"; "Art Therapy"; "Initial Critical Reactions to Henry Miller's Novels." Such subjects involve both library research and outside reading.

It is generally not feasible to work out a paragraph-by-paragraph outline of a long essay. Usually, you will have accumulated too much detail from your research to plot out in advance every single paragraph of the paper. Moreover, to maintain the flow of a long essay, you will have to create transitional paragraphs, which are simply unforeseeable until you actually begin to write the paper (see Chapter 5).

The best way to outline the long essay is to chart an orderly sequence of the topics to be covered by listing the main ideas and subideas. Important examples of a subidea may also be listed in the outline, providing that one example is balanced against another for symmetry. The only difference between this kind of outlining and outlining by paragraphs or key words is that here the logical divisions and entries will be more complex and detailed. The following is an example of an outline for a long essay:

TYPES OF COMEDY

Thesis: Comedy can be divided into two types: comedy to reform the foolish and comedy to entertain the bored.

I. Comedy to reform the foolish
    A. Satire
        1. Ridiculing systems
            a. Swift's "Modest Proposal"
            b. Voltaire's *Candide*
        2. Ridiculing persons
            a. Dryden's "MacFlecknoe"
            b. Newspaper cartoons of political figures
    B. Burlesque
        1. Putting down the sacred
            a. Shaws's *Arms and the Man*
            b. Woody Allen's *Manhattan*
        2. Elevating the lowly
            a. "Ode to a Wart"
            b. Pope's "Rape of the Lock"

II. Comedy to entertain the bored
    A. Comedy of manners
        1. Verbal wit
            a. Wilde's *The Importance of Being Earnest*
            b. Coward's *Private Lives*
        2. Situation comedy
            a. Fielding's *Tom Jones*
            b. Neil Simon's *Chapter Two*
    B. Farce
        1. Exaggerated movements
            a. Charlie Chaplin
            b. The old Sid Caesar television shows

2. Exaggerated costuming
    a. Circus clowns
    b. Milton Berle's female impersonations

The intent here is not to frame out separate paragraphs, but to establish an ordered progression for the essay. With this outline, the writer is obliged to follow a specific series of ideas, but not to translate each idea into a separate paragraph. The actual number of paragraphs this outline will entail is determined by the flow of the narrative, the availability of data, and the number of pages assigned for the essay.

Outlining by topic or by sentence

Some outlines are topic outlines in which the entries are not complete sentences, but fragments that sum up the topic. Other outlines are sentence outlines in which the entries are complete sentences. Your decision on whether to use a topic or a sentence outline depends on how complete a breakdown you need. If your subject is simple and all you need are key words to serve as guideposts so that you will not get sidetracked, or if you merely wish to set down some major trends, categories, or stages, then you should use a topic outline. But if your subject is a difficult one or in an area that is new to you, then you should use a sentence outline. Consider the following topic outline:

THE FUTURE OF OUR CITIES

Thesis: An assessment of the future of our cities reveals two emerging trends.

I. The megalopolis
    A. Definition
        1. Cluster
        2. System
    B. Two major organizational problems
        1. Transcendence
        2. Coordination

II. Shift in decision-making
    A. Local decisions
        1. Facts not known
        2. Outside agencies
    B. Federal government
        1. Increase in power
        2. Local restrictions

This topic outline is of no value to a person not thoroughly familiar with the problems of city government. A student writing a paper based on such a cryptic outline is bound to have difficulty coming to a conclusion. Now consider the following sentence outline of the same subject:

THE FUTURE OF OUR CITIES

Thesis: An assessment of the future of our cities reveals two emerging trends.

I. The megalopolis is replacing the city.
   A. Megalopolis can be defined in two ways.
      1. A megalopolis is a cluster of cities.
      2. A megalopolis is a system of interwoven urban and suburban areas.
   B. Two major organizational problems of the megalopolis will need to be solved.
      1. One problem is how to handle questions that transcend individual metropolitan areas.
      2. Another problem is how to coordinate the numerous activities in the megalopolis.

II. Decision-making is shifting from local control to higher echelons of public and private authority.
   A. The growing scale of the urban world often makes local decisions irrelevant.
      1. Local agencies may not know all of the facts.
      2. National policies may supersede local decisions.
   B. The federal government moves into the picture.
      1. The extent of federal involvement increases as the city grows.
         a. Federal long-range improvement plans are used.
         b. Grant-in-aid programs become necessary.
      2. Federal assistance imposes restrictions.
         a. Federal policies make sure that no discrimination takes place in the areas of housing, employment, and education.
         b. Federal representatives check on local installations to make sure that they are up to federal standards.

A good sentence outline supplies all of the basic information needed to write your paper. Without an outline, you run the risk of treating major ideas like details and details like major ideas; furthermore, you may find yourself moving forward, then backtracking, and then moving forward again, resulting in an incoherent paper. Because a careful outline takes into account the relationships among ideas and their degrees of importance, it keeps a novice from muddled writing.

From outline to essay

In writing your paper you may not use the exact wording of your outline, but you will certainly follow its main direction. The difference between the sentence outline and the completed essay is a matter of expanding, rounding out, and connecting. Compare, for example, the first section of a sentence outline on fairy tales with the development of the topic.

THE USES OF ENCHANTMENT

Thesis: Nothing in the entire range of children's literature can be as satisfying as the folk fairy tale.

I. From the fairy tale a child can learn about the inner problems of man.
   A. The child can acquire the inner resources to cope with the conditions of society.
      1. He can learn to bring order to the turmoil of his feelings.
      2. He can learn the advantage of moral behavior.
   B. The child can find meaning for his life.
      1. In their millennia of being retold, fairy tales relay overt as well as covert meaning to all levels of human thought.
      2. Fairy tales carry important messages to the conscious, the preconscious, and the unconscious mind.
      3. By dealing with universal problems, fairy tales encourage the development of the child's budding ego.
      4. Fairy tales show how to satisfy id pressures in ways that are in line with ego and superego requirements.

In all these respects and many others, nothing in the entire range of "children's literature"—with rare exceptions—can be as enriching and satisfying to child and adult alike as the folk fairy tale. True, fairy tales teach little overtly about the specific conditions of life in modern mass society; these tales were created long before modern society came into being. But from them a child can learn more about the inner problems of man, and about solutions to his own (and our) predicaments in any society, than he can from any other type of story within his comprehension. Since the child is exposed at every moment to the society in which he lives, he will learn to cope with its conditions—provided, that is, that his inner resources permit him to do so. The child must, therefore, be helped to bring order into the turmoil of his feelings. He needs—and the point hardly requires emphasis at this moment in our history—a moral education that subtly, by implication only, conveys to him the advantages of moral behavior, not through abstract ethical concepts but through that which seems tangibly right and therefore has meaning for him. The child can find meaning through fairy tales. Like so many other modern psychological insights, this one was anticipated long ago by poets. The German poet Schiller wrote, "Deeper meaning resides in the fairy tales told to me in my childhood than in the truth that is taught by life." Through the centuries (if not millennia) during which fairy tales, in their retelling, became even more refined, they came to convey overt and covert meanings at the same time; came to speak simultaneously to all levels of the human personality, communicating in a manner that reaches the uneducated mind of the child as well as the sophisticated mind of the adult. In terms of the psychoanalytic model of the human personality, fairy tales carry important messages to the conscious, the preconscious, and the unconscious mind, on whatever level these are functioning. By dealing with universal human problems, and especially with those that preoccupy the child's mind, these stories speak to his budding ego and encourage its development, and at the same time relieve preconscious and unconscious pressures. As the stories unfold, they give conscious credence and body to id pressures and show how to satisfy these in ways that are in line with ego and superego requirements.

—Bruno Bettelheim, *The Uses of Enchantment*

Application: Outlining versus not outlining

Outlining has an odd role in English classrooms. In some, it is a technique students are forced to learn regardless of whether or not they find it helpful. In others, it is merely a device taught those students whose essays, without an outline, would be incoherent and muddled. In some long papers—such as the research paper—students must submit a complete outline even if it is prepared after the fact. But will outlining really help you write a better essay?

That depends on the way you write. The two most common metaphors used to describe the process of writing liken it either to growing a plant or building a house. The first pictures writing as an organic process. The writer begins with a seed, a germ, an idea; slowly, as the idea develops, it takes root, spreads, grows. A sentence flowers into a paragraph, a paragraph into a page, a page into an essay. The second metaphor assumes that writing is a more mechanical, premeditated process. Writers decide ahead of time what they want to write, what they hope to communicate in a written piece. They lay the foundation, frame the main points, fill in the details. No doubt there are writers who neither grow plants nor build houses when they write, but these two metaphors are often mentioned as commonly descriptive of the way most writers work.

If these metaphors accurately describe the way most of us write, it follows that outlining won't help you if you are the purely organic kind of writer. Writing for you is entirely too interior a process to benefit from the kind of structure an outline offers. Indeed, outlining might seriously interfere with the way you naturally work. But if you are the other kind of writer—and one method of writing is not necessarily superior to the other—then you may find outlining not only useful but vitally necessary to the way you work.

Use an outline if it helps you; but if your teacher doesn't require an outline and if it does you no good, then don't use one. If you must submit an outline with your paper but don't use one to write, outline your essay after you've written it. Sometimes constructing an outline after the essay is finished can show up a structural error you would otherwise have overlooked.

In spite of the fact that some people use outlines better than others, the outline does have a significant advantage over other methods of organizing: it allows you to see the entire essay in miniature and to examine its structure as a whole. When you are immersed in an essay, it is easy to become fascinated with individual phrases and sentences and to lose sight of the overall structure. But in an outline all structural defects stand out clearly. Here is an example of a poorly structured essay:

Poor: Thesis: The police have two different roles, law enforcement and public service.

I. The law enforcement role

II. The public service role
    A. Traffic control
    B. Personal counseling
    C. Providing information

If this outline were followed, the essay would be lopsided. Although the thesis states that the police have two roles, the outline virtually ignores the first role, while it develops the second.

Rewrite: Thesis: The police have two different roles, law enforcement and public service.

I. The law enforcement role
    A. Prosecution of lawbreakers
    B. Enforcement of court decisions
    C. Crime prevention

II. The public service role
  A. Traffic control
  B. Personal counseling
  C. Providing information

Finally, we should point out that, while an outline is best used to fix approximate limits to an essay and to set up a sequence of topics to be followed, the outline is simply a means to an end, and not the end itself. If, in the act of writing the essay, an important new idea should occur to you or a better way of treating your subject, do not be inhibited by the thought of deviating from the outline. The outline can always be adjusted. The point is to write a good paper; the outline is simply a means of doing that.

EXERCISES

1. Write a paragraph outline for one of the following theses:

   a. Inflation has had a deteriorating effect on the purchasing power of the dollar.
   b. The essay exam has several advantages over the objects test.
   c. The first three months of an infant's life are crucial to the development of his or her personality.
   d. Public television's *Masterpiece Theatre* caters to a sophisticated and literate audience.
   e. In response to the rapid rise in urban crime, many people with high incomes are moving to residential compounds protected by private guards and other security devices.

2. Identify the key words in the following theses, specifying two or three subtopics into which they may be divided.

   a. Strong diplomatic ties with China would have several advantages for the United States.
   b. An electrical blackout in any major city of the United States would have disastrous results.
   c. The Greek myth of Jason and Medea has modern overtones.
   d. The words *disinterested, inflammable,* and *fortuitous* are often misunderstood.
   e. Various theories have been suggested to explain the black athlete's apparent domination of U.S. sports.

3. In the following outlines delete the entry that destroys the logical order.

   a. Thesis: Because of their cultural traits, the Dobuans are different from other primitive tribes.

      I. The location and environment of Dobuan Island make it difficult for the Dobuans to find sufficient food.

II. The rituals of marriage set the Dobuans apart from other primitive tribes.
III. The Dobuans' reliance on magic makes them more superstitious than other primitive tribes.
IV. The fact that the Dobuans value treachery and ill will sets them apart from other primitive tribes.

b. Thesis: The purpose of the California missions was to Christianize the Indians and to strengthen Spain's claim to California.

I. The mission padres taught the Indians Christian virtues.
II. The padres were concerned with saving the souls of the Indians.
III. The missions were constructed in the form of small cities.
IV. Without its colonists in California, Spain's claim to this territory was weak.
V. Spain was competing with Russia and England for territory in California.

c. Thesis: American political assassins have acted on nonpolitical impulses.

I. They are pathetic loners.
II. Their reality is a fantasy world.
III. The victim is usually a surrogate parent image.
IV. The assassin is seeking the same "fame" that the victim has.
V. European assassinations, unlike ours, have been the results of elaborate plots.

d. Thesis: The major themes in Shakespeare's *King Lear* are comments on somber and sad aspects of life.

I. One theme is that the gods are arbitrary.
II. Another theme is that often human beings embrace their enemies but turn on their friends.
III. A third theme is that things are not always what they seem.
IV. Disguises are used to emphasize the difference between appearance and reality in a theme.
V. Another theme is that divisiveness in families or the state leads to chaos.

4. Scrutinize the following two outlines for errors in form as well as in content. Write an improved version of each. Make the first a sentence outline and the second a topic outline.

a. Thesis: The adult Moses is one of the most commanding and inspirational figures of the Old Testament.

I. Moses was a God-intoxicated man.

A. Moses' faith in God.

B. He created in the Hebrews a religious faith that was to endure after their life as a nation had died.

1. The Babylonian and Persian conquests.
2. The faith endured during the Greek conquest.
3. The faith endured during the Roman conquest.
4. Despite their faith, the Hebrews often worshiped foreign gods.
5. The faith endured during the various diasporas.

II. Moses was a peerless travel guide.

A. During the long sojourn in the wilderness, Moses showed endless patience.

1. Enduring constant grumbling on the part of the tribes.
2. This period of desert wandering symbolizes the age of innocence of any developing nation.
3. He settled quarrels with great patience.

B. His earlier flight in order to escape punishment for having killed an Egyptian made him fully acquainted with the Sinai desert.

1. He knew where to find water.
2. He knew how to avoid dangerous enemy territory.
3. He always followed a magical cloud by day and a pillar of fire by night.

III. Moses was the founder of a complex legal system.

A. He gave the Hebrews the Torah.

1. Parts of the Torah dealt with man's relationship to God.
2. Parts of the Torah dealt with man's relationship to man.

B. He gave the Hebrews the ordinances.

1. Some of the ordinances dealt with matters of social justice.
2. According to one ordinance, a man who knocks out his slave's tooth must let that slave go free.
3. Others of the ordinances dealt with religious ceremonies.
4. Some of the ordinances dealt with plans for building a temple.

b. Thesis: A critical analysis of fiction entails several important elements.

I. The nature of fiction

A. Fiction as an imitation of life
B. Fiction as an apprehension of life

II. The substance of fiction
   A. The subject can be many things
      1. It can be a place
      2. Character
      3. Situation
      4. Quality of life
   B. The theme
      1. Expressed by one major idea
      2. Expressed by one or more motifs
III. The characters of fiction
   A. Protagonist
   B. Antagonist
   C. Foil
   D. Confidant
   E. Romeo and Juliet
IV. The structure of fiction
   A. Plot
      1. Conflict
         a. Internal
      2. Progression
         a. Starting in the middle of the action
         b. Proceeding by flashback
         c. Foreshadowing an event
         d. Revealing the ending first
         e. Using strong diction
   B. Archetype
      1. Connecting the past with the present
      2. Establishing universal experience
V. The point of view of fiction
   A. Omniscient observer
   B. First-person narrator
   C. Central consciousness
VI. The language of fiction is dense
   A. Tone
   B. Imagery
   C. Figurative language
   D. Surprise ending

Part TWO

Writing

5

How do I get from outline to paragraph?

- Uses of the paragraph
- Parts of the paragraph
  - The topic sentence
  - Supporting details
  - Levels of generality
- Characteristics of the well-designed paragraph
  - Unity
  - Coherence
  - Completeness
- Transitions between paragraphs
- Special kinds of paragraphs
  - Introductory paragraphs
  - Concluding paragraphs

Application: Form and function in the paragraph

Exercises

Just as the sentence contains one idea in all its fullness, so the paragraph should embrace a distinct episode; and as sentences should follow one another in harmonious sequence, so the paragraphs must fit on to one another like the automatic couplings of railway carriages.

—Winston Churchill

THE PARAGRAPH DATES FROM THE MIDDLE AGES when scribes made a mark in the margins of hand-copied manuscripts to signal a new idea. With the advent of printing, this mark evolved into the familiar indentation of the modern paragraph.

Paragraphs are unquestionably useful to both writer and reader. From the writer's point of view, they allow the typographical underscoring of major ideas. The writer may block off into separate paragraphs those ideas considered important enough to be set apart. For the reader, the paragraph provides a pause, a chance to absorb one idea before encountering another. "The purpose of paragraphing," says one writer who put the reader's case plainly, "is to give the reader a rest."

Uses of the paragraph

Paragraphing in the essay is the equivalent of long division in arithmetic. The aim is to divide and discuss—to reduce the thesis into a series of smaller, discussable ideas that can be treated in separate paragraphs. From ancient times until today, the primary use of the paragraph has therefore been to signal the introduction of a new idea or the further development of an old one. Here is an example of a paragraph signaling a new idea:

> In the modern formal bullfight or corrida de toros there are usually six bulls that are killed by three different men. Each man kills two bulls. The bulls by law are required to be from four to five years old, free from physical defects, and well armed with sharp-pointed horns. They are inspected by a municipal veterinary surgeon before the fight. The veterinary is supposed to reject bulls that are under age, insufficiently armed or with anything wrong with their eyes, their horns or any apparent disease or visible bodily defects such as lameness.

> The men who are to kill them are called matadors and which of the six bulls they are to kill is determined by lot. Each matador, or killer, has a caudrilla, or team, of from five to six men who are paid by him and work under his orders. Three of these men, who aid him on foot with capes and at his orders place the banderillas, three-foot wooden sharps with harpoon points, are called peones or banderilleros. The other two, who are mounted on horses when they appear in the ring, are called picadors.
>
> —Ernest Hemingway, "The Bullfight"

The shift in discussion between the first and second paragraph is obvious: paragraph 1 is about the bulls; paragraph 2 is about the men who will fight and kill them.

A second use of the paragraph is to add significantly to or elaborate on what has been said in a preceding paragraph. Here is an example:

> The oxen in Africa have carried the heavy load of the advance of European civilization. Wherever new land has been broken they have broken it, panting and pulling knee-deep in the soil before the ploughs, the long whips in the air over them. Where a road has been made they have made it; and they have trudged the iron and tools through the land, to the yelling and shouting of the drivers, by tracks in the dust and the long grass of the plains, before there ever were any roads. They have been inspanned before daybreak, and have sweated up and down the long hills, and across dungas and river-beds, through the burning hours of the day. The whips have marked their sides, and you will often see oxen that have had an eye, or both of them, taken away by the long cutting whip-lashes. The waggon-oxen of many Indian and white contractors worked every day, all their lives through, and did not know of the Sabbath.
>
> It is a strange thing that we have done to the oxen. The bull is in a constant stage of fury, rolling his eyes, shovelling up the earth, upset by everything that gets within his range of vision—still he has got a life of his own, fire comes from his nostrils, and new life from his loins; his days are filled with his vital cravings and satisfactions. All of that we have taken away from the oxen, and in reward we have claimed their existence for ourselves. The oxen walk along within our own daily life, pulling hard all the time, creatures without a life, things made for our use. They have moist, limpid, violet eyes, soft muzzles, silky ears, they are patient and dull in all their ways; sometimes they look as if they were thinking about things.
>
> —Isak Dinesen, *Out of Africa*

In the first paragraph the author points out that oxen have played a key role in civilizing the African continent. In the second paragraph she elaborates on the first by reminding us that all of this patient subservience on the part of the oxen is at a price. They are, after all, castrated animals who have lost their drive and will.

Parts of the paragraph

The topic sentence

A paragraph consists of two parts: a *topic sentence* and *supporting details*. In the topic sentence the writer makes a generalization or claim and attempts to prove it with supporting details. If we could present this arrangement as a diagram, this is what a paragraph would look like:

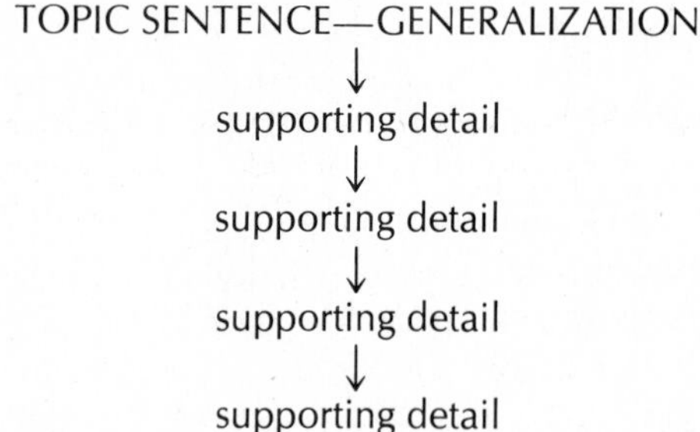

And here is an example of this arrangement with the topic sentence underscored:

> Rotten writing is scarcely a new problem. Napoleon's script was so miserable that one of his generals once mistook a letter of his for battle orders. Charles Hamilton, a Manhattan dealer in autographs and manuscripts, contends that Gertrude Stein's oblique prose style may be explained by the fact that compositors often misread her cryptic script. Poet William Butler Yeats often could not read his own work. Horace Greeley, the editor of the old New York *Tribune*, had a notoriously illegible scrawl. He once scribbled a note to a reporter telling him that he was fired for incompetence; so indecipherable was the missive that for years afterwards the man was able to pass it off as a letter of recommendation.
>
> —"Nowadays, Writing Is Off the Wall," *Time*, January 1, 1980

The topic sentence—the general statement—occurs at the beginning of this paragraph and is followed by supporting details, which consist mainly of examples drawn from history. The diagram of this paragraph vaguely resembles a tabletop supported by a center pedestal. But some paragraphs begin with a generalization and end with one. The first generalization is the topic sentence while the second summarizes what the paragraph is about. If you diagramed such a paragraph, it would look like this:

TOPIC SENTENCE—GENERALIZATION
↓
supporting detail
↓
supporting detail
↓
supporting detail
↓
supporting detail

FINAL SUMMARIZING GENERALIZATION

Writers often use this summarizing sentence if the content of a paragraph is so complex that it requires a summing up. But its use is dictated less by rhetorical necessity than by personal choice and style. Here is an example of this type of paragraph with both the topic sentence and the summarizing generalization underlined:

> A language changes because things happen to people. If we could imagine the impossible—a society in which nothing happened—there would be no changes in language. But except possibly in a cemetery, things are constantly happening to people: they eat, drink, sleep, talk, make love, meet strangers, struggle against natural perils, and fight against one another. They slowly adapt their language to meet the changing conditions of their lives. Although the changes made in one generation may be small, those made in a dozen generations may enormously affect the language. The big and little phases of history—fashions, fads, inventions, the influence of a leader, a war or two, an invasion or two, travel to a foreign land, the demands of business intercourse—may alter a language so much that a Rip Van Winkle who slept two or three hundred years might have trouble making himself understood when he awoke. Even in a relatively quiet society, linguistic change proceeds inexorably.
>
> —J. N. Hook and E. G. Mathews, *Modern American Grammar and Usage*

A single topic sentence can also be developed over the course of two or more paragraphs. This development usually occurs when the topic sentence is too broad or complex to be adequately covered in a single paragraph, or when the presentation of supporting details in several paragraphs is more emphatic. A diagram of a topic sentence developed over two paragraphs would look like this:

TOPIC SENTENCE—GENERALIZATION

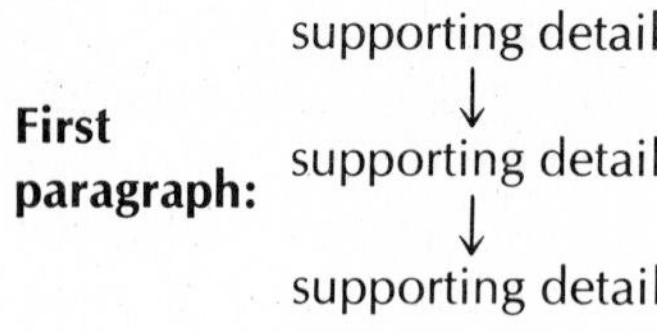

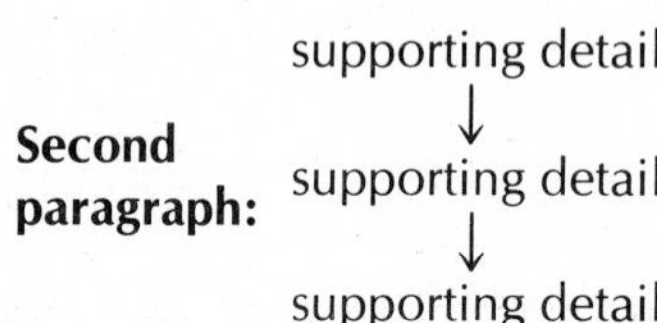

The following is an example of a topic sentence developed over two paragraphs. The topic sentence is underlined:

> There has always been something so fascinating about the mere fact of fatness that men of all nations and of many degrees of wisdom or lack of it have formulated opinions on its state, its origins, and its correction. Shakespeare's characters are at their most eloquent when the topic is obesity. "Make less thy body and hence more thy grace. Leave gormandizing. Know the grave doth gape for thee thrice wider than for other men." And, of course, to Julius Caesar, the Bard attributed the notion of the harmlessness of fat companions in warning against "the lean and hungry look" of "yon Cassius."
>
> In *Coming Up for Air,* George Orwell has the narrator, himself a fat man, sum it up: "They all think a fat man isn't quite like other men. He goes through life on a light-comedy plane . . . as low farce." Sometimes the situation is just as sad and much less tolerable. When W. D. Howells was consul at Venice, he was told by a tall lanky man, "If I were as fat as you, I would hang myself." And Osborn in his otherwise lightly satirical picture-essay, *The Vulgarians*, pontificates, "The fat and the fatuous are interchangeable."
>
> —Jean Mayer, *Overweight: Causes, Cost, and Control*

Covering a topic sentence in more than one paragraph allows for a fuller development of the general idea. But there is a pitfall attendant on this, namely, the temptation to digress. The beginning writer will find it safer to use a separate topic sentence for each paragraph.

As the sum of what a paragraph is about, its topic sentence should naturally occupy a prominent position. And in all our examples so far the topic sentence has come first. Such a paragraph is said to be organized from the general to the particular: the idea first, followed by the particulars. The reverse of this arrangement is the paragraph organized from the particular to the general, where the supporting details come first and the topic sentence last. Here is an example:

> The human population already stands at over 4 billion, and at current growth rates that number will double within thirty-eight years. If the growth rate were to continue unchecked, in fact, the global population would reach about 150 billion within two centuries. Yet nearly two-thirds of the existing inhabitants of the earth are undernourished or malnourished, and they are dying of starvation at the rate of more than 10 million every year. There can be little question that unchecked population growth is the most critical social problem in the modern world, with potential consequences in terms of sheer human misery that are almost unimaginable.
>
> —Ian Robertson, *Sociology*

This arrangement is an uncommon one and somewhat mannered. Before you can cite details in support of an idea, you must first know what the idea is. Consequently, it has become traditional for writers to first state the general idea of a paragraph and then cite details in support of it, since this pattern conforms to the way people usually reason. The paragraph in which the topic sentence appears after the supporting details should be used only as a change of pace, not as a matter of course.

Finally, some paragraphs have topic sentences that come not first or last, but second or third. Paragraphs of this kind of are usually found in the middle of the essay. The initial sentences are used to ensure a smooth transition from the preceding paragraph, and then the topic sentence makes its appearance. Here is an example:

> In our own way, we conform as best as we can to the rest of nature. The obituary pages tell us of the news that we are dying off, while the birth announcements in finer print, off at the side of the page, inform us of our replacements, but we get no grasp from this of the enormity of scale. There are 3 billion of us on the earth, and all 3 billion must be dead, on schedule, within this lifetime. The vast mortality, involving something over 50 million of us each year, takes place in relative secrecy. We can only really know of the deaths in our households, or among our friends. These, detached in our

> minds from the rest, we take to be unnatural events, anomalies, outrages. We speak of our own dead in low voices; struck down, we say, as though visible death can only occur for cause, by disease, or violence, avoidably. We send off flowers, grieve, make ceremonies, scatter bones, unaware of the rest of the 3 billion on the same schedule. All that immense mass of flesh and bone and consciousness will disappear by absorption into the earth, without recognition by the transient survivors.
>
> —Lewis Thomas, "Death in the Open"

The first sentence is for transition—to connect this paragraph with the one before. The second sentence is the topic sentence. It contains the assertion that the supporting details prove.

Supporting Details

The supporting details of a paragraph are specific assertions of fact that support the topic sentence. What sort of details you need will vary with the point you are trying to support. Supporting details may include examples, statistics, and the opinions of authorities. In the paragraph about bad handwriting, the supporting details consist of historical examples, while the paragraph about attitudes toward the obese is supported by the quoted opinions of famous men.

But not every topic sentence contains an assertion that can be supported by examples, statistics, or opinions. Sometimes, in order to support the topic sentence, the writer must carry the argument to its logical conclusion rather than recite facts and figures. Here is an example:

> The question then arises, "What sort of evidence *would* prove the efficacy of prayer?" The thing we pray for may happen, but how can you ever know it was not going to happen anyway? Even if the thing were indisputably miraculous it would not follow that the miracle had occurred because of your prayers. The answer surely is that a compulsive empirical proof such as we have in the sciences can never be attained.
>
> Some things are proved by the unbroken uniformity of our experiences. The law of gravitation is established by the fact that, in our experience, all bodies without exception obey it. Now even if all the things that people prayed for happened, which they do not, this would not prove what Christians mean by the efficacy of prayer. For prayer is request. The essence of request, as distinct from compulsion, is that it may or may not be granted. And if an infinitely

> wise Being listens to the requests of finite and foolish creatures, of course He will sometimes grant and sometimes refuse them. Invariable "success" in prayer would not prove the Christian doctrine at all. It would prove something much more like magic—a power in certain human beings to control, or compel, the course of nature.
>
> —C. S. Lewis, "The Efficacy of Prayer"

In the second paragraph the writer is trying to support an assertion stated in the first: that no empirical proof can ever be found to establish the efficacy of prayer. His supporting details consist not of examples, statistics, or opinions but of an extended argument.

Levels of generality

Because a paragraph contains one topic sentence but many supporting details, its sentences will be found to vary in their *levels of generality*. This expression refers to the degree in which a sentence is either specific or general in the assertion it makes. In the typical paragraph, the most general sentence will be the topic sentence; the more specific sentences will supply supporting details. It is possible to mark the sentences of any well-written paragraph on a general to specific scale, using 1 to denote the most general sentence and 4 the most specific:

> 1. As an historian, I have plowed through state papers, memoirs, diaries, and letters, and I know that the ability to write has only a remote connection with either intelligence, greatness, or schooling. 4. Lincoln had no schooling yet became one of the great prose writers of the world. 4. Cromwell went to Cambridge and was hardly able to frame an intelligible sentence. 3. Another man of thought and action, Admiral Howe, generally refrained from writing out his plan for battle, so as to save his captains from inevitable misunderstanding. 4. Yet Howe managed to win the famous First of June by tactics that revolutionized the art, and led directly to Nelson's Trafalgar plan—itself a rather muddled piece of prose. 2. Let us start with no illusions about an imaginary golden age of writing.
>
> —Jacques Barzun, "How to Write and Be Read"

If you have written a sound, well-supported paragraph, you should be able to work a similar exercise on its sentences, with similar results. For every general assertion in your paragraph, you should have three or four more specific ones. If this proportion is not true of your paragraph, you have failed to provide adequate support for its topic sentence.

Characteristics of the well-designed paragraph

The characteristics of the well-designed paragraph are unity, coherence, and completeness.

Unity

A paragraph is said to have unity when its sentences stick to the topic and do not stray to secondary issues or deal with irrelevancies. All the sentences focus on the topic of the paragraph to the exclusion of everything else. Student writers often have difficulty maintaining unity in the paragraphs they write. They promise one thing in the topic sentence and give something else in the supporting details. Here is an example from a student paper:

> 1. A fairy tale is a serious story with a human hero and a happy ending. 2. The hero in a fairy tale is different from the hero in a tragedy in that his progression is from bad to good fortune, rather than the reverse. 3. <u>In the Greek tragedy "Oedipus Rex," for example, the hero goes from highest fortune to lowest misery, but in the end he recognizes his error in judgment and maintains a noble posture despite profound suffering. 4. The audience watching him is purged of pity and fear through what Aristotle labeled a "catharsis."</u> 5. The hero in a fairy tale usually has a miserable beginning. 6. He is either socially obscure or despised as being stupid and lacking in heroic virtues. 7. But in the end, he has surprised everyone by demonstrating his courage, consequently winning fame, riches, and love. 8. We clearly see this bad-to-good-fortune progress in stories like "Cinderella," "Sleeping Beauty," and "The Frog Prince."

The topic sentence of the paragraph promises to give a definition of a fairy tale, but part of the paragraph drifts away from the definition. The digression begins at the end of sentence 2, when the writer is still attempting the definition by specifying what a fairy tale is not—it is not a Greek tragedy. However, sentences 3 and 4 are entirely beside the point. With the fifth sentence the writer resumes the announced intent of the paragraph—to define a fairy tale.

The possible causes of this fault are several. Some digressions can be traced to a writer's daydreaming; some to boredom with the topic on hand; some to a desire to impress the reader by introducing an interesting but irrelevant point. The cure is not easy to prescribe. What the inexperienced writer needs to remember is that the purpose of the paragraph is announced in the topic sentence, and it is this purpose that the other sentences of the paragraph must carry out.

The beginning writer is most likely to be sidetracked at the end of a paragraph. Usually the digression occurs because, in an attempt to conclude the paragraph, the writer introduces a second topic sentence instead of summarizing what the paragraph is about. Here is an example:

> In America the car has taken on some distinctly religious overtones. The family station wagon is a type of chapel where the family can commune with nature and each other; the weekly car wash is a baptismal ritual or cleansing rite; and the periodic trade-in for a better model is a pilgrimage to find renewal, rebirth, and reaffirmation. The recent crop of religious bumper stickers ("Honk If You Love Jesus"; "Have the Holy Spirit, Will Share"; "Guess Who's Coming Again"; "In Case Of Rapture, This Driver Will Disappear") is undeniable evidence that religion has invaded the automobile. *However, the religious bumper sticker is not necessarily a sign of true religion. It takes more than snappy slogans to be a real Christian.*

The italicized sentences stray from the point of the topic sentence: "in America the car has taken on some distinctly religious overtones." These sentences should be left out or their idea developed in another paragraph.

Coherence

A paragraph has coherence when its sentences are logically connected. But sentences are not automatically linked simply because they follow one after another on the page. Four devices can be used to insure paragraph coherence:

1. Transitional words and phrases
2. Pronoun reference
3. Repeated key terms
4. Parallelism

Transitional words and phrases, which point out the direction of the paragraph, are used to link its sentences. Here is an example:

> <u>In addition</u> to the academic traditionalism in schools, there are other problems. <u>First,</u> there is the problem of coordinating education with the realities of the work. <u>Second,</u> there is the question of how long the schooling period should be. <u>Despite evidence to the contrary,</u> a case can be made for the notion that we not only overeducate our children, but also take too long to do it.

The underlined words and phrases add coherence to the passage. They join sentences, and consequently ideas, in clear and logical relationships. Without the use of transitional words and phrases, the writing would seem choppy and the relationships between sentences unclear. Here is a list of some transitional words and phrases:

after all	in contrast
also	and
in fact	as a consequence
in spite of	nevertheless
finally	for example
next	however
therefore	moreover
furthermore	but

Coherence can also be achieved by *pronoun reference*. A noun is used in one sentence or clause, and a pronoun that refers to it is used in the next sentence or clause. In the following paragraph the pronouns so used are underlined:

> Twenty years ago women were a majority of the population, but they were treated like a minority group. The prejudice against them was so deep-rooted that, paradoxically, most people pretended that it did not exist. Indeed, most women preferred to ignore the situation than to rock the boat. They accepted being paid less for doing the same work as a man. They were as quick as any male to condemn a woman who ventured outside the limits of the roles men had assigned to females: those of toy and drudge.

Key terms may be repeated throughout the paragraph to link sentences. The key terms are underlined:

> Fantasy is not restricted to one sector of the southern California way of life; it is all pervasive. Los Angeles restaurants and their parking lots are such million-dollar structures because they are palaces of fantasy in which the upward-moving individual comes to act out a self-mythology he or she has learned from a hero of the mass media. Often enough, the establishments of La Cienega Boulevard's Restaurant Row are fantasies of history in their very architecture.

Parallelism is also used to ensure coherence, although not nearly so often as any of the other three devices. The principle behind parallelism is that similar ideas are expressed in structurally similar sentences (see also "Parallelism," Section 28 of the handbook). Here is a paragraph that uses parallelism to ensure coherence:

> Now, I will not for a moment deny that getting ahead of your neighbor is delightful, but it is not the only delight of which human beings are capable. There are innumerable things which are not competitive. It is possible to enjoy food and drink without having to reflect that you have a better cook and a better wine merchant than your former friends whom you are learning to cold-shoulder. It is possible to be fond of your wife and children without reflecting how much better she dresses than Mrs. So-and-So and how much better they are at athletics than the children of that old stick-in-the-mud Mr. Such-and-Such. There are those who can enjoy music without thinking how cultured the other ladies in their women's club will be thinking them. There are even people who enjoy a fine day in spite of the fact that the sun shines on everybody. All these simple pleasures are destroyed as soon as competitiveness gets the upper hand.
>
> —Bertrand Russell, "The Unhappy American Way"

Completeness

A paragraph is complete when it has provided enough details to support its topic sentence. A paragraph is incomplete when the topic sentence is not developed or when it is merely extended through repetition. In either case the reader is burdened with useless generalizations. The following paragraph is incomplete.

> Withholding tax is a bad way to go about collecting taxes from the people in our country because this system assumes that the American people are incompetent.

This paragraph hints at an argument, but then comes to a dead stop. The reader will automatically ask, "In what way or by what means does tax withholding assume that the American people are incompetent?" Without further evidence, the paragraph goes nowhere. The paragraph below, although longer, will leave the reader just as dissatisfied.

> Withholding tax is a bad way to go about collecting taxes from the people in our country because this system assumes that the American people are incompetent. By withholding taxes, the federal government is acting as if the American people were a pack of

> irresponsible children who lack any sense of accountability. Tax withholding is a way of showing distrust. How can individuals become dependable citizens when their own government treats them as if they were incapable of doing their duty?

Here the topic sentence has been elaborated on, but no real content has been added. Every sentence repeats the original topic sentence and does not drive the argument forward with convincing support. Now read the paragraph below:

> Withholding is a bad way to go about collecting tax money, even though the figures may show that it gets results. It is bad because it implies that the individual is incapable of handling his own affairs. The government as much as says, We know that, if left to your own devices, you will fritter away your worldly goods, and tax day will catch you without cash. Or it says, We're not sure you'll come clean in your return, so we will just take the money before it reaches you, and you will be saved the trouble and fuss of being honest. This implication is an unhealthy thing to spread around, being contrary to the old American theory that the individual is a very competent little guy indeed. The whole setup of our democratic government assumes that the citizen is bright, honest, and at least as fundamentally sound as a common stock. If you start treating him as something less than that, you are going to get into deep water. The device of withholding tax money, which is clearly confiscatory, since the individual is not allowed to see, taste, or touch a certain percentage of his wages, tacitly brands him as negligent or unthrifty or immature or incompetent or dishonest, or all of those things at once. There is, furthermore, a bad psychological effect in earning money that you never get your paws on. We believe this effect to be much stronger than the government realizes. At any rate, if the American individual is in truth incapable of paying his tax all by himself, then he should certainly be regarded as incapable of voting all by himself, and the Secretary of the Treasury should accompany him into the booth to show him where to put the X.
>
> —E. B. White, "Withholding"

While the reader may not agree with these ideas, the writer has fulfilled his promise to show why he does not like withholding tax. He has provided clear examples and has moved from the general to the specific, keeping in mind the direction of his topic sentence. His paragraph is complete. Make your paragraphs complete by providing enough detail to support their topic sentences.

Transitions between paragraphs

The distance between two paragraphs is measurable by the difference between their ideas. Successive paragraphs dealing with different ideas often need a transition between them to prevent the reader from becoming confused. It is entirely false to assume—as many student writers do—that the use of a new paragraph is itself a kind of transition. Something more is often needed—some formal transition to help the reader follow your discussion.

The transition between two paragraphs may be made through the use of a phrase, a sentence, or even an entire paragraph. Here is an example of a transitional phrase linking two paragraphs:

> Some commanders of ships take their Departure from the home coast sadly, in a spirit of grief and discontent. They have a wife, children perhaps, some affection at any rate, or perhaps only some pet vice: that must be left behind for a year or more. I remember only one man who walked his deck with a springy step and gave the first course in an elated voice. But he, as I learned afterwards, was leaving nothing behind him, except a welter of debts and threats of legal proceedings.
>
> On the other hand, I have known many captains who, directly their ship had left the narrow waters of the Channel, would disappear for some three days or more. They would take a long dive, as it were, into their state-room, only to emerge a few days afterwards with a more or less serene brow. Those were the men easy to go on with. Besides, such a complete retirement seemed to imply a satisfactory amount of trust in their officers, and to be trusted displeases no seaman worthy of the name.
>
> —Joseph Conrad, "Landfalls and Departures"

The phrase that opens the second paragraph, "on the other hand," is transitional. It alerts the reader to the fact that this paragraph is going to describe a very different kind of captain than the preceding paragraph did. Many other phrases and words can be used to signal the shift in discussion from one paragraph to another. If the second paragraph is to make a significant addition to the first, words such as "furthermore," "moreover," or "additionally" might be used. Other kinds of shifts can be indicated by using such common connecting words and phrases as "however," "but," "nevertheless," "in spite of."

Another way to make a transition from one paragraph to another is by using an initial connecting sentence. Here is an example:

> It is beginning to look as if we are deeply connected with our cosmic surroundings. Some of these connections may dictate matters as mundane as the weather. Several British astronomers suggest that the Ice Age may have been triggered by the solar system's having passed through a cloud of dust and gas associated with one of our galaxy's spiral arms.
>
> Still deeper connections between ourselves and the galaxies are being discerned. Astrophysicists studying the chemical composition of stars, and biologists investigating the chemical composition of our bodies, have found that we are made up of much the same allotment of elements as is our galaxy: The metals found in trace elements in our bodies appear to have been formed in the explosions of stars that died before the sun was born, seeding space with the metal-rich dust and gas from which our solar system and, eventually, ourselves were formed.
>
> —Timothy Ferris, "Probing the Mysteries of the Galaxies"

The underlined transitional sentence refers to the content of the first paragraph and predicts the content of the second. To understand the reference to "still deeper connections," for instance, the reader must track back to the first paragraph and recall its discussion there. Yet, at the same time, the sentence is shifting the discussion from the connections mentioned in the first paragraph to those about to be discussed in the second.

A third way to make the transition from one paragraph to another is by using a transitional paragraph:

> It is paradoxical stuff, kitsch. It is obviously bad: so bad that you can scarcely understand how any human being would spend days and weeks making it, and how anybody else would buy it and take it home and keep it and dust it and leave it to her heirs. It is terribly ingenious, and terribly ugly, and utterly useless; and yet it has one of the qualities of good art—which is that, once seen, it is not easily forgotten. Of course it is found in all the arts: think of Milan Cathedral, or the statues in Westminster Abbey, or Liszt's settings of Schubert's songs. There is a lot of it in the United States—for instance, the architecture of Miami, Florida, and the Forest Lawn Cemetery in Los Angeles. Many of Hollywood's most ambitious historical films are superb kitsch. Most Tin Pan Alley love songs are perfect 100 percent kitsch.
>
> There is kitsch in the world of books also. I collect it. It is horrible, but I enjoy it.

> The gem of my collection is the work of the Irish novelist Mrs. Amanda McKittrick Ros, whose masterpiece, *Delina Delaney*. . . .
>
> —Gilbert Highet, "Kitsch"

The second paragraph is a transitional paragraph. It is short and to the point because it simply shifts the discussion from one *major* topic to another. In this case, the discussion is shifted from kitsch in the general arts to kitsch in literature.

Finally, the transition from one paragraph to another can be achieved by repeating a single theme. In the following example, the successive paragraphs are joined by their focus on the theme that "killing for sport is pure evil":

> To me it is inconceivable how anyone should think an animal more interesting dead than alive. I can also easily prove to my own satisfaction that killing "for sport" is the perfect type of pure evil for which metaphysicians have sometimes sought.
>
> Most wicked deeds are done because the doer proposes some good to himself. The liar lies to gain some end; the swindler and the thief want things which, if honestly got, might be good in themselves. Even the murderer may be removing an impediment to normal desires or gaining possession of something which his victim keeps from him. None of these usually does evil for evil's sake. They are selfish or unscrupulous, but their deeds are not gratuitously evil. The killer for sport has no such comprehensible motive. He prefers death to life, darkness to light. He gets nothing except the satisfaction of saying, "Something which wanted to live is dead. There is that much less vitality, consciousness, and, perhaps, joy in the universe. I am the Spirit that Denies." When a man wantonly destroys one of the works of man we call him Vandal. When he wantonly destroys one of the works of God we call him Sportsman.
>
> The hunter-for-food may be as wicked and as misguided as vegetarians sometimes say; but he does not kill for the sake of killing. The rancher and the farmer who exterminate all living things not immediately profitable to them may sometimes be working against their own best interests; but whether they are or are not they hope to achieve some supposed good by their exterminations. If to do evil not in the hope to gain but for evil's sake involves the deepest guilt by which man can be stained, then killing for killing's sake is a terrifying phenomenon and as strong a proof as we could have of that "reality of evil" with which present-day theologians are again concerned.
>
> —Joseph Wood Krutch, "Killing for Sport is Pure Evil"

Special kinds of paragraphs

Most paragraphs have a topic sentence and supporting details, but a few have neither. Generally, these few are highly specialized paragraphs that perform a limited function in the essay. Among them are the following.

Introductory paragraphs

The introductory paragraph has two uses: It must catch the attention of readers and make them want to read on; it must say what the essay is going to do. Such a paragraph consists of two parts: an opener and a thesis—with the thesis occupying its traditional place as the last sentence of the paragraph. Here is an example:

> Man in the Arctic has always defended himself from the forces of nature, from the environment. At times he has had to protect himself from wild animals. Now, however, a new era has dawned, when nature in the Arctic must be preserved from man himself. The animals of the world, the cleanest lakes and rivers, and even the crystal air of the Arctic are threatened.
>
> —Yuri Ryhkheu, "People of the Long Spring"

The first three sentences draw the reader's attention to the Arctic; then follows the thesis as the last sentence of the opening paragraph.

The Lead

"Lead" is the journalistic term for the opening sentence of an article whose aim is to hook and hold the reader. Of such paramount importance is the lead in the world of journalism that students are schooled in its various types. Here are some examples of different types of leads you might consider using as openers in your own essays.

The *bullet lead* is a short sentence aimed at hooking the reader with its dramatic impact. Here are some examples:

> "There is no such thing as a minor nuclear power." (from a newspaper article about the worldwide proliferation of nuclear arsenals)
>
> "Polls show that 21% of wives cheat—or is it 54%? (from a magazine article about the unreliability of statistics about sex)
>
> "Anwar Sadat is dead." (from a student essay about Sadat's assassination)

The bullet lead has a staccato, breathtaking quality that makes it an especially suitable beginning for shocking or weighty topics.

The *spotlight lead* focuses on a scene or event related to the thesis. It has the advantage of opening *in medias res*—in the middle of the action. Here are some examples:

> "First, there is the unspeakable sadness: the image of beautiful Grace Kelly, dead at 52 in the embrace of twisted steel." (from a magazine article about Grace Kelly's death)

> "On the cab of a battered and overloaded Toyota van waiting at the border between Nigeria and neighboring Benin was the unintentionally ironic sign NO CONDITION IS PERMANENT." (from a magazine article about the expulsion of 80,000 Ghanaians from Nigeria)

> "For more than a minute today the sun hung over Los Angeles like a twinkling, slate-blue platter as the moon slid between it and the earth, bathing the city in an awesome half-light that told the amazed audience of scientists and curious onlookers that a total solar eclipse was taking place." (from a student paper about an eclipse)

Done vividly, the spotlight lead wields a quick, effective hook. You begin in the middle with here and now, and trace back to there and then—to explanation, cause, discussion. It is the favorite lead of *Time* magazine.

The *quotation lead* is a quotation related to the thesis of the essay. It may be a quotation from a person featured in the article, from an expert on your subject, or from a literary source. Here are two examples:

> In the revolutionary 1960's, Terry O'Banion, a well-respected educator, stated, "The 'F' grade is an extension of the scarlet letter and represents the wrathfulness of the Protestant ethic in that all who fail must be punished. A student is required to wear his failure on his transcript for all to see for the duration of his life." Following O'Banion's humanizing influence, many teachers gradually abandoned the "F" grade. But today, as the 1980's face a rising tide of mediocrity in our schools, we are witnessing a rebirth of stringent standards with the consequent re-appearance of the "F" grade.
>
> —Elaine Palange

> "'Tis not enough to help the feeble up, / But to support him after,' says the charitable Timon of Athens in Shakespeare's play." (from a student essay about caring for the downtrodden)

Naturally, if you do lead with a quotation, you must give it accurately and identify your source.

The *thesis lead* is simply a forthright statement of the thesis. Consequently, if your thesis is dull, your lead will be dull. So we advise you to use this lead with caution. Saying too much too soon can make your entire essay seem anticlimactic. Here are two examples of good thesis leads:

> "Perhaps the bitterest, most physical and obvious poverty that can be seen in an American city exists in skid row among the alcoholics."
>
> —Michael Harrington, *The Other America*

> "I take it as an article of faith that we humans are a profoundly immature species; that, in fact, we do not know most knowable things; and that we are only now beginning to learn how to learn."
>
> —Lewis Thomas, "On the Edge of Knowledge"

Both these thesis leads are good because they are thought-provoking—they arouse in the reader an immediate curiosity about how the thesis will be proved. Neither thesis is merely a dull, mechanical announcement of a self-evident truth.

Openings to avoid

No book this size can account for every possible way to begin an essay. But the leads described above should at least give you a notion of how to make a fresh start, and should convince you that you do not have to open in the same mechanical way every time.

Just as some openings are good, others are decidedly bad. Among the worst are the following, all from student essays and all—much to the sorrow of English teachers—seemingly gaining in popularity:

1. "I think," "I feel," "In my opinion," or "In my judgment" as an opening:

> "I think the consequences of legalizing marijuana would be far less serious than not legalizing it."

Any opinion, feeling, thought, or judgment you express in an essay is automatically assumed to be yours, unless you say otherwise. It is therefore useless to label them, especially at the beginning of an essay—just as bad (and unnecessary) as prefacing your every utterance with "I am saying."

2. The opening that mechanically announces the topic:

> "My essay is about couples who choose to live together without getting married because they feel this arrangement allows them more freedom."

It is difficult to imagine a reader who would not wince if forced to read an essay with such an uninspired beginning.

3. The opening that merely sums up the topic sentences of the essay:

> "If marijuana were legalized people would be stoned at work and school, drug dealers would become legally rich, and people would begin experimenting with other dangerous drugs."

This is a thesis lead, but a dull and predictable one. It wants some prefacing spice to whet the reader's appetite.

Concluding paragraphs

Effective Endings

If the introductory paragraph should pique a reader's interest, then the concluding one should satisfy it. An effective closing technique is to make the ending sum up the entire essay as did the thesis in its beginning. Here is an example from an essay about a microcephalic baby born to a surrogate mother through artificial insemination. The writer has argued throughout the essay that the baby, though defective, is still human. He ends on the same note:

> The point is simply that these goods are people, however they may be produced. Nor is any child to be judged or treated as a factory reject merely because something is wrong with him. One forgets these things from time to time, lost in pride at our advancement.
>
> —*Time*, 14 February 1983

Another effective ending is to tell the reader what ought to be done. Here is an example from an essay in which the author has argued that the only real technology in medicine is that which comes from a genuine understanding of disease:

> If I were a policy-maker, interested in saving money for health care over the long haul, I would regard it as an act of high prudence to give high priority to a lot more basic research in biologic science. This is the only way to get the full mileage that biology owes to the science of medicine, even though it seems, as used to be said in the days when the phrase still had some meaning, like asking for the moon.
>
> —Lewis Thomas, "Technology of Medicine"

A variation on this sort of ending is the one which details the consequences that are likely to occur if a certain action or program is not carried out. Here is an example. The writer has been arguing that instead of being cut back—as they are—the humanities should be increased on all levels of American education:

> Jefferson was prouder of having been the founder of the University of Virginia than of having been President of the United States. He knew that the educated and developed mind was the best assurance that a political system could be made to work—a system based on the informed consent of the governed. If this idea fails, then all the saved tax dollars in the world will not be enough to prevent the nation from turning on itself.
>
> —Norman Cousins, "How to Make People Smaller than They Are"

Implicit in every beginning is also an ending. And sometimes the best ending is the one that brings the essay full circle in order to answer any questions or doubts left in the reader's mind. Here is an example. First the opening:

> "Will spelling count?" In my first year of teaching freshman composition I had a little act I performed whenever a student asked that inevitable question. Frowning, taking my pipe out of my mouth, and hesitating, I would try to look like a man coming down from some higher mental plane. Then, with what I hoped sounded like a mixture of confidence and disdain, I would answer, "No. Of course it won't."

And then the ending:

> This year I have a little act I perform whenever a student asks, "Will spelling count?" Frowning, taking my pipe out of my mouth, and hesitating a moment, I try to look like a man coming down from some higher plane. Then, with what I hope sounds like a mixture of confidence and disdain, I reply, "Yes. Of course it will."
>
> —Jack Connor, "Will Spelling Count?"

A commonplace but effective ending is one that tells the reader what meaning may be drawn from the essay. Here is an example from an essay on heredity versus environment:

> The extent to which intelligence can be developed may be low, in which case no environment can produce a high IQ; then

> heredity sets a limit on the development. But the child may have inherited a better brain, capable of developing a high IQ, and yet in a poor environment his IQ remains low—just as with a child that inherited a poorer brain.
>
> —Donald Olding Hebb, *Textbook of Psychology*

But probably the best and most effective ending of all is the one that takes the reader slightly by surprise by restating the writer's views with a slight twist. Often brief, this memorable kind of ending is uniquely adapted to each essay and demands a creative turn of mind from the writer. Here is an example:

> Hard as it is for many of us to believe, women are not really superior to men in intelligence or humanity—they are only equal.
>
> —Anne Roiphe, "Confessions of a Female Chauvinist Sow"

And here is a second example (from an essay called "The Sophisticated Man"):

> Some years ago at a large party I met a man whose reputation had preceded him as a brilliant writer and the contented husband of a handsome wife. After fifteen minutes of spirited but impersonal conversation, he took my hand and said very quietly, "I love you." He knew that I knew that he meant it. I knew that he would never leave his wife. We shared a mutual knowledge, separately arrived at.
>
> And that, I think, is the final virtue of sophistication. It is a condition beyond explanation.
>
> —Marya Mannes

This sort of ending, while taking the reader by surprise, should not stun with a bizarre unexpectedness. If the twist doesn't emerge naturally out of your essay, don't try to force it. End on some other note.

Endings to Avoid

Bad endings, like bad beginnings, are classifiable by major, ever recurring types. Do your utmost to avoid endings like the following, all from student essays:

1. "In conclusion, let me say . . ."

> In conclusion, let me say that it's harder for men to assume feminine roles than it is for women to assume masculine roles.

The assignment was to attack or defend this topic: "Our society allows women to assume masculine roles more readily than it allows males to assume roles traditionally called feminine." What makes the ending poor is not its phrasing but its dismal, abrupt predictability. The reader gets the impression that the writer feels like a surly sales clerk who, having put in a minimum stay behind the counter, has decided to close shop and go home. And so down comes the shutter with "In conclusion, let me say." It may bang shut with a variation, such as "Therefore, these are the reasons why I believe" or "Last but not least" or some other pat phrase. But bang shut it does, with rude finality.

2. The ending that repeats the opening almost word for word. Here is the opening:

> Many couples choose to live together without getting married because they feel it allows them more freedom in their relationships and if it doesn't work out all they have to do is leave without any long drawn-out divorce.

And here is its cloned ending:

> Many couples feel living together will bring more freedom to their relationship and less worry about what will happen if it doesn't work out. They don't want to put up with any long drawn-out divorce when they part.

Writers do often end their essays by bringing them full circle. But they try to do so with verve and wit, not by merely tracking stubbornly back to where they began like a determined salmon.

3. "I think," "I feel," "In my opinion." We do not need to give examples of this worst of all possible endings because it is popular enough to be widely known. Do not end with these words. You can, of course, end by saying what you think or feel or hold as an opinion, but you should not do it in such a boring and predictable way. Here is an example in which the student writer gives her opinion, says what she thinks, and shares what she feels about couples who live together, without once using those dull words:

> Although the living together arrangement seems to be working out well for these couples, I couldn't live that way. All their reasons for living together make sense, but if they are going to live and act like married couples, why not get married? Couples should, of course, have the freedom of choice on how they live their lives, but those who choose to live together out of wedlock are making a mistake.

Application: Form and function in the paragraph

To begin with, let us be clear about one thing. A block of words on a page is not a paragraph merely because it looks like one; it must also *function* like one. Here is an example of what we mean:

> Margaret Mitchell's first husband, Clifford Henry, died in World War I, Scarlett O'Hara's first husband, Charles Hamilton, died in the Civil War. (Notice that their initials are the same.)
>
> Margaret Mitchell shocked Atlanta's Junior League when she danced an Apache dance at her debutante ball; Scarlett O'Hara outraged the Confederate Old Home Guard by dancing with Rhett Butler while she was still in mourning.
>
> Margaret Mitchell served as a volunteer nurse during Atlanta's great fire of 1917; Scarlet O'Hara served as a volunteer nurse at the makeshift hospital in war-time Atlanta.

Make point, prove point: in expository writing this is usually the dual function of the paragraph. The topic sentence makes the point; the supporting details contained in the body of the paragraph prove it. The examples above, from an actual student paper, do neither. None contains a topic sentence. The student is not paragraphing; he is dabbling in lay-out.

So it is not enough merely to clothe your sentences in the uniform of the paragraph—the familiar indented first line and blocklike shape. You must make a point in your paragraphs, and then you must prove it. Your points must be related to the big idea of your essay—its thesis. And each paragraph should advance your discussion of the thesis in at least one small step.

To the familiar student query, "How long should my paragraphs be?" the often unsatisfactory answer is, "Long enough to prove your point." And while that answer may seem a vague reply to a definite question, it indicates the relationship between form and function in the paragraph. What you are trying to do in the paragraph—its function—will determine its final size—its form. You cannot both make and prove a point in a paragraph only one or two sentences long. You need at least five or six sentences, perhaps more.

The clearest example of how function alters form in the paragraph is to be found in the writing of journalists. Any newspaper reader has regularly seen paragraphs like these:

> With shuddering regularity, students pull books from Harvard's vast library stacks and find nothing between the covers but dust.
>
> The problem is enormous for Harvard, owner of 9.3 million books. But it is just as painful for lovers of the written word everywhere.

> From humble paperbacks to leather-bound editions, books by the billions are dying in public and private collections across the country. The reason: they are printed on paper that self-destructs.
>
> —Daniel Haney, "Books by Billions are Turning to Dust"

The paragraphs above, like the platypus, are examples of specialized evolution—of form adapting to unique function. Journalists seldom argue or debate in newspapers; they report. And they report to readers who have little time for more than the bare facts. The result is that the journalistic paragraph has gradually shrunk until it is nowadays usually only a sentence or two long. Its obvious advantage is that it can be instantly read and understood by people with varying reading abilities. Journalistic paragraphs also help the appearance of the printed page of newspapers and magazines, which are printed in columns. Long paragraphs in narrow columns produce impenetrable tracts of solid type, with no relief for the eye.

The journalistic paragraph, however, is for journalists, not students. Student writers are expected to do more than merely generalize about a topic or serve up the simplisms of the times for hurried readers: they are expected to define, argue, prove, classify, persuade, and refute. They are expected to deal with ideas and evidence, and to back up assertions with facts, observations, and expert opinion. In short, they are expected to write their papers using the traditional kind of paragraph that has evolved out of expository writing.

EXERCISES

1. Write a suitable topic sentence for a paragraph that would contain the following supporting details:

   a. (1) Cultivate only the best writers.
      (2) You needn't assume that just because something is in print, it is well written.
      (3) If you fall into the habit of reading hacks or writers that have only a dulled sense for the right word, then you are not helping yourself to become a writer who is fresh and original.
      (4) Read those authors who appear in *The New Yorker*, who get good reviews in magazines like *Saturday Review*, and who haven't faded after writing one book or one play.

   b. (1) In primitive tribes this concern was limited to members of the tribe. If a man was not a member, one need not worry about whether one was behaving ethically or unethically toward him.
      (2) But as man started reflecting on his own behavior and how it affected others, he slowly began to realize that his social

concerns—his ethics—must include all human beings with whom he came in contact.

(3) Thus it can be said that a system of ethics evolved in order to assure that man would be at peace with himself.

c. (1) Vaccination for German measles has practically eradicated the incidence of birth defects and other complications resulting from that disease.

(2) Smallpox vaccination has been so effective that doctors have to hunt to find a case of smallpox.

(3) In the last thirty years, the Salk vaccine has substantially reduced the number of polio victims in our country.

(4) While a few people fear that some new and terrible disease will crop up for which no vaccine will be powerful enough, we can rejoice in the fact that at least the major child killers of the past have been vanquished.

2. Create a paragraph based on the topic sentence provided and following the levels of generality as listed.

1. Fashion designers force consumers to spend unnecessary money on clothes by declaring last year's fashions outmoded every new season.
2
3
3
4
2
2

3. Divide the following paragraph into its proper levels of generality by numbering each sentence:

No discussion of maternal fatigue would be complete without mentioning the early evening hours—unquestionably the toughest part of the day for the mother of small children. Much has been written lately about the international "energy crisis," but there is nothing on the globe to parallel the shortage of energy in a young mother between 6:00 and 9:00 p.m.! The dinner is over and the dishes are stacked. She is already tired, but now she has to get the troops in bed. She gives them their baths and pins on the diapers and brushes their teeth and puts on the pajamas and reads a story and says the prayers and brings them seven glasses of water. These tasks would not be so difficult if the children *wanted* to go to bed. They most certainly do not, however, and develop extremely clever techniques for resistance and postponement. It is a pretty dumb kid who can't extend this ten-minute process into an hour-long tug of war. And when it is all finished and Mom staggers through the nursery door and leans against the wall, she is then supposed to shift gears and greet her romantic lover in her bedroom. Fat chance!

—James Dobson, *What Wives Wish Their Husbands Knew About Women*

4. In the following paragraphs, draw a line through any sentence that weakens paragraph unity.

   a. I agree with Thomas Jefferson that there is a natural aristocracy among human beings, based on virtue and talent. A natural aristocrat is a person who shows genuine concern for his fellow human beings and has the wisdom as well as ability to help them improve the quality of their lives. He is the kind of person to whom you would entrust your most important concerns because his decisions would be honest rather than self-serving. A natural aristocrat cannot be bought or manipulated. He will not promise what he cannot deliver. But when he makes a promise, he has virtue backed up by talent to fulfill it. Unfortunately, few political leaders today are natural aristocrats because early in their ambitious careers they get beholden to those powers that helped them up the political ladder.

   b. In medieval society physical strength and animal cunning were the most admired characteristics of human beings, but since the invention of gunpowder, we have come to value other qualities more highly. Now that even a physically weak person can be made strong by carrying a gun, other ingenuities have become the marks of heroic people. Of course, boxing requires physical strength and animal cunning; yet many people today admire good boxers. The qualities most admired today are intellectual acumen, leadership ability, artistic talent, and social adjustment. I find it distressing that we do not prize goodness as much as we should. After all, Lincoln's outstanding feature was goodness. If a person is not good, he is not admirable. The tournament and personal combat have been replaced by the university, the political arena, the stage, and the personality inventory as testing grounds for heroes.

5. Identify the most obvious means used to establish coherence in the following paragraphs.

   a. In general, relevancy is a facet of training rather than of education. What is taught at law school is the present law of the land, not the Napoleonic Code or even the archaic laws that have been scratched from the statute books. And at medical school, too, it is modern medical practice that is taught, that which is relevant to conditions today. And the plumber and the carpenter and the electrician and the mason learn only what is relevant to the practice of their respective trades in this day with the tools and materials that are presently available and that conform to the building code.

—Harry Kemelman, *Common Sense in Education*

b. The extent of personal privacy varies, but there are four degrees that can be identified. Sometimes the individual wants to be completely out of the sight and hearing of anyone else, in solitude; alone, he is in the most relaxed state of privacy. In a second situation the individual seeks the intimacy of his confidants—his family, friends, or trusted associates with whom he chooses to share his ideas and emotions. But there are still some things that he does not want to disclose, whether he is with intimates or in public. Either by personal explanation or by social convention, the individual may indicate that he does not wish certain aspects of himself discussed or noticed, at least at that particular moment. When his claim is respected by those around him, he achieves a third degree of privacy, the state of reserve. Finally, an individual sometimes goes out in public to seek privacy, for by joining groups of people who do not recognize him, he achieves anonymity, being seen but not known. Such relaxation on the street, in bars or movies or in the park constitutes still another dimension of the individual's quest for privacy.

—Alan F. Westin, "Privacy"

c. The motor car is, more than any other object, the expression of the nation's character and the nation's dream. In the free billowing fender, in the blinding chromium grills, in the fluid control, in the ever-widening front seat, we see the flowering of the America that we know. It is of some interest to scholars and historians that the same autumn that saw the abandonment of the window crank and the adoption of the push button (removing the motorist's last necessity for physical exertion) saw also the registration of sixteen million young men of fighting age and symphonic styling. It is of deep interest to me that in the same week Japan joined the Axis, De Soto moved its clutch pedal two inches to the left—and that the announcements caused equal flurries among the people.

—E. B. White, "The Motor Car"

6. Write a provocative introductory paragraph for an essay on one of the following topics:

   a. Admitting women to military schools
   b. Rationing water or gasoline
   c. Automatic capital punishment for terrorists who take hostages
   d. Purging our language of all words with a sexist bias ("he" as a general pronoun, "chairman," "congressman," "businessman," "insurance man")

e. Job prospects for college seniors
f. One of today's most serious urban problems

7. Write a brief paragraph that would function as a smooth transition from one to the other of the pairs of paragraphs listed.

   a. (1) The first paragraph lists activities of a male executive that are the same as activities for which the homemaker is chided (long phone conversations, coffee klatches with colleagues, unnecessary fancy luncheons).
      (2) The second paragraph indicates the differences between the two sets of activities.

   b. (1) The first paragraph provides statistics to demonstrate that thousands of poor people in America live on pet food.
      (2) The second paragraph argues that we must do something in order to solve the problem of hunger and malnutrition in America.

   c. (1) The first paragraph makes the point that many foreign countries consider Americans wasteful, extravagant, and selfish in their insistence on driving big cars.
      (2) The second paragraph holds the automobile industry responsible for shaping America's taste in cars.

8. Combine the sentences below into a coherent paragraph, using any one of the four devices suggested in this chapter.

   a. The crisis of doubt about education as the great leveler of society began in the 1960s after it became clear that schools were not giving equal education to black and Spanish-speaking Americans.
   b. Most educators believed all that was needed was a series of reforms.
   c. Schools should be integrated to wipe out unequal facilities.
   d. Compensatory programs like Head Start were to help poor children do as well as middle-class children.
   e. Billions of dollars were spent in the name of these reforms.
   f. Little concrete evidence of success could be found.
   g. One side felt that the programs were good but needed to be run better.
   h. The other side felt that the fault lay in expecting too much from education.
   i. The Coleman report concluded that family-background differences account for much more variation in achievement than do school differences.
   j. Many educators and policy-makers now no longer view education as the "balance-wheel of the social machinery."

6

What is the best way of following through?

Language is not simply
a reporting device for experience
but a defining framework for it.

—Benjamin Whorf

YOU HAVE DEVISED A THESIS, made an outline, and researched your topic. Now you must develop your ideas and data into an essay. Paradoxically, even at this stage you will be working with parts rather than with the whole essay. The accumulation of smaller elements into larger ones is the basic principle behind all writing. Sentences become paragraphs, paragraphs become pages, and pages become the essay.

Now is when your outline will be most useful. It should predict the approximate number of paragraphs needed and even forecast the function of each paragraph. For example, you may need a paragraph that defines an ambiguous word or phrase. You may need one that gives examples of an idea or concept. You may need another that compares and contrasts two ideas. Every paragraph in the essay will have a specific function, but all the paragraphs will nevertheless work toward the end of amplifying and supporting the thesis.

Each paragraph of an essay is invariably developed around a single purpose. Listed and discussed below are the seven major purposes to which paragraphs may be devoted:

1. Narration
2. Description
3. Example
4. Definition
5. Comparison and contrast
6. Causal analysis
7. Classification

Each of these methods of development corresponds to a particular operation of thought.

Narration

To narrate means to recount an incident or to tell a story. Narration, however, is not limited to simple storytelling. You use a form of narration whenever you relate an experience or present information in purposeful sequence. A short story or a novel is written in narrative form, but so are the minutes of a business meeting.

Your earliest letters to distant relatives were probably embellished narratives of childhood experiences. So are the entries in your journal or diary. Narration is the one kind of writing you are most likely to have practiced. Here is an example of a narrative paragraph:

> He rose and placed his candle unsuspectingly on the floor near the loom, swept away the sand without any change, and removed the bricks. The sight of the empty hole made his heart leap violently, but the belief that his gold was gone could not come at once—only terror, and the eager effort to put an end to the terror. He passed his trembling hand all about the hole, trying to think it possible that his eyes had deceived him; then he held the candle in the hole and examined it curiously, trembling more and more. At last he shook so violently that he let fall the candle, and lifted his hands to his head, trying to steady himself, that he might think. Had he put the gold somewhere else, by a sudden resolution last night, and then forgotten it? A man falling into dark water seeks a momentary footing even on sliding stones; and Silas, by acting as if he believed in false hopes, warded off the moment of despair. He searched in every corner, he turned his bed over, and shook it, and kneaded it; he looked in his brick oven where he laid his sticks. When there was no other place to be searched, he kneeled down again and felt once more all round the hole. There was no untried refuge left for a moment's shelter from the terrible truth.
>
> —George Eliot, *Silas Marner*

One principle of narration is that not all events are treated equally. Instead, the writer emphasizes only those events and incidents important to the story, glossing over those periods of time in which nothing important is presumed to have happened, elaborating on those during which some significant event occurred. This is called *pacing*—the purposeful selection and treatment of episodes according to the degree of importance they have in the story. In real life, every single minute of even an agonizingly boring month must be painfully lived through; in a narrative, an irrelevant and boring month is seldom longer than a few sentences. Here is an example:

> Another month flew by, during which I made such progress in the language that I could understand all that was said to me, and express myself with tolerable fluency. My instructor professed to be astonished with the progress I had made; I was careful to attribute it to the pains he had taken with me and to his admirable method of explaining my difficulties, so we became excellent friends.
>
> —Samuel Butler, *Erewhon*

Aside from learning the language, the narrator had nothing significant happen to him in the month, and so he passes quickly over it. But in another part of this same novel, the events of a few moments are narrated for pages and pages.

In a narrative paragraph, especially one written from the first-person point of view, the language is usually understood to characterize the personality behind it. So it is especially important that the writer practice consistency of voice, and not use words or phrases that would be out of character. If you were telling a story from a child's point of view, you should use the vocabulary of a child. If you used the vocabulary of a pompous banker, the illusion of the child narrator would be destroyed. Here is an example of an obvious lapse:

> We went for a walk and I got hungry. I asked my mommy for some candy. My mommy bought me candy. We sat down on a park bench and ate it. Pigeons came right up to my toes. <u>But because my doctor has repeatedly warned me against the abnormally high level of triglycerides in candy, I decided only to nibble a small piece of it.</u>

Subtler forms of this error are possible. To avoid them, you must remember to tell the story throughout from the same point of view with which it was begun. (For more on narration as fiction writers practice it, see Chapter 11.)

Description

Most beginning writers, when asked to write a description, are seized by an impulse to close their eyes, view the scene mentally, and describe everything in it. The result is usually a bad or hazy description. You cannot tell or show everything about a scene, nor should you attempt to. The best descriptions do not. Instead, they are focussed on and limited to the single strongest impression the thing being described has had on the writer:

> <u>The Spanish night is so deep and pompous as quite to browbeat the noisier light of day.</u> The buildings, which always look

> clearcut and newly built, become, against the dark stress of evening, brilliantly crisp and more brittle than glass. A long line of white buildings will tower up to threaten you with its proud, wave-like bulwarks. At every corner, behind the dark trees that are deep, still areas of water, there will rise up another of those strutting waves out of the depth. In its turn it will draw up, holding itself to full height before it launches a leonine assault on your puny presence. Then it will hold itself back from you before the superior strength of the next glittering wave that you meet, as you walk through the brittle moonlight. In this way the slowest progress through a town will be running the gauntlet of a whole pack of hungry shadows.
>
> —Sacheverell Sitwell, *Southern Baroque Art*

The paragraph is constructed around a single overwhelming impression—a Spanish night so "deep and pompous" that it seems threatening. To support this impression, the writer has marshaled a paragraph of descriptive details and images.

The dominant impression of a descriptive paragraph is stated in its topic sentence, which, in a nondescriptive paragraph, would contain the general idea. But where the descriptive paragraph differs from other kinds of paragraphs is in its use of imagery as supporting detail. The nondescriptive paragraph supports a general idea with examples, statistics, and authority opinions, while the descriptive paragraph supports its dominant impression with imagery:

> Jenny knew that, in reality, her mother was a dangerous person—hot breathed and full of rage and unpredictable. The dry, straw texture of her lashes could seem the result of some conflagration, and her pale hair could crackle electrically from its bun and her eyes could get small as hatpins. Which of her children had not felt her stinging slap, with the claw-encased pearl in her engagement ring that could bloody a lip at one flick? Jenny had seen her hurl Cody down a flight of stairs. She'd seen Ezra ducking, elbows raised, warding off an attack. She herself, more than once, had been slammed against a wall, been called "serpent," "cockroach," "hideous little sniveling guttersnipe." But here Pearl sat, decorously inquiring about Julia Carroll's weight problem. Jenny had a faint, tremulous hope that times had changed. Perhaps it was the boys' fault. Maybe she and her mother—intelligent women, after all—could live without such scenes forever. But she never felt entirely secure, and at night, when Pearl had placed a kiss on the center of Jenny's forehead, Jenny went off to bed and dreamed what she had always dreamed: her mother laughed a witch's shrieking laugh; dragged Jenny out of hiding as the Nazis tramped up the stairs;

> accused her of sins and crimes that had never crossed Jenny's mind. Her mother told her, in an informative and considerate tone of voice, that she was raising Jenny to eat her.
>
> —Anne Tyler, *Dinner at the Homesick Restaurant*

The impression dominating this paragraph is a daughter's memory of her temperamental and often vicious mother. The imagery—from "hot breathed and full of rage" to laughing "a witch's shrieking laugh"—reinforces and focuses the dominant impression.

A paragraph, like a camera, cannot focus on more than one object at a time without some blurring. A writer cannot include several vignettes of a scene in a single paragraph without its effect being scattered and diffuse. In writing a description, resist the impulses to put into it everything that you see or hear. Instead, focus on the dominant impression of the scene, object, or person and build your description around that impression.

Remember too that a dominant impression does not always have to be visual. It can be based on any of the senses. If you wanted to write about a nondescript man who reeked of garlic, you could better describe the impression he made on you by focusing on the way he smelled rather than on how he looked. An airport may be unprepossessing to the eye but unforgettable to the ear, making its noise a better dominant impression for your description. For example, in this description of the last moments of the *Titanic*, a survivor recounts the sounds made by the dying ship:

> Occasionally there had been a muffled thud or deadened explosion within the ship. Now, without warning, she seemed to start forward, moving forward and into the water at an angle of about fifteen degrees. This movement, with the water rising up toward us was accompanied by a rumbling roar, mixed with more muffled explosions. It was like standing under a steel railway bridge while an express train passes overhead, mingled with the noise of a pressed steel factory and wholesale breakage of china.
>
> —John B. Thayer, *The Sinking of the S.S. Titanic*

Example

The example is the best antidote to vagueness in a paragraph. It allows writers to show exactly what they mean. Let us examine the following generalization, "There are many ways in which English can be conventional." Exactly what the writer meant by that is nearly impossible to fathom without some sort of example, which he then provided:

> There are many ways in which English can be conventional. Consider: You are at the police station to identify a culprit. "That's he," you gasp. Have you spoken correctly? No. It will serve you bloody right when a sneering sergeant says, "Whom are you trying to kid? That's a plain clothes cop." "Correct" English is correct conventionally and in context. Down at the police station the correct form is, "That's him."
>
> It is correct, furthermore, not because the policemen don't know the difference but because they *do* know the difference. They will know, if you say, "That's he," that you are being inappropriately formal, rudely calling attention to what you mistakenly deem one of your many merits, and, possibly, insulting them all by your presumption that they need you to set a good grammatical example.
>
> —Richard Mitchell, "The Underground Grammarian"

On every page, in almost every paragraph, writers must back up their assertions with examples if they wish to communicate their meaning well. It is not enough to merely generalize that such and such is the case as one might do in informal conversation. Specific instances must be cited.

Examples are useful in arguments, definitions, and even descriptions. Here an example is used to further an argument:

> Jonah could have been swallowed whole by a sperm whale. . . .
>
> A ship in the South Seas in 1771 had one of her boats bitten in two by a sperm whale. The beast seized one unlucky crew member in her mouth and went down with him. On returning to the surface the whale ejected him on the wreckage of the broken boat, much bruised but not seriously injured. . . .
>
> A worse fate befell another victim in 1891. The *Star of the East* was in the vicinity of the Falkland Islands and the lookout sighted a large sperm whale three miles away. Two boats were launched and in a short time one of the harpooners was enabled to spear the fish. The second boat attacked the whale but was upset by a lash of its tail and the men thrown into the sea, one man being drowned, and another, James Bartley, having disappeared, could not be found. The whale was killed and in a few hours was lying by the ship's side and the crew were busy with axes and spades removing the blubber. They worked all day and part of the night. Next morning they attached some tackle to the stomach which was hoisted on the deck. The sailors were startled by something in it which gave spasmodic signs of life, and inside was found the missing sailor,

doubled up and unconscious. He was laid on the deck and treated to a bath of sea water which soon revived him.

—quoted in Victor B. Scheffer, *The Year of the Whale*

Here, two examples are used to define the meaning of "romantic recognition":

Romantic recognition. Two examples will do. When we were flying from Erivan, the capital of Armenia, to Sukhum, on the Black Sea, a Soviet scientist, who spoke English, tapped me on the shoulder and then pointed to a fearsome rock face, an immeasurable slab bound in the iron of eternal winter. "That," he announced, "is where Prometheus was chained." And then all my secret terror—for a journey among the mountains of the Caucasus in a Russian plane is to my unheroic soul an ordeal—gave way for a moment to wonder and delight, as if an illuminated fountain had shot up in the dark. And then, years earlier, in the autumn of 1914, when we were on a route march in Surrey, I happened to be keeping step with the company commander, an intelligent Regular lent to us for a month or two. We were passing a little old woman who was watching us from an open carriage, drawn up near the entrance to a mansion. "Do you know who that is?" the captain asked; and of course I didn't. "It's the Empress Eugenie," he told me; and young and loutish as I was in those days, nevertheless there flared about me then, most delightfully, all the splendor and idiocy of the Second Empire, and I knew that we, every man Jack of us, were in history, and knew it once and for all.

—J. B. Priestley, "Romantic Recognition"

And here an example is used to help describe John Masefield, the English poet:

One never forgets Masefield's face. It is not the face of a young man, for it is lined and grave. And yet it is not the face of an old man, for youth is still in the bright eyes. Its dominant quality is humility. There were moments when he seemed almost to abase himself before his fellow-creatures. And this humility was echoed in everything he did or said, in the quiet, timid tone of his voice, in the way in which he always shrank from asserting himself.

This quality of his can best be illustrated by his behaviour that night. When the time came for him to read his poems, he would not stand up in any position of pre-eminence but sheltered himself behind the sofa, in the shade of an old lamp, and from there he delivered passages from "The Everlasting Mercy," "Dauber," "The

Tragedy of Nan," and "Pompey the Great." He talked, too, melodiously, and with the ghost of a question mark after each of his sentences as though he were saying, "Is that right? Who am I to lay down the law?" And when it was all over, and we began to discuss what he had said, all talking at the top of our voices, very superficially, no doubt, but certainly with a great deal of enthusiasm, it was with a sudden shock that I realized that Masefield had retired into his shell, and was sitting on the floor, almost in the dark, reading a volume of poems by a young and quite unknown writer.

—Beverley Nichols, *Twenty-Five*

Notice that in some of these paragraphs an introductory word or phrase is used before the example, whereas in others it is not. Whether or not you need to say "for example" or "consider" or "for instance" before you give the example will depend on the context in which it is being used. A prefatory word or phrase is sometimes useful and sometimes not. Remember, however, that your example must be appropriate to the point it is intended to support, and must be sufficiently interpreted for the reader to understand what it is intended to illustrate.

Definition

A great deal of argument is daily waged over the meanings of words and phrases. Some of these arguments are ultimately irresolvable since they presume adherence to one ideological position or another. Yet partisans will nevertheless expend effort and ink in trying to explain what is meant by some term or expression dear to their cause. Such an effort involves a *definition*—an attempt to specify the meaning of a word or phrase. Articles, essays, and books have been written with the sole purpose of defining some abstract and cosmic term.

The writer who wishes to define a term must do at least two things: first, say what the term means; second, make clear what it does not mean. Here is an example of a paragraph in which a writer defines a *plot* and also defines what it is not:

Let us define a plot. We have defined a story as a narrative of events arranged in their time-sequence. A plot is also a narrative of events, the emphasis falling on causality. "The king died and then the queen died," is a story. "The king died, and then the queen died of grief," is a plot. The time-sequence is preserved, but the sense of causality overshadows it. Or again: "The queen died, no one knew why, until it was discovered that it was through grief at the death of

> the king." This is a plot with a mystery in it, a form capable of high development. It suspends the time-sequence, it moves as far away from the story as its limitations will allow. Consider the death of the queen. If it is a story we say, "and then?" If it is a plot we ask, "why?" That is the fundamental difference between these two aspects of the novel. A plot cannot be told to a gaping audience of cave men or to a tyrannical sultan or to their modern descendant the movie-public. They can only be kept awake by "and then—and then." They can only supply curiosity. But a plot demands intelligence and memory also.
>
> —E. M. Forster, *Aspects of the Novel*

Many definitions involve an etymological analysis of the word or phrase to be defined. The writer tries to show how the word came into being and what its earliest meaning was. This kind of information is useful in explaining how the current meaning of a word evolved. Here is an example of an etymological analysis that helps us to understand the meaning of the word *bible*:

> In the derivation of our word *Bible* lies its definition. It comes from the Greek word *biblion,** which in its plural *biblia* signifies "little books." The Bible is actually a collection of little books, of every sort and description, written over a long period of time, the very earliest dating, in part at least, as far back as 1200 B.C. or perhaps even earlier; the latest as late as A.D. 150. In its rich and manifold nature it might be called a *library* of Hebrew literature; in its slow production over a period of many centuries it might be termed a *survey* of that literature to be understood as we understand a survey of English literature, in which we become familiar with types of English prose and poetry from Anglo-Saxon times to our own.
>
> —Mary Ellen Chase, "What Is the Bible?"
>
> **Biblos* was the name given to the inner bark of the papyrus; and the word *biblion* meant a papyrus roll, upon which the Bible was originally copied.

The overriding aim of any defining paragraph or essay is, of course, to make clear the meaning of a certain word or phrase. But the writer may not always be trying to convey the technical or dictionary meaning of a word or phrase. Some definitions may be poetic, as in the following example:

> Home is where you hang your hat. Or home is where you spent your childhood, the good years when waking every morning was an excitement, when the round of the day could always produce something to fill your mind, tear your emotions, excite your wonder or awe or delight. Is home that, or is it the place where the

people you love live, or the place where you have buried your dead, or the place where you want to be buried yourself? Or is it the place where you come in your last desperation to shoot yourself, choosing the garage or the barn or the woodshed in order not to mess up the house, but coming back anyway to the last sanctuary where you can kill yourself in peace?

—Wallace Stegner, *Big Rock Candy Mountain*

You can use a variety of strategies to define a word or phrase. You can analyze its etymology, give examples of its meaning, and discuss its current usage. Here is a paragraph in which the writer used all three devices to define "idiopathic diseases":

We have a roster of diseases which medicine calls "idiopathic," meaning that we do not know what causes them. The list is much shorter than it used to be; a century ago, common infections (EXAMPLES) like typhus fever and tuberculous meningitis were classed as idiopathic illnesses. Originally, when it first came into the language of medicine, the term had a different, highly theoretical meaning. It was assumed that most human diseases were intrinsic, due to inbuilt (ETYMOLOGICAL ANALYSIS) failures of one sort or another, things gone wrong with various internal humors. The word "idiopathic" was intended to mean, literally, a disease having its own origin, a primary disease without any external cause. The list of such disorders has become progressively shorter as medical science has advanced, especially within this century, and the meaning of the term has lost its doctrinal flavor; (CURRENT USAGE) we use "idiopathic" now to indicate simply that the cause of one particular disease is unknown. Very likely, before we are finished with medical science, and with luck, we will have found that all varieties of disease are the result of one or another sort of meddling, and there will be no more idiopathic illness.

—Lewis Thomas, *The Medusa and the Snail*

Comparison and contrast

The odds are that you will not get through college without sometime having to compare or contrast two items, either in an essay exam or in a research paper. For instance, your English exam may read, "Contrast the tragic flaw in the character of Oedipus with that of Othello." Or in your sociology report you may have to "compare the basic demands of the feminist movement with those of the civil rights movement." Similar questions are asked not only in liberal arts studies but also in the sciences.

To compare means to point out how two things are alike, while to contrast means to point out how they are unlike. When you say that both Mark and Allen are wearing purple socks with yellow jumpsuits, you are *comparing* their clothing. When you say that Alice is attired in a flimsy summer dress whereas Martha is sporting an ankle-length fur coat, you are *contrasting* their clothing. Many students do not recognize the difference between these two techniques.

A well-developed comparison or contrast is a study in logic and in composition. Suppose you want to develop the key thought, "My college experience is teaching me that good instructors are a different breed from bad ones." You must first decide on your bases for contrast. You must ask yourself in which areas of instruction you wish to contrast the activities of good teachers with bad teachers. The following three could be your choice: 1. time spent on lesson preparation; 2. willingness to tolerate dissent; 3. personal relationship with students. Having chosen your bases, write down the three areas under consideration on the left side of a sheet of paper and then create two columns (one for good instructors, the other for bad instructors) in which you will place comments, as follows:

	Good instructors	**Bad instructors**
1. Time spent on lesson preparation	Good instructors constantly revise lessons, including up-to-date reviews, newspaper clippings, research results, and other relevant material. Instructors refer to more than one source work and give suggestions for further reading. Lectures and discussions are the result of clear objectives.	Bad instructors give same lectures year in and year out, including the same dead jokes. They do nothing but spell out rudimentary facts, to be memorized verbatim for final tests. They often spend class time on dull workbook assignments. They show as many movies as possible, during which they nap.
2. Willingness to tolerate dissent	Good instructors welcome arguments as a way of bringing life into the classroom and of pointing up alternatives. Like Socrates, they believe that the classroom dialectic is a valid learning method.	Bad instructors see dissent or discussion as a threat to discipline and to their authority, so avoid both. They feel safe only when they are parroting themselves or the textbook.

3. Personal relationship with students	Good instructors spend time beyond office hours listening to student questions or complaints. They willingly clarify difficult problems. They never embarrass or patronize students.	Bad instructors are usually too busy off-campus to spend time in personal consultation with students. They deliver their lecture and disappear. They make students who ask for special help feel inferior.

Once you have made this preliminary sketch, you can develop it simply by adding a few transitional words and phrases, as has been done in the following passage (transitions are underlined):

> My college experience is teaching me that good instructors are a different breed from bad ones. In terms of time spent on lesson preparation, good instructors constantly revise their lessons, including such items as up-to-date reviews, newspaper clippings, research results, or any other related material. They refer to more than one source work and give suggestions for further reading. Their lectures and discussions are the obvious result of clear objectives. In contrast, bad instructors give the same lectures year in and year out, including the same dead jokes. Only the rudimentary facts are spelled out in class, to be memorized verbatim and regurgitated on final tests. They often spend classroom time on dull workbook assignments or, as often as possible, a movie, during which they take a nap.
>
> Another big difference between good and bad instructors is in their willingness to tolerate dissent. Good instructors welcome arguments as a way of bringing life into the classroom and of pointing up alternatives. Like Socrates, they believe that the classroom dialectic is a valid learning method. Bad instructors, however, take the opposite tack. They see dissent or discussion as a threat to their discipline and to their authority, so they avoid both. They feel safe only when they are parroting themselves or their textbooks.
>
> Good and bad instructors differ markedly in their relationship to students. Good instructors spend time beyond office hours listening to student questions or complaints. They willingly clarify difficult problems, and they never embarrass or patronize students. Bad instructors, on the contrary, are usually too busy off-campus to spend time in personal consultation with students. They deliver their lecture and disappear. The student who asks for special help is made to feel inferior.

The example just cited demonstrates the *alternating* method of comparison/contrast. The paragraph is written to alternate back and forth from one side of an issue to the other. Another system—called the *block* method—uses separate paragraphs for each side of the issue, as illustrated in the following passage that contrasts two views of Jewish history:

> On the one hand, the Diaspora* Jews can say that this talk of a predestination drama is a lot of nonsense. What has happened is only an interesting constellation of accidental, impersonal events, which some people have distorted out of all proportions to reality. We were defeated in war, they could say, we lost our land, we were exiled, and now it is our turn to disappear, just as under similar circumstances the Sumerians, the Hittites, the Babylonians, the Assyrians, the Persians—yes, even the Jews in the Kingdom of Israel—disappeared.
>
> On the other hand, they can say that their ancestors could not have been pursuing a mere illusion for 2,000 years. They could say that if we are God's Chosen People as our forefathers affirmed, if we have been placed in an exile to accomplish a divine mission as our Prophets predicted, and since we did receive the Torah, then we must survive to fulfill our Covenant with God.
>
> —Max I. Dimont, *The Indestructible Jews*

The alternating and block methods of comparison/contrast are further clarified in the following two outlines contrasting the Datsun and the Volkswagen on the basis of cost, performance, and looks:

Alternating outline

I. Cost A. Datsun B. Volkswagen	first paragraph
II. Performance A. Datsun B. Volkswagen	second paragraph
III. Looks A. Datsun B. Volkswagen	third paragraph

Block outline

I. Datsun A. Cost B. Performance C. Looks	first paragraph

*Term used for the dispersion of the Jews throughout the world. Eds.

II. Volkswagen
  A. Cost
  B. Performance   second paragraph
  C. Looks

Three rules must be observed in the development of a comparison/contrast.

The items to be compared/contrasted must belong to the same class. Some common ground must exist between items being compared/contrasted or the attempt at comparison will be meaningless. For example, a comparison between a hummingbird and a cement mixer, or between backgammon and Dutch Cleanser would be silly. On the other hand, some usefulness may be derived from a comparison between the Chinese and Japanese languages, or between golf and tennis—pairings that respectively belong to common groups: Oriental languages and sports. Moreover, the expression of the comparison/contrast must be grammatically accurate:

Wrong: Our telephone system is better than Russia.
(Here a telephone system is contrasted with all of Russia.)
Right: Our telephone system is better than *that* of Russia.

or

Our telephone system is better than Russia's.
Wrong: Ed's income is less than his wife.
(Here Ed's income is contrasted with his wife.)
Right: Ed's income is less than *that* of his wife.

or

Ed's income is less than his wife's.

Both sides of the question must be dealt with. All comparisons and contrasts are concerned with two sides, and you must deal equally with both of them. Do not mention one side and assume that your reader will fill in the other side. If you are contrasting the summer weather in Death Valley with the summer weather at Donner Pass, you cannot say,

> In Death Valley the heat is so intense that even lizards wilt.

and assume that your reader will fill in, "but at Donner Pass the summers remain cool." You must draw the contrast fully, as in the following:

> In Death Valley the heat is so intense that even lizards wilt, *whereas* at Donner Pass a cool breeze freshens even the hottest day.

Expressions indicating comparison/contrast should be generously used. Although comparison requires less back and forth movement than contrast, you must nevertheless take both sides into account by stating exactly what traits they have in common. For instance, in pointing out that in some ways high schools are like prisons, you cannot restrict yourself to discussing the domineering principal, the snoopy truant officer, the pass required to leave campus, or the punitive grading system. You must mention both sides, indicating that the domineering principal in high school is *like* the stern warden in prison; that the snoopy truant officer who makes sure that students attend school has much *in common with* the prison guards who make sure that inmates stay in prison; that the pass required to leave campus is *similar* to the formal permission required to leave a locked ward; and that the punitive grading system of high schools is *like* the demerit system of prisons. These expressions serve as signposts in your text, telling your reader how your different points relate.

The following expressions indicate *comparison*:

also
as well as
bears resemblance to
both . . . and
in common with
in like manner
like
likewise
neither . . . nor
similar
too

The following expressions indicate *contrast*:

although this may be true
at the same time
but
for all that
however
in contrast to
in opposition to
nevertheless
on the contrary
on the one hand . . . on the other hand
otherwise
still
unlike
whereas
yet

Contrast emphasizes the separate sides of an issue by pulling them apart as much as possible in order to clarify their differences. Comparison is less two-sided because it tries to draw together both sides of an issue in order to reveal what they have in common. In short, *contrasts diverge* while *comparisons converge*. In the following passage, note how the Egyptian world and the Greek world are placed far apart so that their ideological differences stand out. Note also how the underlined expressions indicating contrast clarify the shift from one side to the other:

> A brief consideration of Egyptian mythology contrasted with the mythology of the Greeks is enough to convince us of the revolution in thought that must have taken place from one age to the other. The Egyptian gods had no resemblance to anything in the real world, whereas the Greek gods were fashioned after real Greek people.
>
> In Egypt the gods that were typically worshiped consisted of: a towering colossus, so immobile and so distorted that no human could imagine it alive; or a woman with a cat's head, suggesting inflexible, inhuman cruelty; or a monstrous mysterious sphinx, aloof from anything we might consider human. The Egyptian artists' interpretations of the divine were horrid bestial shapes that combined men's heads with birds' bodies or portrayed lions with eagle wings—creatures that could inhabit only terrifying nightmares. The monstrosities of an invisible world were what the Egyptians worshiped.
>
> The Greek interpretation of divinity stands in opposition to this dark picture. The Greeks were preoccupied with the visible world. Unlike the Egyptians, they found their desires satisfied in what they could actually see around them. The ancient statues of Apollo, for instance, resemble the strong young bodies of athletes contending in the Olympic games. Homer describes Hermes as if he were a splendid Greek citizen. Generally the Greek artists found their gods in the idealized beauty or intelligence of actual human counterparts. In direct contrast to the Egyptians, they had no wish to create some hideous fantasy that they then called god.

In the next passage, note the funneling effect that emphasizes what whales and human beings have in common. Note how the underlined expressions indicating comparison draw together these two seemingly divergent animals:

> Whales and human beings are like two nations of individuals who have certain characteristics in common. As mammals they both are warm-blooded, giving milk, and breathing air. As social creatures they both have basic urges for privacy as well as for fraternization. As species bent on reproduction they both show similar patterns of aggression during courtship, the male trying to gain the female's attention and the female responding. Finally, as mystical beings they both are caught in the net of life and time, fellow prisoners of the splendor, travail, and secrets of earth.

Comparisons are often used to clarify abstract or complex ideas. For example, in the Bible Jesus remarks:

> The kingdom of heaven is like to a grain of mustard seed, which a man took and sowed in his field: Which indeed is the least of all seeds; but when it is grown, it is the greatest among herbs, and becometh a tree, so that the birds of the air come and lodge in the branches thereof.
>
> —Matthew 13:31–32

In this comparison, the complicated idea of God's kingdom is made understandable to the Jewish people by being compared to a mustard seed, something simple and familiar in their agrarian life. Through this comparison Jesus explains to his listeners something about the power and the influences that a life dedicated to God can exert on those who commit themselves to it.

Causal analysis

Causal analysis involves the ability to see cause and effect relationships between two elements. When you investigate the reason for something, you are either answering the question, Why did this happen? or, What will this do? The answer to the first question we label *cause*; the answer to the second we label *effect*. When you say, "Harold has lost one friend after another because he wears dirty clothes, uses obscene language, and is moody," you are dealing with cause. When you say, "Harold's dirty clothes, obscene language, and moodiness will make lasting friendships impossible," you are dealing with effect. *Cause* explains what has happened in the past; *effect* predicts what will happen in the future.

In a psychology class, you may wish to examine the question, "Why are so many couples unable to discuss their marital problems?" The answer quite naturally leads you to causal analysis. You may come up with the key thought, "Barriers between husbands and wives have two major causes." Such a key thought could be developed as follows:

> Barriers between husbands and wives have two major causes. The first is timidity. Many couples are embarrassed to discuss intimate problems, such as sexual maladjustment, personal hygiene, or religious beliefs. They prefer to let their discontent fester rather than to confront it openly. A wife says, "I wouldn't hurt my husband by telling him that his dirty hands offend me." A husband says, "I

> dislike the way my wife compares me to her father in everything I do, from mowing the lawn to smoking my pipe, but I could never tell her so." Guilt feelings can reinforce this sort of timidity. If a wife or husband knows that a frank talk about sex, for instance, will uncover some past indiscretion, he or she will avoid the confrontation out of guilt on one partner's part or fear of knowing on the part of the other partner. The longer this silence is kept, the stronger it becomes.
>
> The second major cause is pride. Many couples are too proud to admit that they have problems. Their Hollywood view of marriage does not provide for unpleasantness or failure, so they fantasize married bliss instead of admitting and discussing problems that cause pressure and pain. Many wives, for example, whose husbands escape into work because they have lost interest in the home, will give elaborate excuses for this escape in order to avoid the humiliation of friends finding out that the marriage is not idyllic. Similarly, many partners refuse to share such worries as financial losses or job decline, thinking that admitting to such worries somehow makes them look weak. One marriage counselor claims that many divorces could be prevented if only the couples involved would drop their sense of false pride and discuss whatever is making the marriage miserable.
>
> Strange as it may seem, two people can live under the same roof, joined together in life's most intimate relationship, while their timidity or their pride keeps them from discussing problems that vitally affect the quality of their union.

A slight shift in approach could lead you to a discussion of effect rather than cause. If you ask the question, "What happens when two people no longer discuss their marital problems?" you are not interested in the cause of lack of communication, but in its effect. You might develop the key thought, "Barriers between husband and wife result in a tension-filled home," as in the following paragraph:

> Barriers between husband and wife result in a tension-filled home. When marriage partners constantly overlook a problem or pretend it does not exist, they eventually become frustrated and angry. They develop feelings of isolation and rejection as their unfulfilled yearnings become a gnawing hunger. Lacking communication, the marriage is left without an emotional safety valve to let off pent-up frustration. The ensuing strain increases as the angry partners take out hidden, unexpressed resentments on their children, using them as scapegoats for their own great void. In the beginning the tension may show itself only in minor misunderstand-

> ings or brief pout sessions, but as the barriers remain, these little hurts turn into wounds. The husband may become belligerent toward the wife, belittling her in front of friends or ignoring her until she retreats in cold indignation. The wife may feel so rejected and worthless that she seeks another man to comfort her or to treat her with sensitivity. The tension grows. Soon the home has become a place of bitter hostility, where love and warmth are impossible. The cause is their unwillingness to talk and listen.

In order to arrive at a cause, you need to distinguish among three kinds: *necessary, sufficient,* and *contributory.*

A *necessary* cause is one that *must* be present for the effect to occur, but it alone cannot make the effect occur. For instance, irrigation is necessary for a crop of good grapes, but irrigation alone will not cause a good crop. Other factors have to be present, such as enough sunshine, correct pruning, proper pesticides, and good soil.

A *sufficient* cause is one that *can* produce a given effect by itself. For instance, an empty gasoline tank alone can keep a car from running, even though other problems, such as a bad spark plug, a leaking hose, or ignition trouble may be present also.

A *contributory* cause is one that *may* produce an effect, but cannot produce the effect by itself. For instance, vitamin E may help a long-distance runner to win a race, but other factors have to be present also, such as the correct time count, judges to observe the event, and so forth. The runner may also win the race without the help of vitamin E.

Understanding the difference among these three causes will help you in your investigations of cause and effect. First, it will keep you from careless assertions. For example, you will know better than to make either of the following statements:

> Busing will provide equal education and social integration.
>
> Busing will not provide equal education and social integration.

Both of these assertions are wrong because they treat busing as a sufficient cause for equal education and social integration. In reality, busing may be a necessary cause or a contributory cause, but busing alone can provide neither equal education nor social integration. Other factors are necessary, such as enlightened students, teachers, and parents.

Second, understanding the difference among the three causes will keep you from making dogmatic statements, such as:

> A vegetarian diet will prevent cancer.
>
> Acupuncture is the answer to anesthesiology problems in America.

> Violence on television is the cause of today's growing criminal violence.

Rather, you will soften your statements by inserting such phrases as "may be," "is a contributing factor," "is one of the reasons," or "is a major cause." A careful study of cause and effect teaches that few causes are *sufficient*; most are merely *necessary* or *contributory.*

Most writers do not rigidly follow the principles of causal analysis except when they argue a technical question that must be explained according to the rules of logic. The following passage is an example of the free use of the principles of causal analysis:

> The association of love with adultery in much of medieval love poetry has two causes. The first lies in the organization of feudal society. Marriages, being matters of economic or social interest, had nothing whatever to do with erotic love. When a marriage alliance no longer suited the interests of the lord, he got rid of his lady with as much dispatch as he got rid of a horse. Consequently, a lady who might be nothing more than a commodious piece of property to her husband, could be passionately desired by her vassal. The second cause lies in the attitude of the medieval Christian church, where the desire for erotic, romantic love was considered wicked and a result of Adam's sin in the Garden of Eden. The general impression left on the medieval mind by the church's official teachers was that all erotic pleasure was wicked. And this impression, in addition to the nature of feudal marriage, produced in the courtly poets the perverse desire to emphasize the very passion they were told to resist.

The student who wrote this paragraph does not demonstrate cause according to precise rules, but rather shows the common-sense result of her research into why medieval poetry emphasized adulterous love. It is important to be careful in asserting causal connections between events. If a connection is not there, you cannot create one. If a cause appears possible but not certain, use a word like *probable* to protect your credibility:

> Nervous exhaustion is the <u>probable</u> reason for Michael's depressions.

If a cause is not sufficient, but merely contributory, make this clear, as in the statement:

> Motorcycles are <u>one of the reasons</u> for a dramatic increase in noise pollution.

Classification

To write a classification means to analyze a thing according to its constituent parts. For example, if you wrote a paragraph on the kinds of books in your library, or the types of mugs in your beer mug collection, or the elements in Mark Twain's humor, you would be classifying. The purpose of a classification is to discover the nature of a thing by examining its parts. Here is an example of a paragraph developed by classification:

> A simple experiment will distinguish two types of human nature. Gather a throng of people and pour them into a ferry-boat. By the time the boat has swung into the river you will find that a certain proportion have taken the trouble to climb upstairs in order to be out on deck and see what is to be seen as they cross over. The rest have settled indoors to think what they will do upon reaching the other side, or perhaps lose themselves in apathy or tobacco smoke. But leaving out those apathetic, or addicted to a single enjoyment, we may divide all the alert passengers on the boat into two classes: those who are interested in crossing the river, and those who are merely interested in getting across. And we may divide all the people on the earth, or all the moods of people, in the same way. Some of them are chiefly occupied with attaining ends, and some with receiving experiences. The distinction of the two will be more marked when we name the first kind practical, and the second poetic, for common knowledge recognizes that a person poetic or in a poetic mood is impractical, and a practical person is intolerant of poetry.
>
> —Max Eastman, "Poetic People"

Typically, a classification, especially of a complex subject, cannot be contained within a single paragraph. But whether it is short or long, the classification must conform to these rules:

1. It must be based on a single principle.
2. It must be complete.
3. It must exclude one part from another.

The first rule means that you must sort out the parts of your subject according to one criterion. For example, if you were writing a paper on the works written *by* Samuel Johnson, and came up with the following list:

1. Johnson's poetry
2. Johnson's prose

3. Johnson's dictionary
4. Boswell's *Life of Johnson*

you would have broken this rule. Boswell's *Life of Johnson* was not written by Johnson, but *about* him. It doesn't belong in this list, but in a division of works *about* Johnson.

The second rule means that you must include all the parts of the subject in your division. If you omitted Johnson's dictionary from the above list, it would be incomplete. The third rule means that the categories in your division must not overlap. Here is an example of an overlapping division of Johnson's works:

1. Johnson's poetry
2. Johnson's prose
3. Johnson's dictionary
4. Johnson's *Lives of the Poets*

Lives of the Poets is a prose work and is already included under the category of Johnson's prose. If it is listed separately, it overlaps a category.

The student writer of the following passage has broken one of the rules of classification:

> Mass production in American industry is made up of four distinct elements: division of labor, standardization through precision tooling, assembly line, and consumer public. First is the division of labor, which means that a complicated production process is broken down into specialized individual tasks that are performed by people or machines who concentrate on these tasks only. Second is the standardization of parts as a result of precision tooling. This means that each part can be produced by machines both for interchangeability and for assembly by semiskilled workers. Third is the assembly line, which is a method of moving the work from one person to another in a continual chain of progress until the item is completed. This is a way of moving the work to the person, instead of the person to the work. The last element is the consumer public. Without it mass production would be a futile endeavor, for it is the public that buys up all the mass-produced items as fast as they roll off the assembly line.

Clearly, the classification is not based on a single principle. The error shows up immediately. In the key thought, the first three parts are distinctly elements of mass production, but the fourth part, the consumer public, is not part of the mass production process, but comes into the picture only after the item is already on the market. The student has not stuck to the principle of classification, which was to identify the elements of mass production.

Development through classification serves not only to depict parts of a whole, but also to trace steps in the course of a process, as in the following example:

> There is an art also in the sharpening of a scythe, and it is worth describing carefully. Your blade must be dry, and that is why you will see men rubbing the scythe-blade with grass before they whet it. Then also your rubber must be quite dry, and on this account it is a good thing to lay it on your coat and keep it there during all your day's mowing. The scythe you stand upright, with the blade pointing away from you, and you put your left hand firmly on the back of the blade, grasping it: then you pass the rubber first down one side of the blade-edge and then down the other, beginning near the handle and going on to the point and working quickly and hard. When you first do this you will, perhaps, cut your hand; but it is only at first that such an accident will happen to you.
>
> —Hilaire Belloc, "The Mowing of a Field"

What the writer has done is to break down into steps the act of sharpening a scythe and explain them in logical order. This constitutes a kind of classification called *process analysis*.

Combining paragraphs into an essay

At the beginning of this chapter we said that the act of writing involved the accumulation of smaller elements into larger ones. Brief essays as well as bulging tomes are composed on this same principle. The writer adds sentence to sentence to form paragraphs, and paragraph to paragraph to make pages. The paragraph is the level of discourse at which the writer thinks. Each paragraph should represent a writer's single thought on the subject. As the following student essay shows, many different kinds of paragraphs can be used in a single essay:

THE POPULATION BOMB IN YOUR OWN BACKYARD

INTRODUCTION Even as you read this paper you may be stroking or petting a time bomb that will tick the human race into mass famine. Yes, that cuddly ball of fluff on your lap is one of humanity's most unbelievable blunders. THESIS *Owning family domestic animals is a luxury we can no longer afford and a practice we must sharply curtail or discontinue completely within the next ten years.*

DEFINITION

Webster's Collegiate Dictionary defines a pet as "an animal or bird that is cherished." Indeed, the family dog or cat has become as much a part of the American family as apple pie and Thanksgiving dinner. We find pets included in everything from family portraits to presents under the Christmas tree. But let's be serious and mature. If we discount our emotional ties to domestic pets, we are left with a personal liability and an economic drain without any redeeming social value.

ANALYSIS OF EFFECT

The effects of pet ownership on a national scale are mind-boggling. According to Carl Djerassi's article "Planned Parenthood for Pets," which appeared in the January 1973 *Bulletin for Atomic Scientists*, the United States has the highest ratio of pets to humans in the world, with between 70 million and 110 million dogs and cats. Many of these pets receive a much better diet than 1 to 2 billion humans. Each year dogs in the United States alone consume enough protein to feed 4 million human beings. Americans spend an estimated $4.5 billion a year on pet shelters, health care (some pets have hospitalization plans and a few even visit psychiatrists), waste clean-up (40 million pounds of dog dung are deposited each year in New York City alone), pet foods, collars, clothes, vitamins, licenses, doggie and kitty hotels, and funerals. About $1.5 billion was spent in 1971 for pet food, almost four times the $390 million spent on baby food in that same year.

TRANSITIONAL PARAGRAPH USING CONTRAST

One may argue strongly that we need pets as an important form of diversity, to alleviate feelings of loneliness and inadequacy, and as a child substitute, thus helping to limit population growth. It seems clear, however, that we have gone much too far. The massive population explosion of dogs and cats not only drains off valuable nutrients from less fortunate humans, but ironically has resulted in a dramatic rise in abandoned pets.

NARRATION

An experience comes to mind that affirms my stand against domestic pets. While serving in the military, I was attached for training to the 651st desert warfare and survival school at Edwards Air Force Base, California, located ninety miles outside Los Angeles. During my duty there it was reported that a large pack of wild dogs was terrorizing the base housing area, schools, and shopping center, resulting in destruction of property, several animal bites, and, as a consequence, series after series of painful antirabies vaccinations mandatorily administered to the bite victims. The problem came to a crisis when several men working to recover practice bombs from the bombing range were attacked by a pack of wild dogs. One man was severely bitten, and as the men took refuge in their vehicle, one large animal jumped and hit the driver's side window with such ferocity and velocity as to shatter it. Several other men of my squad and I were ordered to search out and destroy these animals. Armed with some of the finest combat-tested equipment in the U.S. arsenal and assisted by helicopter gunships, we located the animals, trapped in a gully, and vaporized them in a display of firepower that rivaled some of the fiercest fire-fights and perimeter defense actions I was to experience less than a year later in the rice paddies of Laos and South Vietnam. Closer inspection of the dead animals revealed that all sixty-one of them were abandoned pets with collars, inoculation marks and name tags proving beyond a doubt that this pack of wild, diseased, rabid dogs had not long ago been "man's best friend." Few Americans are aware that approximately 13.3 million pets are destroyed each year at public and private shelters, at an annual cost of about one hundred million dollars.

EXAMPLES

We must find a better way to limit pet population growth, preferably by sharply lowering the pet birth rate and decreasing our need for so many pets. In fact, all major pet food manufacturers in the United States have begun to diversify and produce food products for human consumption as a hedge against the "dog that may bite its master's hand." Two examples in the Los Angeles basin are Kal-Kan dog food and Ralston-Purina Corporation, both of whom now market frozen T.V. dinners for people. *It is becoming urgent that the family "Fido," "Muffin," or "Lassie" be, to a great extent, eliminated from the American scene.*

BACK TO THESIS

CONCLUSION

My dog Spot must go, and to the avid pet lover who would argue that "she saved my life," etc., etc., I suggest that a thirty-dollar smoke detector or an alarm in the car or house would serve just as well or even better. For the rhapsodizer who points to his doe-eyed Beagle puppy and asks, "How can you be so heartless?" I will immediately produce a picture of an eight-year-old doe-eyed, starving, ragged Appalachian coal miner's daughter and retort, "How can you be so insensitive and cruel?"

An essay could as easily be comprised of paragraphs that all perform more or less the same function. For example, you could write an essay to define a complex term, with each paragraph adding to the definition. Or you could write an essay in which successive paragraphs merely add further examples that support your main idea.

The different kinds of paragraphs contribute to an essay rather in the same way that many different kinds of artisans and workers—carpenters, electricians, masons, and painters—contribute to erecting a building. Each paragraph adds something unique to the essay; each worker, something unique to the building. But all will be devoted toward the fulfillment of the architect's plan which, in the case of the essay, is the thesis.

Application: Rhetorical patterns and the essay exam

The patterns of development covered in this chapter are especially useful in writing essay exams. You will find that most teachers phrase their questions so that the answer will quite naturally fall into one of the rhetorical patterns. Four examples of actual exam questions follow, accompanied by properly developed, actual student answers.

1. Question from an Introduction to Literature exam:

> After reading Katherine Anne Porter's "Flowering Judas," write a 300-word essay in which you analyze the main causes of Laura's emotional paralysis.

The answer requires a *causal analysis:*

> In "Flowering Judas" by Katherine Anne Porter, Laura, a young woman, is living in Mexico and working as an underground agent for the powerful leader of a socialist revolution. She finds herself caught up in a life that causes her deep pain and anguish. Laura is afraid to continue her existence in Mexico for she fears her life is in grave danger, but she also can see no way of escape. Three major causes of Laura's paralyzed condition are her excessive idealism, her disillusionment with life, and her inability to love.
>
> Laura is hopelessly idealistic, especially in her view of the revolution. She had thought the revolution would be glorious—a way to feed the hungry, heal the sick, and free the enslaved. Instead, it was a movement characterized by violence, deceit, and self-interest. She believed also that a revolutionary leader should be "lean, animated by heroic faith, a vessel of abstract virtues." Far from such an image, Braggioni is vain, dishonest, and power hungry. Laura realizes dimly that she expects too much from people and life, but she is unable to give up her idealism.
>
> Related to Laura's idealism is her deep disillusionment with life. All of her hopes have been shattered and she feels that she has been "betrayed irreparably by the disunion between her way of living and her feeling of what life should be, and at times she is almost contented to rest in this sense of grievance as a private store of consolation." Laura has doubts about her own character. It may be true, she muses, that "I am as corrupt, in my own way, as Braggioni, as callous, as incomplete." Reflecting on her situation, Laura realizes that she has promised herself to this place and that she can no longer imagine herself as living in another country. She feels trapped with no hope of escape.

Another cause for Laura's paralysis is her inability to love. Laura is afraid to make herself vulnerable to anyone. It is quite clear that nobody touches her. For example, when a young captain riding horseback with her tries to take her in his arms, she spurs her horse and gallops away. The Polish agitator who talks love to her across café tables gets nowhere. The Indian children to whom she teaches English are very fond of her and bring her fresh garden flowers every day. They write on the blackboard "We lov ar titcher," but Laura does not return their affection, and they remain strangers. Braggioni warns Laura about her coldness, saying, "Wait and see—you will surprise yourself some day!" Laura sits patiently and feels there is nothing she can do but say "No" when the moment comes. Laura is "gradually perfecting herself in the stoicism she strives to cultivate against that disaster she fears, though she cannot name it."

Laura's paralysis is a result of her own character, totally void of any realism that would lend her some flexibility.

—Audrey Harris

2. Question from a Western Civilization exam:

Write a brief paragraph in which you define *Hellenism*.

The answer requires a *definition*:

The term *Hellenism* means "pertaining to the culture, ideals, and life style of classical Greece," that is, Greece during the Age of Pericles (494–429 B.C.), the Athenian statesman largely responsible for the advancement of democracy and for the creation of the Delian League, both of which stressed the splendors of Athens. Thus Hellenism means the kind of art that produced such monuments as the Parthenon, the Acropolis, the Charioteer, and the Venus de Milo. It means great literature like the dramas of Aeschylus, Sophocles, and Euripides. Furthermore, Hellenism also means exorbitant national pride and a belief in the innate greatness of man and his ability to solve life's problems on his own. It involves pagan joy, freedom, and love of life—as contrasted with the stern morality of the Hebrew Old Testament.

—Martha Rodriguez

3. Question from a Marine Biology exam:

In approximately 100 words classify marine organisms according to their modes of life. Briefly describe each category.

The answer requires a *classification*:

All marine organisms may be classified according to their modes of life as 1) nektonic, 2) planktonic, or 3) berthic. Nektonic creatures are those that can swim freely and migrate to other areas. Typical examples are whales, fish, and squid. Planktonic creatures are usually microscopic, have little or no ability to move about, and merely drift or float in the water. Berthic creatures exist on the sea floor and are either permanently attached like sponges and crabs, or they creep like crabs and snails, or they burrow like clams and worms.

—Richard Evers

4. Question from a Psychology of Women exam:

   In a succinct paragraph, indicate how a love bond differs from an ordinary friendship.

   The answer requires a *contrast*:

   A love bond and an ordinary friendship differ in several important aspects. An ordinary friendship can be formed at any age between any acquaintances, whereas bonding takes place in the first seven months of life between the infant and the caretaker (mother or father). If this bonding does not take place in the first seven months or is inconsistent until age 2-3, the child may not be able to form a lasting friendship later in life. A special kind of bonding takes place in marriage. It is the feeling of strong attachment that develops over a period of time and creates a single intimate relationship as a continuing process. Ordinary friendships, on the other hand, are usually multiple and new ones keep being formed throughout life. Most will not last for a lifetime the way a marriage love bond will.

   —Fred Sedley

In using the rhetorical patterns, you must aim, above all, to answer the question properly. If the question (as in the examples above) is worded to demand a specific kind of answer, then you must give it. But where the question allows you to develop your answer in a number of different ways, you should always opt for the rhetorical pattern that will allow you to make the most of what you know about the topic, so that your answer will be purposeful, clear, and detailed.

EXERCISES

1. Which is the most appropriate method for developing the following key thoughts? What information would you include in your development?

a. Since there is no clear-cut medical definition for depression, the term tends to be defined pragmatically by its symptoms.
b. The fact that most candidates for the office of United States Vice President are hastily chosen by only one man and his advisers could have tragic results for our nation.
c. The bright summer moonlight gave the small enclave an eerie look.
d. I agree with the aim of the feminist movement to abolish some of the unnecessary gallantries men are supposed to perform for women.
e. In the last five years our country has witnessed a renewed interest in gold mining.
f. Latin and Anglo cultures reveal several distinct differences.
g. The assassinations of Abraham Lincoln and John F. Kennedy were very similar.
h. When I was eleven years old, a confrontation with a neighbor of ours taught me a lesson about hyprocrisy.

2. Write a one-paragraph description of either the most *serene* or the most *terrifying* scene you have ever witnessed. Base your description on a dominant impression.

3. Write a one-paragraph description of your room based on a dominant impression.

4. In the following description, strike out those words that do not support the dominant impression.

> Desolation and decay are the dominant manifestations of this Navajo wildland. Sound and movement seem to have no place here. As far as the eye can see, the view is one vast yellow and purple corrugated world of canyons and mesas void of citizenry. Only occasionally does the roar of an airplane streaking across the sky interrupt the eerie silence to remind me that another inhabited world exists. As I gaze out into this majestic expanse, I get an insight into the meaning of time as measured by ages. So much of the view is the result of slow corrosion and natural destruction. I can hardly believe my eyes when, accidentally, I discover two blue and white Hamm's beer cans wrapped in sandwich bags and dropped behind a withered bush. A picnic in this wasteland—how incongruous! The miles upon miles of canyon-gashed, billowing slickrock supporting a series of sculptured sandstone buttes are like the monuments of a splendid but vanished past.

5. Which of the following two passages makes better use of examples in developing a key thought? Give reasons for your choice.

a. When I was eleven, I became possessed of an exaggerated fear of death. It started one quiet summer afternoon with an explosion in the alley behind our house. I jumped up from under a shade tree and tailed Poppa toward the scene. Black smoke billowed skyward, a large hole gaped in the wall of our barn, and several maimed chickens and a headless turkey flopped about on the ground. Then Poppa stopped and muttered, "Good Lord." I clutched his overalls and looked. A man, or what was left of him, was strewn about in three parts. A gas main he had been repairing had somehow ignited and blown everything around it to bits.

Then once, with two friends, I had swum along the bottom of the muddy Marmaton River, trying to locate the body of a Negro man. We had been promised fifty cents apiece by the same white policeman who had shot him while he was in the water trying to escape arrest. The dead man had been in a crap game with several others who had managed to get away. My buddy, Johnny Young, was swimming beside me; we swam with ice hooks which we were to use for grappling. The two of us touched the corpse at the same instant. Fear streaked through me, and the memory of his bloated body haunted my dreams for nights.

b. Adultery can strengthen a marriage. For an example of this strengthening, I think of the movie *Bob and Carol and Ted and Alice*. Here an upper-middle-class couple dabble with group sex and extramarital affairs, but this adultery leads them in the end to a greater appreciation of each other because they realize that adultery is really boring and unfulfilling while the richest relationship lies in a marriage where the two partners form a close-knit unit and remain faithful to each other. But they had to learn this truth through adultery.

Another example of this strengthening is a thirty-five-year-old mother of three who once said that when her husband had an affair, he found out that the woman he was going with was far more jealous and tied him down much more than she did. So he came back to being a faithful husband, and their marriage now is better than ever. The husband found out that the grass is not always greener on the other side of the fence.

6. Pick out one outstanding trait in your personality (shyness, generosity, jealousy, temper) and give three specific examples of how this trait has shown up in your life.

7. Develop a 300- to 500-word definition of one of the following terms. Begin with the lexical definition; then extend the definition in any way that best explains the term.

a. Diplomacy
b. Adolescence
c. Tyranny
d. Imagination
e. Panache
f. History
g. Black humor
h. Miracle

8. Using the example on pages 00–00 as a pattern, set up a sketch in which you contrast one of the following pairs:

   a. History and legend
   b. Stupidity and ignorance
   c. American cars and Japanese cars
   d. Classical poetry and modern poetry
   e. Academic learning and practical experience
   f. Believers and atheists
   g. Socialists and Communists

9. List several ways in which the following are alike:

   a. First love and a spring thunderstorm
   b. Psychology and religion
   c. A boy locked in a room and a boy dominated by his mother
   d. Senility and childhood
   e. All wars

10. Label the following causes as either *sufficient, necessary,* or *contributory.* (Use a common-sense approach rather than a technical one.)

    a. A ruptured aorta causes heart failure.
    b. A guppy will die without water.
    c. Arguments can lead to a divorce.
    d. The earth rotates around the sun; consequently, daylight begins.
    e. Vaccination causes a drop in neonatal deaths.
    f. An increase in commercial banks' prime lending rates can cause a recession.
    g. Neglecting to turn in a research paper results in an F grade.
    h. Riding a bicycle is good for your health.
    i. Paying taxes makes you a good citizen.
    j. A rise in temperature causes ice to melt.

11. State what is wrong with the following causal analyses:

    a. A runny nose causes the flu.
    b. I am fat because all the members of my family are fat.
    c. This morning my horoscope said that I should take risks, so I am going to invest my savings in speculative stock.
    d. The baby is crying; his diaper must need to be changed.
    e. You had better stop driving; that scraping noise will certainly wreck your transmission.
    f. If you drink ten glasses of water a day, you will be the picture of rosy health.
    g. Skin color is the cause of racial strife.
    h. Quarreling between husband and wife leads to a divorce.

12. Classify one of the following topics into its major types. Make clear the principle of your classification.

    a. Humor
    b. Rulers (in history)
    c. Marriage ceremonies
    d. Sports
    e. Periodicals
    f. Women (or men)
    g. Music

13. Classify the following terms under headings that will indicate what they have in common:

    a. Swimming
    b. Gliding
    c. Croquet
    d. Tobogganing
    e. Sledding
    f. Flying
    g. Golf
    h. Water polo
    i. Skydiving
    j. Surfing
    k. Lacrosse
    l. Skiing

14. List the main steps involved in one of the following processes:

    a. How to study for a final examination
    b. How to avoid stage fright
    c. How to prepare for a trip overseas
    d. How to be a good listener
    e. How to get along with a domineering mother-in-law.
    f. How to solve some political dilemma (e.g., a home for the Palestinians, quality education for minorities, the possibility of a recession, cooling of détente with Russia)
    g. How to keep up on the news

15. In the following passage, what subject is the author breaking up into two types? What is the principle on which he has based his classification?

> There is one sort of ________ which principally arises from that instinctive, disinterested, and undefinable feeling which connects the affections of man with his birthplace. This natural fondness is united with a taste for ancient customs and a reverence for traditions of the past; those who cherish it love their country as they love the mansion of their fathers. They love the tranquility that it affords them; they cling to the peaceful habits that they have contracted within its bosom; they are attached to the reminiscences that it awakens; and they are even pleased by living there in a state of obedience. This ________ is sometimes stimulated by religious en-

thusiasms, and then it is capable of making prodigious efforts. It is in itself a kind of religion; it does not reason, but it acts from the impulse of faith and sentiment. . . .

But there is another species of ________ which is more rational than the one I have been describing. It is perhaps less generous and less ardent, but it is more fruitful and more lasting; it springs from knowledge; it is nurtured by the laws; it grows by the exercise of civil rights; and, in the end, it is confounded with the personal interests of the citizen. A man comprehends the influence which the well-being of his country has upon his own; he is aware that the laws permit him to contribute to that prosperity, and he labors to promote it, first because it benefits him, and secondly because it is in part his own work.

—Alexis de Tocqueville, *Democracy in America*

7

What is the right word?

The difference between the almost right word
and the right word
is really a large matter—
'tis the difference between
the lightning-bug and the lightning.

—Mark Twain

THE POWER OF WORDS is nearly immeasurable and there is no doubt whatsoever that they can hurt at least as much as sticks and stones. We articulate our wishes, fears, dreams, and ambitions in words. Wars are begun, countries founded, marriages celebrated, and history commemorated with words. Our discussion in this chapter on how words work and how you should use them centers on three main points:

Words are symbols.

Words have contexts.

Words have denotations and connotations.

Words are symbols

A symbol is something that stands for or represents another thing. Words are symbols since they represent objects or concepts. *Hot dog* stands for an object—the particular sausage and bun combination we call by that name; *love* stands for a concept—attraction between people.

Symbols depend on and imply the existence of agreed-on meanings. A word communicates only because it means the same thing to people who speak the same language. Learning any language consists essentially of memorizing how words match up with the objects or concepts they represent. These "match-ups," in turn, are valid and consistent simply because the people who speak the language have implicitly agreed to them. You have learned the language when your response to its words begins to conform to the responses of others who speak it. When you know American English, *hot dog* will cause you to salivate if you are hungry; *halt* will cause you to stop, and *danger!* will cause you to stop and think. Your response in each case is evoked by the object or concept with which each word is matched up in your mind.

S. I. Hayakawa's "semantic triangle" explains how words derive their meanings from being matched up with an object or concept:

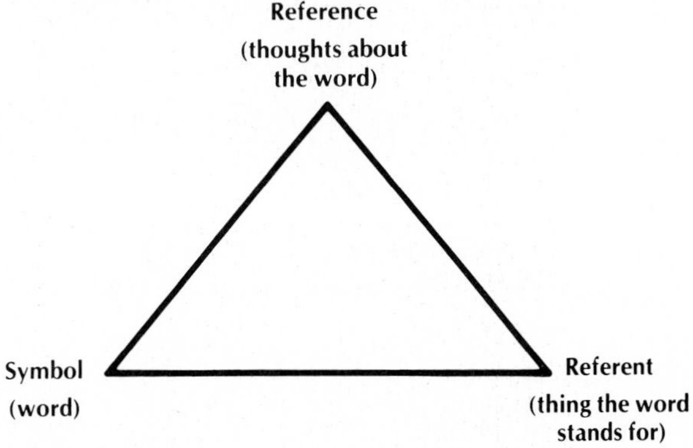

According to this theory, each word operates as a symbol with a referent (thing the word stands for) and a reference (thoughts about the word). In the case of *hot dog*, the triangle looks like this:

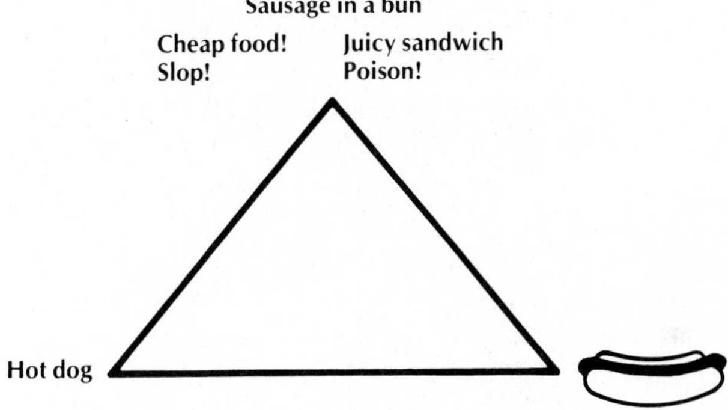

Some words are concrete, and some are abstract. A concrete word has an object as its referent; an abstract word has a concept as its referent. *Hot dog, chair, pencil* and *brick* are all concrete words since each has an object referent that can be produced in case of disagreement over meaning. With an abstract word, however, nothing tangible can be produced to settle disagreements, and the potential for misunderstanding is infinitely greater. For example, examine the semantic triangle for *liberalism* on the next page. Notice that the referent now consists of words that attempt to define the concept of liberalism. An abstract word points to a concept that in turn is defined by more words. Political arguments owe much of their verbiage to this built-in circularity of the abstract word; volumes can be, have been, and will be spoken as contending factions search for a set of words that will

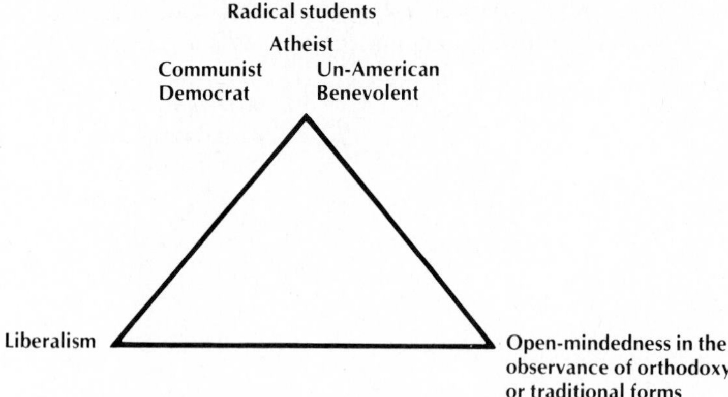

define to everyone's satisfaction a concept like *liberalism*. Possibly no such set of words exists. But communication, and life, would be simpler if, like *hot dog*, an abstract word such as *liberalism* had an object referent that could be displayed on the conference table to settle arguments over its meaning.

Concrete words may also provoke different associations in the minds of different people. *Hot dog* will have a very different reference (thoughts about the word) for a person who was almost poisoned by one than for a person who has consumed hundreds with no ill effects. But in each case the referent will be the same object even though the emotional reaction to it might be vastly different. In contrast, abstract words are likely to have different referents for different people, as well as having different references.

There is a lesson here that applies to your own writing. Many college students tend to write in abstractions. Perhaps they feel that by representing general ideas with abstract words, they sound more learned. Nothing could be further from the truth. The best kind of writing is usually the most concrete because it is most likely to be clearly understood. Sometimes you do have to begin a piece of writing with a general statement, but as soon as you have done this, you should nail it down with concrete words. You might begin by saying, "For the past few months Harry has led a miserable existence." But as soon as possible, you should add, "He suffers sharp pains from an ulcer." In this way you move from abstract *existence* to concrete *ulcer*—from the top to the bottom of the abstraction pyramid on page 125.

The vocabulary available for discussing any conceivable topic ranges from words that are most abstract to words that are most concrete, with intermediate-level words between. In this case, you are being most abstract when you talk about Harry's existence and most concrete when you talk about his ulcer. When you talk about Harry's living condition you are being more abstract than when you talk about his disease, and when you talk

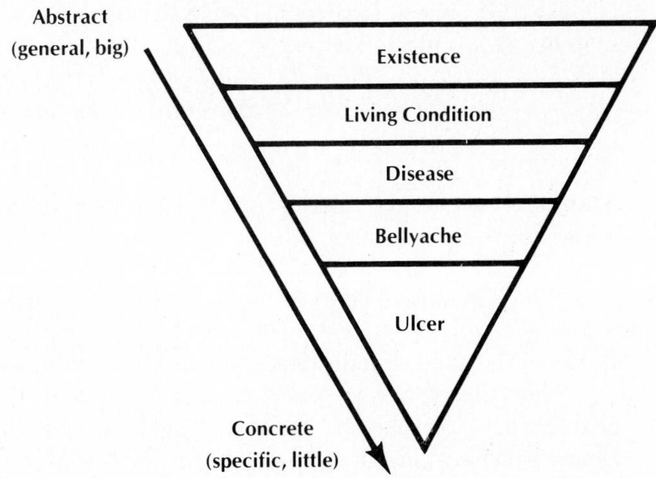

about his bellyache you are being more concrete than both. A similar abstraction pyramid can be constructed for the range of words available in discussing any topic. It is best to keep your writing to the bottom half of the pyramid, to be concrete as frequently as you can.

Words have contexts

No word ever has exactly the same meaning twice. The meaning of each word depends on its context, which includes both the physical and verbal setting or environment in which it is used. And because things are constantly changing in time and space, no word will ever have exactly the same meaning to the person hearing or seeing it repeated.

We understand words differently as their contexts change. The *physical* context of a word is the geographical and historical setting in which the word is *encoded* (spoken or written) or *decoded* (heard or read). Ten years ago, the words "neutron bomb" had no meaning; today they evoke uneasiness and anxiety. Our perception of the word *sex* is different at age ten than at age thirty. Our reaction to the words *iced tea* will be different in 100-degree Texas heat than it will be in subzero arctic cold. And we will attach a totally different meaning to the word *marriage* depending on whether we are happily married, involved in a bitter divorce case, or happily settled as a single. In short, both geography and historical moment have a definite effect on the meaning of words. And since both geography and history change continually, the meanings of words also change continually.

Furthermore, words also depend on their verbal contexts for meaning. The *verbal context* of a word is determined by the words that precede and follow it. Verbal context often allows us to understand words we have never seen before, as in this sentence:

> He reached up to shave his *drundrearies*, which had grown thick on both cheeks.

From the context we guess that the little-used word *drundrearies* means whiskers. And as in this:

> The cows had to be herded back to their *byre* for milking.

Here, as the context indicates, the word *byre* means barn or shed.

The importance of verbal context is clear to foreigners learning English. What we take for granted, they must learn through hard experience—namely, that English is full of words whose meanings change with their verbal contexts. An example is the word *wing*:

1. Lady Macbeth stood in the *wings*, waiting for her cue.
2. My canary has white spots under his left *wing*.
3. She belongs to the left-*wing* faction of the party.
4. Hand me that *wing* nut so that I can screw it on.
5. I haven't studied, so I'll just have to *wing* it.
6. Don't wear your *wing* tips; wear your hush puppies.
7. Betty is a patient in the children's *wing* of the hospital.

Words have denotations and connotations

Every word has a denotation and a connotation. *To denote* means "to point to"; *to connote* means "to imply." The denotation of a word is its bare dictionary definition; the connotation includes all of the emotional overtones suggested by the word. The word *home* denotes a place where one lives, but it connotes much more than that—warmth, shelter, coziness, and all the other qualities that have come to be attached to the total meaning of *home*. Words like *chair, typewriter, clothespin,* and *match* are usually used denotatively, pointing to specific, concrete things and nothing more. But words like *tempest, ghost, Christmas,* and *mother* are used connotatively for the emotional charge they seem to emit. To put this another way: the denotative meaning of a word comes directly from its referent; the connotative meaning is drawn from the ideas that cluster around the reference prong of the semantic triangle. Consider, for example, the semantic triangle on the word *winter*:

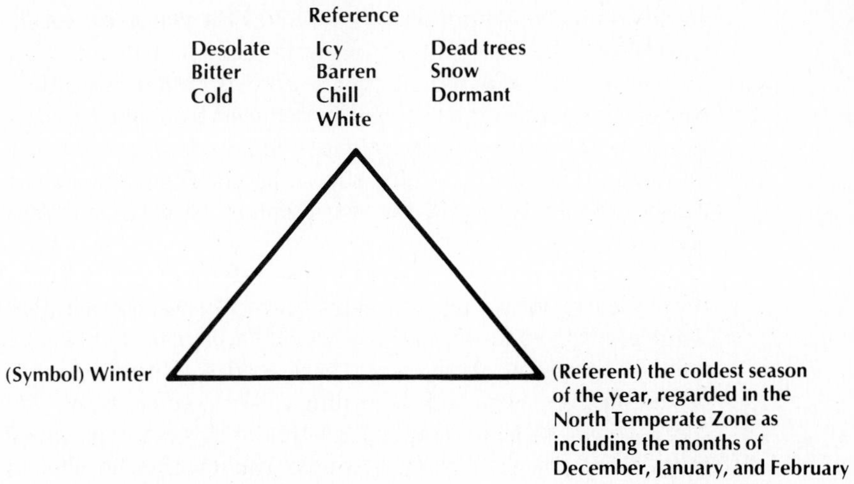

The referent shown was taken from *Webster's New World Dictionary.* The references will vary considerably among individuals but should cluster mainly around images of bleakness, desolation, and dormancy. Nevertheless, there is enough consensus on these various references to make the following connotative uses of *winter* intelligible to most people:

> Laughter drives winter from the mind.
> She is in the winter of her life.
> This is the winter of his discontent.

Quibbles may legitimately be raised over faint shades of meaning, but most people would probably interpret these sentences in the same ways. Here are some possible interpretations:

> Laughter drives bleakness from the mind.

Skiing enthusiasts aside, winter is customarily associated in the minds of most people with dismal weather, storms, blizzards, and gloominess—the characteristics connotatively evoked in this use.

> She is in the waning period of her life.

Winter is the final season of the year, a time when bears hibernate, trees go dormant, and geese fly south. Rhymsters and versifiers therefore traditionally use *winter* to signify old age and death just as they customarily use *spring* to imply youth. Obviously, this poetic meaning is connoted here.

> This is the bitterest period of his disconent.

In this sentence, winter once again takes the rap as a season of bad weather and is used to connote discontent at its very worst.

The denotative meaning of a word is gained from the dictionary; the connotative meaning is ultimately deduced from one's experience. To accurately use a word connotatively, one must not only be aware of its referent meanings, but one must also share the consensus on its reference. If this consensus is not shared, the word cannot be used connotatively with any accuracy.

The connotation of a word whose reference is commonly known will be much clearer than that of a word with a little-known reference. Take the word *pig*, for instance, and the word *okapi*. *Pig* denotes a fat four-legged animal with a curly tail, short ears, and squinting eyes. The referent of *okapi*, on the other hand, according to *Webster's New World Dictionary*, is: "An African animal (Okapia johnstoni) related to the giraffe, but with a much shorter neck." Yet most people would rather be called an okapi than a pig. It is a cliché that the pig is stupid, dirty, and greedy, and these connotations are intended when the term is applied to a person. If the same person is called a lion or a tiger the connotations are more positive, as the person's response is also likely to be, for the lion and the tiger are popularly thought of as hunters and masters in their dominions—a mystique that has transferred favorable connotations to both words. But the lowly okapi is more or less lost on the public consciousness. Its personal habits are unclear, its standards of hygiene or domination are known only to zoologists and zoo keepers. The dictionary definition above, moreover, is of no help whatsoever in clarifying whether one should take insult or rejoice over being called an okapi. The moral of this discussion is that connotative meaning is more subtle and elusive than denotative meaning and requires familiarity with more than the dictionary referent. Or, to put it another way, you know the meaning of a word only when you understand its connotations.

It follows from this discussion that greater semantic skill is required for the connotative rather than the denotative use of words. People who learn another language begin by memorizing the hard and fast denotative meanings of words; only later, as they acquire familiarity with the particular culture, do the reverberations of words—their connotations—become clear. Similarly, a native speaker who first encounters a word and looks up its meaning in a dictionary gains primarily a denotative definition of it. Its connotations will sink in only after the speaker has repeatedly encountered the word in various spoken and written contexts. Because of this lag between acquiring connotative and denotative meanings, the writer who habitually uses a barely familiar vocabulary runs the danger of sounding stilted and wooden. It is better to use only those words whose connotations and denotations you clearly understand.

Literature, especially poetry, uses words largely for their connotative meanings, while technical and scientific writing primarily relies on the denotative use of words, with individual words functioning as concrete indicators of specific referents. Here, for example, is a passage taken from a pamphlet of technical instructions:

> Place the batteries over the band in the battery compartment for easy removal. When not using batteries for one month or more, be sure to remove them. If the batteries become weak, replace them with new ones as soon as possible.

On the other hand, in this stanza from a poem by John Keats, a haggard and heartbroken knight is described with words used chiefly for their connotations:

> I see a lily on thy brow,
> With anguish moist and fever dew;
> And on thy cheeks a fading rose
> Fast withereth too.

The stanza does not mean to literally suggest that a lily grows on the brow of the knight, or a rose on his cheeks. *Lily* connotatively suggests the paleness of the brow of the sorrowing knight; *rose*, likewise, connotatively refers to the pink fading from his cheeks. As might be expected, the language of literature is richer in connotations than the language of science and has contributed many new words to our everyday vocabulary. The following words, for instance, along with numerous others, all originated from literary sources: *Pecksniffian, robot, pandemonium, malapropism, braggadocio*. To find their literary origins, look them up in a dictionary.

Consider, as another example of connotation, any of the number of words that can be used to describe someone's way of walking. Here are a few choices, each connoting a different gait: *trot, sidle, shamble, slouch, amble, march, prance, swagger, saunter, trip, tramp, tiptoe, traipse, waddle, plod, clump*. A writer, wishing to characterize a person's gait, could use one or another of these words in the following sentence:

> John ________ over to where Mary sat on the bench looking thoughtfully out at the river.

If John is an immensely fat old man, *waddle, clump*, or *plod* ought to do; if he is a surly adolescent in the middle of a row over his use of the family car, the choice might be between *traipse, shamble, swagger*, or *slouch*. If John is an airy, light-footed ballet dancer, he might *prance* or *trip*. If he is a military man, ever conscious of his locomotion and posture, he might *march*. If he is a horse, he would no doubt *trot*, and if a conspirator, he would probably *sidle* or *tiptoe*. In any event, the choice of one of these words to express John's gait would vary entirely with what sort of person John is and how the writer wishes to characterize him for the reader.

Good writers will use words both for their denotative effects and for their subtle connotative overtones. As you write, try to be aware of the connotative meanings of words you use. *Tinkle* and *boom* both denote noises. But a sensitive writer will not say, "The silver bell *boomed*," nor "The huge cannons *tinkled*." The writer might, however, quite appropriately say, "The silver bell tinkled," and, "The huge cannons boomed." Consider the following word choices in parentheses; the most appropriate words are italicized:

1. She knew that that black raven circling the sky was a bad (sign, *omen*, thing).
2. Suddenly Belinda's stomach (moved, *turned*, did an about face).
3. Water (hit, bumped, *slapped*) the rickety pylons.
4. With (stuck-up, *haughty*, bragging) grandeur the old duchess arose from her chair.
5. We did not care for the ornate furnishings of the bedroom assigned to us and considered them quite (funny, stupid, *absurd*).

In each case the italicized word is the best choice within the context of the sentence, for it is the atmosphere of any given passage that dictates the choice of words. A dignified atmosphere requires dignified words (Tell the illustrious ambassador that his *dinner* awaits him below); a rough atmosphere requires rough words (Grunting swinishly, the pigs furiously attacked the *swill* in the trough.) Choose words carefully for the atmosphere you wish to create.

Slang

Slang is not the same as profanity, bad grammar, or provincial language. In other words, *damn it, he don't know nothing*, or *I reckon* is not slang. Most slang simply consists of new words and phrases that people invent in their desire to give the language vigor and novelty. Often slang consists of coinages and figures of speech used by special subcultures, occupations, or social groups to communicate among themselves.

Slang is formed in many ways. It can develop by normal linguistic processes, such as compounding (*low-down, sob-stuff*), word shortening (*pro, gym, prof, mike, vet*), abbreviating (*VIP, OK, LSD*), generalizing proper names (*real McCoy, roger, guy, jerry*), or borrowing from other languages (*savvy, pronto, kaput*). Much slang develops through the wit of a single person whose catch phrase is so effective that others use it until it is widespread. Some slang is borrowed from the vocabulary of particular activities, as:

on the beam (aviation)

behind the eight ball (pool)

tune in, tune out (radio)

cop out (underworld)

cash in your chips (poker)

lower the boom (sailing)

wipe out (surfing)

Some slang uses standard vocabulary, but twists its meaning, as:

bread (money)

sweat (trouble)

joint (place, or marijuana)

drip, creep (unattractive person)

sack (bed)

lousy (bad)

The good side of slang is that it is spontaneous and direct. The bad side is that it can be imprecise and ambiguous. Even dictionaries sometimes disagree on the meaning of a slang word or expression. The following exchange, between an advice columnist and one of her readers, illustrates this pitfall of using slang:

DEAR ABBY: As a pro who gets paid for writing scripts, articles, etc., I must be nuts writing to you. However, I can't resist pointing out your misuse of the expression, "lucked out." You wrote (in praise of Gamblers Anonymous): "Many compulsive gamblers have *lucked out* by joining this wonderful group of people."

According to the Dictionary of American Slang (Wentworth & Flexner) "lucked out" means "to be out of luck" or "to have met with ill fortune or disaster."

—MARINA DEL REY MORT

DEAR MORT: According to Webster's New World Dictionary of the American Language, "lucked out" means "to be lucky" or "to have things turn out favorably." So, regardless of whether one buys my authority or yours, it would appear that I "lucked out" either way.

Because of its imprecision and restricted use, slang should not be used in formal writing. An equally important argument against the use of slang is that it tends to give your writing a flippant and insincere tone. Unless this is the tone you are striving for (and it usually is not), you should keep slang out of your writing.

Application: Use, don't abuse, words

In Chapter 2, we urged you to use your oral skills to process your written words. Here we return again to that theme. Give up the notion that to write well you must use big, fancy words that you would never speak. But do not cling too stubbornly to its opposite idea—that any word you would freely say in conversation is also suitable fare for your writing. The middle course is the safest. Write in words that you would comfortably say to an audience of people you respect; avoid words that an overpowering sense of awe might cause you to mumble to the Queen of England or the Pope. Above all, try to use words connotatively, not merely for their dictionary meaning.

Specifically, we advise you to use words in the following ways.

Use short words over long ones

The only exception to this rule occurs when the longer word offers greater precision than the shorter one. But seldom are long words more exact than short ones. More often than not the short word will instantly evoke an image in the reader's mind, while the long one will merely be dense and imageless. Here is an example of an entire paragraph made incomprehensible by the overuse of big words:

> He speaks against a permissive society, yet if it weren't for this society's permissiveness, he wouldn't be able to put forth his socially recidivist views, contumacious to the norm as they are. It is an attitude such as his that made abiogenesis a visible theory for so long.

Translated into plain English, this is what the author probably meant:

> He speaks against our permissive society; yet, if it weren't for this very permissiveness, he would not be allowed to express his own anti-social views. People with his closed-mindedness block scientific and cultural progress.

The motive for deliberately using a big word when a little one would do often springs from the writer's misguided desire to impress. But clarity impresses even more than a dense vocabulary.

Use the correct word

Avoid using words whose meanings you only half remember or do not truly understand. Always check the dictionary for words whose meanings are fuzzy in your memory. Here are some examples of misused words found in a student paper.

Wrong: Everywhere we saw children who had been *depraved* of food.
Right: Everywhere we saw children who had been *deprived* of food.

Wrong: I will be happy to *appraise* you of what happened.
Right: I will be happy to *apprise* you of what happened.

At the heart of much garbled writing lie misspelled words. The old argument that "as long as meaning is clear, spelling does not matter" is at best specious. Misspelled words can play havoc with the meaning of a sentence. Consider the following announcement:

> *Wreckless* drivers pay high insurance premiums.

Here the misspelled word inverts the meaning of the sentence—a *wreckless* driver being one who has had *no* wrecks. What the writer meant to say was quite different:

> *Reckless* drivers pay high insurance premiums.

Consider also this comment from a real estate news bulletin:

> Next month the city will *raze* three new department stores.

The writer meant to say *raise*, which means *to build up*, instead of *raze*, which means to tear down or *demolish*.

Poor spelling can also destroy serious writing. To write, for instance, that Mr. Smith has an *innoculate* (instead of *innocuous*) personality is to completely blunt the force of your opinion. The reader doubtless knows your meaning, yet you must unwittingly appear even more innocuous than your enemy, Mr. Smith. Consider this spelling blunder, "The *predation* of the document had rendered it null and void in this state." A document may be predated, but it cannot commit predation—that must be left to wolves and other wild beasts. Misspelling, as you can see, is so perilously close to malaproprism—the ludicrous misuse of words—that a reader might easily mistake the lesser offense for the greater.

The only cure for poor spelling is diligent proofreading. A knowledge of prefixes, suffixes, and root meanings of words can help, but nothing takes the place of checking the dictionary for the correct spelling of every word about which you have the slightest doubt.

Use concrete words

Good writing deals in particulars. For instance, when you state, "My boss is conceited," you no doubt have details in mind—he brags about his money; he expects his help to grovel; he exaggerates his talents; and so on. Let your readers in on these particulars, or they may supply their own, perhaps inaccurately.

Vague: *Everything* looked inviting.
Concrete: The homemade potato salad and the apple pie looked inviting.

Vague: He wore *unusual* clothes.
Concrete: He wore a red gypsy shirt with blue denim overalls topped by a paisley turban.

Note that often you can make a vague sentence concrete by adding particulars:

Vague: White people *deceived the Indians*.
Concrete: White people deceived the Indians by breaking treaties, stealing pastureland, and herding them into sterile reservations.

Vague: She stole the show with her *fine dancing*.
Concrete: She stole the show with her fine dancing, a combination of well-executed pirouettes, bows, leaps, and half-twists.

Use appropriate words

Your own good judgment and sensitivity to connotation and context must guide you here. Obvious lapses in tone and style will give anyone's writing an awkward, erratic quality, as the following examples show:

Awkward: Students who hope for a scholarship grant to continue their education will not *blow it* by rude attacks on the school board.
Better: Students who hope for a scholarship grant will not *ruin their chances* by rude attacks on the school board.

Awkward: Foolproof statistics about sex are difficult to compile, but one fact is evident: girls *end up in the sack* just as often as boys.

Better: Foolproof statistics about sex are difficult to compile, but one fact is evident: girls *have as much sex* as boys.

NOTE: For emphasis, a writer will sometimes deliberately use a word that is slightly out of character with the rest of the words in the sentence:

> I hate the idea of causes, and if I had to choose between betraying my country and betraying my friend, I hope I should have enough *guts* to betray my country.
>
> —E. M. Forster

Guts is obviously a more colloquial word than the other words in the sentence, but it is also more emphatic than *courage* or *resolution* or some other more formal synonym.

Use words that sound right

Words that rhyme in a single sentence and words used in an alliterative cluster may make your writing sound unintentionally comical. Sentences with an internal rhyme are easily corrected by rewriting:

Rhyme: At dawn, from behind drawn curtains, we saw her mow the lawn.
Better: At dawn we looked out the window and watched her mow the grass.

Rhyme: The shop looked like a prop on the top of the mountain.
Better: The shop seemed toylike on the brow of the mountain.

Alliteration is a poetic device of grouping words together that begin with the same sound, like "*f*ine, *f*renzied *f*ellow." Here the alliterative sound is the repeated initial *f* sound. Alliteration is well suited to poetry, but an obstruction to clear prose. Again, it is easy to correct an alliterative sentence:

Alliterative: Perhaps his puny profits pose no persistently serious problem.
Better: It is unlikely that his small profits will become a serious difficulty.

Alliterative: Sloppy, slovenly, slatternly speech and inept, incoherent writing sometimes characterize students' work.
Better: Students are occasionally careless and inept in their speech, while in their writing they are often incoherent.

Both alliteration and rhyme draw attention to themselves and therefore away from your meaning. They should consequently be avoided.

Use figures of speech

The figure of speech, when deftly used, will delight your readers with its concrete freshness. The two most common figures are the *metaphor* and the *simile*. The metaphor hinges on an implicit comparison:

> This is the hour of lead.
>
> —Emily Dickinson.

The simile, on the other hand, uses an explicit comparison, often introduced by "like" or "as":

> To see him act is like reading Shakespeare by flashes of lightning.
>
> —Samuel Taylor Coleridge

Aptly done, the figure of speech can make ideas and concepts vivid and concrete. Consider, for example, this abstract, imageless assertion:

> He was the sort of teacher who presented his students with one fact after another in quick succession, thinking that facts would make them mature quickly.

Here is the same idea presented metaphorically:

> . . . he seemed a kind of cannon loaded to blow them [his students] clean out of the regions of childhood at one discharge.
>
> —Charles Dickens, *Hard Times*

The second version is not only more vivid and memorable, it is also curiously more concrete than the first.

Writers who can use such figures well have a device at their fingertips that will save them time and endless numbers of words. Here is an example in which the writer uses a combination of metaphor and similes to explain viruses:

> The viruses, instead of being single-minded agents of disease and death, now begin to look more like mobile genes. Evolution is still an infinitely long and tedious biologic game, with only the winners staying at the table, but the rules are beginning to look more flexible. We live in a dancing matrix of viruses; they dart, rather like bees, from organism to organism, from plant to insect to mammal and to me and back again, and into the sea, tugging along pieces of

> this genome, strings of genes from that, transplanting grafts of DNA, passing around heredity as though at a great party.
>
> —Lewis Thomas, "The Lives of a Cell"

Both the metaphor and the simile are used to make writing vivid by transferring the pictorial quality of an object to a non-pictorial fact. For instance, if you have difficulty describing the inhuman quality of your boss, you might say, "He is like a computer." The ominous quietness of a room filled with angry people can be described as "the quietness of the eye of a hurricane."

Use metaphors and similes to throw light on a dark passage or to make an abstract concept vivid, but use them sparingly. Prose dripping with them quickly becomes cloying, like too sweet fruitcake. Furthermore, some figurative expressions—most coined long ago—have become trite enough to numb. Listed below are a few of these that ought to be carefully scrubbed from your writing:

busy as a bee

white as a sheet

cold as ice

green with envy

slow as molasses

by the sweat of his brow

over my dead body

EXERCISES

1. Create an abstraction pyramid (like the one on page 125) for the following words:

   a. pencil
   b. tooth
   c. cat
   d. rose

2. The words in the sets that follow have approximately the same denotations. Underline the word you would prefer to be called. Identify what connotation leads you to reject one member of the word pair.

   a. Fanatical/enthusiastic
   b. Politician/statesman
   c. Prying/curious
   d. Frigid/cold
   e. Compliant/servile
   f. Foolhardy/daring
   g. Gullible/trusting
   h. Modest/prudish
   i. Gabby/talkative
   j. Relaxed/loose

3. Explain the differences in connotation among the words in the groups below. Suggest contexts for the use of each word.

   a. Confess, grant, come clean
   b. Obese, plump, bulky
   c. Frighten, intimidate, startle
   d. Apparel, outfit, costume
   e. Grave, cemetery, final resting place
   f. Earthy, terrestrial, mundane
   g. Eager, anxious, yearning
   h. Champion, back, advocate
   i. Catching, infectious, communicable
   j. Fragile, brittle, crisp

4. The italicized words in the following sentences tend to evoke negative feelings. Replace them with words that are less negative.

   a. She is one of the most *bullheaded* people I know.
   b. Have you noticed that he always plays the role of *henchman*?
   c. Let us make sure that he is *blackballed* from our club.
   d. She has *hoarded* a great fortune.
   e. Please ask him to wait before *butting in* again.
   f. We would appreciate it if you would *procrastinate* no longer.
   g. His *dipsomania* should be curbed.
   h. If he were not quite so *bizarre*, he would make a good minister.
   i. We shall interview only people who have demonstrated that they are *pushy*.
   j. We have special jobs set aside for *crippled* people.

5. From the words in parentheses, choose the one that seems most appropriate.

   a. Great leaders are constantly aware of the supreme power of the (mob/crowds/group).
   b. Like a true aristocrat, he lived in elegant (plainness/straightforwardness/simplicity).
   c. A (wisp/bundle/fragment) of cloud trailed across the moon.
   d. Understood as a central consolidated power, managing and directing the various interests of society, all government is (wicked/bad/evil).
   e. God moves in (odd/strange/peculiar) and mysterious ways.
   f. His most obvious character fault was a tendency to (wallow, slouch, crouch) in self-pity.
   g. President Theodore Roosevelt is associated with the American tradition of (rough/tough/rugged) individualism.
   h. If an earthquake were to (swallow/engulf/absorb) us tomorrow, we would have lived to the fullest.

i. The television series *The Winds of War*, based on Herman Wouk's epic novel, was (captivating/tremendous/attractive).

6. Reword the following sentences to avoid all slang.

   a. That really gets my goat.
   b. The students sat around and shot the breeze.
   c. It's time that the Congress talked turkey about nuclear waste.
   d. Banks must stop handing out loans willy-nilly.
   e. Bjorn Borg beat the pants off Jimmy Connors.
   g. There was something fishy about the numbers he presented.
   h. What a cheapskate that millionaire is!
   i. You pay through the nose if you want to buy a Mercedes-Benz station wagon.
   j. It boggles the mind to think of how many planets there are in the universe.

8

Why doesn't it make sense?

Not wrung from speculations and subleties,
but from common sense and observation.

—Sir Thomas Browne

LOGIC IS A PUBLIC METHOD OF REASONING. It differs from other varieties of thought, such as intuition or hunch, because it requires that both the *process* and the *evidence* behind a conclusion be shown. The distinction between process and evidence is this: process asserts a relationship between ideas; evidence supports or denies the validity of the asserted relationship. For instance, the statement "Cigarette smoking can be harmful to your health" is asserting a causal relationship between smoking and poor health, in effect claiming that the one can cause the other. The validity of this relationship is supported by overwhelming evidence, such as the following mortality statistics listed in *Smoking and Health: Report of the Advisory Committee to the Surgeon General of the Public Health Service*: cigarette smokers have a 70% higher death rate from coronary artery disease; a 500% higher death rate from chronic bronchitis and emphysema; and a 1000% higher death rate from lung cancer, than nonsmokers. This evidence, along with numerous other facts, supports the contention that cigarette smoking can be harmful to a smoker's health. The rules of logic demand that all statements linking ideas together in relationships must be similarly supported by evidence.

Your argument is logical when you can demonstrate that anyone using the same reasoning process and the same evidence must inevitably come to the same conclusion. It is illogical if it is based on a private process of reasoning, or if it fails to consider all the relevant evidence. Logic is simply the result of an attempt to create a method of reasoning that functions independently of any one person; it is essentially neutral and works for interchangeable minds so long as its rules are followed. The opposite of logic is mysticism, magic, or any other system whose claim to truth depends on the special talents of one person.

The reasoning process of a logical argument typically relates ideas by cause, consequence, category, or alternative. Usually, the ideas are connected by link words, such as *therefore*, *because*, and *since*. Logic requires that the relationship asserted between the connected ideas be valid, be supported by evidence, and be made clear by the link word.

When ideas are related by *consequence*, if the first idea is true, then the second idea is also true as a consequence.

> The Constitution declares that all people are equal in the sight of the law. It is *therefore* illegal for any state to discriminate against any of its citizens.

An idea may be related to another by being its *cause*.

> I vote Democratic *because* that is the way I was brought up to vote.

When ideas are related by *category*, one idea is classified under another.

> From the pouch on this animal that it uses to nurse its young, we *infer* that it belongs to the marsupial order.

An idea may be related to another by being its *alternative*.

> *Either* we do something about pollution now on a gradual basis or we shall be faced later on with a massive clean-up bill.

The process of reasoning: Deduction and induction

The process of reasoning involves two principal forms of logic—deductive and inductive logic. Deductive logic is reasoning that proceeds from the general to the specific, from something known to something unknown. Here is an example:

All oranges have vitamin C.	(*major premise*)
This fruit is an orange.	(*minor premise*)
Therefore, this fruit has vitamin C.	(*conclusion*)

The above formula is known as a *categorical syllogism*—a three-part logical statement that deduces a conclusion in the third part from information expressed in the preceding two parts. The syllogism is the mainstay of deductive logic and features commonly in our daily thinking. For instance, if you tell a friend, "Avoid buying a Speedmobile because Speedmobiles have bad ignitions," you are unconsciously using a shortened form of the categorical syllogism, called the *enthymeme*.

Inductive logic, on the other hand, proceeds not from a major premise to a specific conclusion, but from specific facts and evidence to a generalization. Here is an example: In 1750, James Lind, a surgeon's mate aboard the British ship H.M.S. *Salisbury*, decided to experiment with the effects of diet on scurvy—a disease that was then the terror of seamen all over the world. Lind isolated twelve scurvy victims, separating them into six groups of two. Each group was fed the daily rations of the Royal Navy along with different dietary supplements. Four groups were given cider, vinegar, and ordinary seawater to drink. The fifth group received a gruel recommended by a hospital surgeon, while the sixth group was given two oranges and a lemon each day. Of the twelve stricken men, only two recovered from the disease—the two given the oranges and lemon daily. Lind therefore generalized that the citrus fruit contained some substance beneficial to the cure of scurvy. Further tests confirmed this hypothesis.

Our daily operations in logic involve both deduction and induction. For instance, deductive logic persuades us that lightning, whether it flashes in Los Angeles or in Bangkok, is always electricity; that gravity will be found in Sydney, Australia, as well as in Reno, Nevada; and that the ostrich on the Serengeti Plain of Tanzania can no more fly than its counterpart in the Baltimore Zoo. In each case, deductive logic simply attributes to the individual occurrence or animal the characteristics known to apply to the category to which it belongs.

Inductive logic, on the other hand, provides us with new hypotheses to be used as major premises in deductions. For instance, before the Lind experiment, the policy of the British Admiralty, based on the premise that only malingerers contracted scurvy, was to flog any sailor complaining of its symptoms. After the Lind findings were published, the Admiralty abandoned its policy of flogging scurvy victims and, instead, fed them with daily doses of lemon juice. The shift in treatment represented the Admiralty's abandonment of its former major premise on the disease. Ideally, all reasonable people should react in a like manner to the introduction of any new hypothesis that is supported by substantial evidence.

No logical method is error free. Operations of deduction as well as induction are subject to common flaws. Here is an example of an erroneous categorical syllogism:

> All dogs have four legs
> This animal has four legs.
> Therefore, this animal is a dog.

But the animal could also be a rabbit, a camel, or even a hippopotamus, to mention a few other possibilities. Here is a similar error, taken from a student paper:

> I agree that the professor who refused to sign the loyalty oath of the university should be fired. If he was loyal, he would have signed the oath. Communists never want to sign loyalty oaths. And since the professor did not want to sign the oath, it is obvious to me that he is a communist.

The syllogism, once untangled, reads:

> Communists don't sign loyalty oaths.
> The professor didn't sign the loyalty oath.
> Therefore, the professor is a communist.

This is a faulty conclusion, one that does not follow from the major premise. Every four-legged animal is not necessarily a dog, neither is everyone who refuses to sign a loyalty oath a communist. If the major premise of the syllogism had been, all who refuse to sign loyalty oaths are communists, then it would have followed that the professor, by refusing to sign, must also be a communist. But such a major premise would have been silly and patently untrue.

The presence of undefined, ambiguous terms in the major premise is another error of student syllogisms. For instance, consider the following:

> Anyone who is against preserving our environment is obviously a right-winger who wants only to make money. For instance, it has been shown that the big oil companies have one goal and that is to discover more oil in our hills or beneath our oceans. They are always against cleaning up the environment or preserving it. To me this proves that big oil companies are right-wingers interested only in company profits.

"Right-winger" is an ambiguous term. No amount of logical exertion will make this syllogism more than a mechanism for name-calling. The category of "right-wingers" has to be more clearly defined before the reader can understand the characteristics being imputed to big oil companies.

Inductive logic, on the other hand, suffers from a common error known as *hasty generalization*. Consider, for instance, the following experience: A man goes to a movie one evening during which a patron wearing a bowler hat goes berserk in the theatre. The following day at a baseball game, our man witnesses a fan in a bowler hat who runs onto the field and attacks the shortstop. Driving home from the game, our man pulls alongside a Cadillac at a stoplight and sees the driver, wearing a bowler hat, hitting a companion. Our man generalizes hastily from these three instances: All bowler-hatted men are dangerous. This becomes a major premise in his library of beliefs that he will use from now on to deductively implicate anyone he comes across who wears a bowler hat. Should a bowler-hatted person wish to move into his neighborhood, trouble will no doubt result.

The hasty generalization is an error caused by a misinterpretation of evidence. It cannot logically be induced from three examples that all bowler-hatted men are dangerous. The evidence is simply not sufficient to support such a broad generalization. A generalization, to be reasonably accurate, must be based on what statisticians term an adequate sample—

one large enough to be truly representative. The next time someone comes to you and admonishes, "Don't take a class from Professor X; he's a very tough grader," ask to see the evidence on which this generalization is founded. More likely than not, you'll find that the generalization is based on a cursory talk with two students, both of whom got D's from Professor X. A more reasonable interpretation of this evidence is that the two students deserved to get D's. Even if the evidence of Professor X's hardheartedness is based on the gloomy testimony of twenty students—all of whom got D's—this is still not sufficient evidence to convict Professor X of cruelty to students. Perhaps Professor X teaches a mammoth course that enrolls 1,000 students—in which case a mere 20 D's might be enough to charge him with excessive leniency. Or perhaps the course Professor X teaches is an intrinsically difficult course, such as calculus. Or the 20 D's given out by Professor X—compared to 100 D's for the same course given by Professor Y—make him by far the easier grader of the two. The point is that evidence is complicated and susceptible to being misread.

In student essays, hasty generalizations are often found masquerading as major premises in concealed syllogisms as, for instance, in the following student paragraph:

> When I was a freshman in college, a student from Saudi Arabia sat next to me in biology class. We became friendly and often discussed our daily assignments. Then, one day he brought me a lovely hand-embroidered purse as a gift. I didn't accept it because I just knew that the next step would be for him to ask me to cheat on our biology exams by giving him the answers. All Arabian students cheat; it is a way of life with them.

Imbedded in this paragraph is the following syllogism:

> All Arabian students cheat on college exams.
> This seatmate of mine is an Arabian student.
> Therefore, this seatmate must cheat on college exams.

The major premise proposes a hasty generalization and is consequently faulty. A closer investigation of Arabian culture and ethics would have revealed that honesty in taking college examinations is required in Saudi Arabia just as it is in the United States. Likewise, our man with the prejudice against bowler-hatted men would have found enough decent bowler-hatters to outfit an army.

The fairness and accuracy of any categorical syllogism rest on the accuracy of the information expressed in its major premise. An inaccurate major premise will unerringly lead to an inaccurate deduction. Carried to the extreme of inaccuracy, the categorical syllogism leads to stereotyping and prejudice. During the nineteen-sixties, for instance, it was commonly believed that people's political sentiments could be deduced from their appearance. Long hair on a man was thought to indicate a radical/liberal; short hair, a conservative. Studies have shown that this is a false notion; hair length does not indicate political leaning. The shallow evidence suggests that it does; deep evidence denies any connection. Deep evidence is not merely observational but is formally gathered and assembled by impartial research. All other evidence is shallow. Hasty generalizations are usually supported by shallow evidence but contradicted by deep evidence. Anyone who wishes to think logically must override any generalizations that are denied by valid, deep evidence.

Many arguments begin with an assumption that is based on an unproved generalization. This assumption is usually not stated, but implied:

Argument: Capital punishment should be abolished because it has been proven to have no deterrent effect on crime.

Unstated assumption: Capital punishment exists because people believe it to have a deterrent effect on crime.

Argument: Violence on television should be censored before all our young people become criminals.

Unstated assumption: Violence on television contributes to criminal acts among young people.

Argument: I am a Democrat because I am a liberal.

Unstated assumption: Democrats are liberal.

The assumption with which it begins is the jugular vein of any argument. The following arguments are weak because they begin with an initial assumption that is questionable:

Argument: We need more punishment, not less. All the statistics reveal that crime rates are up and are continuing to rise. What we need are more prisons, more guards, and most of all, severer punishment for criminals.

Questionable assumption: Punishment deters crime.

Argument: Pornography must be held in check unless we are willing to tolerate the rising incidence of rape.

Questionable assumption: Pornography causes rape.

Argument: The speaker, like all Republicans, was a conservative, and so it is to be expected that he will adopt a conservative position on this issue.

Questionable assumption: All Republicans are conservative.

Breakdowns in the process of reasoning

A valid argument links ideas together in a valid relationship. Most errors in reasoning are caused by a breakdown in the linkage between ideas. Consequently, an argument is invalid if the relationship expressed by a link between ideas is false, if the link between ideas is blurred by poor wording, or if the argument fails to focus on the point of contention. The three most common errors in reasoning are, therefore:

Poor linkage caused by a faulty relationship

Poor linkage caused by poor wording

Poor linkage caused by the failure of an argument to focus

Faulty relationship

A breakdown in the reasoning process occurs when one idea is linked to another in a faulty cause, consequence, category, or alternative relationship. Here are some examples:

> For many years baseball players have sported mustaches and long sideburns, and in my opinion they played better baseball. The batting averages were twice what they are today. I might add that with their mustaches and long sideburns the Oakland A's won the World Series. So, if long hair affects the players' performance, then all players should have long hair and mustaches.

In this example, the causal relationship is faulty. The link implies that long hair and a mustache cause a player to play better baseball. There is no evidence to substantiate such a relationship. A baseball player may simultaneously have long hair and a high batting average without the one causing the other.

> Women are by nature superior homemakers. Their natural talents lie in the realm of cooking and interior decorating. Therefore a woman's place to excel is in the home.

The consequence relationship in this argument is faulty. The fact that some of the greatest cooks and interior designers are men is evidence to the contrary.

> The reason the Swiss are such good watchmakers is that they live in a small country; thus they become accustomed to working with diminutive machinery and tools.

This is an example of a faulty causal relationship. It is more likely that the watchmaking ability of the Swiss is due to years of careful individual training.

> A man who has had even one homosexual experience must be termed a homosexual.

The category relationship in this argument is faulty. According to the studies carried out by Alfred Kinsey and others, a majority of American men have had at least one exploratory homosexual experience before establishing a stable heterosexual relationship. Sociologists do not categorize such men as *homosexuals*; if they did, homosexuality would be the norm, rather than a minority form of sexual expression.

> Either we stop the publication of *Hustler* magazine or we accept the fact that our children will be perverted.

This is an example of a faulty alternative relationship, also termed a faulty dilemma. The relationship suggests only two alternatives, when more are available.

A special kind of faulty relationship between ideas can occur when they are equated through the use of an analogy. Two ideas may be brought into relationship with each other despite the fact that they involve different values and principles. The result is likely to be an oversimplification of the argument.

> You wouldn't change surgeons in the middle of a difficult operation. Likewise, let us not change governors in these days of severe crisis.

The analogy here is simplistic and misleading. Governing a state has little in common with a surgical operation to justify the analogy. The following analogy is also simplistic:

> The Federal government and its budget are like a household and its budget. Either the spending is held to conform with the amount of money both have, or both will have to go bankrupt.

The Federal government is vaster and subjected to many more complex variables than a household.

Analogies serve a useful and explanatory purpose where they are used to illuminate minor points of an argument. It is, however, risky to frame a massive argument in the language of an analogy. Instead, deal directly with the issues of the argument, and use analogies to explain minor points.

Poor wording

Fuzzy wording blurs the relationship between the linked ideas:

> Should parents spend time openly discussing sex with their children? The advocates of this idea say that it is definitely part of *good parental training*.

The ambiguous wording of this argument implies that the parents are being trained by the children, rather than the other way around. Here is the same argument rewritten:

> Should parents spend time discussing sex with their children? The advocates of this idea say that it is definitely part of *the sound upbringing of any child*.

Here is another example:

> The theory of evolution is a complex idea wherein all living things are related to one another *since* they all come from the same common ancestor far back in geologic times. Through evolution new species arise from preceding species of plants and animals that were simpler. This has been happening since plants and animals first existed on earth, and it is still going on. *Therefore*, all living things bear relationship to one another and this is called the theory of evolution.

This argument is hazy because the writer uses two link words when there are only two ideas to be linked: the theory of evolution and what it states. Here is the rewritten paragraph with only one link word, *consequently*, and the relationship between the ideas is clearer:

> The theory of evolution states that all living things are related through a common ancestor. New species of plants and animals are believed to have evolved from simpler species. Evolutionists contend that the process has always occurred and is still occurring, and that *consequently* all living things bear a relationship to each other.

The following statement implies that policemen, guards, and private citizens are doing the murdering. It also unnecessarily divides the population into three overlapping groups:

> Studies show that *the murder rates* for policemen, guards, and private citizens are lower in states without the death penalty.

The rewritten paragraph eliminates the false implication and the unnecessary division:

> Studies show that the murder rates are lower in the states without the death penalty.

Failure of an argument to focus

If you attack an opponent instead of the opponent's logic, you are committing an error of process by failing to focus your argument on the point of contention. In a sense, you are linking ideas that really have no bearing on the issue. The commonest error of this type is called an *ad hominem* argument, meaning an argument against the person. Here is an example:

> Senator Smith's opposition to this bill can only be understood after an examination of the Smith voting record. He has voted for every radical proposal before this body. He has openly championed the causes of known criminals and political renegades. In the light of his long-held radical views, the opposition of Senator Smith is understandable.

Ad hominem arguments are frequently resorted to by debaters and writers probably because they allow a vent of passions at little expense to the mind. However, from a logical point of view, they falsely link ideas that bear on personality, rather than on the issue.

Other evasions of process are cataloged by logicians under a variety of colorful names. An argument that "begs the question" is one that moves in circles. It neither says nor adds anything new to the proposition, as:

> I am against prostitution because it causes women to sell themselves.

The "red herring" is the introduction of a subsidiary, emotionally loaded issue that draws attention away from the real one. For instance, in an argument about whether or not schools should be allowed to lead children in group prayer, someone might stand up and say:

> The question here is whether or not we intend to allow atheists to dictate school policy, whether or not we intend to allow the opinions of atheists to dominate our lives.

That, of course, is not the question. Nor does it follow that an opponent of public school prayer is necessarily an atheist. But the assertion is so emotionally loaded that it is apt to distract attention away from the real issue and, perhaps, to put the opponents of public prayer on the defensive.

The *ad populum* argument is an appeal to common feelings, passions, and prejudices through the selective use of unflattering phrases, such as "creeping red socialism," "robber baron businessmen," or "demagogue tendencies," to describe an issue to which one is opposed. Conversely, the favored issue is described with flattering phrases, such as "for our beloved country," "freedom to choose," and "good for the common man":

> There are fascists who will encourage rampant slobbiness in our public parks. They will not stop the careless boobs who dump eggshells, beer cans, and waste paper in a spreading desecration of the purple mountains' majesty of our American landscape. I say the park should be fenced for the sake of loyal American patriots who love their land and want to keep it beautiful.

A logical argument must meet the following demands of process:

Its initial assumption must be true.

It must focus on the subject and not on personalities or side issues.

Ideas must be linked to express accurate, concise, and valid relationships between them.

Evidence in reasoning

Evidence is the bond between a reality and its representation by an idea. The student who wrote, "I believe that capital punishment should be continued because it deters murders" was making an assertion about a reality—that a person on the verge of committing a murder could be deterred from doing it by the existence of a death penalty. If the evidence bears out his assertion, then he has accurately represented the reality; if it does not, then the reality is misrepresented in the assertion. The proof is to be found in evidence.

Evidence consists of the following:

Facts

Experience

Witnesses

Authority

Facts

A fact is information that accurately represents the reality. Facts are subjected to but unchanged by interpretation. For instance, the *Encyclopaedia Britannica* lists the following statistic on capital punishment as a fact:

> Between 1930 and 1965 . . . 50% of those executed for murder, 90% of those executed for rape, and 50% of those executed for some other crime were nonwhite.

One student may interpret this fact to mean that nonwhites were more harshly treated by the courts because of their lower status; another may conclude that nonwhites had a higher capital crime rate because of their poverty. But in either case, the statistic itself remains the same. To state that "American religion has been practical, pious, sentimental, childlike" cannot qualify as a fact because the statement is impossible to verify against reality. On the other hand, the statement that in 1976 the Hare Krishna religion numbered 2500 core members can qualify as a fact because presumably this sect keeps records that can confirm or refute the accuracy of the number.

The following rules govern the use of facts:

Facts must be accompanied by a traceable source. It is not permissible to list an item as a fact without listing its source. The reader must have the opportunity to investigate a suspect source of facts. (An exception to this rule is facts of common knowledge, such as "John F. Kennedy was assassinated.")

Facts must be relevant to the argument. If you are writing a paper arguing for conservation of the bald eagle, you should list appropriate facts dealing with the decline of the eagle population. It is useless to include the metabolic rate of the bald eagle as a subsidiary fact unless this has some bearing on your argument.

Facts must either be current or still valid. If, for instance, you are quoting figures from a book, they should come from its latest edition unless they are unchanged from those in the previous edition. It is improper to quote an old study where a revised version with new data exists, unless you specify in a footnote what you are doing. An old study may be quoted so long as its information is still regarded as valid by experts in the discipline.

Facts must be used with integrity. While it is easy to distort, suppress, or misrepresent a fact, writers must resist all such temptations if they value their reputation.

Experience

Experience, where relevant to the issue being argued, is acceptable evidence. You can appeal to experience when a contention cannot be settled by facts and statistics but must be decided by common sense. Here, for example, an appeal to experience is made by an author who is arguing against the belief that punishment deters crime:

> This misplaced faith in punishment may rest on the unrealistic theory that people consciously decide whether to be criminal—that they consider a criminal career, rationally balance its dangers against its rewards, and arrive at a decision based on such pleasure-pain calculations. It supposedly follows that if the pain element is increased by severe punishments, people will turn from crime to righteousness. A little reflection reveals the absurdity of this notion. How many of the readers of this textbook can recall when they seriously considered a criminal career, not as a vague daydream but as a concrete possibility? How many weighed this possibility and, after balancing all the considerations, "decided" against it? For most law-abiding citizens this decision is not a conscious, rational choice, thoughtfully made at some crucial moment; it is an unconsciously developed way of life, a set of values, and a group of expectations, all emerging from the thousands of events and incidents forming their social experience. Nor is it likely that the professional criminal ever makes such a conscious choice.

An appeal to experience must involve a general and shared experience that is recognizable to typical readers. This kind of appeal is asking for common-sense reflection; if it is based on an esoteric experience few readers have had, it cannot evoke reflection.

A personal experience can strengthen an argument if the experience typically reflects a common condition. For example, the following Vietnamese student used her personal experience to support the thesis that war refugees face serious problems in their adopted countries:

> My father was a pharmacist in Vietnam, but since he could not use his degree in the United States, he had to work as a janitor for a small printing shop. While he did this work gratefully, he felt that he was no longer achieving his career goals. My mother, because of the language handicap, could not find any job. She worried day and

> night about the financial state of the family. Moreover, because she could not speak the language and did not understand the customs of Americans, she had a very difficult time making any friends. Even though our entire family was better off materially in America, we all secretly admitted to ourselves that we had been happier in Vietnam.

Witnesses

Witness testimony is also acceptable evidence. A preamble to the testimony should identify and place the witness at the scene, and list his or her claim to credibility. Here, for example, is witness evidence used in a paper arguing for the existence of UFO's:

> Lonnie Zamora of Socoro, New Mexico, was a police officer for five years. His record indicated that he was a stable and honest person. He sighted a UFO on one of his patrols. He described the spaceship as "taking off straight up" with a deafening roar.

The fact that a witness is a police officer adds to his credibility and is therefore worth mentioning.

Some witness evidence will not require a direct quotation, but merely a paraphrase of what witnesses said they saw:

> In every major city in the world our air is full of smoke and smog. When the Apollo 10 astronauts flew over Los Angeles about 25,550 miles away, they saw a yellow smudge.

Most of the witness testimony you use will come from other sources, which must be plainly documented. In using witness testimony, you should bear these other points in mind:

Quoted testimony must not be edited to slant it in favor of your argument. If you use a partial quotation from witness testimony, you should place three dots (called ellipsis) before or after your quotation to indicate that something has been left out:

> Alma Atkins, an off-duty nurse who witnessed the riot, was quoted in *Harper's* magazine as saying: "The police seemed to come from nowhere. A brick was suddenly hurled by one of the demonstrators. . . ."

The dots indicate that further testimony following *demonstrators* has been omitted.

Quotations should be brief and relevant to your argument. Long quotations of witness testimony tend to clog the flow of your writing.

Discredited witnesses must not be quoted. If you use the original testimony of a witness who has since then been discredited, you should notify your reader either in a note or in your commentary.

Authority

Quoting an authority whose position coincides with your own can be an effective source of evidence. Its usefulness, however, will vary with the prestige of the authority. If he or she is an expert on the subject under discussion, quoting can add substantially to your evidence; if the authority is relatively obscure, quoting may add nothing. The credentials of your authority should be mentioned as preamble to your quotation. Here are some sample statements introducing authorities about to be quoted from:

> As Professor Harold A. Thomas, Jr. of Harvard's Center for Population puts it . . .
>
> Another scientist, Colin M. MacLeod, formerly of the U.S. Office of Science and Technology, says . . .
>
> Research by the late anthropologist Margaret Mead on this subject indicates that . . .

An authority may also be anonymous. The opinions stated in reputable dictionaries and encyclopedias are also acceptable as authority evidence.

It may take some detective work on your part to verify the credentials of your chosen authority. Just because someone has published and has a degree, it does not follow that this person is necessarily an authority. The final criterion is whether or not the person is recognized as an authority by peers. Some common-sense research may therefore be necessary into the credentials and accomplishments of your chosen authority. An excellent reference source for this sort of information is the *Who's Who* series, which lists noted specialists in a variety of subject areas.

If the individual is not listed in *Who's Who*, you should check such items as the school at which he or she was trained, membership in recognized professional organizations, publications, and academic honors. While it is easy enough to check on the publications of a chosen authority, it is more difficult to assess the quality and reputation of the journals in which these publications may have appeared. The simplest thing to do in that case is to ask someone in the field. For instance, if you want to know whether a certain history journal is regarded highly, ask a history instructor. Bear in mind also that a person may be trained in one field and considered an authority in another. Ralph Nader, for instance, is trained as a lawyer, but is widely regarded as an authority in consumer affairs. Conversely, a person may be highly qualified in one area, but definitely no authority in another. It would be a waste of time, for instance, to quote Nader as an authority on theology. His standing in the field of consumer affairs gives him no particular authority in theological matters.

Authority evidence, like witness testimony, should be used to supplement data uncovered by your own research. It cannot replace factual evidence. Argumentative papers call for original probing of your own; a student who simply catalogs a variety of opinions from authorities and then quotes them in good reportorial fashion is evading the assignment and is likely to be rebuffed by the instructor. The ideal is to intersperse your own findings with those of authorities.

A good argumentative paper will draw on various kinds of evidence. It will amass facts of its own, support interpretations of them with quotations from authorities, appeal to experience where common sense can add to an understanding of the issue, and quote witnesses where appropriate.

Breakdowns of evidence

Various breakdowns of evidence can occur. We will deal with the more common failings:

Congested and unnecessary evidence
Uninterpreted evidence
Dogmatic generalizing from evidence
Vague evidence
Distorted evidence

Congested and unnecessary evidence

Congestion occurs when too much evidence is incoherently marshaled behind the line of an argument. Bear in mind that evidence is merely backing for a contention; it should support the thesis of your argument, not usurp it. This example is drawn from a paper arguing for the legalization of prostitution:

> In Paris there are an estimated 10,000 prostitutes. In London, estimates have placed the prostitute population at 6,500. In Hamburg, Germany, there are an estimated 5,000 prostitutes. In New York City, the "hooker" population has been put at 8,000 by police. The

> prostitute population of Plato's Athens has been estimated in the hundreds. In Egypt, during the reign of the Pharaohs . . .

And on to China, Hong Kong, and Babylon. The point? A frail "There have always been prostitutes." The evidence overproves the point; moreover it bogs down the line of argument. Here is a rewritten version:

> Evidence indicates that prostitution flourished in Plato's Athens, in ancient Egypt, dynastic China, and even in the Babylon of Biblical times. Today, the prostitute population ranges from an estimated 10,000 in Paris, 8,000 in New York City, to 6,500 in London. Prostitution is likewise found in every major urban area of the world.

Sometimes evidence is simply unnecessary. One student accumulated an impressive battery of statistics to prove that obesity is due to a high caloric food intake—a contention readily accepted today by most people. An argument will sink with too much evidence, just as it will float away with too little. In short, use evidence to support little-known facts, debatable statements, or easily misunderstood opinions. Self-evident truths and universally accepted facts need no evidence.

Any evidence used must have a direct bearing on the thesis of an argument. Here, for instance, in a paper arguing that the United States should not sell grain to Russia, a student becomes fascinated with Soviet agriculture after the Second World War. The reader is deluged with unnecessary information:

> After the Second World War the idea of collectivization was obnoxious to the Russian, Ukrainian, and Turkic peasants of the U.S.S.R. and was opposed by them. For instance, instead of working the land in large brigades, collective farm workers preferred smaller work units, consisting of members of one household, which in essence meant operating an individual farm within the collective system. Some peasants went so far as to illegally increase their private plots to the detriment of the collective property. This eventually led the government to transform the collective farms into amalgamated collective farms called *sovkhozy*.

These facts, while providing the reader with interesting information about agrarian Russia, have no direct bearing on the main argument. The student's side excursion merely dulls the force of the thesis.

Students sometimes believe that a wealth of evidence showing diligent research will make a better paper. This is not necessarily so. You should deploy only the evidence required to reinforce your major contention. Most likely, you will not be able to use all the evidence your research turned up. Some of it will have to be left out.

Uninterpreted evidence

Uninterpreted evidence is meaningless. You should immediately blend all evidence into the thrust of your argument by interpreting it. Furthermore, evidence stockpiled in one paragraph and then interpreted two paragraphs later loses its impact on the reader. All evidence should be interpreted as soon as it is given. The interpretation should answer the question, So what? immediately after the evidence is given. Here is an example:

Evidence: In 1830 there were 1 billion people on earth. By 1930 there were 2 billion, and by 1960 there were 3 billion. Today the population is 3½ billion persons. By the end of the century or within the next thirty years the population will be approximately 7 billion persons.

So what? Many experts believe that a population of 7 billion persons would exert such a drain on our resources that the species itself might be imperiled.

Dogmatic generalizing from evidence

Nevertheless, it pays to be cautious in interpreting the meaning of evidence. Too often, students base dogmatic and rash assertions on frail and inconclusive evidence. Most of the time, an assertion almost as strong could be made from the evidence if it were properly worded to allow a cautious edge. Here are some examples:

Dogmatic: The evidence means, finally and flatly, that UFO's do exist, and that they are surveying the earth and its life-forms.

Cautious: Indications are firm and strong from the evidence that UFO's do exist and are possibly involved in surveying the earth and its life-forms.

Dogmatic: And so, from the evidence, evolution is shown to be dead wrong, and the Bible's account of how life began on earth is shown to be the correct version.

Cautious: The evidence indicates that, once the premise of the Bible is accepted, a strong case can be made for the accuracy and consistency of its version of how life began on this earth.

Few things are flatly one way or the other. Most of us have to pick our way cautiously through complex and often conflicting evidence. Dogmatism in a conclusion is therefore most often seen as an indication not of foolproof evidence but of a closed mind.

Vague evidence

The best evidence is the most specific; the worst is the most vague. Here is an example of vague evidence:

> Every year, tons and tons of pollution caused by human beings enter the air in the United States.

The assertion is undoubtedly true, but vague. Here is a better version of the same sentence:

> It is estimated that some 200 million tons of pollution caused by human beings enter the air in the United States each year.

Numbers have a finite, visible, and persuasive effect. Use specific evidence wherever possible.

Distorted evidence

Evidence, properly orchestrated, highlighted, or suppressed, can be manipulated as proof for almost any assertion. Statistics are especially vulnerable to distortion. A bank may advertise that the amount of money it will lend is high but will not mention that its interest rates on saving accounts are low. A law school may proudly proclaim that more of its students have passed the bar this year than in any previous year but will neglect to add that this year's enrollment is also larger. Political candidates occasionally brag about the revenue they have brought to their states, conveniently overlooking any outrageous expenditures. Statistical evidence is especially easy to distort because of its inaccessibility to most readers, who will simply accept an author's statistics as accurate. The more specific the statistic looks, the more believable it seems. To illustrate how facts can be distorted, we offer the following piece of nonsense:

> Pickles are associated with all the major diseases of the body. Eating pickles breeds war and communism. They can be related to most airline tragedies. Auto accidents are caused by pickles. There exists a positive relationship between crimes and consumption of this fruit of the cucumber family. For example:

1. Nearly all sick people have eaten pickles. The effects are obviously cumulative.
2. 99.9% of all people who die from cancer have eaten pickles.
3. 100% of all soldiers have eaten pickles.
4. 96.8% of all communist sympathizers have eaten pickles.
5. 99.9% of the people involved in air and auto accidents ate pickles within 14 days preceding the accident.
6. 93.1% of juvenile delinquents come from homes where pickles are served frequently.

Evidence points to the long-term effects of pickle eating:

1. Of all the people born in 1869 who later dined on pickles, there has been a 100% mortality rate.
2. All pickle eaters born between 1879 and 1889 have wrinkled skin, have most of their teeth missing, have brittle bones and failing eyesight, if the ills of pickle eating have not already caused their death.

Even more convincing is the report of a noted team of medical experts:

3. Rats fed 20 pounds of pickles per day for 30 days developed bulging abdomens and their appetite for wholesome food was destroyed.

In spite of all the evidence, pickle growers and packers continue to spread their evil. More than 120,000 acres of fertile soil are devoted to growing pickles. Our per capita consumption is nearly four pounds. Eat orchid petal soup. Practically no one has as many problems from eating orchid petal soup as they do from eating pickles.

Ignoring the context of an assertion is another way to distort evidence. A word or sentence meaning one thing when quoted alone can easily mean something quite different when surrounded by other words or sentences. Advertisements for movies frequently use out-of-context quotes from reviews. For example, the review might say: "For about five minutes *Fruits of Desire* is a topnotch movie, brilliantly acted and magnificently photographed. After that it degenerates into a dismal spectacle of Hollywood hokum." But the advertisement quotes: "topnotch movie, brilliantly acted and magnificently photographed." The point is that you must not take other people's words out of context to make them support your point of view.

The use of evidence

Evidence should not only be used to support a thesis; it should also play a part in the selection of a thesis. An initial assumption should always be tested for deep evidence before it is used as the premise of an argument. The evidence will indicate whether or not the assumption is defensible as a premise. For instance, if you were writing a paper arguing in favor of capital punishment, you could adopt various premises. Your argument is immediately indefensible, however, if it opens with the premise that capital punishment is worth saving because it deters crime. The evidence shows clearly that capital punishment does not prevent crime. For your argument to be convincing, a new premise must be adopted. Ideally, if you were in favor of capital punishment because you mistakenly believed that it did deter crime, you should be prepared to abandon your support after reviewing the evidence. However, if you continue to be in favor of capital punishment, you must find a new premise for your argument. The new assumption, in turn, will influence the kind of evidence you must gather. Your new defense of capital punishment could be based on a calculation of the cost of executing incorrigible criminals versus the cost of locking them up for life. The argument now rests on the assumption that some lives have no value and should not be maintained at the taxpayer's expense. And evidence can be gathered to show the greater cost to taxpayers if a criminal is given life imprisonment over the death penalty.

Some ideas cannot be supported with evidence. Cosmic generalizations cannot be proven either true or false by evidence; neither can value judgments. Here are some examples of insupportable ideas:

> The bathtub is the most dangerous place in the world.

This is insupportable because the assertion calls for an absurd comparison. What is a "place"? Can the bathtub be compared with the pinnacle of Mt. Everest as a place of potential danger? The rewritten sentence makes an assertion that is supportable with evidence. It may or may not be true, but statistics can be tracked down that show where most home accidents occur.

> Accidents are more likely to occur in a bathtub than anywhere else in the home.

The following statement is insupportable because there is no agreed-on measure of "God-fearingness":

> Americans are the most God-fearing people in the world.

The rewritten statement can now be supported with evidence. Presumably such statistics are kept by someone and can be researched:

> Church attendance in America is among the highest of any nation.

Bear in mind that an issue cannot be argued unless it is so worded that it is finite, measurable, and arguable.

Persuasive arguments

The primary function of logic is to persuade. If you observe the demands of logic to show process and evidence, your argument will be logical, but it may not be persuasive. Being persuasive involves more than being logical; it takes in the whole range of writing skills—conciseness, clarity, and the ability to infuse a prose style with personality. We will end this chapter by listing some characteristics of a persuasive argument.

A persuasive argument begins at the point of contention. Here are two sample beginnings from student papers arguing against offshore drilling for oil:

Bad: I oppose offshore drilling for oil. But before I give my reasons why I oppose this project, I would like to review the various present sources of crude oil in our country. . . .

Better: I oppose offshore drilling for oil because such a project could, in the name of oil, destroy thousands of miles of our oceans, adding to the already staggering amount of pollution on earth.

Your opening sentence should concisely state the thesis of your argument and your position.

A persuasive argument draws its evidence from multiple sources. This rule is self-evident, yet frequently ignored. Sometimes a student will draw on a single authority for the bulk of evidence to support a thesis. Ideally, the direction and force of your research should lead you to different kinds of evidence. Many students, however, in a nonideal manner, confine their research to the minimal number of sources demanded by the instructor. The cure for this is to select a topic that you are really interested in.

A persuasive argument is concise and focused. It does not drift off into side issues. If your thesis is *The polarization of sex roles in American society contributes to the high incidence of divorce*, your essay should marshal facts and evidence to substantiate that contention, ignoring such secondary issues as sex discrimination in employment or why many housewives are pursuing employment outside the home. A concentrated and focused argument is generally more persuasive than an argument that strays and wanders.

A persuasive argument has discernible movement. It does not become clogged with evidence nor bogged down with hair-splitting. We suggest that you bear in mind the typical reader's reactions to any argumentative essay or speech:

Ho-hum!	(Wake up your reader with a provocative introduction.)
Why bring that up?	(State your argument in clear, forceful language.)
For instance?	(Supply evidence and facts.)
So what?	(Restate the thesis; say what you expect the reader to do.)

A persuasive argument begins with an assumption that is either grounded in evidence or defensible. It confines itself to issues that can be supported with evidence, does not attempt to argue the unarguable, nor try to prove the unprovable. While the realm of the arguable is constantly shrinking before an onslaught of mysticism and fantasy, many instructors would nevertheless find the following theses entirely unacceptable in an argumentative essay:

> Hell exists as a place of punishment for sinners to atone for wrongdoing committed on earth.
>
> The Great Depression of the 1930s was caused by a destructive astrological conjunction between the planets Venus and Mars.
>
> Cats and all manner of feline creatures are despicable, nauseating beasts.
>
> Arthur Conan Doyle, creator of Sherlock Holmes, was the greatest detective story writer of all times.

All four propositions are based on personal belief and therefore unprovable in a strictly logical sense.

A persuasive argument anticipates the opposition. For instance, if you are arguing that a controversial cancer drug should be legalized, you must not only marshal evidence to show the effectiveness of the drug, you must also answer the arguments of those opposed to its legalization. You might, for instance, introduce these arguments this way: "Opponents to the legalization of this drug claim that its use will prevent the cancer patient from using other remedies proven effective against cancer. This claim, however, misses the point." And then you get down to the point that has been missed.

A persuasive argument will sometimes supplement facts, statistics, and evidence with emotional appeal. This must, however, be used with discretion and caution. Emotional appeal is no substitute for reasoned argument or solid evidence. But used in supplementary doses, emotional appeal can starkly dramatize an outcome or condition in a way that evidence and facts alone cannot. Here is an example. A speaker is trying to persuade an audience to donate blood for the benefit of hemophiliacs. A hemophiliac himself, he spends the first half of his speech explaining factually what hemophilia is—reciting statistics about its incidence and discussing its symptoms. Then, to dramatize the awfulness of the disease, he resorts to an emotional appeal, using his own experience with the pain of hemophilia:

> Because medical science had not advanced far enough, and fresh blood not given often enough, my memories of childhood and adolescence are memories of pain and heartbreak. I remember missing school for weeks and months at a stretch—of being very proud because I attended school once for four whole weeks without missing a single day. I remember the three long years when I couldn't even walk because repeated hemorrhages had twisted my ankles and knees to pretzel-like forms. I remember being pulled to school in a wagon while other boys rode their bikes, and being pushed to my table. I remember sitting in the dark empty classroom by myself during recess while the others went out in the sun to run and play. And I remember the first terrible day at the big high school when I came on crutches and built-up shoes carrying my books in a sack around my neck.
>
> But what I remember most of all is the pain. Medical authorities agree that a hemophilic joint hemorrhage is one of the most excruciating pains known to mankind. To concentrate a large amount of blood into a small compact area causes a pressure that words can never hope to describe. And how well I remember the endless pounding, squeezing pain. When you seemingly drown in your own perspiration, when your teeth ache from incessant clenching, when your tongue floats in your mouth and bombs explode back of your eyeballs; when darkness and light fuse into one hue of gray; when day becomes night and night becomes day—time stands still—and all that matters is that ugly pain. The scars of pain are not easily erased.

The appeal is moving and effective and contributes to the persuasiveness of the speaker's plea.

A persuasive argument ends on a strong note. The conclusion forcefully sums up what the evidence was intended to prove.

Weak: And so, those are the reasons why I favor government subsidy of all campaigns for political office.

Better: Clearly, then, a government subsidy of all campaigns for political office would make sure that our elected officials represent people and not money.

Application: Cause versus correlation

Most of us understand the concept of cause, but only dimly grasp the difference between cause and correlation. The two kinds of relationships show up often in scientific studies but do not have the same meaning. When we say that one event correlates with another, we mean that a predictable relationship may be observed between the two. But it is not necessarily a relationship of cause. The newspaper article below, which appeared just before the 1980 Presidential race between Jimmy Carter and Ronald Reagan, illustrates this point.

Series may be key to presidential race

By WYCHE FOWLER

If you're looking for a sure way to predict who will be our next president, forget about public opinion polls, the stock market, Jimmy the Greek, or newspaper columnists.

It is often said that American presidential elections really don't begin until the World Series is over. But after looking at the record, I have come to the conclusion that it would be more accurate to say that the election might well be decided the moment this year's World Series winner is crowned.

Since 1952, every time the American League team has won the World Series (1952, 1956, and 1972) a Republican president has been elected a few weeks later.

Every time the National League champion triumphed (1960, 1964, and 1976) the Democrats won the White House.

Not convinced? Well, if you check all the way back to 1908, the first year to see both a presidential election and a World Series, you discover that of six National League victories, only one has been followed by a Republican president. That was in 1908, when the winners were the Chicago Cubs and William Howard Taft.

The record following American League triumphs is less clear: Five wins for Democrats and seven for Republicans. However, of the Democratic victories, two were by Franklin Roosevelt in 1932 and 1936, and two by Woodrow Wilson in 1912 and 1916.

The league championships are also variables. This year's presidential race might have gone differently had not the Yankees—who've been involved in eight World Series during presidential election years—lost to Kansas City in the American League playoffs.

The Yankees won the first five series (1928, 1932, 1952 and 1956) with Republican presidents following three of these, the Democrats winning two. But the Yankees have lost the last three election-year World Series—1960, 1964 and 1976—and the Democrats have won following every Yankee loss.

Philadelphia's dramatic victory over the Houston Astros for the National League pennant placed the Phillies in the World Series for the first time since 1950. However, it is their only World Series appearance in an election year, and if I were President Carter, I'd be waving Phillie banners on the campaign trail.

The year 1948 was the last time this World Series pattern of National-Democratic and American-Republican victories was broken.

The conclusion is inevitable even if questionably just: If the Philadelphia Phillies win the World Series, you can count on another term for Jimmy Carter. If the Kansas City Royals win, the betting on Ronald Reagan should prove much safer.

Can the outcome of the World Series predict the results of a Presidential race? Common sense says no. Yet the article points to a strong relationship between the team that wins on the field and the party that wins at the polls. The most likely explanation is coincidence.

But if coincidence can often explain a correlation, it generally cannot account for a causal relationship. Cause means that one event leads directly or indirectly to another. Obvious causal links can be observed between the two. Sometimes the link is direct and outright—a tire blows out and the car turns over; sometimes it is subtle and indirect—exposure to asbestos and, many years later, lung cancer. Correlation, on the other hand, merely means that two events seem to occur in a predictable relationship. It may hint at some causal connection between them but does not necessarily demand one. Your daily departure from your house probably correlates significantly with your neighbor's, since most people leave around the same time in the morning. But your neighbor's routine is obviously not the cause of your own, nor yours of your neighbor's.

Correlation relationships must therefore always be interpreted with caution. Cause may be involved, but so may coincidence. Or there may be a common third factor to explain the relationship between two correlated events. You leave your house early every morning because you need to earn a living; but so does your neighbor. A common economic need is the third-factor explanation for both your actions.

Confusing correlation with cause leads to superstition and fallacy. Baseball players—who are notoriously superstitious—have been known to wear the same socks for weeks or sit firmly in the same place on the bench, so long as their team is winning. But does any baseball player really think that sitting in one special place, or wearing a certain pair of socks, can cause his team to win? If so, he is guilty of mistaking a correlation for a causal relationship.

Cause is necessary, certain, inevitable. Correlation is less certain, less predictable. Because one event has occurred many times in conjunction with another is no guarantee that the relationship will always hold true. According to the pattern predicted by the Fowler article, a win for the Phillies should have been followed by a second term for President Carter. The Phillies did win—in six games; President Carter lost to Ronald Reagan—by a landslide.

EXERCISES

1. Critically analyze the logic of the following generalizations. What objections could you raise? What are the assumptions underlying the statements? Why might a person make such a statement? With what biases?

a. Culture is dead in our time. There are no Bachs, Mozarts, or Leonardo da Vincis; art now is just manufactured for cheap mass consumption; there are no values or discrimination left in the arts.
b. I do not know what the world is coming to: nothing but crime and violence in daily newspaper headlines and television news programs; the old values are disregarded shamefully; no one these days has any moral sense, and the world is filled with swindlers.
c. What the world needs now is love.
d. If there were not so many foreigners in this country, there would not be so much crime.
e. Considering the money involved, it is obvious that the only sort of person who goes into the teaching profession is the kind who cannot make a success out of anything else.
f. Prisoners have an easy life—three meals a day, air-conditioned cells, television, and nothing to worry about.
g. If only we could live forever! Then we would be *really* happy.
h. New Yorkers are more sophisticated than Californians, as is a well-known fact.
i. Wine is better than beer.
j. Social protesters make America appear to have a lot more problems than it really does. They threaten our way of life.

2. The following arguments do not center on the real issue. How do they get diverted?

a. I will never understand what movie critics see in Richard Pryor. He is rude, conceited, and immoral. His drug use is scandalous.
b. The Pure Food and Drug Act has prevented the sale of food and drugs that are harmful to the body. In the same way, Congress should investigate ways to eliminate unscrupulous publishers.
c. Nobody can be healthy without exercise. And certainly to a nation, a just and honorable war is the true exercise. A civil war, indeed, is like the heat of a fever; but a foreign war is like the heat of exercise and serves to keep the nation healthy.

3. The following arguments are weak because of flimsy evidence. Explain what is wrong with the evidence in each case.

a. Naturally she is delinquent. She reads ten comic books a week.
b. Obviously, a marriage works out better if the couple lives together first on a trial basis.
c. I usually vote the way my banker tells me, since bankers are conservative.
d. Once criminals get out of jail, in a few months they kill again and get thrown back into jail. This does not make sense to me.
e. Los Angeles has more alcoholics than any city in the world, as

anyone who walks through MacArthur Park on a Sunday afternoon can plainly see.

4. In the following arguments the relationship between the connected ideas is invalid. Identify the problem in each case.
   a. If big business cannot have tax loopholes, then the consumer will eventually pay the cost of the big business tax loopholes.
   b. If people were virtuous, there would be no need for government. But people are not virtuous; therefore government is necessary.
   c. A rise in juvenile delinquency became noticeable after the Second World War. It is clear that war causes juvenile delinquency.
   d. Industrialism was not established until after the Protestant Reformation; therefore, Protestantism was one of the causes of industrialism.
   e. My parents were like yours: plain, simple, hardworking folks. And if you vote for me, you can be sure that the rights of the common people will be safeguarded.
   f. Ivan Ivanovich has to be a communist. You can tell by his name.
   g. She could not have killed her husband because she is the mother of two darling children.
   h. Car dealers are dishonest. They are dishonest because they never give you a fair deal.
   i. *Master of the Game* must be a good book; it outsold all the other novels at the bookstore last week.

5. Below is an eleventh-century proof of the existence of God. Analyze its logic.

   > God is, by definition, an infinitely perfect being. Such a being must have all the essential properties, since it is infinitely perfect. Existence is an essential property. Therefore, God must have existence.

6. Below are three student arguments written on the following assignment: "Would you vote for a female candidate for President? Explain why you would or why you would not." Analyze the logic of each argument. Give reasons for your view.

   a. I would vote for a female candidate for President. In fact, I think a woman would make a great President. Women are fairer than men, more patient and less aggressive. These are exactly the qualities our country desperately needs: fairness, patience, and peacefulness.

   b. I would vote against a female candidate for President, not because I have anything against women, but because I think that a President needs to put forward an image of strength, and men project more strength than women.

c. I would not vote for a woman because she is a woman; and I would not vote for a man because he is a man. Being a woman or a man has nothing to do with being a good President. The job demands character, strength, and moral leadership. These are sexless qualities which are as likely to be found in a woman as in a man. If given the choice to vote between two candidates, one a woman and the other a man, I would vote for the more qualified.

7. Analyze the logic of the following argument:

> In the dawn of human civilization, asserts the Biblical record, a man named Cain rose up and murdered his brother, Abel, in a fit of rage (Genesis 4:1–8). What was the punishment which God imposed on Cain for this first recorded homicide? Interestingly, it was not the death penalty.
>
> Rather, as you read the account, you will discover that Cain was banished from society—exiled into the wilderness of Nod (verses 9–16). In this case, God allowed Cain to live; the world's first murderer was not put to death.
>
> After those days, according to the Biblical account, men began to multiply on the earth. And soon there followed the second recorded murder in history, when Lamech, a descendant of Cain, slew a young man who apparently had fought with him (Genesis 4:23). No mention is made of Lamech being put to death for his homicide (verse 24).
>
> But as men began to multiply, the earth became filled with increasing violence (Genesis 6:1, 11–12). A cursory study of the Biblical account shows that, in the absence of a death penalty for crimes, the earth became filled with violence! One might conclude that since criminals were not speedily executed or dealt with appropriately, the world experienced a spiraling crime epidemic!

8. The following are poorly worded assertions. Rewrite them to make them more effective.

a. The editor raises the question, Do parents have the right to defend their children against harm? In defense of this idea he states that the Supreme Court has determined that states have the right to protect the moral development of children.

b. It has been determined that most murders are passion murders, and therefore they should not be executed.

c. The great majority of crimes have absolutely no relation to drugs. I am not saying none do, for there is a great deal of drug traffic involving crime.

d. As for the parents, I feel that they have no authority to decide that the embryos will never have the opportunity to experience life, just as they had.

e. The senator has consistently pursued an evenhanded policy between Israel and the Arab states.
f. The state university has no business using the taxpayers' money to buy books for the library, which they have not read a lot of that are already in the library.

9. Label and explain the fallacies in each of the following arguments:

a. The Bible is divinely inspired because God spoke to the prophets of old, who wrote down His Word.
b. Since our nation is a big business, it should be run by qualified business executives.
c. Let me tell you what is wrong with the concept of compulsory medical insurance. It is a half-baked plan cooked up by people who are more interested in giving in to the pressures of creeping red socialism than they are in providing better medical care. These people will sacrifice everything to their bigoted faith in a system of fascist regimentation that is abhorrent to the American people.
d. I will never vote for Bixel's proposed tax reforms because he was a personal friend of Petro Giardelli, a man suspected of Mafia ties.

10. Analyze the logic of the following syllogistic statements:

a. No well-educated person would ever pass up an opportunity to travel to Paris. Since Mr. Smedley traveled to Paris, he must be well educated.
b. Wise men hate violence and crime. Robert Collins hates both of these, which just proves to me that he must be very wise.
c. Chess is a game played by many brilliant people. When I found out that the Democratic candidate plays chess, I immediately decided to vote for him because he is obviously brilliant.
d. Tomboys love football. Marjorie loves football. Therefore Marjorie is a tomboy.
e. My test of whether or not a person is an intellectual is to ask the person about football. If the person likes the game, I know that he or she is not an intellectual. If the person hates football, then I know that he or she is obviously an intellectual.

9

How do I edit?

Make your title descriptive
Begin with a simple sentence
Prune deadwood
Do not overexplain
Be specific
Avoid trite expressions
Use the active voice
Make your statements positive
Keep to one tense
Place key words at the beginning
or end of a sentence
Prune multiple *of*'s
Break up noun clusters
Use exclamation marks sparingly
Vary your sentences
Keep your point of view consistent
Use standard words
End with impact

Application: Editing an actual essay

Revising is part of writing.
Few writers are so expert that they can
produce what they are after on the first try.

—William Strunk, Jr. and
E. B. White

GOOD PROSE IS 1% WRITING AND 99% REWRITING. Indeed, the majority of writers do not produce good copy on the first try. After the initial draft is written, hours and hours are spent in revising. Deadwood is patiently pruned, sentences recast for variety and rhythm, paragraphs reworked for coherence and effect. If you are not a Shakespeare, who was reported to have never blotted a line, or a Sir Walter Scott, who customarily delivered first drafts unread to the printer, you will find yourself spending more time rewriting than writing. This is how it is with most writers—great, good, or indifferent. You should therefore revise as often as you think necessary until you are pleased with the copy.

This chapter is a checklist of rules that catalog some fundamental tips on style and usage. You should have your paper in front of you and go over it as you read. If your writing suffers from such mechanical problems as fragments, comma splices, dangling modifiers, and the like, you should consult your instructor, read the handbook section of this text, and do all the exercises in it.

1. Make your title descriptive

The title of a paper should describe its content. Avoid puffy, exotic titles like this one on a paper dealing with the use of fantasy in Keats' poetry:

Keats: The High Priest of Poetry

Rewrite: The Use of Fantasy in Keats' Poetry

2. Begin with a simple sentence

It is stylistically good sense to open your paper with a short and simple sentence. A long and involved opening will repel, rather than attract, a reader:

> The problem that has come up again and again before various workers in the social sciences, and especially before sociologists and anthropologists, and one that has been debated at length in the journals of both disciplines as well as in the classrooms of various universities and colleges across the country, and one to which various answers, none satisfactory, have been proposed, is this: Are social scientists politically neutral, or are they *ipso facto* committed by their research?

To open with such a cumbersome sentence is like compelling a friend to view a clear landscape through a dirty windowpane. It is better to begin with an easily grasped sentence:

> The question is this: Are social scientists politically neutral, or are they committed by their research?

3. Prune deadwood

Deadwood refers to any word, phrase, or sentence that adds bulk without meaning. It accumulates wherever the writing is roundabout and indistinct. Some styles of writing are so vested in wordiness that it is impossible to assign blame to any single word or phrase:

> There are many factors contributing to the deficiencies of my writing, the most outstanding being my unwillingness to work.

Rewrite: I write badly mainly because I am lazy.

> Anthropologists carrying their studies of primate behavior deep into the tropical forests of Malaysia contribute, through the pursuit of their specialized interest, to the one field that in fact gives us our broadest perspective of human beings.

Rewrite: Anthropologists add to our knowledge of human beings by studying primate behavior in the forests of Malaysia.

The solution to wordiness is to be plain and direct—to state your ideas without fluff or pretension.

Aside from wordiness there are other, more specific kinds of deadwood:

a. Cut *there are* and *there is* whenever possible, thereby tightening a sentence.

> There are many reasons why businesses fail.

Rewrite: Businesses fail for many reasons.

There is a cause for every effect.

Rewrite: Every effect has a cause.

b. Cut *I think, I believe,* and *in my opinion*. Such phrases make the writer sound insecure.

I think that Freud's approach to psychology is too dominated by sex.

Rewrite: Freud's approach to psychology is too dominated by sex.

I believe that women should be paid as much as men for the same work.

Rewrite: Women should be paid as much as men for the same work.

In my opinion, marriage is a dying institution.

Rewrite: Marriage is a dying institution.

c. Cut all euphemistic expressions.

He went to Vietnam and paid the supreme sacrifice.

Rewrite: He was killed in Vietnam.

Last year for the first time I exercised the right of citizens on election day.

Rewrite: Last year I voted for the first time.

d. Cut *-wise*, *-ly,* and *-type* word endings. Such words, easily concocted from adverbs and adjectives, have become popular in college writing.

Poor: Moneywise, she just didn't know how to be careful.
Better: She didn't know how to be careful with her money.

Poor: Firstly, let me point out some economic problems.
Better: First, let me point out some economic problems.

Poor: A jealous-type man annoys me.
Better: A jealous man annoys me.

e. Eliminate all redundant phrases or expressions that can be rewritten more concisely. Here are some typical examples followed by suggested substitutes:

Redundant	Rewrite
owing to the fact that	because
plus the fact that	and
prior to	before
at the present time	now
at this point in time	now
as of this date	today
in this day and age	today
subsequent to	after
along the lines of	like
in the area of	don't use "area" in this way
in the field of	don't use "field" in this way
in a satisfactory manner	satisfactorily

f. Cut all preamble phrases such as *the reason why . . . is that.*

The reason why wars are fought is that nations are not equally rich.

Rewrite: Wars are fought because nations are not equally rich.

The thing I wanted to say is that history has shown the human being to be a social predator.

Rewrite: History has shown the human being to be a social predator.

The point I was trying to make is that reality is sometimes confused with fantasy in Keats' poetry.

Rewrite: Reality is sometimes confused with fantasy in Keats' poetry.

In all such cases the rewrite principle is the same: Lift out the heart of the idea and state it plainly.

g. Cut most rhetorical questions.

That illusion though deceptive is more consoling and less hostile to human needs than reality, appears to be a central theme in Keats's poetry. Why would anyone feel this way? Why did Keats himself feel this way? Possibly because he had tuberculosis and knew he was going to waste away and die.

Rewrite: That illusion though deceptive is more consoling and less hostile to human needs than reality, appears to be a central theme in Keats's poetry. Keats possibly felt this way because he had tuberculosis and knew he was going to waste away and die.

h. Use the right words. Often, the right word will do the work of two words, three, or even an entire phrase.

There is no doubt that the labor force will suffer.

Rewrite: *Doubtless* the work force will suffer.

The money will be used for purposes of promoting the arts.

Rewrite: The money will be used *to promote* the arts.

Senator Bugsby has a benighted view in relation to France.

Rewrite: Senator Bugsby has a benighted view *of* France.

In spite of the fact that Byron's letters reflect an immoral view of the world, I still love to read them.

Rewrite: *Though* Byron's letters reflect an immoral view of the world, I still love to read them.

i. Strike unnecessary words. Less is often more when it comes to using words.

For many days, Laura has been living in painful unhappiness and deep misery.

Rewrite: For days, Laura has been living in deep misery.

Some scholars have claimed with insistence that the word *caste* originated in the country of Persia.

Rewrite: Some scholars have *insisted* that the word *caste* originated in Persia.

The compliment was genuine and sincere in effect.

Rewrite: The compliment was genuine.

4. Do not overexplain

Some critics sneered at Keats for being an apothecary-surgeon, which is what he was trained for.

Rewrite: Some critics sneered at Keats for being an apothecary-surgeon.

If Keats was an apothecary-surgeon, then that is obviously what he was trained to be.

As president of the company, which is an executive-type position, he never scheduled work for himself during April.

Rewrite: As president of the company, he never scheduled work for himself during April.

The term *president* already lets the reader know that the position is an executive one.

The watch is gold in color and costs $300 in price.

Rewrite: The watch is gold and costs $300.

That gold is a color and that $300 is the price are self-evident.

5. Be specific

Lack of specific detail will infect your prose with a pallid vagueness.

The effect of the scenery was lovely and added a charming touch to the play.

Rewrite: The scenery, which consisted of an autumn country landscape painted on four flats extended to cover the entire background of the stage, added a charming touch to the play.

Being specific is simply calling things by their proper names. In speech, it might pass as cute to call things "thingamajigs" or "thingamabobs" or "widgets," but the presence of such fudge words on the page hints at the writer's ineptitude. Any sort of vagueness caused by the writer's not calling things by their proper names will leave a bad impression.

James Boswell, the famous writer, died from living badly.

Rewrite: James Boswell, the famous *biographer,* died of *uremia following a gonorrheal infection*.

Browning wrote poetry in which a speaker talked either to himself or to someone else.

Rewrite: Browning wrote *dramatic monologues*.

The writer of the second sentence, who has simply named Boswell's terminal infection, appears more competent than the writer of the first vague sentence. In the third sentence, for want of a name, the writer is forced into a roundabout description of the kind of poetry Browning wrote. A little research on Browning would have yielded the term "dramatic monologue."

6. Avoid trite expressions (see also Chapter 2)

Some words, phrases, or expressions through overuse have become unbearably hackneyed and should be avoided. Following are some of the most glaring offenders:

in conclusion, I wish to say
last, but by no means least
in terms of
each and every
slowly but surely
to the bitter end
it goes without saying
by leaps and bounds
few and far between
first and foremost
in the final analysis

7. Use the active voice

The active voice is more vigorous than the passive because it allows a subject to stand in its familiar position in front of its verb.

I took a walk.

The subject *I* occupies the position immediately in front of its verb, *took*. With the passive voice, below, immediacy between subject and verb is denied. Moreover, the familiar positions are reversed. The verb stands at one end of the sentence; the subject is shunted to the other end. A *by* intervenes between them.

A walk was taken by me.

In some passive constructions, the subject is dropped and the verb orphaned.

> My last trip to Jamaica will always be remembered.

Converting to the active voice reunites subject and verb in their familiar and immediate constructions and makes the prose more vigorous.

Rewrite: I will always remember my last trip to Jamaica.

The use of the passive voice is stylistically justified only when an action or the object of an action is more important than the subject.

> There, before our eyes, two human beings were burned alive by gasoline flames.

In this case, human beings are more important than gasoline flames. The passive voice is therefore effective.

8. Make your statements positive

Statements that hedge, hesitate, or falter in the way they are worded tend to infuse your style with indecision. Whenever possible, word your statements positively.

Poor: He was not at all a rich man.
Better: He was a poor man.

Poor: "The Cherry Orchard" is not a strong play; it does not usually sweep the audience along.
Better: "The Cherry Orchard" is a weak play that usually bores its audience.

Poor: A not uncommon occurrence is for rain to fall this time of the year.
Better: It commonly rains this time of the year.

9. Keep to one tense

Once you have decided to summarize an action or event in one tense, you must thereafter stick to that tense. Don't start in the past and shift to the present, nor start in the present and shift to the past. Notice the corrections in the following passage.

Here is what I saw: For two acts the ballerina pirouetted, leapt, and floated like a silver swallow; then suddenly, she ~~falls~~ **fell** to the ground like a heavy boulder. Her leg ~~is~~ **was** fractured. For years before I observed this spectacular drama, I ^**had** often heard of this artist's brilliant career. Now I ~~am watching~~ **had watched** her final performance.

10. Place key words at the beginning or end of a sentence

Workers today have forgotten the meaning of the word *quality*, so most craftsmen tell us.

Rewrite: Workers today, so most craftsmen tell us, have forgotten the meaning of the word *quality*.

Generally speaking, wars turn civilized nations into barbaric tribes.

Rewrite: Wars, generally speaking, turn civilized nations into barbaric tribes.

11. Prune multiple *of*'s

A double *of* construction is tolerable; a triple *of* construction is not.

The opinions *of* the members *of* this panel *of* students are their own.

Rewrite: The opinions expressed by this panel of students are their own.

A good way to break up an *of* construction is to add another verb. In the above example the verb *expressed* is inserted in the sentence.

12. Break up noun clusters

A noun cluster is any string of noun+ adjective combinations occurring at length without a verb. The cluster is usually preceded by either *the* or *a*. Noun clusters contribute a tone of unarguable objectivity to writing and have consequently found favor in the writing styles of textbooks, the government, and the social sciences. Note the italicized noun clusters in the following:

> We therefore recommend *the use of local authorities for the collection of information on this issue.*
>
> *The increased specialization and complexity of multicellular organisms* resulted from *evolution according to the principles of random variation and natural selection.*
>
> *The general lessening of the work role in our society* does not mean that we have abandoned *the work basis for many of our values.*
>
> One cannot doubt *the existence of polarized groups in America.*

The test for a noun cluster is whether or not it can be replaced by a single pronoun. Each of the above can be.

To rewrite noun clusters, convert one of the nouns to an equivalent verb form.

Rewrite: We therefore recommend the use of local authorities to collect information on this issue.

> Multicellular organisms specialized and evolved in complexity by the principles of random variation and natural selection.
>
> Because people today work less than they used to is no reason to believe that we have abandoned work as a basis for many of our values.
>
> One cannot doubt that polarized groups exist in America.

Noun clusters clot the flow of a sentence. Avoid them by being generous in your use of verbs.

13. Use exclamation marks sparingly

The exclamation mark should be used rarely and only when urgency or strong emotion is being expressed, as in the following:

> This is what we fought our wars for!

Otherwise, it adds a forced breeziness to your prose.

> We must have urban renewal; and we must have it now!

14. Vary your sentences

Do not begin two sentences in a row with the same word or phrase unless you are deliberately aiming for an effect.

> The true Keats scholar is as familiar with the poet's life as with his poetry and can instantly relate any stage of the two. The true Keats scholar has a tendency to use Keats's poetry to explicate his life, and to use his life to explicate his poetry.

Rewrite: Scholars of Keats know the poet's life as well as they know his poetry and can instantly relate any stage of the two. They use Keats's poetry to explain his life, and his life to explain his poetry.

Vary the length of your sentences.

> The man was angry and wanted his money back. But the officer would not give it back and told him to leave. That made the man angrier, and he threatened to call the police.

Rewrite: The man was angry; he wanted his money back. But the officer would not give it back to him, and told him to leave, which made the man angrier. He threatened to call the police.

The rewrite is more effective because the sentences have a greater variety in length and style.

15. Keep your point of view consistent

When you begin a sentence by referring to *I*, but end it by referring to *one*, you have made the error known as shift in point of view. Such shifts can occur because there are several ways in which you can refer to yourself, your audience, and people in general. You can refer to yourself as *the writer*, *I*, or *we*. You can refer to your audience as *you*, *we*, or *all of us*. You can refer to people in general as *people*, *one*, and *they*. The rule is that once you have chosen your point of view, it must remain consistent.

Wrong: Do not buy Oriental rugs at an auction because if we do, we may get cheated.

Better: Do not buy Oriental rugs at an auction because if you do, you may get cheated.

Wrong: I try to take good care of my car, for when one does not, they usually pay a big price.

Better: I try to take good care of my car, for when I do not, I usually pay a big price.

Wrong: Everyone stood aghast when I told them about the accident.
Better: They all stood aghast when I told them about the accident.

16. Use standard words

College students can be unrelenting in their invention of newfangled vocabulary and often fall prey to the excesses of neologisms—new or coined words. Voguish words fade as quickly as they appear. By the time this book sees print, such words as *nerd, cool, groovy, vibes, stoned, grody, jive,* and *fox* will begin to sound dated and old-fashioned. You should use neologisms sparingly—if at all—in your writing. Instead, draw your primary stock of words from the vocabulary established over the centuries.

Remember, too, standard words must be written in standard spelling. Double-check any doubtful spelling in a dictionary.

17. End with impact

In Chapter 5, we covered in detail various good and bad endings, but we warn you again here against some of the worst kinds of endings. The ending of your essay should either clinch your argument, summarize your main point, reassert your thesis, urge some kind of action, or suggest a solution. Avoid committing the following common errors in your ending.

a. Endings that are trite:

> In conclusion I wish to say . . .
>
> And now to summarize . . .

Such endings are too obvious. If your essay has been properly developed, no special announcement of the conclusion is necessary.

b. Endings that introduce a new idea:

> Wealth, position, and friends, then, made him what he is today, although his father's death may also have influenced him.

If an idea has not been covered earlier, do not be tempted to introduce it as a novelty item in the final paragraph.

c. Endings that are superfluous:

> And so these are my thoughts on the subject.
>
> As you can see, my essay proves that carbohydrates are bad for our health.
>
> From these thoughts you will clearly see that Diaghilev was a dominant figure in modern ballet.

These endings do not reflect thoughtfulness on the part of the writer; they are useless in an essay.

Application: Editing an actual essay

Beyond the 17 rules listed in this chapter, polishing an essay involves smoothing out rough spots, shifting ideas, elaborating on a point, or substituting more precise wording. Once you become adept at this kind of doctoring, you will find it enjoyable because it allows you to see your product blossom into excellence. Following is the first draft of a student paper, with revisions marked in boldface. In the left margin is the number of the rule broken.

The Loss of Horror in Horror Movies

rule 1 ~~Goosepimples, Where Are You?~~

rule 6 ~~For various and sundry reasons~~ Audiences are no longer scared as they once were by the old-fashioned horror movies. Over the years people

vampires, werewolves, zombies, and mummies

rule 5 have been exposed to so many ~~monsters~~ that such creatures have lost their effectiveness as

rule 3g objects of terror. ~~Why do you think this happened?~~

Lack of novelty has produced indifference. Originally, a movie monster, such as the one

created by Frankenstein, terrified audiences
simply because the concept of a man creating
was
rule 9/3e human life ~~is~~ new. ~~Plus the fact that~~ Frankenstein's monster had a sinister plausibility that
people of the 1930s had not experienced. But
then the public was inundated by a deluge of
other film monsters as studios tried to capitalize
on the success of the original. Gradually audiences grew bored as these creations became
trite and shopworn. Fearing loss of business,
ambitious movie producers tried to invent fresh
lure
rule 3d/5 ~~type,~~ grisly shapes that would ~~bring~~ moviegoers
back into the theaters. But their attempts had no
effect on a public surfeited with horror, so
Frankenstein's monster, Wolfman, and Dracula
eventually became comic creatures in Abbott
and Costello films.

to produce
rule 3i Most modern horror films fail ~~in the pro-~~
~~duction of~~ genuine, goosepimply terror in their
audiences. Of course, it may be argued that
films like "The Exorcist" and "Jaws" scared
hysterical screams.
rule 5 many people—even to the point of ~~great fear.~~
But these films relied heavily on shock rather

differs from fear.
rule 8 than on fear. Shock ~~and fear are not the same.~~
Genuine fear involves the unknown or the
It
unseen. ~~Genuine fear~~ seduces the imagination
and appeals
rule 14 into fantastic realms~~, Genuine fear appeals~~ to
our innate store of nightmares. But shock is
merely synonymous with repulsion. People are
shocked when they see something they don't
want to see. For example, the scene of a man
being devoured by a shark will shock. The flaw
here is that the shock value of such a scene
repulse or offend
rule 16 serves more to ~~give the creeps or the heebie-jeebies~~ than to frighten.

Today shock devices are used far too frequently in motion pictures; yet, the sad truth is
that these graphic displays of blood and gore
lack imagination. In older horror movies, the
audience was not privy to the horrible details of
murder. Scenes ~~which~~ merely suggested evil
rule 7 ~~were used~~ instead, and the ~~details were~~
audience's imagination supplied the details.
~~supplied by the audience's imagination.~~ This
rule 4 approach is more effective ~~in its results~~ than
shock because it spurs the viewers to conjure up
their own images of the unseen. The old movie

formulas did not have to use shock devices,

such as bloody murders, to achieve a pinnacle

of horror. Unfortunately, today's audiences have

become "shock-proof" in the sense that it takes
bigger and more bizarre doses of horror **One**
rule 5 ~~more and more~~ to scare them. ~~In conclusion,~~
wonders what the ultimate horror movie will be.
rule 17a ~~horror movies have truly lost their effect.~~

Here is the polished version of the paper, ready to be submitted to the instructor.

The Loss of Horror in Horror Movies

Audiences are no longer scared as they once were by the old-fashioned horror movies. Over the years people have been exposed to so many vampires, werewolves, zombies, and mummies that such creatures have lost their effectiveness as objects of terror.

Lack of novelty has produced indifference. Originally, a movie monster, such as the one created by Frankenstein, terrified audiences simply because the concept of a man creating a human life was new. Frankenstein's monster had a sinister plausibility that people of the 1930s had not experienced. But then the public was inundated by a deluge of other film monsters as studios tried to capitalize on the success of the original. Gradually audiences grew bored as these creations became trite and shopworn. Fearing loss of business, ambitious movie producers tried to invent fresh, grisly shapes that would lure moviegoers back into the theaters. But their attempts had no effect on a public surfeited with horror, so Frankenstein's monster, Wolfman, and Dracula eventually became comic creatures in Abbott and Costello films.

Most modern horror films fail to produce genuine, goosepimply terror in their audiences. Of course, it may be argued that films like "The Exorcist" and "Jaws" scared many people—even to the point of hysterical screams. But these films relied heavily on shock rather than on fear. Shock differs from fear. Genuine fear involves the unknown or the unseen. It seduces the imagination into fantastic realms and appeals to our innate store of nightmares. But shock is merely synonymous with repulsion. People are shocked when they see something they don't want to see. For example, the scene of a man being devoured by a shark will shock. The flaw here is that the shock value of such a scene serves more to repulse or offend than to frighten.

Today shock devices are used far too frequently in motion pictures; yet, the sad truth is that these graphic displays of blood and gore lack imagination. In older horror movies, the audience was not privy to the horrible details of murder. Scenes merely suggested evil, and the audience's imagination supplied the details. This approach is more effective than shock because it spurs the viewers to conjure up their own images of the unseen. The old movie formulas did not have to use shock devices, such as bloody murders, to achieve a pinnacle of horror. Unfortunately, today's audiences have become "shock-proof" in the sense that it takes bigger and more bizarre doses of horror to scare them. One wonders what the ultimate horror movie will be.

Part
THREE

Special assignments

10

The research paper

Errors, like straw, upon the
Surface flow;
He who would search for pearls
Must dive below.

—John Dryden

WRITING A GOOD RESEARCH PAPER will teach you many useful skills. You will learn how to use a library, track down sources, take notes, and make acknowledgments. You will learn to sift through conflicting opinions, to assess contradictory data, and to arrange all your researched material into a coherent paper. You will also learn to distinguish between useful and useless information, to evaluate opinion, and to blend the differing views of the many in support of a single thesis. A long-term benefit—one that hardly occurs to anyone actually struggling to write such a paper—is the discipline the effort teaches.

What the research paper is and what it is not

The research paper is a paper that presents and develops a thesis supported by multiple sources of opinion. You stake out a subject narrow enough to be researched and you steep yourself in it. Then you formulate a thesis—your own attitude or opinion on the subject—and present it either in argumentative or reportorial form along with the facts, opinions, and information that prove it true. The word re*search* is nearly self-explanatory of the major work involved in such a paper: you must search out ideas, facts, information, and opinions that support your thesis.

It follows that a research paper is not a personal essay based solely on experiences from your past. It is not a book report summarizing a single work. It is not a piece of creative writing where you strive for dramatic effect, vivid figurative language, or emotional impact. Your final paper will rely more on the opinions of others than on your own. The line of argument you adopt, the emphasis of your paper will be wholly your own; the materials you find to support your views or justify your emphasis will come entirely from the work of others. Our indebtedness to others is one of the valuable lessons about knowledge and scholarship the research paper teaches.

The seven common errors of the research paper

Students tend to make these seven common errors in writing their research papers, which we hope we can persuade you to avoid:

1. Your paper should not be a mass of choppy, undigested quotations strung one after another on the page.
2. Your paper should not be a summary of one source.
3. Your paper should not be plagiarized. That is, you must not borrow the ideas and opinions of others and pass them off as your own. (See pages 215–16.)
4. Your paper should not include irrelevant material to pad it out to a minimum length.
5. Your paper should not be filled with vague and self-evident statements.
6. Your paper should not be sloppy and hard to read.
7. Your paper should not ignore the rules of documentation.

Kinds of research papers

College research papers fall into two categories: the argumentative paper and the report paper. The argumentative paper takes a stand on a debatable issue and supports it with research. Here are some examples of the theses of argumentative papers:

> Chiropractors deserve the right to practice with the same freedom, merit, and respect as do doctors of medicine.
>
> Despite the fact that his brief term in office has today been all but forgotten, Zachary Taylor was still the most effective president of all time.
>
> Diabetic mothers should be allowed to bear children only after they have been fully informed of the many complications associated with their disease.

The report paper, on the other hand, surveys information on a subject and sums up prevailing opinion. It may report on an incident, classify information, list the origin of a problem, or analyze cause and effect. Here are some theses from report papers:

> With proper therapy and understanding, an autistic child can learn to lead a reasonably normal life.
>
> The definition of *sovereignty* is a complex issue in the Palestinian negotiation for a homeland.

The migratory pattern of whales is a fascinating phenomenon in the Sea of Cortez.

Your instructor will specify whether you should write an argumentative or report paper. Both are valid college assignments. Some instructors assign the argumentative paper because they believe it better measures the student's ability to evaluate conflicting opinions. Others assign the report paper because they feel that it more properly emphasizes accurate research.

Whatever kind of paper you do, it will consist of three main parts:

1. An introduction, including a thesis or statement of purpose.
2. A body made up of supporting evidence for the thesis uncovered by your research and assembled convincingly with proper documentation.
3. A conclusion that summarizes your main points or restates your thesis.

The paper must also be preceded by an outline and followed by notes and a bibliography.

What follows is a step-by-step guide to writing the research paper.

Step 1: Choosing a restricted topic

The first and most important step in writing a research paper is to choose a subject narrow enough to be handled in five to ten double-spaced and typed pages—generally the length assigned. Do not tackle the job haphazardly. Listen to your instructor's explanation of the kind of work expected of you. If your instructor assigns a specific topic, your job is made easier. But suppose your instructor has given you the freedom to choose a topic. Here are some suggestions for doing it:

Choose a subject you enjoy. Subjects chosen for ease alone may bore you and make the assignment intolerable. Browse among the library stacks; pick books that look interesting; leaf through them to discover their contents. Check the magazine racks and reference department for subjects that arouse your curiosity. If you are interested in its topic, your research paper will seem more of a challenge than a burden. Your chances for producing a respectable piece of work are also increased if you have some expertise in your chosen subject. For instance, if you spent last summer visiting the Navajo wildlands, the trip could be the basis for a paper on the Navajo Indians.

Narrow the topic. The choice of too broad a topic can cause student, paper, and instructor to founder in a bog of unassimilated facts, misunderstood notions, and irreconcilable theories. Avoid such gargantuan topics as: The History of the Feminist Movement; Great Opera Singers of the World; The Career of Napoleon Bonaparte; Reasons for Wars; The History of the Renaissance. If you have a general subject in mind but not a narrow enough application of it to fit into a paper, you should begin to browse in the subject area. Eventually, some suitably narrow aspect of the subject will catch your interest and lead you to a topic for the paper.

The narrowing of a topic is illustrated below:

Broad topic	**Narrow topic**	**Narrower topic**
The Russian Revolution	The Tsar's family during the Russian Revolution of 1917	The fate of the Grand Duchess Anastasia during the 1918 Ekaterinburg massacre
The feminist movement	The feminist movement and birth control	Margaret Sanger's role in the struggle for birth control
American poets	Edgar Allan Poe	The beauty-death theme in Edgar Allan Poe's poetry
Henry David Thoreau	Henry David Thoreau and nature	Henry David Thoreau as a pioneer of wilderness conservation
The Great Depression of 1929	Financial aspects of the Great Depression of 1929	The results of "Black Thursday" on the 1929 job market

Choose a topic for which information is available. If the topic is obscure, new, or specifically related to a foreign country, most of your time will be spent tracking down information instead of assimilating it. It is better to choose a subject about which plenty of information can be located in your school or local public library. If you have doubts about the availability of material, consult your instructor or college librarian.

Choose an appropriate topic

Your topic should be both intellectually respectable and within your ability to understand. The following topics are generally unsuitable for college research papers:

a. A paper that is merely a collection of trivial information. The subject of your paper should be meaty enough for you and your instructor to learn something from. The following topics, for example, are not worth doing a research paper about:

Diets that beautify the face
How dogs react to various brands of dog food
Where to find good shoe sales

b. A subject that depends on personal opinion, values, or judgments is a waste of time and effort researching. Here are some examples:

Premarital intercourse—right or wrong?
Jesus is our best friend
Who is the greater artist, El Greco or Dali?

c. A paper that is too technical or that belongs to an esoteric field of knowledge is impossible for most instructors to evaluate fairly. For example, if you have a passionate interest in the use of photovoltaic cells in solar energy programs but your teacher has little or no knowledge of that topic, then it would be a poor choice for a paper. Conversely, if you lack a solid background in medicine, you would be ill advised to attempt a paper on the benefits of ammonium chloride for elderly emphysema patients. As a general rule, avoid topics that involve technical terms, complicated statistics, or specialized concepts.

d. Papers based on a single source defeat the purpose of the research assignment, one of whose aims is to expose students to a wide range of authors and opinions. Besides being trivial, many how-to topics fall in this category. Here are some examples:

How to grow vegetables indoors
The art of silk screening
Five steps to creating a community hot-line for battered children

A good research paper must use a variety of sources, quote a healthy mix of opinion, and reflect conscientious and diligent library research.

Step 2: Discovering the library

Most libraries provide specific written instructions on how to use their facilities. Some instructors invite the librarian to give an annual orientation lecture. In any event, an adequate library should have these materials:

1. Books cataloged according to subject matter
2. Reference works, such as encyclopedias, indexes, atlases, yearbooks, and dictionaries
3. Magazines, newspapers, and periodicals

Generally, the best sources to begin reading on a subject are general works—articles in encyclopedias, chapters in textbooks, histories, biographical references, and dictionaries.

Most American college libraries arrange their materials according to the Dewey Decimal Classification System or the Library of Congress System. Descriptions of the major divisions of these systems should be found at the main desk of the library. Each row of bookshelves will be labeled with the proper catalog numbers. The main divisions of the Dewey system of classification are:

000–099	General works
100–199	Philosophy and psychology
200–299	Religion
300–399	Social sciences
400–499	Languages
500–599	Pure sciences
600–699	Applied sciences
700–799	Fine arts and recreation
800–899	Literature
F	Fiction in English (listed alphabetically by the author's last name)
900–999	History, travel, collected biography
B	Individual biography (listed alphabetically by subject)

The above numbers are expanded by adding decimal places, each with a specific meaning. (For instance *811.52* is the code for *The Complete Poems of Carl Sandburg*, revised and expanded edition.)

The main divisions of the Library of Congress classification are:

A	General works
B	Philosophy, psychology, religion
C–D	History and topography (except America)
E–F	America
G	Geography, anthropology, sports and games
H	Social sciences
J	Political sciences
K	Law

L	Education
M	Music
N	Fine arts
P	Language and literature
Q	Science
R	Medicine
S	Agriculture, forestry
T	Engineering and technology
U	Military science
V	Naval science
Z	Bibliography

This system is expanded by adding letters and arabic numerals. (For instance, *PS 3537.A618 1970* is the code for *The Complete Poems of Carl Sandburg*, revised and expanded edition.)

We do not suggest memorizing the cataloging system of the library you intend to use, but you should become familiar with the general number of the subject you have chosen. In many books published in 1972 and later you will find Cataloging in Publication (CIP) data printed on the copyright page. This entry includes all the information on the Library of Congress card except the number of pages in the book and the year of publication, which appear on the same page in the copyright notice. CIP data can be used in making full and accurate records about the materials you have used without having to go back to the card catalog. Since it includes all the classification numbers and tracings (see next page), you can determine in which categories you will find other useful materials.

Most materials in a library are registered in the card catalog, which consists of an alphabetical file of 3 x 5 cards describing the books the library contains. In addition, some large libraries provide users with printed book catalogs to use in deciding which materials they want to read. You will find three main kinds of cards in a card catalog: author, title, subject.

Bear in mind the following traditions in library filing:

1. *Periodicals*. Alphabetically arranged according to titles, current periodicals, such as *Time*, *Newsweek*, *The New Yorker*, *Sports Illustrated*, and *National Geographic*, are not listed in the card catalog but are usually shelved in a special place in the library.
2. *Clippings*. Many libraries maintain a file of clippings from magazines or newspapers. These are listed not in the card catalog but in special files according to subject.
3. *Microform*. Many libraries have *microfilm* or *microfiche* copies of books, magazines, and newspapers. Microfilm is kept on a spool; microfiche is framed in a card. Both reproductive methods require a

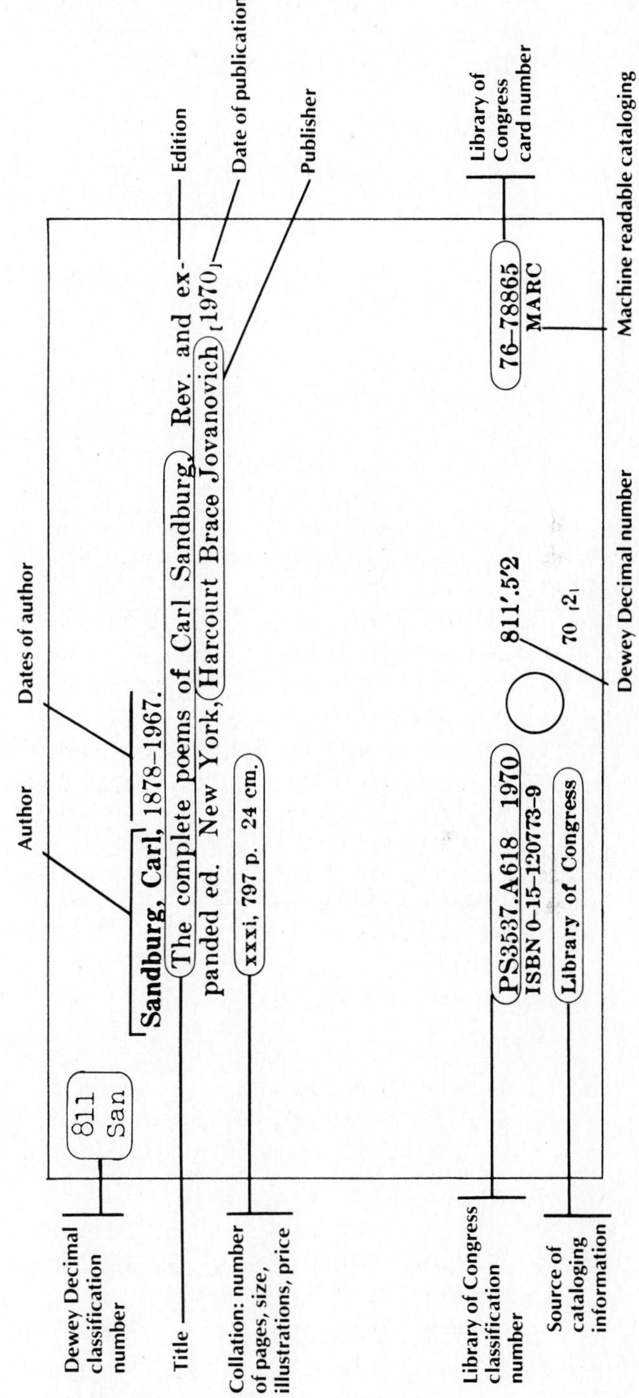
Author card
Author
Dates of author
Edition
Date of publication
Publisher
Library of Congress card number
Machine readable cataloging
Dewey Decimal number
Dewey Decimal classification number
Title
Collation: number of pages, size, illustrations, price
Library of Congress classification number
Source of cataloging information
811
San
Sandburg, Carl, 1878–1967.
The complete poems of Carl Sandburg. Rev. and ex-
panded ed. New York, Harcourt Brace Jovanovich [1970]
xxxi, 797 p. 24 cm.
PS3537.A618 1970
ISBN 0-15-120773-9
811'.52
70 [2]
Library of Congress
76–78865
MARC

Title card

811 The complete poems of Carl Sandburg
San

Sandburg, Carl, 1878–1967.
The complete poems of Carl Sandburg. Rev. and expanded ed. New York, Harcourt Brace Jovanovich [1970]
xxxi, 797 p. 24 cm.

PS3537.A618 1970 811'.5'2 76–78865
ISBN 0–15–120773–9 MARC
Library of Congress 70 [2]

Subject card

811 Poetry -- Collections
San

Sandburg, Carl, 1878–1967.
The complete poems of Carl Sandburg. Rev. and expanded ed. New York, Harcourt Brace Jovanovich [1970]
xxxi, 797 p. 24 cm.

PS3537.A618 1970 811'.5'2 76–78865
ISBN 0–15–120773–9 MARC
Library of Congress 70 [2]

mechanical viewer through which a magnified version of the film can be read. Since microform takes up only six percent of the space previously required by regularly bound volumes, it is becoming increasingly popular. Microform is sometimes listed in the card catalog. When in doubt, consult your librarian.

4. *Library Co-ops*. Libraries in the same vicinity generally cooperate with each other in lending material. If a document you need is not available in your library, ask if it can be acquired through a library co-op.

5. *The Reader's Guide to Periodical Literature*. This is perhaps a researcher's most valuable tool. It is an index to most magazine articles published since 1923. Articles in this index are alphabetically arranged by subject and author as the accompanying facsimile from the 1983 volume shows.

In Step 2 we cannot anticipate every problem you might encounter in doing your library research, nor can we tell you everything you should know about using a library. But students do have some common, recurring prob-

***Readers' Guide to Periodical Literature*—June, 1983**

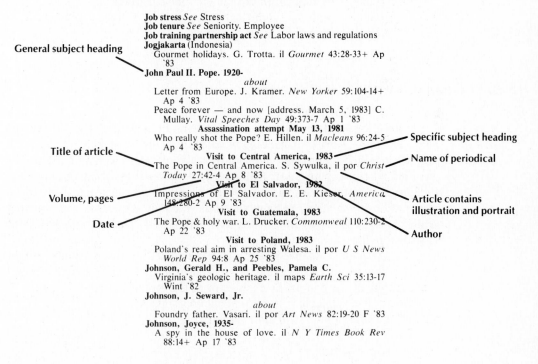

Job stress *See* Stress
Job tenure *See* Seniority. Employee
Job training partnership act *See* Labor laws and regulations
Jogjakarta (Indonesia)
Gourmet holidays. G. Trotta. il *Gourmet* 43:28-33+ Ap '83
John Paul II. Pope. 1920-
about
Letter from Europe. J. Kramer. *New Yorker* 59:104-14+ Ap 4 '83
Peace forever — and now [address. March 5, 1983] C. Mullay. *Vital Speeches Day* 49:373-7 Ap 1 '83
Assassination attempt May 13, 1981
Who really shot the Pope? E. Hillen. il *Macleans* 96:24-5 Ap 4 '83
Visit to Central America, 1983
The Pope in Central America. S. Sywulka, il por *Christ Today* 27:42-4 Ap 8 '83
Visit to El Salvador, 1982
Impressions of El Salvador. E. E. Kieser, *America* 148:280-2 Ap 9 '83
Visit to Guatemala, 1983
The Pope & holy war. L. Drucker. *Commonweal* 110:230-2 Ap 22 '83
Visit to Poland, 1983
Poland's real aim in arresting Walesa. il por *U S News World Rep* 94:8 Ap 25 '83
Johnson, Gerald H., and Peebles, Pamela C.
Virginia's geologic heritage. il maps *Earth Sci* 35:13-17 Wint '82
Johnson, J. Seward, Jr.
about
Foundry father. Vasari. il por *Art News* 82:19-20 F '83
Johnson, Joyce, 1935-
A spy in the house of love. il *N Y Times Book Rev* 88:14+ Ap 17 '83

lems with library research, and we have included samples of these below along with their solutions.

PROBLEM: The back issues of a magazine are not among the bound volumes.
SOLUTION: Past issues are available on microfilm.

PROBLEM: You wanted to take home a magazine or book that has been placed on reserve.
SOLUTION: Photocopy the section you need.

PROBLEM: An important source is not available in the school library.
SOLUTION: Get it from a library co–op.

PROBLEM: You want to know if a certain book is available for purchase.
SOLUTION: Look it up in *Books in Print*.

PROBLEM: You want to know if a certain author is considered an expert.
SOLUTION: Check the various *Who's Who* volumes, which are arranged according to subject matter and geographical area.

PROBLEM: You want to know if a certain author has published works besides those listed in your library catalog.
SOLUTION: Check *Books in Print*. Most college libraries now have a computer link-up with the Library of Congress, which can call up complete publication data on any author published in the United States. Ask the computer technician to call up information on your author.

Step 3: Building a working bibliography

After selecting a narrowed topic and becoming familiar with the library, the next task is to assemble a *working bibliography*—a list of sources you think you will use. (The *final bibliography* is a list of references actually used.) Your efforts to work up a useful bibliography may yield nothing or may yield too much. If no information is available, shift to a new subject; if too much information is on hand, narrow the topic further. Assemble the working bibliography with care. Don't clutter it with entries that have only a faint chance of helping your cause.

Learn to make an intelligent guess as to whether or not a source might be useful by scanning the tables of contents and indexes of books and the bibliography at the end of the chapter or at the end of the book.

Record each usable reference in ink on a separate 3 x 5 card. Each card should contain the following information:

1. Name of author

2. Title of work
3. Facts of publication: Name of publisher, date and place of publication
4. The library the work is from (public or personal)
5. The library's call number for the work
6. A notation of why the work is likely to be useful and which part (article, chapter, pages) is especially so

A sample bibliography card is included below.

Most research sources will be books or articles. However, a personal interview, a public lecture, or a recording that sheds light on your subject may also be part of your bibliography.

You will delete or add cards as you sharpen the focus of your paper in preparation for formulating a thesis. Never throw away a bibliography card; set it aside in an inactive pack. Later, you may wish to include it.

Your instructor may require you to submit the bibliography cards with the paper, so make them as neat as possible. You will find the cards easier to use if you make them uniform, using our sample card as a model. You can also save yourself time and effort by entering information about your

Sample bibliography card

Library call number

Where the book was located

All information necessary for the bibliography and notes

A personal note about why the book seems useful

613.94
S225M

College library

Sanger, Margaret. My Fight for Birth Control. New York: Doubleday and Company, Inc., 1955.

This is an important source because it is autobiographical and tells the reader what motivated Sanger to fight for family limitation. The section on Sanger's nursing experience is especially significant.

sources on the cards in the style required by the final bibliography. To prepare your final bibliography, all you then have to do is alphabetize the cards and transcribe them onto the page. Remember that different kinds of sources require slightly different entries. Consult the Final Bibliography section of this chapter to ensure that you're correctly listing the information you need for each source.

Step 4: Reading

Once you have your sources, you need to begin reading them. Your reading will be mainly of two kinds: scanning and careful reading.

Scanning

Scanning means to inspect a page or chapter quickly to see whether it contains information essential to the narrowed topic. The aim of scanning is to give you a working familiarity with the sources available on the topic. Don't take notes as you scan. Pay attention to chapter headings of books, topic sentences of paragraphs, headings of magazine articles, and summarizing entries in reference works. And don't allow yourself to be sidetracked by a source. Remember that what you are after is an overview of your subject. Cull those sources that look promising and put them aside for careful reading.

Careful reading

Now you focus on details. Your aim is to uncover the evidence and information you need to turn the narrowed subject into a paper with a definite thesis. Now you must take notes as you read.

Step 5: Taking notes

Note-taking—the groundwork of research—should be done accurately, intelligently, and economically. The best way to keep notes is on 4 x 6 cards. The experience of numerous researchers and scholars has verified the superiority of note cards over sheets of paper. Cards can be easily shuffled, discarded, and added while sheets of paper must be cut into strips and pasted in order. Every note card should contain a headnote and an abbreviated source from which the note is taken. (For the full source, you will refer to your bibliography cards.) On the facing page are two sample note cards.

Sample note cards

Headnote

Source

Sanger, p. 125 Origins of birth control

The father of family limitation was Thomas Robert Malthus, who in 1798 concluded: "The grand practical problem is to find the means of limiting the number of births."

Direct quotation

Coigney, p. 180 First success

In 1914 Margaret Sanger published a monthly magazine, The Woman Rebel. The magazine drew wide attention to birth control, but it caused Sanger to be arrested for sending birth control information through the mail. Before she could be placed in jail, Sanger escaped to Europe.

Learn to take notes sparingly. Include in your notes only information crucial to the paper and directly related to the narrowed subject. (See sample note cards accompanying the student paper at the end of this chapter.) If, after prudent scrutiny, you remain doubtful, include the note; you can always discard it, but trying to find it again later may be time-consuming. As with bibliography cards, never throw away a note card; simply place it in a separate inactive pack, in case you need it later. Each note card should be limited to one idea. If you cannot squeeze the idea onto one card, then continue on a second card labeled B. The information contained on your note cards will be of four kinds:

1. Quotation
2. Paraphrase
3. Summary
4. Personal comment

The first three kinds of information must be documented—that is, for ideas not your own, you must give credit in notes or parentheses. Passing off as your own the ideas of another is called *plagiarism* (see pages 215–16), which is a serious offense punishable in many schools by an automatic F for the course and/or suspension or expulsion from school. Some plagiarism is unintentionally committed by students who are unaware of how to properly use the ideas of others. In the following discussion we will try to clear up any possible confusion about what information must be documented.

Direct quotations

When you use the exact words of other writers or speakers, you are quoting them, and you must name them as the source. Short quotations must be placed in quotation marks and must fit into your text coherently. If you take care of this during the note-taking stage, you will save yourself considerable editing later.

Incoherent: The novel arose at a time when "culture which, in the last few centuries, has set an unprecedented value on originality, on the novel; and it is therefore well named."[1]

Better: According to Ian Watt, the novel is well named because it is "the logical literary vehicle of a culture which, in the last few centuries, has set an unprecedented value on originality, on the novel."[1]

Long quotations (exceeding three lines) are not placed in quotation marks but are double-spaced and indented ten spaces. They should be introduced unless they are syntactically part of your own sentence. Following is an example of how to introduce a long quotation:

> In analyzing the temper of England during the mid-19th century, Wyn Craig Wade emphasizes the startling and transforming rush of new inventions:
>
> > By 1840, the steam engine alone had transformed England's industries into sprawling, whirling beehives, and no part of her culture was free from the dizzying influence of a leaping technology. The telephone was invented; then came mechanical refrigeration. Faraday's electrical dynamo, then Edison's electrical light permitted factories to stay open all night long, swelling production to a hitherto unimaginable degree. The turbine and internal combustion engines appeared. In time, the sorcery of Marconi's wireless telegraphy. As Winston Churchill recalled, "Every morning when the world woke up, some new machinery had started running. Every night while the world had supper, it was running still."[2]

The quotation opens at the beginning of a paragraph, and therefore its first line is indented three spaces to indicate this fact. Had the quotation come from the middle of a paragraph, no such indention of its initial line would have been necessary. A quotation within a long quotation is surrounded by regular quotation marks; a quotation within a short quotation is surrounded by single quotation marks. (See Handbook, page 400.) If you wish to omit irrelevant words or lines from a quoted passage, do so by using ellipses. Use three spaced dots when the omission is at the beginning or in the middle of a sentence:

> "All of the functions of language . . . in some ways affect the most basic need of any living organism, survival."[3]

> According to John C. Condon, language is personal; it is ". . . determined by the training, whims, and historical accidents of our culture, community, and family."[4]

Use four spaced dots (with no space before the first dot) when the omission occurs at the end of a sentence.

> "By the age of five the child knows the sound and structure of its language better than most foreign students with years of training. . . ."[5]

Use a full line of spaced dots to indicate the omission of an entire paragraph or more.

Do not overuse quotations. A paper riddled with quotations does not read well because each quotation reflects a different style, causing a choppy effect. The overuse of quotations also makes you look unsure, as if you lacked the ability to say anything on your own. In fact, you should use quotations only when an author has stated an important idea in an original way or when the statement is controversial or obscure. Facts that are common knowledge need not be documented or quoted. As a rule of thumb, if you have read five sources making the same point, that point may be considered general knowledge. For instance, "American jails contain many prisoners arrested for the crime of burglery" is a commonly known fact and does not need to be quoted. So is the statement, "Neil Armstrong was the first man to set foot on the moon." In contrast, the statement, "Children in America are often subjected to unnecessary surgeries because Medicaid is there to pay the bill," is controversial since critics disagree in their views on the subject. We need to know who made the statement and where. Again, a little-known fact such as, "Ten thousand people in the United States are equipped with artificial heart valves made of dacron mesh" needs to be quoted accurately and its author identified.

Paraphrase

To paraphrase is to say in your own words what someone else has said. You read an author's material, you digest the idea, and then you restate the thought, using approximately the same number of words as the original, but using your own vocabulary and your own way of expressing yourself. Paraphrasing does *not* mean using an author's words in a different order so they will not be recognized and then passing them off as your own. Proper paraphrasing is a vital and legitimate part of research. In fact, most of your research papers will consist of paraphrasing—thoroughly digested information presented in your personal style but faithfully documented. Paraphrasing achieves two purposes: First, it indicates that you are on top of your information, having assimilated it thoroughly. Second, it gives your paper a smooth, consistent style. In the example below the original passage is on the left, and the paraphrase is on the right.

Original

It is no longer sufficient for Johnny to understand the past. It is not even enough for him to understand the present, for the here-and-now environment will soon vanish. Johnny must learn to anticipate the directions and rate of change. He must, to put it technically, learn to make repeated, probabilistic, increasingly long-range assumptions about the future. And so must Johnny's teacher.[6]

Paraphrase

In a world where present customs and values quickly give way to new customs and values that have no recognizable connection with what went on before, it is no longer sufficient for a student or teacher to know history and current events. Both student and teacher must become future-oriented by learning to anticipate and project advancing trends and to guess the rate at which change will occur.[6]

In the event that you want to preserve key words or phrases from the original text, a combination of paraphrase and quotation may be used. Below we have changed the paraphrase from Alvin Toffler to a combination paraphrase and quotation:

> As Alvin Toffler points out, in a world where "the here-and-now environment" quickly vanishes, giving way to new customs and new values, it is no longer enough for a student or a teacher to know history and current events. Both student and teacher must become future-oriented by learning to make "repeated, probabilistic, increasingly long-range assumptions" about advancing trends and the rate at which change will occur.[6]

Summary

A summary is a condensation of a piece of writing. The extent of the condensation varies. You may want to condense an entire book into one paragraph, as in this summary of Arnold Toynbee's *Study of History*, Volume IV:

> Arnold Toynbee argues that nothing is more conducive to the decay of a civilization than worldly success. As soon as a nation has reached a peak and begins to rest on its laurels, it is on the downward grade, because it is then no longer willing to respond to new challenges as they present themselves. It begins to mark time instead of to go forward. Inertia sets in as the leaders dream about the glory of their past achievements instead of blazing new trails. Toynbee refers to this tendency for the very success of a civilization to make it unfit for further growth as "the intoxication of victory." (IV, 505) Examples of it can be seen in the self-adulation of Persia, of Greece, and of Rome. The creative energies of these three civilizations hardened into self-stultifying idolatry, which then was followed by a decay of the civilization.[7]

The purpose of such a tight summary is to set in relief the main ideas of a work, usually in order to give weight to your own thesis by citing an important source, or to present in uncluttered and direct form an otherwise complicated or verbose argument. Note that you must tell the reader, either in the text or in a note, exactly what work you are summarizing.

Most often you will want to summarize one or several pages into a single paragraph, maintaining the essential nature of the original work, its context, connotation, and purpose, but using your own language. If the original passage was ironic or satirical, this tone should be reflected in your version. A good way to do this is to quote key words or phrases typical of the author's attitude. The following is a summary of Willie Morris's "Miss Abbott":

> Willie Morris's reminiscence of a terrifying grade school teacher leaves the reader frightened and

amused. "Miss Abbott" emerges as a red-eared religious fanatic who talks through her pink nose, makes fawning slaves out of her girl students, and teaches all of her classes to learn by rote. When she is "knocked out cold" by a student's stray softball, we hardly blame the little boy who wrote: "I wich the old bich had been hit by a hard ball," nor do we condemn the author when he confesses, "I prayed that she would die." But, of course, Miss Abbott revives to continue her academic harassment, which all of us who have ever hated a grade school teacher view with remembered terror.[8]

Summaries are particularly useful when you are trying to capture concisely a factual report. In such a case, you must be meticulous about the accuracy of your facts and be extremely careful about what you leave out when you condense. The following paragraph summary of the bulky Walker Report concerning the riots in Chicago during the 1968 Democratic National Convention is a good example of careful condensation.

According to the Walker Report three factors were mainly responsible for the violent confrontations between the Chicago police and the demonstrators during the 1968 National Democratic Convention:

1. Various real and imagined threats to the city were inferred from inflammatory statements and from informants.
2. The city responded to the threats by refusing the permits for marches and meetings and by deploying armed troops.
3. The city had officially ignored police violence in earlier demonstrations and riots.

Next, the report stresses eyewitness accounts that accused the Chicago police of using unnecessary force in dealing with media representatives as well as demonstrators, especially at the Hilton Hotel, in Lincoln Park, and in Old Town.

Finally, the report recommends that disciplinary action be taken against policemen who lost control, since the problem is a matter of worldwide concern.[9]

Personal comments

Personal comments on the research you have done are an indispensable part of your paper. They will consist of introductions to the ideas of others, reactions to problems, insights into situations, clarification of issues, transitions from one thought to the next, or conclusions drawn from the evidence presented. You also may point up inconsistencies and unanswered questions, or you may suggest solutions. Whatever your comments are, as they present themselves to your mind, write them down on your note cards. Any work of this sort accomplished during the note-taking stage will save time later. The following are three sample personal comments.

Reaction to the reviews by critics of Erich Segal's *Love Story*: In their attacks on Segal's slick plot, stereotyped characters, and excessive sentimentality, critics seem to ignore two aspects of Segal's work: 1. the lucid style, and 2. the uncluttered purpose. Both of these qualities, after all, are important ingredients of good art.

Reasons why, according to one study, the number of academic underachievers in grade school is higher among bright boys than bright girls: It seems reasonable to assume that one cause for the difference in achievement patterns between girls and boys is family expectation. Since the male in our society is still the one who "must" achieve and "get ahead," more parental pressure may be placed on the male than on the female. This difference in motivation might well result in achievement differences. In other words, the pressure produces a paralytic effect.

Transitional paragraph for moving from one stage to the next in the development of Joan Miró's art: The third and last stage in Miró's art is a shift away from the representational element characterizing his second stage to a new surrealistic approach, reflected in strong primary colors and curved lines. A layman looking at Miró's paintings from this period might well compare them to drawings of multicolored amoebas, except that on close scrutiny, the forms approach real-life subjects.

Unless your personal comments contain quoted words, they need no documentation.

Plagiarism

Plagiarism is the use of another's words and ideas as though they were your own. You are guilty of plagiarism in the following instances:

- Using another's work—whether word-for-word, with slight variations, paraphrased, or summarized—without acknowledging your debt in a note.
- Copying another's words and phrases exactly, acknowledging the use with a note, but failing to enclose the copied material in quotation marks.
- Taking an original idea from someone else and using it in your paper without an acknowledging note.

Here is an original passage followed by these three most common instances of plagiarism:

Original	**Plagiarism**
The policy of repression of ideas cannot work and never has worked. The alternative to it is the long difficult road of education. To this the American people have been committed. — Robert M. Hutchins	The practice of repressing ideas cannot work and never has worked. The alternative to repression is education, which may be a long, difficult road. But the American people are committed to this way.

This is blatant plagiarism. A word or two has been changed in the original passage, but most of the text has been lifted nearly intact from the original. No accompanying note admits this borrowing. But even if the writer had included a superscript number and a note acknowledging the source, the passage would still be considered plagiarized because it is too close to the original to be a paraphrase.

Original	**Plagiarism**
The policy of repression of ideas cannot work and never has worked. The alternative to it is the long difficult road of education. To this the American people have been committed. — Robert M. Hutchins	The policy of repression of ideas cannot work and never has worked. The alternative to it is the long difficult road of education. To this the American people have been committed.[1]

In spite of the note, the passage is still plagiarized since it is nothing more than a word–for–word copy of the original. An acknowledging note is not a license to copy. A direct quotation—as this is—must be surrounded by quotation marks *as well as* acknowledged in a note.

Original

It is because Africa figures as a paradise lost -- both in Dinesen's life and in the life of Europe -- that Out of Africa is an authentic pastoral, perhaps the best prose pastoral of our time.

-- Robert Langbaum

Plagiarism

Isak Dinesen's autobiographical Out of Africa derives its power and impact from the myth of a lost paradise of Africa that was implicitly a part of her own life and the life of Europe.

The passage is plagiarized because it attempts to pass off the insight of a critic as the writer's own. One may plagiarize as much by stealing another's idea as by stealing another's words.

To immunize yourself from the charge of plagiarism, be sure to specify in a note the source of the following:

- Any borrowed idea or insight.
- Any borrowed fact or data.
- Any especially clever expression or phrase you got from someone else.
- Any material lifted verbatim from another's work.
- Any paraphrased or summarized information used in the paper.

Step 6: Choosing the thesis and shaping the outline

The thesis will not leap ready-made from your research, but will dawn on you slowly as you sift through evidence, data, and opinions on your narrowed topic. An answer to a question will occur to you. You will spot a trend. You will arrive at your own opinion. For instance, let us assume that your narrowed topic is "the effect of handicapped children on the life of their families." As you began your research, you had this question in the back of your mind: "What are some of the major problems encountered by families with handicapped children?" Four major points emerge from your notes:

1. The handicapped child may suffer from a poor self–image.
2. The parents of a handicapped child may blame themselves for their child's handicap and suffer intense feelings of guilt.
3. Families of handicapped children may feel isolated and lonely because no one else around them is in the same situation.
4. The parents may be reluctant to discipline a handicapped child.

Another question occurs to you: "Is it possible for a handicapped child to be an asset to a family?" Your notes indicate three main points as an answer:

1. The families of handicapped children may develop an admirable sensitivity to human suffering in general.
2. The handicapped children and their families may realize the beauty of life itself.
3. Families of handicapped children often develop an amazing resilience and flexibility that help them adapt to situations that would overwhelm normal families.

From these major points you can now easily extract an appropriate thesis and a simple outline:

Thesis: The presence of a handicapped child in the family need not cause guilt, fear, and isolation if both the handicapped children and their families can rise above the handicap by adjusting to it and reaffirming the essential beauty of life.

I. Families of handicapped children confront some major problems.
  A. The handicapped child may suffer from a poor self-image.
  B. The parents of a handicapped child may experience intense feelings of guilt as they blame themselves for the handicap of their child.
  C. Families of handicapped children may feel isolated and lonely because no one around them is in their same situation.
  D. The parents of a handicapped child may be reluctant to discipline their child.

II. Having a handicapped child can be turned into a family asset.
   A. The family of a handicapped child may develop great sensitivity to human suffering.
   B. The handicapped children and their families may realize the beauty of life itself.
   C. Families of handicapped children often develop an amazing resilience and flexibility that help them adapt to situations that would overwhelm normal families.

In its developmental stage, your outline will reveal areas that have been under–researched and therefore require more information, or areas that have been over–researched and need thinning.

Review Chapter 4 for guidelines on how to create a balanced, logical, complete, and visually accurate outline.

Step 7: Writing the rough draft

When you are ready to begin the rough draft, you are further along than you think. But do not delay your writing until the night before your paper is due. As we said earlier, for most people writing is a demanding task. Paragraphs that express in a smooth style exactly what you want to say will not miraculously flow from your pen, but will require reworking and editing. Be prepared to write at least two drafts—one rough and one final. Deliberate *care* is your watchword. Slow down, think, and construct with exactness.

Most of the time you will have to reword your notes to fit into the context of the paper. Occasionally, a note can be used as originally set down. When this is the case, do not waste time by copying, but staple the entire note card to your typing sheet. When additional transitions, observations, or personal comments are needed, work these in with a view toward purposeful progression, constantly asking yourself, Is my thesis being supported? Am I expressing myself clearly? Am I placing the emphasis where it belongs? When you confront a particularly complex idea, work it out on scratch paper first; this will keep your rough draft from being illegibly messy. Keep a dictionary and a thesaurus handy to look up the meaning and spelling of words and to make your vocabulary more varied.

Since your first draft will suffer considerable handling, shuffling, penciling, and erasing, use a heavy bond paper rather than flimsy scratch paper. Also, leave wide margins and spaces between lines so that you have plenty of room for revisions. Type or write on one side of your paper only.

Three styles of documentation: Footnotes, endnotes, and parenthetical references

The aim of all documentation is to enable a writer to state concisely where a cited source may be found. Scholarly societies and associations try to agree on a uniform style for such citations so that writers may—in the shortest space possible—make their sources intelligible to readers. And for the most part, the use of an agreed-on, uniform style of documentation is a helpful shorthand for writers and scholars. The style tells you what publication facts you should include, in what order you should place them, and where you should put the note. Standardizing such details relieves the drudgery of documentation.

The field of English mainly follows the style laid down by the Modern Language Association (MLA). And recently, MLA has announced a change in its style of documentation. The association now proposes to use a style of parenthetical documentation, where references are placed not in endnotes or footnotes but in parentheses within the text itself. The parenthetical note refers the reader to a bibliography entry, which includes complete publication details on the source.

Simplicity is the main virtue of this new style. In the past, beleaguered students had to perform double labor in documenting their papers. First, they had to laboriously type out footnotes on the bottoms of their pages, often ruining otherwise good pages because they had miscounted the number of lines a note required. Next, they had to repeat the nearly identical information in a bibliography citation. The use of endnotes required the same double labor. But the new style calls for only one complete citation—the bibliography entry. Within the text itself the parenthetical reference consists merely of a name and page number, for example, (Jones 103).

Though the new parenthetical style voted on and approved in 1982 by the MLA is an improvement over both footnotes and endnotes, it will not be formally and widely put into use until publication of the new edition of the *MLA Handbook*, anticipated in 1984—the year this book itself will be published. In the meantime, we have solved our quandary about which style to adopt by deciding to include all three: endnotes, footnotes, and parenthetical references. Our personal preference is for the new style. Its simplicity will endear it to writers and typists everywhere. But until simplicity carries the day and the new parenthetical style has become the standard for English classes, ask your instructor which documentation style you should use in your paper.

Endnotes

Endnotes appear on a separate page at the conclusion of the text. They are numbered consecutively, double-spaced, and listed under the centered title "Notes." The following diagram illustrates the use of endnotes:

Format for Endnotes [collected on separate page]

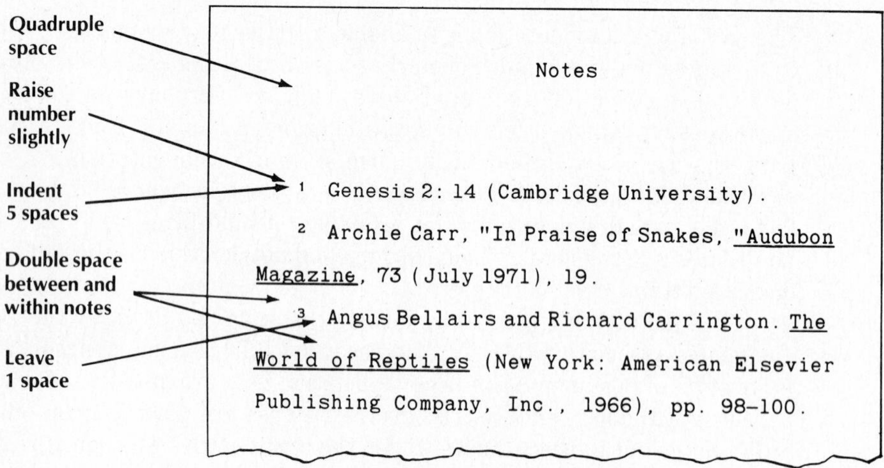

Quadruple space
Raise number slightly
Indent 5 spaces
Double space between and within notes
Leave 1 space
Notes
1 Genesis 2: 14 (Cambridge University).
2 Archie Carr, "In Praise of Snakes, "Audubon
Magazine, 73 (July 1971), 19.
3 Angus Bellairs and Richard Carrington. The
World of Reptiles (New York: American Elsevier
Publishing Company, Inc., 1966), pp. 98-100.

Footnotes

The following diagram illustrates the use of footnotes:

Format for Footnotes [appear at bottom of page]

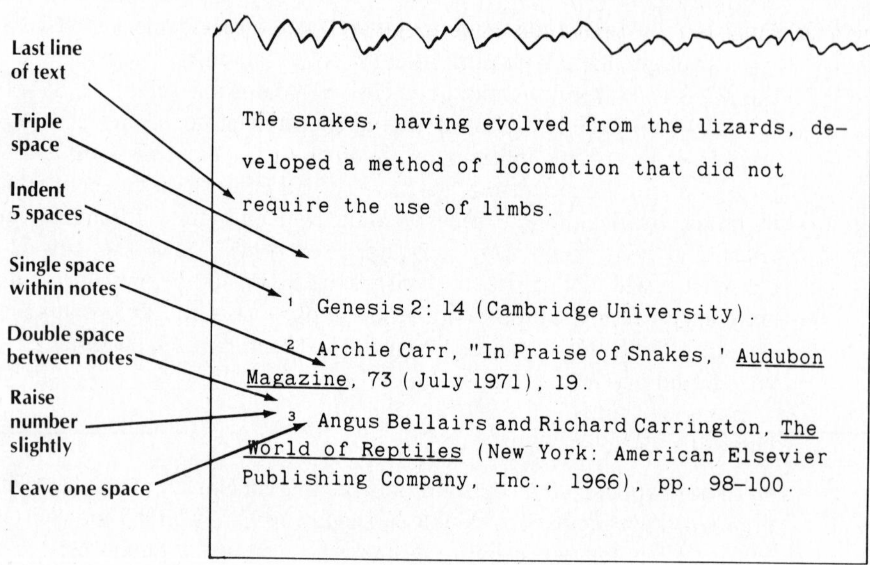

Last line of text
Triple space
Indent 5 spaces
Single space within notes
Double space between notes
Raise number slightly
Leave one space
The snakes, having evolved from the lizards, de-
veloped a method of locomotion that did not
require the use of limbs.
1 Genesis 2: 14 (Cambridge University).
2 Archie Carr, "In Praise of Snakes,' Audubon
Magazine, 73 (July 1971), 19.
3 Angus Bellairs and Richard Carrington, The
World of Reptiles (New York: American Elsevier
Publishing Company, Inc., 1966), pp. 98-100.

Footnotes require special attention. At the bottom of each page you will need to leave enough room for the required number of footnotes. If the length of a footnote requires that it be continued on the following page, type a solid line across the new page one full line below the last line of the text, double-space twice, and continue the note. Footnotes pertaining to this new page should immediately follow the completion of the note continued from the previous page. The following technique will help you save enough space for footnotes at the bottom of a page:

1. Count the number of lines needed for each footnote.
2. Add five lines for the bottom margin of the page.
3. Add three lines to separate the first footnote from the body of the paper.
4. Add two lines for each space between footnotes.

Footnoting is simple when you keep a model in front of you. It is easier, and more accurate, to check your style sheet each time you write a footnote than to try to memorize the proper format. Note entries are different from bibliography entries, as the list of forms on pages 223–41 shows.

Parenthetical References

The new style of parenthetical references provides a citation to a source either in the text itself or in parentheses within the text. Let us assume that a paper on F. Scott Fitzgerald alludes to a critical work by Milton Hindus. Using the endnote style of documentation, the writer might have treated the citation in this way:

> According to Milton Hindus, Fitzgerald's exposure of the savagery of the super rich in America is often tinged with deep satirical indignation.[3]

The superscript 3 would then refer the reader to the following note at the end of the paper:

> [3] Milton Hindus, <u>F. Scott Fitzgerald: An Introduction and Interpretation</u>, American Authors and Critics Series (New York: Holt, Rinehart and Winston, Inc., 1968), p. 102.

In the new system suggested, all of the important documentary information would appear in the text, with only a short reference in parentheses:

> Fitzgerald's exposure of the savagery of the super rich in America is often tinged with a deep satirical indignation (Hindus 102).

or, better yet:

> According to Milton Hindus (102), Fitzgerald's exposure of the savagery of the super rich in America is often tinged with deep satirical indignation.

For the full Hindus reference, the reader then consults the bibliography at the end of the paper, where the following entry would be found:

> Hindus, Milton. <u>F. Scott Fitzgerald: An Introduction and Interpretation</u>. American Authors and Critics Series. New York: Holt, Rinehart and Winston, Inc., 1968.

If two or more works by Hindus were cited in the paper, a key word from the title referred to would be included in the parentheses: (Hindus, <u>Fitzgerald</u> 102).

The advantage of the new style lies in its simplicity. Whereas the endnote style requires a full note as well as a full bibliographical entry, the parenthetical style requires only the latter.

The other documentation changes to be included in the *MLA Handbook* are mainly in bibliography citations. In the main, these changes are minor and may be summed up briefly:

> Arabic numerals are to replace Roman numerals wherever possible in references to volume numbers of books and journals, parts and chapters of books, stanzas of poems, acts of plays, and so forth.
>
> Names of foreign cities are to be cited as they appear on the title page or copyright page of the source. English names may be added in brackets if the use of a foreign name is likely to confuse a reader.
>
> Lower case is to be used for *vol.* and *no.*
>
> *p.* or *pp.* is to be deleted in front of page numbers unless to do so will cause confusion.

l. and *ll.* are to be written out (*line, lines*) until repeated references throughout the text make it clear that a line (or lines) is being cited, in which case *l.* and *ll.* may then be eliminated altogether.

A colon rather than a comma is to separate volume number from page number; the comma after the journal title is to be eliminated; and spaces between volume, year, and page are to be eliminated: *The American Scholar* 20(Summer 1951):279 (not *The American Scholar, XX (Summer 1951), 279*).

For journals that paginate each issue separately, only the issue number is to be given immediately following the volume number: *NEA Journal* 55.5(1966):35 (not *NEA Journal*, 55, No. 2 (1966), 35).

In the following section, we have used the current style of documentation, and in the bibliography citations we have indicated when and how the new style differs markedly from the old style. The student paper at the end of the chapter uses both footnotes and endnotes, and we have reproduced two pages of it using parenthetical references.

Endnote forms for books

Information provided in an endnote citation of a book should always appear in the following order:

> Author, Title (with continuous underlining between separate words of a title), Editor or translator, Edition, Series (publication facts), Volume, page.

If no information is available for one item, skip it and go on to the next. The examples that follow are all given in the endnote format, but the same order of information applies to footnotes. Naturally, footnotes will differ from endnotes in placement and spacing, as shown in the diagrams on page 220.

AUTHOR Name of author or authors, in normal order, followed by a comma.

Book with one author

> [1] J. Hillis Miller, The Disappearance of God: Five 19th-Century Writers (New York: Schocken Books, 1965), p. 8.

Book with more than one author

> [2] Harold Barlow and Sam Morgenstern, A Dictionary of Musical Themes (New York: Crown Press, 1948), p. 84.

For three authors, separate the authors by commas. If there are more than three authors, use the first author, followed by *et al.* (or "and others").

> [3] Evan J. Crane et al., A Guide to the Literature of Chemistry, 2nd ed. (New York: John Wiley & Sons, Inc., 1957), p. 10.

TITLE Title of the book, underlined and followed by a comma unless the next item is enclosed in parentheses.

> [4] Edith Hamilton, Mythology: Timeless Tales of Gods and Heroes (New York: Mentor Books, 1942), pp. 30–33.

Internal titles

In a collection of essays or a book with chapters or sections by different authors, the title of the essay or chapter is followed by a comma and enclosed in quotation marks, and the title of the larger work is preceded by *in*.

> [5] R. W. Short, "Melville as Symbolist," in Interpretations of American Literature, ed. Charles Feidelson, Jr. and Paul Brodtkorb, Jr. (New York: Oxford Univ. Press, 1959), pp. 106–07.

EDITOR OR TRANSLATOR Name of editor or translator, in normal order, preceded by *ed.* or *trans.*, followed by a comma unless the next item is enclosed in parentheses.

> [6] William Hamilton, "The Death of God," in Contemporary Religious Issues, ed. Donald E. Hartsock (Belmont, Calif.: Wadsworth Publishing Company, Inc., 1968), pp. 14–15.
>
> [7] Nathaniel Hawthorne, The Scarlet Letter, ed. Kenneth S. Lynn (New York: Harcourt, Brace & World, Inc., 1961) p. 31.
>
> [8] Homer, The Iliad, trans. Richmond Lattimore (Chicago: Univ. of Chicago Press, 1962), p. 10.

If you wish to cite a complete edited collection, use the following format:

> [9] Gerald W. Haslam, ed., Forgotten Pages of American Literature (Boston: Houghton Mifflin Company, 1970), p. 43.

EDITION Edition used, whenever it is not the first, followed by a comma unless the next item is enclosed in parentheses.

> [10] Laurence Perrine, Sound and Sense, 5th ed. (New York: Harcourt Brace Jovanovich, Inc., 1969), pp. 134–35.
>
> [11] Everard M. Upjohn, Paul S. Wingert, and James G. Mahler, History of World Art, 2nd ed., rev. and enl. (New York: Oxford Univ. Press, 1958), p. 58.

SERIES Name and number of series, followed by a comma unless the next item is enclosed in parentheses.

> [12] William van O'Connor, William Faulkner, rev. ed., University of Minnesota Pamphlets on American Writers, 3 (Minneapolis: Univ. of Minnesota Press, 1964), p. 36 ff.

PUBLICATION FACTS Place, publisher, and date of publication within parentheses. A colon separates the place of publication and the publisher's name, and a comma separates the publisher's name and the date. Another comma follows the end parenthesis to precede the page reference.

> 13 Alvin Toffler, Future Shock (New York: Bantam Books, 1970), pp. 219–21.

If necessary for clarity, include the name of the state or country.

> 14 Andrew Wright, A Reader's Guide to English and American Literature (Glenview, Ill.: Scott, Foresman and Company, 1970), p. 15.

If more than one place of publication appears, choose the major city (usually New York). Also, if more than one copyright date is mentioned, use the most recent, unless your study is specifically concerned with an earlier edition. If the place or date of publication is not provided, insert n.p. or n.d. If only a publisher's name is provided, look up the location of the publisher's office (the place of publication) in the publisher's catalog available in any library or bookstore.

VOLUME Number of the volume from which you are citing if the work contains more than one volume with the same title, in Roman numerals, followed by a comma.

> 15 Charles W. Dunn, "Geoffrey Chaucer," in Major British Writers, ed. G. B. Harrison, enl. ed. (New York: Harcourt, Brace & World, Inc., 1959), I, 3.

PAGE Page number(s) in Arabic numerals, followed by a period.

> 16 Horatio Alger, Jr., Adrift in New York and The World Before Him, ed. William Coyle (New York: The Odyssey Press, Inc., 1966), p. 69.

If you are citing one volume of a multivolume work, leave out the p. or pp.:

> [17] Northrop Frye, "George Gordon, Lord Byron," in Major British Writers, ed. G. B. Harrison, enl. ed. (New York: Harcourt, Brace & World, Inc., 1959), II, 159.

Small Roman numerals are often used in books for numbering the pages of prefaces or introductions.

> [18] Milton Hindus, F. Scott Fitzgerald: An Introduction and Interpretation, American Authors and Critics Series (New York: Holt, Rinehart and Winston, Inc. 1968), p. vii.

Notice the following common usage when giving page numbers: pp. 92–93, *not* pp. 92–3; but pp. 215–18, *not* pp. 215–8 or pp. 215–218.

Endnote forms for periodicals

In endnotes citing a periodical, information is arranged in the following order:

AUTHOR Author, "Article Title," Periodical Title, Volume, date, page.

Name of author, in normal order, followed by a comma.

> [1] Stephen Spender, "Is a New Literature Possible?" Saturday Review, 22 Sept. 1962, pp. 16–19.

If there is more than one author, follow the same rules suggested earlier for books with more than one author.

ARTICLE TITLE Title of article, followed by a comma and enclosed within quotation marks.

[2] Stanley Kunitz, "Frost, Williams and Company," Harper's, Oct. 1962, p. 23.

PERIODICAL TITLE

Name of the periodical, underlined, followed by a comma.

[3] Paul Engle, "Paean for a Poet by a Poet," Life, 15 June 1959, pp. 65–66.

VOLUME AND DATE

Omit the volume number for weekly or monthly periodicals that are paged anew in each issue. Give instead the complete date, set off by commas.

[4] Leon Edel, "Spirals of Reason and Fancy," Saturday Review, 5 Sept. 1964, p. 23.

If pagination of the issue is separate and the month is not given, supply volume and issue number in Arabic numerals, or volume and year of publication.

[5] William R. Elkins, "Thoreau's Cape Cod: The Violent Pond." Oklahoma English Bulletin, 2, No. 2 (1965), 15.

[6] Robert Frances et al., "On Robert Frost," Massachusetts Review, 4 (1963), 238.

PAGE

Page number(s), in Arabic numerals, followed by a period. Note the format for an editorial.

[7] "The Election that Nobody Won," Editorial, Time, 13 Nov. 1972, pp. 32–35.

When the volume number is included, omit p. or pp.

[8] Dorothy Dudley, "The Acid Test," Poetry, 23 (March 1925), 328–35.

Endnote form for newspapers

The endnote form for a newspaper item is the same as that for a periodical, except that in addition to giving the date and page on which the newspaper article appeared, you will also provide the column number and special section.

> [9] John Peterson, "Assault on Heart Disease," National Observer, 20 July 1970, Sec. 1, p. 1, cols. 4–5; p. 17, cols. 1–6.
>
> [10] Jim Murray, "Please Pass the Iguana," Los Angeles Times, 9 Nov. 1972, Sec. 3, p. 1, col. 1.

Endnote forms for special items

As with bibliographical forms, we cannot provide examples for all the eventualities that may occur, but where no examples are given, use your common sense, consult a style manual such as the *MLA Handbook*, or ask your instructor how to handle specific note problems. In all cases, be consistent.

Classical works

For long classical works that appear in several editions, you must give the reader more than just the page number. Include in parentheses the number of the book, part, act, scene, and line, separated by a period. Books, parts, and acts appear in Roman numerals; scenes appear in small Roman numerals; lines appear in Arabic numerals.

> [1] Homer, The Iliad, trans. Richmond Lattimore (Chicago: Univ. of Chicago Press, 1951), p. 101 (III. 38–45).
>
> [2] Plato, The Republic, trans. Paul Shorey (Cambridge, Mass.: Harvard Univ. Press, 1937), p. 225 (III. vi).

When one underlined title is followed by another, separate the titles with the word *in*.

[3] Sophocles, Oedipus the King, in The Complete Greek Tragedies, ed. David Grene and Richmond Lattimore (Chicago: Univ. of Chicago Press, 1959), II, 52 (II. 955–83).

[4] William Shakespeare. Antony and Cleopatra, in The Comedies and Tragedies of Shakespeare, ed. Warren Chappell (New York: Random House, 1944), II, 934 (II. vi. 13–19).

If you are making numerous subsequent citations to a work, you may place an abbreviated version of the reference in parentheses in your text.

Even near death, Antony has no thought but for Cleopatra:

I am dying Egypt, dying; only
I here importune death awhile, until
Of many thousand kisses the poor last
I lay upon thy lips. (Antony IV. xv. 18–21)

Encyclopedias

[5] E. F. Kook, "Stage Design," Encyclopaedia Britannica, 1963 ed.

Authors of encyclopedia articles are usually identified by initials that are interpreted in the encyclopedia index. Endnotes to unsigned articles begin with the title of the article.

[6] "Sitting Bull," Encyclopedia Americana, 1962 ed.

References to sections that are alphabetically arranged need not be identified by volume and page. It is not necessary to give the names of the editors of an encyclopedia or the name and location of the publisher.

Critical reviews

> [7] Charles Rolo, rev. of <u>The Status Seekers</u>, by Vance Packard, <u>The Atlantic</u> (May 1959), p. 91.
>
> [8] Eve Auchincloss, rev. of <u>Sex in History</u>, by Ray Tannahill (New York: Stein & Day, 1980), <u>Time</u>, 3 March 1980, pp. 81, 86.

Poems

> [9] T. S. Eliot, "The Love Song of J. Alfred Prufrock," in <u>Modern American Poetry and Modern British Poetry</u>, ed. Louis Untermeyer (New York: Harcourt, Brace, and Company, 1950), pp. 398–401.

In the case of long classical poems, follow the form for classical works given above.

The Bible

The names of sacred scriptures, both Christian and non-Christian, are not underlined, nor are the names of the individual books. Chapter and verses are indicated by Arabic numerals, separated by a colon.

> [10] Psalms 14:5.

The King James version of the Bible is assumed to have been used unless otherwise indicated.

> [11] Acts 13:42 (J. B. Phillips).

Subsequent references

Once you have provided full information for a reference, your subsequent notes for that same source will be brief. The use of Latin abbreviations, such as *op. cit.*, *loc. cit.*, and *ibid.*, is out of style. In most cases, the last name of the author and the page number will suffice. The *MLA Handbook*, 1977 edition, allows subsequent brief references to appear in parentheses within the text.

> [2] Miller, p. 76.
>
> (Miller, p. 76) within the text

However, if you are citing more than one title by the same author, use the author's last name, followed by a key word from the title, followed by the page number. (The whole title is *The Raven and the Whale.*)

> [2] Miller, Raven, p. 26.

If you are citing authors with identical surnames, you must add the given name to each reference:

> [2] Perry Miller, p. 20.

If two or more authors are involved, use the last names of both, or *et al.*:

> Barlow and Morgenstern, p. 20.
>
> Crane et al., p. 15.

Content notes

Occasionally you may wish to use a note not for documentation, but for special comment. Such a comment may consist of a definition, explanation, judgment, or cross-reference. The purpose is to avoid distracting your reader from the main thrust of your paper. Here are some examples of content notes:

> [1] Briefly, archetype is a term brought into literary criticism as a result of the work of psychologist Carl Jung, who held that behind each "unconscious" lies the "collective unconscious," that is, the blocked-off memory of our racial past. This racial memory, according to Jung, is expressed in repeated images, which are found in early myths, religions, and dreams.

```
     2 Unfortunately, this comment was not made
until after the author's death.

     3 For an explanation of this seeming contra-
diction, see p. 3 of this paper.

     4 Cf. the following lines from Wordsworth's
"Lines Written in Early Spring":

     To her fair works did Nature link
     The soul that through me ran;
     And much it grieved my heart to think
     What man has made of man.

     5 This veiled reference is probably to Sir
Joshua Reynolds.
```

Content footnotes are the same as content endnotes except that they are single spaced and appear at the bottom of the page on which the idea to be clarified occurs.

Step 8: Preparing the final bibliography

It is in preparing your final bibliography that the minor changes of the new MLA style (listed on pages 222–23) will be most obvious. Where the old style and the new MLA style differ in the examples that follow, we have indicated the difference in a note, and we have provided two bibliography pages for the sample paper—one in the old style, the other in the new.

Bibliography form for books

The information in a bibliographical entry for a book should always appear in the following order:

> Author. Title. Editor or translator. Edition. Series. Volumes. Publication facts.

If any of these items are not pertinent to a given entry, simply omit them.

AUTHOR Author's surname, followed by given name or initials, followed by a period.

Book with one author

> Highet, Gilbert. The Art of Teaching. New York: Vintage Books, 1958.

Book with more than one author

If the book has more than one author, invert the name of the first author only:

> Barzun, Jacques, and Henry F. Graff. The Modern Researcher. 3rd ed. New York: Harcourt Brace Jovanovich, Inc., 1977.

For three authors, separate the authors by commas. If there are more than three authors, use the first author, followed by *et al.*:

> Baugh, Albert C., et al. A Literary History of England. New York: Appleton-Century-Crofts, Inc., 1948.

TITLE Title of the book, underlined, followed by a period.

> Seton, Anya. Devil Water. New York: Avon, 1962.

Internal titles

When a book contains separate articles or chapters by different authors, the article or chapter referred to appears in quotation marks, followed by a period. The word *In* precedes the title of the collection.

> Bettelheim, Bruno. "Violence: A Neglected Mode of Behavior." In Violence: A Reader in the Ethics of Action. Ed. George Estey and Doris Hunter. Waltham, Mass.: Xerox College Publishing, 1971.

EDITOR OR TRANSLATOR Name of the editor or translator, preceded by *Ed.* or *Trans.*, followed by a period.

> Yerby, Frank. "Health Card." In Black Literature in America. Ed. Raman K. Singh and Peter Fellowes. New York: Thomas Y. Crowell Company, 1970.
>
> Defoe, Daniel, Moll Flanders. Ed. J. Paul Hunter. New York: Thomas Y. Crowell Company, 1970.
>
> Dante, Alighieri. The Purgatorio. Trans. John Ciardi. New York: New American Library, 1961.

If you wish to cite a complete edited collection, the editor's name appears in the position of the author's name, followed by *ed.* (See Hardin Craig entry below.)

EDITION Edition used, whenever it is not the first, followed by a period.

> Van Doren, Carl C. The American Novel: 1789–1939. 2nd ed. New York: The Macmillan Company, 1940.
>
> Craig, Hardin, ed. The Complete Works of Shakespeare. Rev. ed. Glenview, Ill.: Scott, Foresman and Company, 1964.
>
> Dixon, Raymond J., ed. Granger's Index to Poetry. 4th ed., rev. and enl. New York: Columbia Univ. Press, 1953.

SERIES Name and number of the series followed by a period.

> Unger, Leonard. T. S. Eliot. University of Minnesota Pamphlets on American Writers, 8. Minneapolis: Univ. of Minnesota Press, 1961.

VOLUMES Number of volumes under this title, in Arabic numerals, if all the volumes have been used.

```
Harrison, G. B., et al., eds. Major British
    Writers. 2 vols. New York: Harcourt Brace
    Jovanovich, Inc., 1959.
```

If all the volumes have not been used, indicate the ones that have been used after the publication information.

```
Baker, Ernest A. The History of the English
    Novel. London: H. F. and G. Witherly, 1924-39.
    Vols. II and III.

New style: Vols. 2 and 3.
```

For volumes with separate titles, use the following format:

```
Seton-Watson, Hugh. The Russian Empire 1808-1917.
    Vol. III of Oxford History of Modern Europe.
    Oxford: Clarendon Press, 1967.

New style: Vol. 3 of
```

PUBLICATION FACTS Place, publisher, and date of publication, followed by a period. Use a colon to separate the place from the publisher, and a comma to separate the publisher from the date. If more than one place of publication appears, choose the major city (usually New York). If more than one copyright date is mentioned, cite the most recent one, unless your study is specifically concerned with an earlier edition.

```
James, Henry. The Portrait of a Lady. New York:
    Washington Square Press, Inc., 1963.
```

If necessary for clarity, include the name of the state or country.

```
Hilles, Frederick W., ed. The Age of Johnson. New
    Haven, Conn.: Yale Univ. Press, 1964.
```

If the place or date of publication is not provided, insert n.p. or n.d. for "no place" or "no date." If only a publisher's name is provided, look up the location of the publisher's office (the place of publication) in the publisher's catalog, available in any library or bookstore.

Bibliography form for periodicals

The information in an entry for a periodical should appear in the following order, leaving out items for which no information is available and going on to the next item:

Author. "Article Title." Periodical Title, date, pages.

AUTHOR Author's surname, followed by given name or initials, followed by a period.

```
Reid, Ron. "Black and Gold Soul with Italian
    Legs." Sports Illustrated, 11 Dec. 1972, pp.
    36-37.

New style: Sports Illustrated (11 Dec. 1972):
    36-37.
```

If there is more than one author, follow the same rules suggested earlier for books with more than one author.

ARTICLE TITLE Complete title of article, enclosed in quotation marks and followed by a period.

```
Spender, Stephen. "Is a New Literature Possible?"
    Saturday Review, 22 Sept. 1962, pp. 16-19.

New style: Saturday Review (22 Sept. 1962):16-19.
```

PERIODICAL TITLE Name of periodical, underlined and followed by a comma.

```
"The War: A Shattering Disappointment." Editori-
    al. Time, 25 Dec. 1972, p. 9.

New style: Time (25 Dec. 1972):9.
```

DATE Date of monthly or weekly periodicals, followed by a comma.

Yee, Min. "Chinatown in Crisis." Newsweek. 23 Feb. 1970, pp. 57-58.

New style: Newsweek (23 Feb. 1970):57-58.

If the periodical does not appear regularly on a specified date, then supply the month and year.

Riesman, David. "Where Is the College Generation Headed?" The Atlantic, April 1961, pp. 39-45.

New style: The Atlantic 207(April 1961):39-45. Note that the new style requires the volume number, 207.

If the periodical is paged anew for each issue and the exact date of publication is not given, then supply the volume and number of the issue in order to simplify the reader's search for the journal.

Elkins, William R. "Thoreau's Cape Cod: The Violent Pond." Oklahoma English Bulletin, 2, No. 2 (1965). 57-59.

New style: Oklahoma Bulletin 2.2(1965):57-59.

If a periodical uses continual pagination throughout the annual volume, supply volume number and page reference.

Ramsey, Jarold W. "The Wife Who Goes Out Like a Man, Comes Back as a Hero: The Art of Two Oregon Indian Narratives." PMLA, 92 (1977), 9-18.

New style: PMLA 92(1977):9-18.

PAGES Page numbers for the entire article, not just for the specific pages cited, followed by a period.

> Fetterman, John. "The People of Cumberland Gap." National Geographic. Nov. 1971, pp. 591–621.
>
> New style: National Geographic 140(Nov. 1971):591–621.
>
> Note that the new style requires the volume number, 140.

When a volume or issue number is given, the pp. in front of the page numbers is omitted. If the article is an unsigned editorial, use the following format:

> "The Stature of a Genius." Editorial. House Beautiful, 101 (Oct. 1959), 208, 275–77.
>
> New style: House Beautiful 101(Oct. 1959):208, 275–77.

Bibliography form for newspapers

The bibliographical listing for a newspaper item is the same as for a periodical, except that in addition to giving the date and page on which the newspaper article appeared, you will also give the special section and column number:

> Getze, John. "Alaskan Oil to Overflow West." Los Angeles Times. 28 August 1977, Part VIII, p. 1, col. 5.
>
> New style: Los Angeles Times (28 August 1977): Part 8, p. 1, col. 5.

If the article is an unsigned editorial, use the following format:

> "A Card, a Simple Card." Editorial. Los Angeles Times, 28 August 1977, Part IV, p. 2, cols. 1–2.

New style: Los Angeles Times (28 August 1977): Part 4, p. 2, cols. 1–2.

Bibliography form for special items

Since the nature of published as well as unpublished documents is infinitely varied, we cannot provide standardized forms of citation for all types. Use common sense in giving sufficient information so that your reader can locate the reference or at least understand it. The following are examples of types of references you may wish to cite.

Critical review

Gray, Paul. Rev. of The Bloody Chamber, by Angela Carter. New York: Harper & Row, 1980. Time, 10 March 1980, p. 82.

New style: Time (10 March 1980):82.

Mimeographed item

Witt, Charles B. "The Common Cold." Los Angeles, 1976. (Mimeographed)

Letter

Wood, Miriam. Letter to author. 19 Feb. 1976.

Interview

Bietz, Arthur L. Telephone interview. 4 Nov. 1975.

Recording

Eagle, Swift. The Pueblo Indians. Caedmon, TC 1327, n.d.

Cassette

Beckhofer, Robert. Death of History. University of Michigan, n.d.

More and more libraries are treating and cataloging cassette tapes as books.

Television or radio program

World of Survival. Narr. John Forsythe. CBS Special. 29 Oct. 1972.

"Chapter 2." Writ. Wolf Mankowitz. Dickens of London. Dir. and prod. Marc Miller. Masterpiece Theater. Introd. Alistair Cooke. PBS, 28 August 1977.

Pamphlet

Registrar-Recorder for County of Los Angeles. County Counsel's Analysis, Arguments for, and Proposed Charter Amendments. Pamphlet enclosed in official Sample Ballot, Los Angeles, California, 1972.

Public document

Cong. Rec. 7 Feb. 1977, pp. 3830-35. U.S. Const. Art. 1, sec. 2.

Encyclopedia article

Swinburne, Algernon Charles. "Marlowe, Christopher." Encyclopaedia Britannica, 1963 ed.

When copying your cards for the final bibliography, follow the format used in the sample paper in this chapter.

Abbreviations

Use abbreviations often and consistently in your notes and bibliography, but avoid them in your text. In notes you should abbreviate dates (Jan., Feb.) and institutions (Univ., Assn.). The following are abbreviations commonly encountered or used.

A.D. *Anno Domini*. Refers to years after Christ's birth, as "A.D. 200."
anon. Anonymous.
art., arts. Article(s).
B.C. Before Christ. Refers to years before Christ's birth, as "50 B.C."
bk., bks. Book(s).
ca. *Circa*. *About*, used to indicate an approximate date, as "ca. 1730."
cf. *Confer*. *Compare* one source with another.
ch., chs. Chapter(s).
col., cols. Column(s).
comp. Compiled by or compiler.
diss. Dissertation.
ed., eds. Editor(s), edition, or edited by.
e.g. *Exempli gratia*. *For example*, preceded and followed by a comma.
enl. Enlarged, as in "enl. ed."
et al. *Et alii*. *And others*, as in "John Smith et al."
f., ff. Page(s) following, as "pp. 8 f." meaning page 8 and the following page.
i.e. *Id est*. *That is*, preceded and followed by a comma.
l., ll. Line(s).
MS, MSS Manuscript(s).
n.d. No date.
no., nos. Number(s).
n.p. No place.
p., pp. Page(s).
passim *Here and there throughout the work*, as "pp. 67, 72, et passim."
pseud. Pseudonym.
pt., pts. Part(s).
rev. Revised, revision, reviewed, review.
rpt. Reprint, reprinted.
sec., secs. Section(s).
sic *Thus*, placed in brackets to indicate that an error exists in the passage being quoted, as "sevral [sic]."

st., sts. Stanza(s).
trans. Translator, translated, translation.
vol., vols. Volume(s).

Step 9: Writing the final copy

When your rough draft has been completed, set it aside for a day or two to give your mind some rest from the subject. Then pick it up again with fresh objectivity and give it one final, ruthless criticism. Do not be soft on yourself. It is better to catch errors and clumsy passages yourself than have your instructor catch them for you. After careful review and editing, type the final copy according to the format used in the sample paper in this chapter. Unless your instructor wishes you to follow a specific format, the rules that follow should prove helpful.

The outline

Your outline precedes the text of your paper and should look uncluttered and balanced. You need not number the pages of your outline. See the outline preceding the sample paper.

The body of the paper

1. Hire a typist if your typing is sloppy. Too many erasures or typographical errors prejudice the reader. All good stationery stores stock Liquid Paper or Ko-Rec-Type, which allow neat corrections to be made easily.
2. Use heavy 8½ x 11 white bond paper, observing 1-inch margins at the top, bottom, and both sides of the paper. Avoid erasable bond as it smudges and will not take corrections in ink.
3. Double-space throughout your paper, including quotations and endnotes. Footnotes require double-spacing between notes but single-spacing within. Triple space to separate the first footnote from the body of the paper. See sample student paper.
4. A research paper does not need a title page; instead, the author's name, instructor's name, course number, and date should appear on the first page of the outline and again on the first page of the text in the upper right-hand corner. The title should be centered and double-spaced below the date. See sample student paper.
5. Number pages consecutively throughout the paper in the upper right-hand corner. Do not follow page numbers by hyphens, parentheses,

periods, or other characters. Do not number the first page of the paper, but begin with 2.

6. If your paper contains subdivisions, use subtitles aligned with the left margin and underlined but not capitalized.
7. Place footnote/endnote numerals within the text of your paper one half space above the line. Each numeral immediately follows the material to which it refers.
8. Each footnote at the bottom of the page must appear on the same page as the numeral referring to it. Indent the first line of each footnote five spaces, but align the second and subsequent lines with the left margin. Single-space each footnote, and double-space between footnotes.
9. In a typed manuscript, italics are indicated by underlining. Generally, italicize any title that appears on the outside cover of a work, and place in quotation marks titles that appear inside the cover. (Exceptions are plays, long poems, movies, and operas, which are always underlined.) Do not, however, underline or place in quotation marks the title of your own paper.
10. If possible, use pica type, since it is easier to read than elite.
11. Proofread your paper again and again. Regardless of who types your paper, you alone are responsible for the final copy. Failure to proofread may result in careless errors that will lower your grade. If you cannot retype pages that contain errors, make corrections neatly in black ink.

The bibliography

Bibliography entries are arranged alphabetically according to surname of the author (or first word in entry where no author appears). Double-space between and within entries. If an entry has more than one line, indent the second and subsequent lines five spaces. Start the bibliography on a new page and type "Bibliography" or "Selected Bibliography," centered at the top of the page. See student sample.

Checklist

____ 1. My introduction is strong and includes my thesis.
____ 2. My paper follows my outline.
____ 3. My paragraphs are coherent.
____ 4. The language sounds like me.
____ 5. I have not quoted excessively.
____ 6. I have not plagiarized.
____ 7. My thesis is supported by evidence in the paper.

___ 8. My paper looks neat.
___ 9. I have proofread for mechanical errors.
___ 10. My notes and bibliography are accurate in content and in form.

Sample paper

Following is a facsimile of a student paper, complete with sentence outline, body, notes, and bibliography. For your convenience in studying the development of the paper, we have supplied the appropriate note cards from which each page was developed. And in the right-hand margin, we have noted where each Roman numeral of the outline begins.

Mitch McDiffett
Professor McCuen
English 101
December 16, 1983

Agatha Christie's Hercule Poirot

THESIS: Although Agatha Christie eventually tired of her greatest creation, Hercule Poirot, his unique personality and techniques of solving crimes made him one of the finest and most loved fictional detectives of all time.

I. Hercule's unique personality and character set him apart from other fictional detectives.
   A. His physical appearance was unique.
      1. He was 5′4″, had a black handlebar mustache, an egg-shaped head, and catlike eyes that grew greener as the solution to a crime drew near.
      2. He wore a black coat, pin-striped pants, a bow tie, shiny black boots, and, usually, a coat and muffler.
   B. Hercule Poirot was extremely egotistical and self-centered.
      1. He thought of himself as the greatest detective.
      2. He belittled his sidekick, Hastings, for his extreme lack of intelligence.
      3. He took great pride in his mustache.
   C. His mannerisms were eccentric.
      1. He gestured extravagantly while he spoke.
      2. While speaking, he would switch from French to English without warning.

II. Hercule's techniques of solving crimes made him one of the greatest fictional detectives.
   A. He used common sense and logic in solving his cases.
      1. He suspected everyone until the case was solved.
      2. He claimed that no crime was impossible to solve.
      3. He used a step-by-step process.
   B. His techniques of solving cases involved more than just the use of physical evidence.
      1. He liked to sit and sip his chocolate while he sifted through the information in his head.
      2. He relied on the "little grey cells" in his brain to figure out the case.

        3. He considered himself a specialist because he used a combination of mathematical precision and applied psychology.

III. Agatha Christie's greatest creation was Hercule Poirot.
    A. Hercule Poirot began to be a part of Agatha.
        1. Three of her books were adapted to plays without him because the actor playing him was not what Christie had imagined him to be.
        2. Gradually Christie came to feel that her invention was hanging around her neck.
        3. She began to realize that Hercule would be with her until she died.
    B. Christie began to tire of Hercule Poirot.
        1. She began to see him as an anachronism.
        2. Hercule Poirot vanished.

Time, p. 75 Introduction

Agatha Christie (1891–1976) was called "Queen of the Maze," "The Mistress of Murder," "Woman with God-like Genius."

Her accomplishments:

Earned over $20 million (most money made on murder since Lucrezia Borgia)

83 books, 17 plays, 9 vols. of short stories, autobiographical report, Mousetrap (longest-running play in theatrical history), creation of Marple and Poirot

The Mysterious Affair at Styles introduced Hercule Poirot for the first time.

Murdoch, p. 20 Introduction

The Mysterious Affair at Styles, Christie's first book (1920's), was the result of a challenge by Christie's sister—to write a book with an unguessable solution. Poirot is born. When Christie tired of him, she created Miss Jane Marple.

Mitch McDiffett
Professor McCuen
English 101
December 18, 1983

Agatha Christie's Hercule Poirot

Dame Agatha Christie (1891-1976) has been called "Queen of the Maze," "The Mistress of Murder," and a "Woman with God-like Genius."[1] She earned over twenty million dollars, more money made on murder by any woman since Lucrezia Borgia. A Dame of the British Empire, her accomplishments include eighty-three books, seventeen plays, nine volumes of short stories, an autobiographical report about her experiences on a field study with her archeologist husband, the longest running play in theatrical history (Mousetrap), and the creation of two famous fictional detectives, Miss Jane Marple and Hercule Poirot.[2]

Dame Agatha wrote her first book in the early 1920's after she was challenged by her sister to write a mystery with an unguessable solution.[3] This book, The Mysterious Affair at Styles, introduced her most famous creation, Hercule Poirot, a retired police officer from Belgium.[4] In the thirties,

[1] "Dame Agatha: Queen of the Maze," Time, 26 Jan. 1976, p. 75.

[2] "Dame Agatha," p. 75.

[3] Derrick Murdoch, The Agatha Christie Mystery (Toronto: Pagurian Press Limited, 1976), p. 20.

[4] "Dame Agatha," p. 75.

Keating, p. 41. Hercule Poirot's personality

Known as the greatest sleuth ever (except for Sherlock Holmes).
Born in 1844, 14 years after Belgium separated from Holland.
Died in 1974, still completely alert.
His final appearance is in Curtain, whispering "cher ami" to Hastings, his sidekick of many years. He had begun his career with the words "mon ami, Hastings."

Bailey, p. 87 Hercule Poirot's looks

"A diminutive five foot four inches tall and slender."

Keating, p. 41, 103 Hercule Poirot's looks

His hair was an "unrepentant" black--slicked down with tonic.
His greatest pride was his handlebar mustache (made him look like a dandy).

2

after writing about Poirot for ten years, she began to tire of him, so she created a new character, Miss Jane Marple, an old spinster lady who enjoyed solving crimes.[5] Although Christie eventually tired of her greatest creation, Hercule Poirot, his unique personality and techniques of solving crimes made him one of the finest and most loved fictional detectives of all time.

Hercule Poirot is known as the greatest sleuth ever, with the exception of Sherlock Holmes. He was born in about 1844, fourteen years after Belgium had broken away from Holland. He died in 1974, in a book called <u>Curtain</u>, his admirable qualities not in the least dimmed. No one knew his exact age because he was always reluctant to reveal it. Poirot's last words were "cher ami," which he whispered to his associate of many years, Hastings. These words were most fitting considering that he had begun his infallible career with the words, "mon ami, Hastings."[6]

Hercule's unique personality and character set I
him apart from other fictional detectives. One of the memorable features of his personality and character was his physical appearance. He was "a diminutive five foot four inches tall and slender."[7] His hair was an "unrepentant" black, neatly groomed with hair tonic. His upper lip displayed his pride

[5] Murdoch, p. 92.

[6] H. R. F. Keating, "A Sleuth For All Seasons," <u>The Saturday Evening Post</u>, March 1978, p. 41.

[7] O. L. Bailey, "On the Docket," <u>Saturday Review of the Arts</u>, Jan. 1973, p. 87.

Bailey, p. 87 — Hercule Poirot's looks

He had catlike eyes that grew greener as the solution to a crime became clearer. Poirot has been referred to as a "mustachioed Humpty-Dumpty."

Keating, p. 103 — Hercule Poirot's looks

He was an "extraordinary looking little man, who carried himself with immense dignity."

His outfit mostly consisted of the same items: black jacket, striped pants, bow tie, overcoat, muffler, dazzling patent leather boots.

Duffy, p. 88 — Personality traits of H.P.

Boundless egotism and arrogance. In Curtain he belittles Hastings: "Since you cannot use your grey cells as you do not possess them, use your eyes, your ears and your nose if need be insofar as the dictates of honor allow."

Excessive pride in his "waxlike mustache," which he was constantly grooming.

3

and joy and his most distinctive feature, a small black handlebar mustache.[8] He had catlike eyes that grew greener as the solution to a crime drew near and a head the shape of an egg. Thus Poirot has been referred to as a "mustachioed Humpty Dumpty."[9] This "extraordinary looking little man, who carried himself with immense dignity," almost always wore the same outfit, consisting of a black jacket, striped pants, a bow tie, and, in all but the hottest weather, an overcoat and muffler. He also wore patent leather boots that almost always displayed a dazzling shine.[10]

Another characteristic feature of Poirot was his boundless egotism and arrogance. He was convinced beyond doubt that he was the greatest detective of all time -- a fact that he announced to everyone. In _Curtain_, where as usual he was paired up with Captain Hastings, he reveals his arrogance by belittling the Captain, to whom he sneers: "Since you cannot use your grey cells as you do not possess them, use your eyes, your ears and your nose if need be insofar as the dictates of honor allow."[11] Another focus of Poirot's overweening pride was his black "waxlike mustache," which he groomed constantly.[12] Despite his arrogance, Poirot was im-

[8] Keating, pp. 41, 103.

[9] Bailey, p. 87.

[10] Keating, p. 103.

[11] Martha Duffy, "The Sweet Sleuth Gone," _Time_, 15 Sept. 1975, p. 88.

[12] Duffy, p. 88.

My own observation — Personality traits of H.P.

He was impeccably polite, even to the criminal.

He often says, "merci," "excusez-moi," "I beg your pardon."

Keating, p. 103 — Personality traits of H.P.

Eccentric mannerisms:

1. Extravagant gestures. (Once he knocked the suspected murderer's girlfriend's glasses off her nose, replacing them with a pair belonging to the real murderer without her noticing—confirming that she in fact was the real murderer).
2. Eccentric speech—switching from French to English
3. Often demolished the language of Shakespeare.

Duffy, p. 88 — Personality traits of H.P.

Normally Poirot intermittently used broken English. But whenever he announced the solution to a crime, he did so in beautifully correct English.

4

peccably polite, never breaking the rules of acceptable conduct and always performing the courtesies required by society. "Merci," "excusez-moi," "I beg your pardon" were part of his standard vocabulary. Even when he had determined who the criminal was, that person would be treated with as much deference as a law-abiding duke or duchess.

Perhaps Poirot's most characteristic feature was his eccentric mannerisms.[13] He often horrified British society by gesturing extravagantly while speaking. Once, while conversing with the suspected murderer's girlfriend, he accidentally knocked her sunglasses off her nose. When, however, she did not notice that he replaced them with a pair worn by the real murderer, he confirmed his "already formed hypothesis" that she in fact was the murderer.[14] His speech was unforgettably eccentric.[15] He would switch from French to English while speaking and was known to demolish the language of Shakespeare. In his normal speech he would often use broken French or English, but would switch to beautiful and correct English when announcing the solution to a crime.[16] The amazing fact about Poirot is that despite his exaggerated narcissism and his queer habits, he is somehow believable. Each reader has the freedom to imagine Poirot the way he wants to see him, and though two individual readers may have two

[13] Keating, p. 103.

[14] Keating, p. 103.

[15] Keating, p. 103.

[16] Duffy, p. 88.

Ulam, p. 23 <u>Hercule Poirot's techniques</u>

Ulam states that if, like Poirot, we had used common sense and logic (our "little grey cells") to handle the Cuban missile crisis and the Vietnam war, we might have been spared the suffering of the last decade. But, instead, we consulted "stultifying models" in the form of our "best and brightest professors."

Duffy, p. 88 <u>Hercule Poirot's techniques</u>

Poirot suspected everyone and believed no one until the case was completely solved. He never allowed himself to become biased.

<u>Hercule Poirot's techniques</u>

Cite the Buckley case in <u>Peril at End House</u> as an example of Poirot's use of logic and deductive reasoning to solve a crime.

5

disparate views of Poirot, for both of them he will fulfill their highest expectations of a top-notch sleuth.[17]

Hercule Poirot's techniques of solving crimes made him one of fiction's superb detectives. Poirot always relied on common sense and logic to solve his cases. In discussing Poirot's techniques, Adam Ulam states that it would have been helpful if the United States had used his techniques in handling the Cuban missile crisis and the Chinest Communist invasion of Southeast Asia. We should have consulted our "little grey cells" and used our common sense instead of consulting our "best and brightest professors." If, like Poirot, we had used our common sense rather than trust "stultifying models," we might have been spared many of the travails of the recent past.[18] II

One of Poirot's methods of approach was to suspect everybody and not believe a word that was spoken until the case was completely solved.[19] For example, in <u>The Peril at End House</u>, Poirot's client, Miss Buckley, the supposed victim of several near-deaths, was actually the murderess. Because she had supposedly been shot at, she sent for her cousin to come and comfort her. Her cousin was then shot and killed, supposedly being mistaken for the original victim. As the plot unfolds, the unsuspecting reader finds out that the cousin was ac-

[17] Murdoch, p. 89.

[18] Adam Ulam, "Murder and Class," <u>The New Republic</u>, 31 July 1976, p. 23.

[19] Duffy, p. 88.

Grant, p. 20 — Hercule Poirot's techniques

Step-by-step process

He starts with the barest facts and keeps discovering more facts until the truth appears.

Poirot does not rely on physical clues as much as Sherlock Holmes.

Poirot likes to think, think, think—ponder the evidence.

Grant, p. 108 — Hercule Poirot's techniques

In Third Girl Poirot gets confused by the mass of evidence. So he just sits and sifts the evidence through his "little grey cells" until the pieces all fit.

Grant, p. 108 — Hercule Poirot's techniques

Poirot considered himself a specialist "because each of his cases required a mixture of mathematical precision and applied psychology."

6

tually shot by Miss Buckley, the supposed victim. By deductive reasoning and close observation, Poirot finally figured out this crime. He always claimed that no crime was impossible to solve. This egotistical Belgian used a step-by-step reasoning process, and he never rushed into a case. He just started with the barest facts available and kept discovering more facts until the truth came to light. Unlike Sherlock Holmes, who used a magnifying glass and searched around for every possible clue, Poirot solved his cases with more than just the use of physical evidence.[20] He liked to sit and sip his chocolate while he sifted through the information in his head. The reader often observes him in deep thought sitting on the beach, in a train compartment, or at his desk -- reviewing the facts and poring over the evidence -- thinking, pondering.[21] For instance, in _Third Girl_, there were many times when Poirot was so confused about the case that he would just sit and run all the information through his head until he stumbled upon a clue that he could pursue profitably. In working on these clues he used the "little grey cells," a phrase that emphasized his brainy use of common sense and logic and became his famous trademark. Poirot considered himself a specialist "because each of his cases required a mixture of mathematical precision and applied psychology."[22] The combi-

[20] Ellsworth Grant, "A Tribute to Agatha Christie," _Horizon_, Autumn 1976, p. 108.

[21] Grant, p. 108.

[22] Grant, p. 108.

Murdoch, p. 98 Christie and Poirot

Christie was determined not to model Poirot after the famous Sherlock Holmes. The problem was that Doyle had "picked such an effective formula that it was difficult not to move in his wake."

Murdoch, p. 63 Christie and Poirot

Christie was not satisfied when actors tried to play the part of Poirot. (In the plays adapted from her books, she deleted the part of Poirot.)

Murdoch, p. 63 Christie and Poirot

Christie was always "profoundly unhappy at the striking difference between the appearance of any actor considered an attractive box office name to play Poirot and her own distinct image of what her detective looked like. For example, the last man who played Poirot on the London stage was Francis J. Sullivan, a man who was six foot one inch tall."

7

nation of his methods of solving crime helped him become one of the greatest of all detectives.

In time, Hercule Poirot began to become so much III
a part of Agatha Christie that to think of her was to think of Poirot as well. In inventing her little detective, Christie claims that she tried to make him distinct from any other detective, especially from Sir Arthur Conan Doyle's Sherlock Holmes. The problem she faced was that Doyle had "picked such an effective formula that it was difficult not to move in his wake."[23]

Christie had such a vivid mental image of Poirot that she had a hard time seeing any actor try to portray him.[24] In three plays adapted from her books, she deleted the part of Poirot. According to the critic Merrick Murdoch, she could not trust a hack writer to make his dialogue sound like Poirot. Murdoch also mentions that Christie was always

> profoundly unhappy at the striking difference between the appearance of any actor considered an attractive box office name to play Poirot and her own distinct image of what her detective looked like. For example, the last man who played Poirot on the London stage was Francis J. Sullivan, a man who was six foot one inch tall.[25]

As the years passed, Agatha Christie began to be recognized not only as a general mystery writer

[23] Murdoch, p. 98.

[24] Murdoch, p. 63.

[25] Murdoch, ph 63.

Christie, p. 268 | Christie and Poirot

As the years passed, Christie was seen more and more as the creator of Hastings and Poirot.

Christie, p. 263 | Christie and Poirot

Eventually, Poirot became such a vital part of Christie's life that she often felt him as a living presence—a presence that grew too real and became her "Belgian invention hanging around her neck, firmly attached there like the albatross of the 'Ancient Mariner.'"

Christie, p. 421 | Christie and Poirot

When Michael Morton was turning *The Murder of Roger Ackroyd* into a play, he suggested turning Poirot into a young "Beau Poirot" so that the girls could fall in love with him. Christie stubbornly refused. She realized how much she liked Poirot just as she had created him.

8

but specifically as the creator of Hastings and Poirot.[26] She herself admits to having felt the physical presence of Hercule Poirot, a presence that grew almost too real. Often when talking to her husband, Archie, at home, the presence of a third party seemed to intrude and to demand attention. It was her "Belgian invention hanging around her neck, firmly attached there like the albatross of the 'Ancient Mariner'."[27] When Michael Morton was adapting The Murder of Roger Ackroyd, one of Christie's popular stories, for the stage, he suggested taking twenty years off her creation, calling him "Beau Poirot" and making the girls fall in love with him. Christie stubbornly refused, and at this point realized how much she liked Poirot and how much a part of her life he had become.[28]

Despite Christie's artistic involvement with Poirot, she began to get tired of him as time passed and he kept reappearing regularly. She sensed, quite correctly, that he had become an anachronism, a thing of the past. Her common sense told her that no modern person of consequence would take an interesting crime to an investigator, and she doubted whether an investigator could even make a decent living.[29] Furthermore, she began to feel that her readers preferred books about present-day life to

[26] Agatha Christie, An Autobiography (New York: Dodd, Mead & Company, 1977), p. 268.

[27] Christie, p. 263.

[28] Christie, p. 421.

[29] Murdoch, p. 92.

Murdoch, p. 92 The end of Poirot

Christie eventually tired of Poirot. Also, her common sense told her that he had become an anachronism. Interesting crimes were no longer taken to private investigators. Thus Poirot vanished, to be replaced by Miss Jane Marple.

My own observation Conclusion

Christie was an exceptional woman.
Loved her profession
Prolific writer (one book per year)
Still had time for plays, short stories, and travel
Considered one of the best detective story writers of all time

9

books about the past and that some new protagonist needed to be invented. Thus Hercule Poirot simply vanished from Christie's books as quickly as he had surfaced, to be replaced by an equally popular sleuth, the spinster Miss Jane Marple.[30]

Dame Agatha Christie was an exceptional woman, who loved her profession. She averaged one book a year, but somehow still found time to visit different places, write plays and short stories, and accept various awards. She was, and still is, considered one of the best detective-story writers of all time, and Hercule Poirot was the character who brought her the most fame. His unique personality and techniques of solving crime made him one of the most memorable fictional detectives ever invented.

[30] Murdoch, p. 92.

Notes

[1] "Dame Agatha: Queen of the Maze," Time, 26 Jan. 1976, p. 75.

[2] "Dame Agatha," p. 75.

[3] Derrick Murdoch, The Agatha Christie Mystery (Toronto: Pagurian Press Limited, 1976), p. 20.

[4] "Dame Agatha," p. 75.

[5] Murdoch, p. 92.

[6] H. R. F. Keating, "A Sleuth For All Seasons," The Saturday Evening Post, March 1978, p. 41.

[7] O. L. Bailey, "On the Docket," Saturday Review of the Arts, Jan. 1973, p. 87.

[8] Keating, pp. 41, 103.

[9] Bailey, p. 87.

[10] Keating, p. 103.

[11] Martha Duffy, "The Sweet Sleuth Gone," Time, 15 Sept. 1975, p. 88.

[12] Duffy, p. 88.

[13] Keating, p. 103.

[14] Keating, p. 103.

[15] Keating, p. 103.

[16] Duffy, p. 88.

[17] Murdoch, p. 89.

[18] Adam Ulam, "Murder and Class," The New Republic, 31 July 1976, p. 23.

[19] Duffy, p. 88.

[20] Ellsworth Grant, "A Tribute to Agatha Christie," Horizon, Autumn 1976, p. 108.

[21] Grant, p. 108.

[22] Grant p. 108.

[23] Murdoch, p. 98.

[24] Murdoch, p. 63.

[25] Murdoch, p. 63.

[26] Agatha Christie, An Autobiography (New York: Dodd, Mead & Company, 1977), p. 268.

[27] Christie, p. 263.

[28] Christie, p. 421.

[29] Murdoch, p. 92.

[30] Murdoch, p. 92.

Bibliography

Bailey, O. L. "On the Docket." *Saturday Review of the Arts*, Jan. 1973, pp. 87–89.

Christie, Agatha. *An Autobiography*. New York: Dodd, Mead & Company, 1977.

Duffy, Martha. "The Sweet Sleuth Gone." *Time*, 15 Sept. 1975, pp. 88, 90.

Grant, Ellsworth. "A Tribute to Agatha Christie." *Horizon*, Autumn 1976, pp. 106–09.

Keating, H. R. F. "A Sleuth for All Seasons." *The Saturday Evening Post*, March 1978, pp. 41, 100, 103, 105–07.

Murdoch, Derrick. *The Agatha Christie Mystery*. Toronto: Pagurian Press Limited, 1976.

Ulam, Adam. "Murder and Class." *The New Republic*, 31 July 1976, pp. 21–23.

"Dame Agatha: Queen of the Maze." *Time*, 26 Jan. 1976, p. 75.

SAMPLE PAGES WITH NEW-STYLE
PARENTHETICAL DOCUMENTATION

Mitch McDiffett
Professor McCuen
English 101
December 18, 1983

Agatha Christie's Hercule Poirot

Dame Agatha Christie (1891–1976) has been called "Queen of the Maze," "The Mistress of Murder," and a "Woman with God-like Genius" (Time, 26 Jan. 1976, 75). She earned over twenty million dollars, more money made on murder by any woman since Lucrezia Borgia. A Dame of the British Empire, her accomplishments include eighty-three books, seventeen plays, nine volumes of short stories, an autobiographical report about her experiences on a field study with her archeologist husband, the longest running play in theatrical history (Mousetrap), and the creation of two famous fictional detectives, Miss Jane Marple and Hercule Poirot (Time 75).

Dame Agatha wrote her first book in the early 1920's after she was challenged by her sister to write a mystery with an unguessable solution (Murdoch 20). This book, The Mysterious Affair at Styles, introduced her most famous creation, Hercule Poirot, a retired police officer from Belgium (Time 75). In the thirties, after writing about Poirot for ten years, she began to tire of him, so she created a new character, Miss Jane Marple, an old spinster lady who enjoyed solving crimes (Murdoch 92). Although Christie eventually tired of her greatest creation, Hercule Poirot, his unique personality and techniques of solving crimes made him one of the finest and most loved fictional detectives of all time.

With the exception of Sherlock Holmes, declared the critic H. R. F. Keating (41), Hercule Poirot was known as the greatest sleuth ever. Keating goes on to say that Poirot was born in about 1844, fourteen years after Belgium had broken away from Holland. He died in 1974, in a book called Curtain, at the ripe old age of 130, his admirable qualities not in the least dimmed. No one knew his exact age because he was always reluctant to reveal it. Poirot's last words were, "cher ami," which he whispered to his sidekick of many years, Hastings. These words were most fitting considering that he had begun his infallible career with the words, "mon ami, Hastings" (Keating 41).

Hercule Poirot's unique personality and character set him apart from other fictional detectives. One of the memorable features of his personality and character was his physical appearance. He was "a diminutive five foot four inches tall and slender" (Bailey 87). His hair was an "unrepentant" black, neatly groomed with hair tonic. His upper lip displayed his pride and joy and his most distinctive feature, a small black handlebar mustache (Keating 41, 103). He had catlike eyes that grew greener as the solution to a crime drew near and a head the shape of an egg. Thus Poirot has been referred to as a "mustachioed Humpty Dumpty" (Bailey 87). This "extraordinary looking little man, who carried himself with immense dignity," almost always wore the same outfit, consisting of a black jacket, striped pants, a bow tie, and, if weather permitted, an overcoat and muffler. He also wore patent leather boots that almost always displayed a dazzling shine (Keating 103).

Bibliography

Baily, O. L. "On the Docket." Saturday Review of the Arts 11 (Jan. 1973):87–89.

Christie, Agatha. An Autobiography. New York: Dodd, Mead & Company, 1977.

Duffy, Martha. "The Sweet Sleuth Gone." Time (15 Sept. 1975):88, 90.

Grant, Ellsworth. "A Tribute to Agatha Christie." Horizon 18 (Autumn 1976):106–09.

Keating, H. R. F. "A Sleuth for All Seasons" The Saturday Evening Post 31(March 1978):41, 100,103,105–07.

Murdoch, Derrick. The Agatha Christie Mystery. Toronto: Pagurian Press Limited, 1976.

Ulam, Adam. "Murder and Class." The New Republic (31 July 1976):21–23.

"Dame Agatha: Queen of the Maze." Time (26 Jan. 1976):75.

Select list of reference works

This list has been compiled to help you find general background material for your research paper. The list is in two main parts: general reference works and reference works in subject fields.

General reference works

Unabridged English-Language Dictionaries

Craigie, Sir William A., and James R. Hulbert, eds. *A Dictionary of American English on Historical Principles*. 4 vols. 2nd ed. Chicago: Univ. of Chicago Press, 1960.

Funk & Wagnalls New Standard Dictionary of the English Language. New York: Funk & Wagnalls, 1980.

Murray, Sir James A. H., et al., eds. *A New English Dictionary on Historical Principles*. 13 vols. New York: Oxford Univ. Press, 1888–1933.

The Oxford English Dictionary. 12 vols. London: Oxford Univ. Press, 1961. Supplements in progress.

Random House Dictionary of the English Language. New York: Random House, 1966.

Webster's New International Dictionary of the English Language. 2nd ed. Springfield, Mass.: G & C. Merriam, 1959. The third edition (1961) contains many thousands of new expressions, but for all-round use the second edition is preferred by many teachers.

Abridged English-Language Dictionaries

The American College Dictionary. rev. ed. New York: Random House, 1957.

The American Heritage Dictionary. Boston: Houghton Mifflin, 1981.

Funk & Wagnalls Standard College Dictionary. rev. ed. New York: Funk & Wagnalls, 1980.

Random House Dictionary. New York: Random House, 1980.

The Concise Oxford Dictionary, 6th ed., Oxford, Eng.: The Clarendon Press, 1976.

The Shorter Oxford English Dictionary. 3rd ed., rev. Oxford, Eng.: The Clarendon Press, 1959. Also known as *The Oxford Universal Dictionary,* this one-volume work is based on the "historical principles" that distinguish the larger work in thirteen volumes.

Webster's New Collegiate Dictionary. 8th ed. Springfield, Mass.: G. & C. Merriam, 1973.

General Encyclopedias

The Encyclopaedia Britannica. 30 vols. Chicago: Encyclopaedia Britannica, 1980.

The Encyclopedia Americana. 30 vols. New York: Grolier, 1982.

General Indexes

Annual Magazine Subject Index: A Subject Index to American and English Periodicals. 43 vols. Comp. F. W. Faxon. Boston: Boston Book, 1908–52. Ceased publication.

Book Review Digest. New York: H. W. Wilson, 1946– . Monthly, except February and July.

International Index. New York: H. W. Wilson, 1913– . Quarterly with annual and two-year cumulations. First published (1907) as a supplement to the *Readers' Guide* in order to index more scholarly and technical periodicals. Since 1955 it has carried the subtitle, "A Guide to Periodicals in the Social Sciences and the Humanities."

New York Times Index. New York: The New York Times, 1913– . Semi-monthly, with annual cumulations.

Nineteenth-Century Readers' Guide to Periodical Literature, 1890–1899. 2 vols. New York: H. W. Wilson, 1944. Author and subject index to some fifty periodicals published in the 1890s.

Readers' Guide to Periodical Literature. New York: H. W. Wilson, 1900– . Semimonthly from September to June, monthly in July and August, with annual and five-year cumulations. Indexes about 125 periodicals of a general nature, by author, title, and subject. Scientific periodicals have been included since 1953.

Biographical Aids—Living Persons

Biography Index: A Cumulative Index to Biographical Material in Books and Magazines. New York: H. W. Wilson, 1947– . Quarterly, with annual and three-year cumulations.

Current Biography: Who's News and Why. New York: H. W. Wilson, 1940– . Monthly, except in August, with annual cumulation.

Webster's Biographical Dictionary. Springfield, Mass.: Merriam, 1972.

Who's Who in America. Chicago: A. N. Marquis, 1899– . Biennial. Includes noteworthy persons in all fields.

Who's Who of American Women. Chicago: A. N. Marquis, 1958– . Issued biennially.

World Biography. 5th ed. Bethpage, N.Y.: Institute for Research in Biography, 1954.

In addition to the foregoing, there are "who's who" publications by country, by region, by race, and by profession.

Biographical Aids—Persons No Longer Living

Dictionary of American Biography. Published under the auspices of the American Council of Learned Societies. 21 vols. New York: Scribner's, 1928–46. Supplements 1–4, 1944–74.

Dictionary of National Biography. Ed. Leslie Stephen and Sidney Lee. 63 vols. London: Smith, Elder, 1885–1900. Supplements at ten-year intervals; the latest, covering 1941–50, published in 1959. Includes notable persons of Great Britain and the colonies from the earliest historical period.

Who Was Who in America. Chicago: A. N. Marquis, 1967. Covers the years 1607–1896.

Atlases and Gazetteers

Collocott, T. C. and J. O. Thorne, eds. *Macmillan World Gazetteer and Geographical Dictionary.* rev. ed. New York: Macmillan, 1957.

Encyclopaedia Britannica World Atlas. Chicago: Encyclopaedia Britannica, 1970.

Goode, John Paul. *Goode's World Atlas.* 13th ed. Chicago: Rand McNally, 1970. Frequently revised.

Rand McNally Standard World Atlas. Chicago: Rand McNally, 1958.

The Atlas of the Earth. London: Mitchell Beazley Ltd., 1972.

Miscellaneous Handbooks and Yearbooks

Bartlett, John, ed. *Familiar Quotations.* 14th ed., completely rev. Boston: Little, Brown, 1980.

Collier's Year Book. New York: Collier, 1938– .

Great Treasury of Western Thought, Ed. Mortimer Adler and Charles van Doren. New York: Bowker, 1977. Contains statements by great western thinkers.

Kane, Joseph N. *Famous First Facts.* rev. and enl. ed. New York: H. W. Wilson, 1950.

The Oxford Dictionary of Quotations. 3rd ed. New York: Oxford Univ. Press, 1979. Popularity, not necessarily merit, has determined the quotations contained.

Peterson, Houston, ed. *A Treasury of the World's Great Speeches.* New York: Simon & Schuster, 1965.

Statesman's Yearbook. New York: Macmillan, 1864– . Gives statistical and historical information about the countries of the world and about international organizations such as NATO and the United Nations.

World Almanac and Book of Facts. New York: World Telegram and Sun, 1868– .

Bibliographies

American Book Publishing Record. New York: R. R. Bowker, 1960– . Monthly. Provides a complete record of American books published.

American Book Publishing Record Annual Cumulatives. New York: R. R. Bowker. Annual volumes.

N. W. Ayer & Son's Directory of Newspapers and Periodicals. Philadelphia: N. W. Ayer & Son, 1880– . Annually. Covers the United States and its possessions, Canada, Bermuda, Panama, and the Philippines.

Books in Print. 3 vols.: Author, Title, Subject. New York: R. R. Bowker, 1957– . Annual.

The Bibliographic Index. New York: H. W. Wilson, 1938– . Semiannual. Includes foreign-language works.

Publishers' Weekly. New York: Publishers' Weekly, 1872– . Includes both books published and those announced for publication.

Ulrich's International Periodicals Directory. 21st ed. New York: R. R. Bowker, 1982. Includes foreign periodicals.

Winchell, Constance M. *Guide to Reference Books*. 9th ed. Chicago: American Library Assn., 1951. Supplements, in progress.

Government Publications

Boyd, Anne Morris, and Rae E. Rips. *United States Government Publications*. 3rd ed., rev. New York: H. W. Wilson, 1950.
Explains the nature, distribution, catalogs, and indexes of U.S. Government publications; lists and describes important publications of departments of the U.S. Government: the executive, legislative, and judicial branches, Congress, the Courts, etc.

U.S. Superintendent of Documents. *United States Government Publications, Monthly Catalog*. Washington, D.C.: U.S. Government Printing Office, 1895– .

Subject fields

Fine Arts—Dance and Drama

Baker, Blanch, M. *Theatre and Allied Arts: A Guide to Books Dealing with the History, Criticism, and Technic of the Drama and Theatre and Allied Arts and Crafts*. New York: H. W. Wilson, 1952.

Dramatic Index. Boston: Boston Book, 1910–49. Now published as Part II of the Annual Magazine Subject Index. Ceased publication. Good for articles about the history of the stage.

Ewen, David, ed. *Complete Book of American Musical Theater*. New York: Holt, 1958. Pertinent information concerning more than three hundred productions since 1886.

Gassner, John and Edward Quinn. *The Reader's Encyclopedia of World Drama.* New York: Crowell, 1979.

Hartnoll, Phyllis. *The Oxford Companion to the Theatre.* 3rd ed. New York: Oxford Univ. Press, 1967.

Logasa, Hannah. *Index to One-Act Plays,* 1900–1924. Boston: F. W. Faxon, 1924. Four supplements cover the period from 1924 to 1957.

Nicoll, Allardyce. *A History of English Drama,* 1660–1900. 6 vols. rev. ed. Cambridge, Eng.: Cambridge Univ. Press, 1952–59.

Shipley, Joseph T. *Guide to Great Plays.* Washington, D.C.: Public Affairs Press, 1956. Covers all periods, giving history, production, themes, casts.

Fine Arts—Music

Apel, Willi. *Harvard Dictionary of Music.* Rev. enl. ed. Cambridge, Mass.: Harvard Univ. Press, 1969.

Baker, Theodore, *Biographical Dictionary of Musicians.* 6th ed., completely rev. by Nicholas Slonimsky, New York: G. Schirmer, 1978.

Duckles, Vincent, et al. *Guide to Reference Materials on Music.* 3rd ed. Berkeley, Calif.: Univ. of California Press, 1974.

Ewen, David. *Living Musicians.* New York: H. W. Wilson, 1940. First supplement, 1957. Lists the most important works of each composer, with biographical information.

——. *Ewen's Musical Masterworks.* 2nd ed. New York: Arco, 1954. Includes every field of music; summarizes plots of operas and evaluates composers and their works.

——, ed. *Complete Book of American Musical Theater.* New York: Holt, 1958.

Feather, Leonard G. *Encyclopedia of Jazz.* New York: Horizon Press, 1960.

New Grove *Dictionary of Music and Musicians.* 20 vols. Ed. Stanley Sadie. New York: Macmillan, 1980.

Music Index. Detroit: Information Service, 1949– . Monthly, with annual cumulations.

New Oxford History of Music. Vols 1–5 (additional volumes in progress). London: Oxford Univ. Press, 1974– .

Scholes, Percy A. *The Oxford Companion to Music.* 10th ed., completely rev. New York: Oxford Univ. Press, 1970. Covers all phases of music, with long encyclopedic articles, including some 1,500 biographies.

Song Index: An Index to More than 12,000 Songs. Comp. Minnie E. Sears and Phyllis Crawford. New York: H. W. Wilson, 1926. Supplement. New York: H. W. Wilson, 1966.

Thompson, Oscar. *International Cyclopedia of Music and Musicians.* 5th ed., rev. and enl. by Nicholas Slonimsky. New York: Dodd, Mead, 1949.

Fine Arts—Painting, Sculpture, and Architecture

American Art Annual. Washington, D.C.: American Federation of Arts, 1898– .

Art Index, New York: H. W. Wilson, 1933– . Quarterly with annual and two-year cumulations. Includes both fine and applied arts.

Chamberlin, Mary W. *Guide to Art Reference Books*. Chicago: American Library Assn., 1959.

Encyclopedia of Painting. Ed. Bernard S. Myers, New York: Crown, 1955.

Encyclopedia of World Art. New York: McGraw-Hill, 1959–68. 15 vols. A comprehensive work, covering all phases of art.

Gardner, Helen, *Art Through the Ages*. 7th ed. Revised by Horst de la Croix and Richard G. Tansey. New York: Harcourt Brace Jovanovich, 1980.

Monro, Isabel S., and Kate M. Monro. *Index to Reproductions of American Paintings*. New York: H. W. Wilson, 1964.

——. *Index to Reproductions of European Paintings*. New York: H. W. Wilson, 1956.

Reinach, S(alomon). *Apollo: An Illustrated History of Art throughout the Ages*. Completely rev., with a new chapter by the author. New York: Scribner's, 1935.

Upjohn, Everard M., Paul S. Wingert, and Jane G. Mahler. *History of World Art*. 2nd ed., rev. and enl. New York: Oxford Univ. Press, 1958.

Who's Who in American Art. New York: R. R. Bowker, 1937– . Includes bibliographies of both American and Canadian artists, with a geographical index and a list of open exhibitions.

Poetry

Arms, George, and Joseph M. Kuntz. *Poetry Explication: A Checklist of Interpretations since 1925 of British and American Poems Past and Present*. New York: Swallow Press and Morrow, 1950.

Courthope, William J. *A History of English Poetry*. 6 vols. New York: Macmillan, 1895–1910. A standard work.

Granger's Index to Poetry. Ed. William J. Smith. 4th ed. New York: Columbia Univ. Press, 1953. Supplements in progress.

Granger's Index to Poetry and Recitations. 3rd ed., Chicago: A. C. McClurg, 1940. Indexes both standard and popular collections. Supplements in progress.

Sell, Violet, et al., comps. *Subject Index to Poetry for Children and Young People*. Chicago: American Library Assn., 1957.

Tate, Allen. *Sixty American Poets, 1896–1944*. rev. ed. Washington, D.C.: Library of Congress, General Reference and Bibliographic Division, 1954. Includes bibliographies of their writings.

Literature

Baker, Ernest A. *The History of the English Novel*. 11 vols. London: H. F. and G. Witherly, 1977.

Baker, Ernest A., and James Packman, eds., *A Guide to the Best Fiction, English and American, including Translations from Foreign Languages*. new and enl. ed. London: G. Routledge, 1967. Includes an index of authors, titles, subjects, historical names and allusions, places, characters, and so forth.

Baugh, Albert C., ed. *A Literary History of England*. New York: Appleton-Century-Crofts, 1948.

Bell, Inglis F., and Donald Baird. *The English Novel, 1578–1956: A Checklist of Twentieth-Century Criticisms*. Denver: A. Swallow, 1959.

Benét, William Rose, ed. *The Reader's Encyclopedia*. 2nd ed. New York: Thomas Y. Crowell Company, 1965. Deals with world literature and the arts and includes mythology and legend.

Blanck, Jacob. *Bibliography of American Literature*. New Haven, Conn.: Yale Univ. Press, 1955– . Work in progress.

Bond, Donald F. *A Reference Guide to English Studies*. 2nd ed. Chicago: Univ. of Chicago Press, 1971.

The Cambridge Bibliography of English Literature. Ed. F. W. Bateson. 4 vols. Cambridge, Eng.: Cambridge Univ. Press; New York: Macmillan, 1941. Supplements in progress.

Cassell's Encyclopedia of World Literature. Ed. J. Buchanan Brown. 3 vols. London: Cassell, 1973.

Coan, Otis W., and Richard G. Lillard. *America in Fiction: An Annotated List of Novels that Interpret Aspects of Life in the United States*. 5th ed. Stanford, Calif.: Stanford Univ. Press, 1966.

Columbia Dictionary of Modern European Literature. Ed. Horatio Smith. New York: Columbia Univ. Press, 1947. Treats only the literature of continental Europe of the twentieth century and immediately before.

The Concise Cambridge Bibliography of English Literature, 600–1950. Ed. George Watson. Cambridge, Eng.: Cambridge Univ. Press, 1958.

Dickinson, Asa D. *The World's Best Books*. New York: H. W. Wilson, 1953.

Fiction Catalog: Seventh Edition, 1960: A List of 4,097 Works of Fiction in the English Language, with Annotations. Ed. Estelle A. Fidell and Esther V. Flory. New York: H. W. Wilson, 1961. First published in 1908. Annual supplements, cumulated periodically.

Hackett, Alice Payne. *Sixty Years of Best Sellers, 1895–1955*. New York: R. R. Bowker, 1956.

Hart, James D. *The Oxford Companion to American Literature*. 4th ed., New York: Oxford Univ. Press, 1965.

Harvey, Sir Paul. *The Oxford Companion to Classical Literature*. Oxford, Eng.: The Clarendon Press, 1961.

——. *The Oxford Companion to English Literature*. 4th ed. Oxford, Eng.: The Clarendon Press, 1967.

Kunitz, Stanley J., and Howard Haycraft, eds. *American Authors, 1600–1900*. New York: H. W. Wilson, 1938.

——. *British Authors before 1800*. New York: H. W. Wilson, 1952.

——. *British Authors of the Nineteenth Century*. New York: H. W. Wilson, 1936.

——. *The Junior Book of Authors*. 2nd ed. New York: H. W. Wilson, 1951.

——. *Twentieth Century Authors*. New York: H. W. Wilson, 1959.

Literary History of the United States. Ed. Robert E. Spiller et al. 4th ed. New York: Macmillan, 1978. Supplements in progress.

Magill, Frank N., ed. *Masterplots*. New York: Salem Press, 1955– . Updated annually.

Modern Language Association of America. *MLA International Bibliography of Books and Articles on the Modern Languages and Literature*. New York: Modern Language Association, 1921– .

The Oxford History of English Literature. Ed. Frank P. Wilson and Bonamy Dobree, New York: Oxford Univ. Press, 1945– . Supplements in progress.

Shipley, Joseph T., ed. *Dictionary of World Literature*. New York: Philosophical Library, 1943.

——. *Encyclopedia of Literature*, 2 vols. New York: Philosophical Library, 1946.

Short Story Index: An Index to 60,000 Stories in 4,320 Collections. Comp. Dorothy E. Cook and Isabel S. Monro. New York: H. W. Wilson, 1953. Supplements in progress.

Thrall, William F., and Addison Hibbard, eds. *A Handbook to Literature*. 3rd ed. New York: The Odyssey Press, 1980. Explains terminology of literary study and includes an outline of the literary history of England and America.

Van Doren, Carl C. *The American Novel*, 1789–1939. 2nd ed. New York: Macmillan, 1940.

Myth and Folklore

Benét, William Rose, ed. *The Reader's Encyclopedia*. 2nd ed. New York: Thomas Y. Crowell Company, 1965.

Diehl, Katherine S. *Religions, Mythologies, Folklores: An Annotated Bibliography*. 2nd ed. New York: Scarecrow Press, 1962.

Frazer, Sir James G. *The Golden Bough: A Study in Magic and Religion*. 12 vols. 3rd ed. New York: Macmillan, 1907–15. See also: *Aftermath: A Supplement to*

"The Golden Bough." New York: Macmillan, 1936. And an abridgment, *The New Golden Bough*. Ed. Theodore H. Gaster, New York: Criterion Books, 1959.

Harvey, Sir Paul. *The Oxford Companion to Classical Literature*. Oxford, Eng.: The Clarendon Press, 1961. Includes Greek and Roman mythology.

Hastings, James, ed. *Encyclopaedia of Religion and Ethics* . . . 13 vols. in 7. New York: Scribner's, 1928. Includes mythology and folklore.

Larousse Encyclopedia of Mythology. New York: Prometheus Press, 1959. Worldwide in coverage.

Mythology of All Races. Ed. Louis H. Gray and John A. MacCulloch. 13 vols. Boston: Marshall Jones, 1916–32.

Thompson, Stith. *Motif-Index of Folk Literature: A Classification of Narrative Elements in Folktales, Ballads, Myths, Fables, Mediaeval Romances* . . . 6 vols. rev. and enl. ed. Bloomington, Ind.: Indiana Univ. Press, 1955–58.

Philosophy and Psychology

Baldwin, James Mark. *Dictionary of Philosophy and Psychology*. 2nd ed. New York: Macmillan 1961.

Cattell, Jacques, ed. *American Men of Science*. 9th ed. New York: R. R. Bowker, 1956. Volume III: *The Social and Behavioral Sciences*.

Contributions to Modern Psychology: Selected Readings in General Psychology. Ed. Don E. Dulany et al. New York: Oxford Univ. Press. 1958.

Dictionary of Philosophy and Psychology. Ed. James M. Baldwin et al. 3 vols. new ed. New York: Macmillan, 1925–33. A work that is still useful, although it does not include modern developments.

Encyclopaedia of the Social Sciences. Ed. Edwin R. A. Seligman and Alvin Johnson. 15 vols. New York: Macmillan, 1930–35. A comprehensive work that brings out the relationships among the sciences. *The International Encyclopedia of the Social Sciences* complements this work.

English, Horace B., and Ava C. English. *A Comprehensive Dictionary of Psychological and Psychoanalytical Terms*. New York: Longmans, Green, 1958.

Good, Carter V., and Douglas E. Scates. *Methods of Research: Educational, Psychological, Sociological*. New York: Appleton-Century-Crofts, 1954.

Harriman, Philip L., ed. *Encyclopedia of Psychology*. 2nd ed. New York: Philosophical Library, 1965.

Harvard List of Books in Psychology. Ed. Edward G. Boring. Cambridge, Mass.: Harvard Univ. Press, 1955. Supplements in progress.

Louttit, Chauncey M. *Handbook of Psychological Literature*. Bloomington, Ind.: The Principia Press, 1932.

Miller, Hugh. *An Historical Introduction to Modern Philosophy.* New York: Macmillan, 1947.

Russell, Bertrand. *A History of Western Philosophy.* New York: Simon and Schuster, 1945.

Schneider, Herbert W. *A History of American Philosophy.* New York: Columbia Univ. Press, 1946.

Social Sciences Index. New York: Wilson, 1974– . Quarterly with annual cumulations.

Urmson, J. O., ed. *The Concise Encyclopedia of Western Philosophy and Philosophers*. New York: Hawthorn Books, 1960. Treats philosophy from Abelard to the present time; includes up-to-date bibliographies.

U.S. Library of Congress, Reference Department. *Philosophical Periodicals: An Annotated World List*. Washington, D.C.: U.S. Government Printing Office, 1952.

Religion

Attwater, Donald, ed. *The Catholic Encyclopaedic Dictionary.* New York: Macmillan, 1958.

Barrow, John G. *A Bibliography of Bibliographies in Religion*. Austin, Tex.: By the Author, 716 Brown Bldg., 1955.

The Catholic Encyclopedia: An International Work of Reference on the Constitution, Doctrine, Discipline, and History of the Catholic Church. 16 vols. New York: Catholic Encyclopedia Press, 1907–14. Supplements in progress.

Coulson, John, ed. *The Saints: A Concise Biographical Dictionary.* London: Burns and Oates, 1958.

Encyclopaedia of Religion and Ethics. Ed. James Hastings, et al. 12 vols. New York: Scribner, 1908–27.

Hastings, James, et al., eds. *Dictionary of the Bible*. 5 vols. New York: Scribner's, 1905–09.

Joy, Charles R., comp. *Harper's Topical Concordance*. New York: Harper & Brothers, 1940. Topical index of the King James version of the Bible.

Miller, Madeleine S., and J. Lane Miller. *Harper's Bible Dictionary.* 6th ed. New York: Harper & Brothers, 1959. Addresses all levels of readers.

The Oxford Dictionary of the Christian Church. Ed. F. L. Cross. New York: Oxford Univ. Press, 1957. Second corrected impression, 1958.

Schaff, Philip. *The New Schaff-Herzog Encyclopedia of Religious Knowledge . . .* Ed. Samuel Jackson et al. 12 vols. New York: Funk & Wagnalls, 1908–12. Supplements in progress.

Zaehner, Robert C., ed. *The Concise Encyclopedia of Living Faiths*. New York: Hawthorn Books, 1959.

Biological and Physical Sciences—General

The American Yearbook. Publisher varies, 1929– . Summarizes progress in the sciences.

Hawkins, Reginald R., ed. *Scientific, Medical, and Technical Books Published in the United States of America*. 2nd ed. New York: R. R. Bowker, 1958.

The McGraw-Hill Encyclopedia of Science and Technology. 4th ed. New York: McGraw-Hill, 1977. Supplements in progress.

Technical Book Review Index. New York: Special Libraries Assn., 1935– . Monthly, except July and August.

Biological Sciences

Agricultural Index. New York: H. W. Wilson, 1916– . Monthly.

Blake, Sidney F. *Geographical Guide to Floras of the World: An Annotated List with Special Reference to Universal Plants and Common Plant Names*. Washington, D.C.: U.S. Government Printing Office, 1942.

Cattell, Jacques, ed. *American Men of Science*. Vol. II: *The Biological Sciences*. 9th ed. New York: R. R. Bowker, 1956. Living persons.

Comstock, Anna B. *Handbook of Nature-Study*. 24th ed. New York: Comstock, 1939.

Henderson, Isabella F., and W. D. Henderson. *Dictionary of Scientific Terms . . . in Biology, Botany, Zoology, Anatomy, Cytology, Embryology, Physiology*. 4th ed., rev. by J. H. Kenneth. Princeton, N.J.: D. Van Nostrand, 1949.

Jordan, E. L. *Hammond's Nature Atlas of America*. New York: C. S. Hammond, 1952. For the layman nature lover.

Palmer, Ephraim L. *Fieldbook of Natural History*. New York: Whittlesey House, 1949.

Willis, J. C. *Dictionary of Flowering Plants and Ferns*. 6th ed., rev. Cambridge, Eng.: Cambridge Univ. Press, 1931.

Physical Sciences

American Institute of Physics Handbook. Ed. Dwight E. Gray et al. New York: McGraw-Hill, 1957.

Ballentyne, D. W. G., and L. E. Q. Walker. *A Dictionary of Named Effects and Laws in Chemistry, Physics, and Mathematics*. 2nd ed. New York: Macmillan, 1961.

Cattell, Jacques, ed. *American Men and Women of Science*. New York: R. R. Bowker, 1971– .

Condon, Edward U., and Hugh Odishaw. *Handbook of Physics*. New York: McGraw-Hill, 1958.

Considine, Douglas M. *Encyclopedia of Chemistry.* 4th ed. New York: Reinhold, 1983.

Gray, H. J., *Dictionary of Physics*. New York: Longmans, Green, 1958.

International Dictionary of Physics and Electronics. Ed. Walter C. Michels et al. 2nd ed. Princeton, N.J.: D. Van Nostrand, 1961.

Mellon, Melvin Guy. *Chemical Publications*. 3rd ed. New York: McGraw-Hill, 1958. A survey, with explanations of ways to use such publications to advantage.

U.S. Department of Interior, Bureau of Mines. *Minerals Yearbook*. Washington, D.C.: U.S. Government Printing Office, 1933– .

Social Sciences—General

Cattell, Jacques, ed. *American Men of Science*. Vol. III: *The Social and Behavioral Sciences*. 9th ed. New York: R. R. Bowker, 1956. Living persons.

Encyclopaedia of the Social Sciences. Ed. Edwin R. A. Seligman and Alvin Johnson. 15 vols. New York: Macmillan, 1930–35.

International Index. New York: H. W. Wilson, 1913– . Quarterly, with annual and two-year cumulations. First published (1907) as a supplement to the *Readers' Guide* in order to index more scholarly and technical periodicals. Since 1955 it has carried the subtitle, *A Guide to Periodicals in the Social Sciences and the Humanities*.

Zadrozny, John T., ed. *Dictionary of Social Science*. Washington, D.C.: Public Affairs Press, 1959.

Social Sciences—Education

Alexander, Carter, and Arvid J. Burke. *How to Locate Educational Information and Data*. 4th ed., rev. New York: Bureau of Publications, Teachers' College, Columbia Univ., 1958.

Education Index. New York: H. W. Wilson, 1929– . Monthly, except July and August, with annual cumulations. Covers the entire field and includes British publications.

Encyclopedia of Education. 10 vols. Ed. by L. C. Deighton. New York: Macmillan, 1971.

Monroe, Paul, ed. *A Cyclopedia of Education*. 5 vols. New York: Macmillan, 1911–13. Valuable for its presentation of the history and philosophy of education. Needs updating.

Rivlin, Harry N., ed. *Encyclopedia of Modern Education*. New York: Philosophical Library, 1943. Explains some of the problems of present-day education.

Who's Who in American Education. Nashville, Tenn.: Who's Who in American Education, 1928– . Biennial.

Social Sciences—Geography

Bartholomew, John W., ed. *Advanced Atlas of Modern Geography.* 3rd ed. New York: McGraw-Hill, 1956.

Hammond's Ambassador World Atlas. Maplewood, N.J.: C. S. Hammond, 1961. Includes the 1960 census figures.

Webster's Geographical Dictionary, rev. ed. Springfield, Mass.: G. & C. Merriam, 1959. (See also "Atlases and Gazetteers.")

Social Sciences—History

Adams, James Truslow, ed. *Dictionary of American History.* 6 vols. 2nd ed., rev. New York: Scribner's, 1961.

Barzun, Jacques and Henry F. Graff. *The Modern Researcher.* Rev. ed. New York: Harcourt Brace Jovanovich, 1970.

Morison, Samuel Eliot. *The Oxford History of the American People.* New York: Oxford Univ. Press, 1965.

The Cambridge Ancient History. Ed. J. B. Bury et al. 12 vols. Cambridge, Eng.: Cambridge Univ. Press, 1923–39.

The Shorter Cambridge Medieval History. Ed. C. W. Previte-Orton, 2 vols. Cambridge, Eng.: Cambridge Univ. Press, 1953.

The Cambridge Modern History. Ed. A. W. Ward et al. 13 vols. and atlas. Cambridge, Eng.: Cambridge Univ. Press, 1902–26. (See also *New Cambridge Modern History.*)

Current, Richard N., T. H. Williams, and Frank Freidel. *American History: A Survey.* New York: Random House, 1961.

Handlin, Oscar, et al. *Guide to American History.* Cambridge, Mass.: Harvard Univ. Press, 1954.

Keller, Helen Rex. *Dictionary of Dates,* 2 vols. New York: Macmillan, 1934. Historical events through 1930.

Lord, Clifford L., and Elizabeth H. Lord, eds. *Historical Atlas of the United States,* rev. ed. New York: Holt, 1953.

New Cambridge Modern History. Cambridge, Eng.: Cambridge Univ. Press, 1957–70. Supplements in progress.

The New American Nation Series. Ed. Henry S. Commager and Richard B. Morris. New York: Harper & Brothers, 1954– . Work in progress. Sixteen volumes have appeared, each by a different author.

Schlesinger, Arthur M., and Dixon R. Fox, eds. *History of American Life: A Social, Cultural, and Economic Analysis*. 13 vols. New York: Macmillan, 1929–44.

U.S. Library of Congress, Reference Division. *A Guide to the Study of the United States of America*. Washington, D.C.: U.S. Government Printing Office, 1960.

Other Social Sciences

Burchfield, LaVerne. *Student's Guide to Materials in Political Science*. New York: Holt, 1935.

Clark, Donald T., and Bert A. Gottfried. *Dictionary of Business and Finance*. New York: Thomas Y. Crowell Company, 1957.

Dictionary of Sociology. Ed. D. G. Mitchell. Chicago: Aldine, 1968.

Dictionary of Economics and Commerce. 3rd ed. London: Macdonald, 1969.

Patterns of Government: The Major Political Systems of Europe. Ed. Samuel H. Beer and Adam B. Ulam. New York: Random House, 1958.

Schlesinger, Arthur M., and Dixon R. Fox, eds. *History of American Life: A Social, Cultural, and Economic Analysis*. 13 vols. New York: Macmillan, 1929–44.

Smith, Edward C., and Arnold J. Zurcher, eds. *New Dictionary of American Politics*. rev. ed. New York: Barnes & Noble, 1955.

Van Royen, William, ed. *Atlas of the World's Resources*. Vol. I: *The Agricultural Resources of the World*. Vol. II: *The Mineral Resources of the World*, by William Van Royen and Oliver Bowles. Englewood Cliffs, N.J.: Prentice-Hall, for the University of Maryland, 1952–54.

EXERCISES

Documentation problems

1. Convert the following information into the proper bibliography form.
   a. A book by Geoffrey Ashe entitled King Arthur's Avalon, copyrighted in 1957 and published by Collins, whose address is St. James's Place, London.
   b. A book called Limits and Latitudes, copyrighted 1965, written by Kevin G. Burns, Edward H. Jones, and Robert C. Wylder, and published in Philadelphia and New York by the J. B. Lippincott Company.
   c. The seventh edition of a book whose title is Writing with a Purpose, authored by James M. McCrimmon and published by Houghton Mifflin Company of Boston, copyrighted 1972.
   d. A two-volume edition of a work called American Literature: The Makers and the Making, edited by Cleanth Brooks, R. W. B. Lewis,

and Robert Penn Warren, published in New York by St. Martin's Press, Inc., copyrighted in 1973.

e. Sculley Bradley, and others' edition of The Scarlet Letter by Nathaniel Hawthorne, published in New York by W. W. Norton & Company, Inc., in the year 1962.
f. A translated version of the novel Crime and Punishment by Fyodor Dostoevsky. The translator is Constance Garnett; the copyright date is 1964, published by Bantam Books in New York.
g. Lionel Trilling's article The Meaning of a Literary Idea, reprinted in a book called Exploring Literature, which is edited by Lynn Altenbernd and published by The Macmillan Company in New York, copyrighted 1970.
h. An article entitled The Historical Roots of our Ecologic Crisis, found in a journal called Science, Volume 155, pages 1203 to 1207. That particular issue of the magazine came out on March 10 of 1967.
i. An unsigned news article in the newspaper Los Angeles Times, headlined Nader Links Candles and Lead Poisoning, found in the December 7, 1973 issue, Part I, page 5, columns 1 and 2.
j. An entry from the Encyclopaedia Britannica entitled Seleucid Dynasty. The author is E. R. Bevan. The encyclopedia edition year is 1963.

2. Using page numbers that you make up, turn the previous bibliography entries into proper footnotes, numbered consecutively 1–10.

Note-taking problems

1. Summarize the following paragraph into no more than twenty-five words.

> All the objectively observable characteristics of the goose's behavior on losing its mate are roughly identical with those accompanying human grief. This applies particularly to the phenomena observable in the sympathetic nervous system. John Bowlby, in his study of infant grief, has given an equally convincing and moving description of this primal grieving, and it is almost incredible how detailed are the analogies we find here in human beings and in birds. Just as in the human face, it is the neighborhood of the eyes that in geese bears the permanent marks of deep grief. The lowering of the tonus in the sympathicus causes the eye to sink back deeply in its socket and, at the same time, decreases the tension of the outer facial muscles supporting the eye region from below. Both factors contribute to the formation of a fold of loose skin below the eye which as early as in the ancient Greek mask of tragedy had become the conventionalized expression of grief. My dear old greylag Ada, several times a widow, was particularly easy to recognize because

of the grief-marked expression of her eyes. A knowledgeable visitor who knew nothing about Ada's history standing beside me at the lake suddenly pointed her out among many geese, saying, "That goose must have been through a lot!"

—Konrad Lorenz, *On Aggression*

2. Paraphrase the following passage, using approximately the same number of words as the original.

In many ways (though by no means in all), Napoleon was insensitive to the forces that were shaping the future. Except in some scattered remarks made at St. Helena, when he had time to reflect on the age, he was blind to the potentialities of steam power and of other inventions that were changing the world. A conservative by temperament, he distrusted innovations of any sort. He sought to establish a dynasty when monarchy was beginning to go out of fashion—and the dynasty he wished to establish was based on the Carolingian model, at that; he created a nobility after a revolution had been fought to abolish it; and in restoring the Church he gave it a position which, as subsequent history has shown, was out of keeping with modern trends.

—J. Christopher Herold, *The Age of Napoleon*

11
Writing about literature

The SQIF format for writing about literature

What to say about fiction

- Point of view
- Plot and theme
- Tone
- Mood
- Character

What to say about drama

- Point of view
- Plot and theme
- Tone
- Mood
- Character

What to say about poetry

- Point of view
- Plot and theme
- Tone
- Mood
- Character

Assume that since your reader is already familiar with the text you are discussing, he will be bored with commonplace perceptions–as you yourself would be–and will feel insulted if you retell him the plot.

—John R. Trimble

HAVE POINT, MAKE POINT, PROVE POINT: all who write essays must observe this threefold rule. It applies to an essay about literature just as much as it does to a narrative or an argument. All the techniques you've already learned in this book, as well as the above rule, apply.

The essay analyzing a literary work is unique only in its focus and sources of support. The focus of the essay about literature is generally on the interpretation of a work or its use of certain literary techniques. You may have to analyze a theme or a symbol, explain figurative language, or provide historical perspective. It is from the work, too, that you should draw supporting details for your interpretation. To say that a certain poem has this meaning or that is not enough; you must also prove it by quoting the author's actual words.

The SQIF format for writing about literature

The cardinal rule for writing about literature is simply this: you should analyze and write about the most significant feature of the work. If you are writing about a poem that uses elaborate imagery but says little or nothing about its speaker, you should focus your analysis on its imagery and ignore its speaker. If the story has a threadbare plot but a well-developed character, then you should focus on that character. First, you determine by common sense what is most significant about the literary work; then you analyze and write about that using the SQIF format: Summarize, Quote, Interpret, and discuss Form.

Begin your analysis with a *summary* of the work's theme—what you take to be its dominant idea. Naturally, if you are wrong about the theme, your entire analysis is wrong. However, if you use the SQIF format, your instructor will have the opportunity to reconstruct your thinking and examine the evidence that led you to your mistaken conclusion. Most instructors are gentle with erroneous themes so long as they can trace the thinking process behind them.

If you feel a preamble to your essay is necessary, at least make sure the theme is stated in your opening paragraph. Your summary of theme will serve as a thesis for your analysis and lend structure and direction to it.

Quotations from the literary work serve as evidence for your version of its theme. They anchor your analysis to the text of the work and keep you from going adrift on the sea of speculation. But do not simply string one quotation after another as padding for a skimpy analysis. Use the sandwich principle—bread, then meat, then bread; interpret, then quote, then interpret again. Here is an example:

> The speaker, however, is not so optimistic. He sees that there are "no more clowns . . . no more children . . . no more old ladies" left to inspire the poet/artist. If we take the clowns to mean the ability to laugh in the middle of tragedy, the children to mean innocence in the midst of guilt, and the old ladies to mean gentleness in the middle of cruelty, we can then anticipate the ending of the poem, which is the speaker's conclusion that artists have lost their magic—that is, their illusive talents—and "soon shall be dead." In short, the savagery of war annihilates hope and along with it the artist's inspiration.

Notice that the writer imbeds her quotations between interpretation. Sandwich quotations interfere less with the flow of writing than blob quotations. Here is an example of a blob quotation:

> The speaker seems to be very depressed, as when he says:
>
> i said
>   no denying
> essentially, this fact—
>   no denying in places like bergen-belsen
> the world's hope died there—
>   which is narrow, but—
>   maybe true—
> the world's hope died
> when auschwitz opened its gates—

A frail point backed up by a massive quotation is a clear signal of padding, to which most instructors respond negatively. Quote to prove your theme, not to lengthen your essay.

Interpretation consists of applying the extracted theme to the body of work and demonstrating that it fits. In short, you trace the way the theme is developed throughout the work. Summarizing the theme puts your interpretation in thesis form: the rest of the analysis consists of expanding on the theme and proving it with evidence from the text. If your summary of theme is concise and accurate, the follow-through interpretation should be easy.

Form refers to the mechanics of a literary work—to its physical characteristics. The form of a poem is its meter, rhyme scheme, imagery, stanza structure, and shape; the form of a play is its division into acts and scenes, its plot, dialog, and setting. Form refers to what a literary work is made up of; content refers to what the work means. This conceptual difference between form and content is frequently used in the analysis of literature. It is possible to analyze a work for its form or its content. When you write about theme you are analyzing content; when you scan a poem for its meter, you are analyzing form.

Most essays about literature do not call for long, ponderous commentary on form. The idea is simply to mention and underscore those elements of form that are prominently used to convey theme. If the poem uses a distinctive rhyme to reinforce its theme, you should mention it in your analysis. If a play makes use of the flashback technique (where a character relives a memory for the benefit of the audience) to advance its plot, that, too, should probably be mentioned in your analysis. Only the major elements of form need to be discussed.

What to say about fiction

Whichever genre of literature you choose to write about, the central principle remains the same: you should focus on the most significant feature of the work and analyze that. Some stories emphasize character; others emphasize mood, and others plot. With still others, tone may be more significant than either character, mood, or plot. In each case, you should concentrate on the emphasis in the work and focus your analysis on it.

One or more of the following features is generally touched on in any analysis of fiction: point of view, plot and theme, tone, mood, and character. We will discuss these features as they apply to both the short story and the novel.

Point of view

Point of view refers to the perspective from which a story is told. The main points of view are: omniscient, first-person, and stream of consciousness.

With the *omniscient* point of view, the story is narrated from the perspective of an invisible author who refers to the characters as "he" or "she." Here is an example:

> The old gentleman at the tea-table, who had come from America thirty years before, had brought with him, at the top of his baggage, his American physiognomy; and he had not only brought it with him, but he had kept it in the best order, so that, if necessary, he might have taken it back to his own country with perfect confidence. At present, obviously, nevertheless, his journeys were over and he was taking the rest that precedes the great rest.
>
> —Henry James, *Portrait of a Lady*

The omniscient point of view allows an author to observe and comment on the behavior of a character. The author can describe a character's appearance, tell what he or she is thinking, then move to another character and do the same. The effect is one of shifting intimacy that carries the reader from one character to another through the invisible presence of the author. In many short stories and novels the author focuses on one major character as the central consciousness of the fiction.

Where the omniscient point of view is used, the author's attitude toward the story or characters is sometimes revealed through tone. We will discuss this point later when we deal with tone.

The *first-person* point of view tells the story through the mind of a single character who refers to himself or herself as "I." Here is an example:

> I'm a sick man . . . a mean man. There's nothing attractive about me. I think there's something wrong with my liver. But, actually, I'm not even sure what it is about my sickness; I'm not even sure what it is that's ailing me.
>
> —Feodor Dostoevsky, *Notes from the Underground*

A first-person narrative is colored by the personality of the character who tells it. We see everything through the eyes of the character; every event, thought, or occurrence in the story is a reflection of the character's personality. A chief difficulty with this point of view is judging and evaluating the reliability of what the narrator says or does. Other implications for characterization also follow from the use of this point of view. We will discuss these when we deal with character.

The *stream of consciousness* point of view is an extension of the first-person point of view, but it involves an unusual technique. Stream of consciousness is an attempt to reconstruct the mental processes of a character on a page, to show how his or her mind actually sounds inside. The idea is not simply to capture the conscious or rational side of a character's mind, but to plumb the unconscious and irrational side of it as well. Here is an example:

> Through the fence, between the curling flower spaces, I could see them hitting. They were coming toward where the flag was and I

> went along the fence. Luster was hunting in the grass by the flower tree. They took the flag out, and they were hitting. Then they put the flag back and they went to the table, and he hit and the other hit. Then they went on, and I went along the fence. Luster came away from the flower tree and we stopped and I looked through the fence while Luster was hunting in the grass.
>
> —William Faulkner, *The Sound and the Fury*

This is the description of a golf game as seen through the mind of an idiot. Notice the simplicity of his language and his descriptions. He perceives everything as occurring in rigid sequence.

Here, in contrast, is a recollection in the mind of a suicidally depressed character:

> I didnt look back the tree frogs didnt pay me any mind the grey light like moss in the trees drizzling but still it wouldnt rain after a while I turned went back to the edge of the woods as soon as I got there I began to smell honeysuckle again I could see the lights on the courthouse clock and the glare of the town square on the sky and the dark willows the light still on in Benjys room and I stooped through the fence and went across the pasture running I ran in the grey grass among the crickets and honeysuckle getting stronger and stronger and the smell of water then I could see the water the colour of grey honeysuckle I lay down on the bank with my face close to the ground. . . .
>
> —William Faulkner, *The Sound and the Fury*

Stream of consciousness writing typically abandons traditional grammar and sentence structure on the assumption that these are superficial devices not observed by the mind in the thought process. In the above passage, the character is reliving a traumatic and painful memory; his thoughts are jumbled with vivid impressions that run through his mind almost incoherently. The passage recreates the experience as the character lived it in his mind.

A story written from a stream of consciousness point of view cannot be read literally. Such a point of view does not attempt to be factual or rational since it is based partly on the Freudian notion that the mind is subjected to irrational and absurd forces. You therefore have to infer about the character, rather than simply accept what he or she says literally.

To sum up, point of view in fiction is analogous to camera angle in a movie. Each of the different points of view allows an author to process and construct information about a character and his or her world in a slightly different way. It is important, therefore, that you begin your analysis of fiction with a clear idea about who is telling the story, what his or her attitude toward the narrative is, and whether or not his or her version of the story can be taken as factual and honest.

Plot and theme

Plot refers to the sequence of events or actions in a story. Plots are as numerous as the imagination of writers allows and vary in importance from one story to another. At the heart of plot is conflict—a character in opposition either to himself or herself, to something or someone else, or to the environment. The formula is:

PLOT + CONFLICT = THEME

For instance, if the plot recounts a "second honeymoon" trip taken on a fiftieth wedding anniversary, and the conflict exists in the husband between the demands of his wife and his personal need for privacy, the overall theme can probably be expressed as a criticism of marriage, depending on how the story turns out. If it turns out badly—the husband feels cramped, the wife is unhappy, yet they decide to spend the rest of their lives together in spite of their personal misery—then the theme may be the brutalization of romantic feeling by marriage. The idea is not to be glib, but to sum up plot and conflict into a major idea that becomes the theme.

A caution: do not ramble on for pages about plot. Many instructors regard this as a padding device. Here is an example from a student paper on Melville's *Bartleby the Scrivener*:

> The story is about a man who is hired as a scrivener or clerk by the narrator. At first, he seems a little sluggish, but does what he's told. Then, after a while, he begins to object to doing little things that are part of his job. For instance, on the third day when the narrator asks Bartleby to help him examine a paper, he refuses and says, "I would prefer not to," which is what he always says when he refuses to do as he's asked. At first, his boss could hardly believe his ears, but he was so busy that he decided to forget the incident and asked Nippers to help him examine the papers instead.

The paper goes on in this vein for a couple of pages, unnecessarily so, because the instructor has obviously read the story and does not need to have it retold. What the assignment calls for is a statement of the major idea in the story and a tracing of this idea throughout the narrative using the SQIF format. Here is the opening sentence of a better analysis:

> The theme of *Bartleby the Scrivener* is society's inability to deal with a nonfunctioning human who withdraws and becomes cut off from its materialistic values.

This opening touches on plot, conflict, and theme. The plot is Bartleby's gradual withdrawal; the conflict is between him and his society; the theme is the sum of the two—how a function-conscious society that evaluates its members for their work is at a loss to deal with an individual on a solely human basis.

Combine plot and conflict and formulate a statement of theme that will become your thesis. After that, follow the SQIF format as you document your thesis by referring directly to passages in the story.

Tone

Tone is an abbreviation for *tone of voice*. A writer tells a story and does it in a voice. Because we must read rather than hear the story, the tone of voice of its teller may be hard to detect. However, it is vital that you understand the author's tone, since it affects the way a story can be validly interpreted.

Tone is used both to project the personality of a character on the page and to reveal the attitude of the author toward the narrative. Tone will signal whether the author is taking the story seriously, comically, bitterly, ironically, or otherwise. Compare these openings from two different novels:

> Studs Lonigan, on the verge of fifteen, and wearing his first suit of long trousers, stood in the bathroom with a Sweet Caporal pasted in his mug. His hands were jammed in his trousers' pockets, and he sneered. He puffed, drew the fag out of his mouth, inhaled and said to himself: "Well, I'm kissin' the old dump goodbye tonight."
>
> —James T. Farrell, *Studs Lonigan*

> In the last years of the seventeenth century there was to be found among the fops and fools of the London coffee-houses one rangy, gangling flitch called Ebenezer Cooke, more ambitious than talented, and yet more talented than prudent, who, like his friends-in-folly, all of whom were supposed to be educating at Oxford or Cambridge, had found the sound of Mother English more fun to game with than her sense to labor over, and so rather than applying himself to the pains of scholarship, had learned the knack of versifying, and ground out quires of couplets after the fashion of the day, afroth with "Joves" and "Jupiters," aclang with jarring rhymes, and string-taut with similes stretched to the snapping point.
>
> —John Barth, *The Sotweed Factor*

Both openings draw introductory portraits of the main characters. In the first example, the writer uses slang to describe Studs Lonigan; for example, "his mug" for "his face," and "the fag" for "the cigarette." Notice that when Studs Lonigan speaks, his language follows the same city slang the author used to describe him. The tone of the description adds to the portrait by giving us the flavor of Studs' personality—his tough-guy mask. That is the function of the slang words in the description, to inflect the language with a tough-guy tone that implies something about Studs' personality.

In the second example, the language is archaic and burlesque, the sentence long and cumbersome. The major character is referred to as "one rangy, gangling flitch . . . more ambitious than talented, and yet more talented than prudent." He is a poet pretender who "grinds out quires of couplets." The comic, burlesque tone of the passage obviously reflects the author's attitude toward Ebenezer, not Ebenezer's attitude toward himself. Once the stage is set, the satire operates because of the chasm between the way Ebenezer regards himself and the way he is regarded by his author. Ebenezer considers himself a serious poet and writes passionately after the fashion of the day. His author takes him for a mock poet and delights in poking fun at his versification. And the signal to the reader that the author is treating Ebenezer as a comic figure is given through the tone of the passage.

Both of these examples are taken from contemporary novels. In the first, the tone is used to project and imply the personality of the major character; in the second, tone is used to set comic distance between the author and the major character. The point is this: you must be sensitive and alert to tone, or you will miss the undercurrents of fiction. There are no hard and fast rules when it comes to recognizing tone. Most native speakers of English have an intuitive sense for the appropriate language on any occasion. The subtleties of tone are ordinarily achieved by an author twisting language in such a way that it deviates from what is appropriate and causes slight reverberations that we call tone. Consider this example:

> Braggioni loves himself with such tenderness and amplitude and eternal charity that his followers—for he is a leader of men, a skilled revolutionist, and his skin has been punctured in honorable warfare—warm themselves in the reflected glow, and say to each other: "He has a real nobility, a love of humanity raised above mere personal affections." The excess of this self-love has flowed out, inconveniently for her, over Laura, who, with so many others, owes her comfortable situation and her salary to him.
>
> —Katherine Anne Porter, *"Flowering Judas"*

In the story, the description of Braggioni is given from Laura's point of view, and the tone of the language is inflected with irony, to convey her dislike for him. It is ironic overkill to say that someone loves himself with "tenderness and amplitude and eternal charity." The same applies to the phrasing "his skin has been punctured in honorable warfare." If we rewrite the passage in more appropriate language, much of the ironic tone will disappear:

> Braggioni loves himself. He is a leader of men, a revolutionist. He has been injured in the war. His followers warm themselves in his

> glow and say to each other, "He has a real nobility, a love of humanity raised above personal affection." He likes Laura who, like so many others, owes her comfortable situation and her salary to him.

But, as it stands in the short story, the description of Braggioni is ironic; that is, it says one thing but means another. The ironic tone sums him up as a cynical and egotistic opportunist, implies that his followers are duped by his humanitarian pretensions, and conveys Laura's dislike for him.

Good dialog will also convey a separate tone of voice for each character. Sometimes, tone in dialog is inflected to reveal conflict, as in this example from a Hemingway story, "Hills Like White Elephants" (1927):

> "And we could have all this," she said. "And we could have everything and every day we make it more impossible."
>
> "What did you say?"
>
> "I said we could have everything."
>
> "We can have everything."
>
> "No, we can't."
>
> "We can go everywhere."
>
> "No, we can't. It isn't ours any more."
>
> "It's ours."
>
> "No, it isn't. And once they take it away, you never get it back."
>
> "But they haven't taken it away."
>
> "We'll wait and see."
>
> "Come back in the shade," he said, "You mustn't feel that way."
>
> "I don't feel any way," the girl said, "I just know things."
>
> "I don't want you to do anything that you don't want to do . . ."
>
> "Nor that isn't good for me," she said. "I know. Could we have another beer?"

The couple are somewhere in Spain where the woman is about to undergo an abortion. The man tries to humor and reassure her and seems on the surface as if he would give in to her wish not to have the abortion. But he really wants her to go through with it, and in spite of his assertions to the contrary, she knows it. The conflict between them is subtly conveyed through tone. At the end, she even anticipates one of his pat lines:

> "I don't want you to do anything that you don't want to do . . ."
>
> "Nor that isn't good for me," she said. "I know. Could we have another beer?"

A tone-sensitive reader will hear the resigned sarcasm in her final line.

In writing about tone in fiction, several common tacks are:

1. To analyze and write about the tone in the work as it indicates the attitude of the author
2. To analyze tone as it reveals personality and conflict
3. To analyze tone as it is used to depict characters

Whether or not you analyze the literary work strictly for its tone, you should be alert to its use in fiction in these ways.

Mood

Mood is the dominant impression to come out of scenery descriptions in the work. It usually functions in fiction about the same way as setting does in a play, to provide a backdrop for the action and an external equivalent for the conflict taking place in the story. Here, for instance, is how Joseph Conrad's *Heart of Darkness* (1902) begins:

> *The Nellie*, a cruising yawl, swung to her anchor without a flutter of the sails, and was at rest. The flood had made, the wind was nearly calm, and being bound down the river, the only thing for it was to come to and wait for the turn of the tide.
>
> The sun-reach of the Thames stretched before us like the beginning of an interminable waterway. In the offing the sea and the sky were welded together without a joint, and in the luminous space the tanned sails of the barges drifting up with the tide seemed to stand still in red clusters of canvas sharply peaked, with gleams of vanishing flatness. The air was dark above Gravesend, and farther back still seemed condensed into a mournful gloom, brooding motionless over the biggest, and the greatest, town on earth.
>
> The Director of Companies was our captain and our host. We four affectionately watched his back as he stood in the bows looking to seaward. On the whole river there was nothing that looked half so nautical. He resembled a pilot, which to a seaman is trustworthiness personified. It is difficult to realize his work was not out there in the luminous estuary but behind him, without the brooding gloom.

Heart of Darkness tells the story of a man who goes to Africa and while there succumbs to the darkness inside himself and becomes the leader of a cannibal tribe. Notice how the opening descriptions emphasize a mood of becalmed gloom. The air is described as "condensed into a mournful gloom, brooding motionless over the biggest, and the greatest, town on earth."

Later on in the novel, the words *gloom* and *brooding* occur again and again in the descriptive passages.

Mood is usually consonant with the conflict in the story. If the story is about a man who succumbs to an internal darkness, we expect that the author will set up an external equivalent in the description of the landscape to prepare us for the character's downfall. Obviously, it would seem incongruous to tell a story about a man who falls victim to an inner dark force and have the whole affair take place in clear sunlight at the foot of a pink mountain. The mood must be modulated to be consistent with the line of conflict. The same is true of mood manipulation in movies. Vampires come out on dark overcast nights when black clouds hang over a sinister moon. But when the sun comes out and flowers are blooming, Mary Poppins flies down on the end of her umbrella. The mood is manipulated through the use of appropriate background scenery. Some stories are known as mood stories because they emphasize mood to the exclusion of everything else. A mood story generally turns on a minimal plot, has little action, and projects its characters' state of mind and conflict into the imagery used to describe scenery.

The key principle in writing about mood is to locate and identify the correspondences between the mood in the descriptive passages and the theme of the story.

Character

Most writing about character involves an analysis of action and motive. The writer must expand on evidence in the text that implies something about the character. We have already talked about how tone can be inflected to depict character and how mood can provide an external equivalent to the conflict. All parts of fiction—point of view, plot, theme, tone, and mood—generally have some bearing on, or meet in, the central character. A story written from the first-person point of view has the mind of the character who tells it as a common denominator to all its parts. A story written from an omniscient point of view will orchestrate all its parts to be consistent with the conflict experienced by its main character. It follows that analysis of character must take account of the context in which the character operates and will most likely have to touch on one or more of the other features of fiction. The use of the SQIF format will force you to observe the context of the story as you discuss its main character.

A caution: beware of identifying with a character. This is a common student error. Here is an example excerpted from a student paper on Hemingway's "Hills Like White Elephants":

> The woman was such a beautiful person. I really liked her. I personally thought that her lover, at least I think that that was what he

> was or he would not have wanted her to have the abortion, was very patronizing to her. He didn't understand her point of view, and all he could do was try to agree with her. I hated his attitude. But she had more pride than he did, because even though she knew that he was lying to her all the time, she didn't try to force him to accept the baby. He reminds me of a lot of callous men I know.

In addition to its other flaws, the excerpt suffers from an overidentification by its writer with the woman in the story. There is no point in moralistically condemning one character while adulating another. The idea is to analyze the character in such a way that your analysis of him or her sheds light on the story.

There are a finite number of methods available to an author in drawing a character. Characterization comes about by:

1. What a character does, says, or thinks
2. What an author says about a character
3. What a character says about himself or herself
4. What another character says about him or her

In most novels written from the omniscient point of view, all four combine to produce a single picture of a character. In James's *Portrait of a Lady*, for instance, Isabel Archer is partly drawn by what she does, thinks, and says. This dialog occurs on her first meeting with her aunt:

> . . . And then, since the girl [Isabel] stood there hesitating and wondering, this unexpected critic said to her abruptly: "I suppose you're one of the daughters?"
>
> Isabel thought she had very strange manners. "It depends upon whose daughters you mean."
>
> "The late Mr. Archer's—and my poor sister's."
>
> "Ah," said Isabel slowly, "you must be our crazy Aunt Lydia!"

We are therefore led to infer that Isabel can be blunt and outspoken.

She is also characterized by what the author tells us about her.

> It may be affirmed without delay that Isabel was probably very liable to the sin of self-esteem; she often surveyed with complacency the field of her own nature; she was in the habit of taking for granted, on scanty evidence, that she was right; she treated herself to occasions of homage. Meanwhile her errors and delusions were frequently such as a biographer interested in preserving the dignity of his subject must shrink from specifying.

What she says about herself also characterizes her:

> "I don't like everything settled beforehand," said the girl, "I like more unexpectedness."
>
> Her uncle seemed amused at her distinctness of preference.
>
> "Well, it's settled beforehand that you'll have great success," he rejoined, "I suppose you'll like that."
>
> "I shall not have success if they're too stupidly conventional. I'm not in the least stupidly conventional. I'm just the contrary. That's what they won't like."

Other characters add to her characterization. For example, the aunt comments:

> I don't know whether she's a gifted being, but she's a clever girl—with a strong will and a high temper. She has no idea of being bored.

And a friend notes:

> I call people rich when they're able to meet the requirements of their imagination. Isabel has a great deal of imagination.

All combine to give a multiangled camera shot of Isabel's personality and her struggle to become unconventional.

In contrast, when a story is written from the first-person point of view, characterization must come from a single source: what the character says and what can be inferred about his or her personality from the way he or she tells the story. Here, for instance, is an excerpt from Ring Lardner's short story "The Golden Honeymoon" (1926) that suggests something about the personality of the narrator:

> We went to Trenton the night before and stayed at my daughter and son-in-law and we left Trenton the next afternoon at 3:23 PM.
>
> This was the twelfth day of January. Mother set facing the front of the train, as it makes her giddy to ride backwards. I set facing her, which does not affect me. We reached North Philadelphia at 4:03 PM and West Philadelphia at 4:14 but did not go into Broad Street. We reached Baltimore at 6:30 and Washington, D.C. at 7:25. Our train laid over in Washington two hours till another train come along to pick us up and I got out and strolled up the platform and into Union Station.

He is trite, orderly, and bored; his life is taken up with pointless trivia such as the arrival and departure times of the train he is riding on. Notice that what conclusions we come to about him have to be inferred from the way he sees and reports on his world, and not from anything an outside narrator directly tells us. Plot, theme, mood, conflict, tone, and point of view all cluster into a single source: the personality of the "I" who tells the story.

In summary, bear in mind that you should analyze the work of fiction for its most significant feature. If a story turns on an intricate plot to the exclusion of everything else, then its plot should be the focus of your analysis. The most significant and highly developed feature of a story, whether its point of view, plot, tone, mood, or character, is frequently the source of its main idea or theme, and that is what your analysis should develop.

What to say about drama

Much of what we said about fiction also applies to drama. Both make use of plot, tone, mood, and character, although in slightly different ways.

Point of view

Generally, a play is not mounted from a single point of view. A play may tell a story about a character, and it may focus on the character's interrelationships with people and the world. But the author customarily does not intervene with comments on behalf of the character or to tell all his or her intimate thoughts, nor does a narrator tell all or most of the story to the audience.

The essence of drama is interaction of characters with each other, played out through action and dialog on a stage. Some modern plays distort characterization and action for effect and have an implied point of view that is linked with the playwright's theme. Ionesco's *The Bald Soprano* (1948), for instance, opens with the following:

> Mrs. Smith: There, it's nine o'clock. We've drunk the soup, and eaten the fish and chips, and the English salad. The children have drunk English water. We've eaten well this evening. That's because we live in the suburbs of London and because our name is Smith.
>
> Mr. Smith: (*Continues to read, clicks his tongue.*)
>
> Mrs. Smith: Potatoes are very good fried in fat; the salad oil was not rancid. The oil from the grocer at the corner is better quality than the oil from the grocer across the street. It is even better than the oil from the grocer at the bottom of the street. However, I prefer not to tell them that their oil is bad.

This version of reality is uniquely the playwright's, and implies the equivalent of a first-person point of view. Ionesco is parodying the smug and shallow life in the English suburbs, which accounts for the peculiar and banal dialog. As a rule, however, serious drama operates on the "slice of life" that is arranged to accord with all the probabilities of conventional reality. Satirical and absurd plays are exceptions in which the playwright frequently distorts the drama until it symbolically reflects the version of reality seen from his or her point of view.

Plot and theme

Early dramatists conceived of a play as having unity. Whatever occurred at the end of a play must be caused by something that existed in its beginning. This concept of plot gave rise to the technique of foreshadowing—a means by which dramatists hint the presence of something that will later play a significant part in the outcome of the plot. For instance, in Odets's *Awake and Sing!* (1935), Jacob suddenly introduces the fact that he has an insurance policy on his life:

> Jacob: (*Taking a large envelope from pocket.*) Please, you'll keep this for me. Put it away.
> Morty: What is it?
> Jacob: My insurance policy. I don't like it should lay around where something could happen.
> Morty: What could happen?
> Jacob: Who knows, robbers, fire . . . they took next door. Fifty dollars from O'Reilly.
> Morty: Say, lucky a Berger didn't lose it.
> Jacob: Put it downtown in the safe. Bessie don't have to know.
> Morty: It's made out to Bessie?
> Jacob: No, to Ralph.
> Morty: To Ralph?
> Jacob: He don't know. Some day he'll get three thousand.

Later in the play, Jacob will commit suicide in his attempt to bequeath Ralph the three thousand and a new beginning. By introducing the insurance policy before it was needed to resolve the complications of the plot, the playwright foreshadowed the significant part it would later have. When the suicide eventually takes place and the policy comes up, we are not surprised. It seems a natural turn of events.

Foreshadowing is part of standard plotting technique in almost all drama, both on stage, in film, and on television. If, at the opening of a segment in a television series, a character makes mention of an umbrella for no apparent reason, it means that the umbrella is destined to play a part in the outcome of events before the half hour or hour is up. The failure to foreshadow causes a *deus ex machina* effect. This Latin term means "god from a machine," and comes from the Greek playwrights' occasional use of a machine to lower a god onto the stage to resolve difficult and sticky plots.

To this day, melodrama continues to call on *deus ex machina* devices to solve its peculiar problems. After showing the misery and poverty of a family—the wolf and bill collector at the door and the starving children—the play is then resolved by the entrance of a long-lost and wealthy cousin, thereby resorting to a *deus ex machina*. The cousin would be the equivalent of the god from a machine whose presence was unaccounted for at the beginning of the play and whose abrupt entrance into the play signals that the playwright is imposing a moralistic and improbable solution on its plot.

The formula we gave earlier, plot+conflict=theme, is generally equally applicable to drama. The plots of many three-act plays have the following arrangement: Act I introduces the conflict; Act II complicates it; Act III resolves it. In addition, there may be a subplot branching off the main plot. Some plays do not observe this simple three-act arrangement; others have no subplots, only a main plot. Most plays, however, will have at least one speech somewhere, usually toward the end, in which a character sums up its theme. At the end of *Awake and Sing!* for instance, Ralph's final speech sums up the exhortation to live that is both the play's theme and title:

> Ralph: Right here in the house. My days won't be for nothing. Let Mom have the dough. I'm twenty two and kickin'! I'll get along. Did Jake die for us to fight about nickels? No! "Awake and Sing," he said. Right here he stood and said it. The night he died, I saw it like a thunderbolt! I saw he was dead and I was born! I swear to God, I'm one week old! I want the whole city to hear it—fresh blood, arms. We got 'em. We're glad we're living.

A play may also state its theme symbolically, as in Ionesco's *Rhinoceros* (1959) where the grotesqueness of conformity is expressed through the gradual metamorphosis of its characters into rhinoceroses.

Tone

As in fiction, tone of voice in drama is inflected in dialog to reveal the character's personality. Here, for example, is what George Bernard Shaw's version of a poet sounds like:

> Octavius: Jack; we men are all coarse: we never understand how exquisite a woman's sensibilities are. How could I have done such a thing!

Tanner: Done what, you maudlin idiot?
Octavius: Yes, I am an idiot, Jack: If you had heard her voice! If you had seen her tears! I have lain awake all night thinking of them. If she had reproached me, I could have borne it better.

—George Bernard Shaw, *Man and Superman*

Notice the exaggerated emotional tone used by Octavius, the poet. The burden of tonal characterization in drama rests entirely with dialog since the characters are on stage and must talk for themselves.

Mood

Mood is partly a function of physical setting and partly of descriptive language. If you are reading a play rather than seeing it performed, you must take into account the descriptions of setting as given by the playwright. These, in part, imply the mood the scene is written to be played in. If you are seeing a play, the stage setting, lighting, and pace of dialog will all operate to evoke the desired mood. Early playwrights who wrote for stages lacking in setting and lighting facilities often built descriptions of scenery into the character's dialog to create an appropriate mood. Here, for instance, from Shakespeare's *Macbeth*, Lennox describes the night of the king's murder:

Lennox: The night has been unruly. Where we lay.
Our chimneys were blown down, and as they say,
Lamentings heard i' th' air, strange screams of death.
And prophesying, with accents terrible,
New hatched to th' woeful time. The obscure bird
Clamoured the livelong night. Some say, the earth
Was feverous, and did shake.

Again, the principle is the same as in fiction: to create a mood equivalent to the conflict through the use of description. To the Elizabethan, the storm would mirror the unnaturalness of the king's murder and imply a breach of the cosmic order; it is also a good mood equivalent to the turbulence in Macbeth's mind.

The playwright also manipulates dialog and action on stage to create and evoke mood. Here, for example, from Chekhov's *The Cherry Orchard* (1904), is part of a scene dominated by a dreamy, wistful mood:

Mme. Ranevskaya: Now you want giants! They're only good in fairy tales; otherwise they're frightening.
(Yepihodov crosses the stage at the rear, playing the guitar.)

Mme. Ranevskaya: (Pensively.) There goes Yepihodov.
Anya: (Pensively.) There goes Yepihodov.
Gayev: Ladies and gentlemen, the sun has set.
Trofimov: Yes.

When you read a play, you should be alert to the fluctuations of mood indicated by the content and pace of its dialog.

Character

Characterization in drama is achieved by what a character does or says and by what other characters say about him. Dramatic characters vary widely in individuality. Some are used symbolically to stand for an idea and have no unique identity outside of the concepts they represent. Others are sharply drawn and uniquely constituted as separate personalities. Extreme examples of these two are to be found in Mrs. Smith from Ionesco's *The Bald Soprano*, who is a stereotype of the English suburbanite, and in Shakespeare's Hamlet, who plays his own agonized self. Mrs. Smith's speech is stuffed with banalities, which suit her representational nature:

Mrs. Smith: Mrs. Parker knows a Rumanian grocer by the name of Popesco Rosenfeld, who has just come from Constantinople. He is a great specialist in yogurt. He has a diploma from the school of yogurt-making in Adrianople. Tomorrow I shall buy a large pot of native Rumanian yogurt from him. One doesn't often find such things here in the suburbs of London.

Hamlet's dialog, in contrast, is edged with his personal torments:

Hamlet: O that this too too solid flesh would melt,
Thaw, and resolve itself into a dew,
Or that the Everlasting had not fixed
His canon 'gainst self-slaughter. O God, God,
How weary, stale, flat, and unprofitable
Seem to me all the uses of this world!
Fie on't, ah, fie, 'tis an unweeded garden
That grows to seed. Things rank and gross in nature
Possess it merely.

The use of characters to stand for ideas is a technique both of serious and satiric drama, although it is more widely found in the second. Early morality plays of the Middle Ages used characters in serious drama to symbolically personify the war between the forces of good and evil in Biblical stories. The technique has survived even today in serious drama. In

Arthur Miller's *Death of a Salesman*, for example, Uncle Ben represents to Willy Loman both the lure of success and missed opportunity. A typical line is the following:

> Ben: William, when I walked into the jungle, I was 17. When I walked out I was twenty-one. And, by God, I was rich!

A play's theme may also be wholly embodied in its characters as in *The Bald Soprano* where the characters both act out and stand for the thematic ideas. You need to decide early in your analysis of a play whether its characters are more representational than real.

Writing about drama is not significantly different from writing about fiction. The difference is primarily one of approach and emphasis.

What to say about poetry

When analyzing poetry, you should follow our general rule: analyze the poem for its most significant feature. Poetry is more compressed than either fiction or drama, and makes use of rhythm and rhyme as a means of conveying tone. Poetry has also evolved some further conventions of its own. In general, however, poetry is as analyzable through the use of the five features of literature—point of view, plot and theme, tone, mood, and character—as is either fiction or drama.

Point of view

The convention in poetry assumes that behind each poem is a speaker who speaks the poem and provides its point of view. Occasionally, the speaker may be identified with the poet, especially when the subject of the poem seems obviously related to the poet's life as deduced from its title. Theodore Roethke's poem "Elegy for Jane My Student, Thrown by a Horse" falls into this category, as its title implies. An elegy is a poem lamenting the death of someone, and since the poet tells us in the title of the poem that the lamented someone was once his student, we can assume that the grief is his own, and not a speaker's. But even this cannot be assumed to be true of all elegies. In the past, it was customary for a bereaved family to pay a poet to write an elegy for its deceased member. The resulting poem would also have a speaker called "I," who would lament the passing of the family member in a most personal way.

More often than not the speaker's attitude does not necessarily coincide with the poet's. It is more usual to assume that the speaker, who almost always refers to himself as "I," is simply a point of view constructed for the sake of the poem. There are at least two good reasons for assuming that the speaker's point of view is not the poet's. First, many poems are too brief and contain too little evidence on either the speaker or the poet for it to matter. Second, even if the contrary is assumed—that the speaker and the poet are the same—the assumption usually adds nothing to understanding either the speaker, the poet, or the poem. Take for instance, this poem by William Carlos Williams:

THIS IS JUST TO SAY

I have eaten
the plums
that were in
the icebox

and which
you were probably
saving
for breakfast

Forgive me
they were delicious
so sweet
and so cold

If the speaker is assumed to be the poet, all we know is that he has raided an icebox at one time or another. Nothing else comes out of the assumption that the speaker is the poet. Moreover, whether it was the poet or the speaker who ate the plums is insignificant.

Plot and theme

Most poems do not have a plot, but every poem has a context that is related to its theme. A poem's context is the frame of reference it begins with. It must begin somewhere, with some idea, act, event, or discovery as its initial frame. From then on, it proceeds within this assumed context. Consider this poem:

DESIGN

I found a dimpled spider, fat and white,
On a white heal-all, holding up a moth
Like a white piece of rigid satin cloth—
Assorted characters of death and blight
Mixed ready to begin the morning right,

Like the ingredients of a witches' broth—
A snow-drop spider, a flower like a froth.
And dead wings carried like a paper kite.

What had that flower to do with being white,
The wayside blue and innocent heal-all?
What brought the kindred spider to that height,
Then steered the white moth thither in the night?
What but design of darkness to appall?—
If design govern in a thing so small.

—Robert Frost

The context of this poem is provided in its first two lines: "I found a dimpled spider, fat and white, On a white heal-all, holding up a moth." These lines mean exactly what they say: that the speaker found a spider and a dead moth. The rest of the poem is made up of the speaker's elaboration on his discovery and his speculation on what it means. We cannot call this a plot: plot refers to a sequential series of events, one thing happening as the result of another. But this discovery, though it is too static to be a plot, is the initial context of the poem; from then on, we expect the poem to stay within the context of that discovery, and it does.

But even if a poem has no plot, it will have a theme—a dominant idea that all its parts add up to. Frequently, the theme of a poem will be stated in its imagery. The theme of Frost's poem is partly hinted at by its title, "Design," and is expressed through the images it uses to describe the spider and the moth. The spider is described as "fat and white"; the moth is also "white"; the flower, normally blue, as the speaker tells us, is also "white." White is the color we associate with innocence, which leads the poet to ask:

What had that flower to do with being white,
The wayside blue and innocent heal-all?
What brought the kindred spider to that height,
Then steered the white moth thither in the night?

The entire cosmos seems implicated, by coincidence, in the murder of a mere moth. Having raised the question, the poet then answers it with another question: "What but design of darkness to appall?" and then questions his own answer: "If design govern in a thing so small." The imagery assembles a scene of fantastic coincidence: a dead white moth in the clutches of a white spider on top of a white flower. And all three came together in a dark night. We are left speculating about innocence versus destiny—and that is the dominant idea or theme of the poem.

The initial context in which a poem opens will often be implied by its title. Below are the titles of various poems together with a paraphrase of the context of each poem:

"Snake," by D. H. Lawrence: The speaker describes his encounter with and reaction to a snake.

"To His Coy Mistress," by Andrew Marvell: The speaker is berating his mistress for being coy.

"On Looking at Stubb's *Anatomy of the Horse*," by Edward Lucie-Smith: The speaker has a daydream as he examines a book titled *Anatomy of the Horse* by Stubb.

Many poems will use their titles in this way—to establish an initial context or frame that the first line of the poem will then abruptly plunge the reader into. Frequently, a reader who misses the implications of a poem's title will miss its starting point and be unable to follow it. This use of title partly accounts for the conciseness of poetry. While a short story will often expend the first few paragraphs or pages establishing the context for the narrative to follow, a poem will simply flash a title, take its context for granted, and begin.

We began by saying that most poems do not have a plot, but all poems have a context. A few poems, however, do have a plot. The ballad is a poem that tells a story, and therefore generally has a plot, much like a short story does. "Ringo" and "Frankie and Johnny" are two well-known ballads that have been set to music. Plot poems, or ballads, while being more terse than fiction, will often use their plots similarly. Much of what we said about plots in the fiction section therefore applies to ballad poetry.

Some poems are skimpy in length, and consequently contain very skimpy themes. While the size of a poem does not necessarily reflect the complexity of its theme or main idea, it is generally a factor. Students, however, are seldom content to accept the shallowness of a poem's theme at its face value. Generally, they cling to the belief that there must be more, and it must be probed for in the poem's symbolism. Every poem is believed to have some vast "hidden meaning." This is not so: some poems mean exactly what they say. There is a surface meaning, and nothing underneath. Here, for example, is one such poem:

THE EAGLE

He clasps the crag with crooked hands;
Close to the sun in lonely lands,
Ringed with the azure world, he stands.

The wrinkled sea beneath him crawls;
He watches from his mountain walls,
And like a thunderbolt he falls.

—Alfred, Lord Tennyson

The poem is a vivid, poetic rendering of an eagle, almost like a word painting. It is nothing more than that. If you hunt for symbols in it, you will produce nothing but a forced and artificial interpretation.

In writing about a poem's theme, you should:

1. Identify the poem's initial context
2. Trace the development of the poem from its context to its conclusion
3. Study the imagery the poem uses.

Tone

As in fiction or drama, tone in poetry is inflected to vary with the seriousness of the subject and to project the personality of the speaker. Poetry, however, uses rhythm and rhyme to convey tone. Compare this stanza:

> Break, break, break,
> On thy cold gray stones, O Sea!
> And I would that my tongue could utter
> The thoughts that arise in me.
>
> —Alfred, Lord Tennyson

with this one:

> A sweet, a delicate white mouse,
> A little blossom of a beast,
> Is waltzing in the house
> Among the crackers and the yeast.
>
> —Stanley Kunitz, from "The Waltzer in the House"

The difference in tone between these two stanzas is partly a result of what their words mean, and partly a result of the way they sound. There is a complex interplay between the rhythm of the words and their meanings. Poetic rhythm is this manipulation of words in a line to produce a sound that underscores the subject of the poem. If the poem deals with a gloomy and weighty topic, as in the first example above, we expect its lines to sound heavy and laborious; if its subject is light and frothy, as in the second example, we expect its lines to sound likewise. As the poet Alexander Pope once put it, "The sound must seem an echo to the sense." This principle of modulating the sound of a poem to produce a tone appropriate to its subject is basic to the use of rhythm in poetry.

Frequently, the rhyme of a poem will similarly underscore its meaning. Here is an example:

DADDY

You do not do, you do not do
Any more, black shoe
In which I have lived like a foot
For thirty years, poor and white,
Barely daring to breathe or Achoo.

Daddy, I have had to kill you.
You died before I had time—
Marble-heavy, a bag full of God,
Ghastly statue with one grey toe
Big as a Frisco seal

And a head in the freakish Atlantic
Where it pours bean green over blue
In the waters off beautiful Nauset.
I used to pray to recover you.
Ach, du.

—Sylvia Plath, from "Daddy"

The poem goes on in this vein for sixteen stanzas. Notice, however, that in the three stanzas reprinted above the primary rhyme is on the "do, shoe, Achoo, you," sound. The title of the poem is "Daddy" and the speaker in it addresses her father in rhymes that capture the gurgle of baby talk. The rhyme underscores the psychological conflict of the speaker, who seems caught between a simultaneous impulse to hate and love her father.

In addition to its use of rhythm and rhyme, poetry also uses other devices common to both fiction and drama, such as appropriate diction and phrasing, to convey its speaker's tone. Most poems are written from the vantage point of a speaker who refers to himself or herself as "I"; the tone of voice in the poem is therefore his or hers, and is partly the means by which we are convinced of the credibility of the speaker, and therefore of the poem. If the speaker's tone and statements are at odds with one another, the poem will seem artificial and false, as if the speaker were contriving to be poetic for our benefit. For the poem to convince us, we must be convinced of the sincerity of its speaker, and that sincerity is partly a function of an appropriate tone. Consider this poem:

UNLUCKY BOAT

That boat has killed three people. Building her
Sib drove a nail through his thumb, and died up by
Bunged to the eyes with rust and penicillin.
One evening when the Bring was a bar of silver

Under the moon, and Mansie and Tom with wands
Were putting a spell on cuithes, she dipped a bow
And invited Mansie, his pipe still in his teeth,
To meet the cold green angels. They hauled her up
Among the rocks, right in the path of Angus,
Whose neck, rigid with pints from the Doundy market,
Snapped like a barley stalk . . . There she lies.
A leprous unlucky bitch, in the quarry of Moan.

Tinkers, going past, make the sign of the cross.

—George MacKay Brown

We have no way of knowing who the speaker is, but the tone of the poem implies that he is a simple person, probably a fisherman, who lives somewhere in the British Isles. We infer this first, from the names of the people associated with the boat: "Sib, Mansie, Angus"; second, from the place names used in the poem: "Doundy market, quarry of Moan"; and finally, from his diction and phrasing, "when the Bring was a bar of silver"—*Bring* apparently meaning *sea*—and from his neck "rigid with pints," which is an Anglicized way of saying that he was drunk either on beer or ale. The reference to the sign of the cross in the last line suggests, more particularly, southern Ireland, which is predominantly Roman Catholic. The fisherman's story of the unlucky boat is believable because it is exactly what we would expect from the point of view of a simple and superstitious fisherman. We would probably not believe the poem if it were inflected with the tone of a sophisticated New Yorker. But as it stands, the tone of the poem adds to the speaker's credibility and convinces us of his sincerity.

In summary, tone in poetry is commonly achieved by the use of rhyme and rhythm appropriate to the subject of the poem, and the use of diction and phrasing appropriate to the speaker of the poem.

Mood

The function of mood in some narrative poetry remains the same as in fiction and drama—to provide an external equivalent for the conflict taking place in the mind of the speaker. Here, for example, is a poem by John Keats:

LA BELLE DAME SANS MERCI

O what can ail thee, knight-at-arms,
Alone and palely loitering?
The sedge has withered from the Lake,
And no birds sing!

O what can ail thee, knight-at-arms,
So haggard, and so woe begone?
The Squirrel's granary is full
And the harvest's done.

I see a lily on thy brow
With anguish moist and fever dew,
And on thy cheeks a fading rose
Fast withereth too—

I met a Lady in the Meads,
Full beautiful, a faery's child
Her hair was long, her foot was light
And her eyes were wild—

I made a Garland for her head,
And bracelets too, and fragrant Zone
She look'd at me as she did love
And made sweet moan—

I set her on my pacing steed
And nothing else saw all day long
For sidelong would she bend and sing
A faery's song—

She found me roots of relish sweet
And honey wild and manna dew
And sure in language strange she said
I love thee true—

She took me to her elfin grot
And there she wept and sigh'd full sore,
And there I shut her wild wild eyes
With kisses four.

And there she lulled me asleep
And there I dream'd, Ah Woe betide!
The latest dream I ever dreamt
On the cold hill side.

I saw pale Kings, and Princes too
Pale warriors, death pale were they all;
They cried, La belle dame sans merci
Thee hath in thrall.

I saw their starv'd lips in the gloam
With horrid warning gaped wide,
And I awoke, and found me here
On the cold hill's side.

And this is why I sojourn here
Alone and palely loitering;
Though the sedge is withered from the Lake
And no birds sing.

The title translates, "The beautiful woman without mercy," and the poem tells of a knight's seduction by an illusive woman who abandons him on a hillside. Notice the description of his surroundings: "the sedge has withered from the Lake/And no birds sing"; and, "the Squirrel's granary is full/And the harvest's done." The knight's story is told against a backdrop of autumn, the season that poetically corresponds to old age and is therefore a suitable equivalent for his disillusionment. His loss of the beautiful woman is complexly echoed throughout the poem in its descriptions. As he says, he awoke and found himself on "the cold hill's side," which invites a comparison in the reader's mind between the desolation the knight feels and the desolation he describes. The one is mirrored in and intensified by the other. The same principle of mood manipulation is at work that we talked about in fiction, where the descriptions of landscape reflect the conflict and feelings in the mind of the speaker.

Mood is an important feature in narrative or ballad poetry, but less so in other shorter poems. For instance, the poem "This Is Just to Say" discussed earlier does not use description to reflect conflict, which is a primary technique for evoking mood. When this technique is used in poetry, as in "La Belle Dame sans Merci," it differs very little from the way it is used in fiction or drama. The principle is the same in all three genres, to use description to provide an external equivalent for the conflict and feelings of the speaker or character.

Character

Some poems are not simply told from the point of view of an undifferentiated speaker, but are full-blown characterizations. It is, however, difficult to distinguish between when a poem is characterizing and when it is simply using a speaker to make comments about the external world. Poetry, as we said earlier, generally is written from the first-person point of view. The convention assumes that this first person who calls himself "I" is simply a point of view constructed for the sake of the poem. This convention evolved partly because most poems are too brief for us to conclude anything about their speaker's personality or character traits. We said that nothing could be concluded about the speaker of the poem "This Is Just to Say" except that he likes to eat plums. And about "Unlucky Boat," we concluded from its tone only that the speaker is probably a fisherman somewhere in the British Isles. What else can we know about him from the poem? Very little. The focus in the poem is on the boat and its history, and not on the speaker.

There are other poems, however, where the speaker's vision is so peculiarly his or her own that we come away thinking that what we have read is more symptomatic of the speaker's mind than of an external reality. Such poems are generally long, and have a chance to articulate the speaker's point of view more completely. Frequently, the character-study poem takes the form of a dramatic monologue—a long speech delivered to a person who never responds. In the process, the speaker reveals a full range of foibles and quirks. In such cases, the person behind the poem is called a *persona*, from the Latin word meaning "mask." The assumption is that the poet has, for the duration of the poem, put on the mask of this person, for the sake of laying bare his or her character.

Many poets have written dramatic monologues, but none better than the English poet Robert Browning (1812–1889), who is the acknowledged master of the form. Here is an example:

MY LAST DUCHESS

Ferrara

That's my last Duchess painted on the wall,
Looking as if she were alive. I call
That piece a wonder, now; Frà Pandolf's hands
Worked busily a day, and there she stands.
Will't please you sit and look at her? I said
"Frà Pandolf" by design, for never read
Strangers like you that pictured countenance,
The depth and passion of its earnest glance,
But to myself they turned (since none puts by
The curtain I have drawn for you, but I)
And seemed as they would ask me, if they durst,
How such a glance came there; so, not the first
Are you to turn and ask thus. Sir, 'twas not
Her husband's presence only, called that spot
Of joy into the Duchess' cheek; perhaps
Frà Pandolf chanced to say "Her mantle laps
Over my Lady's wrist too much," or, "Paint
Must never hope to reproduce the faint
Half-flush that dies along her throat." Such stuff
Was courtesy, she thought, and cause enough
For calling up that spot of joy. She had
A heart—how shall I say?—too soon made glad,

Too easily impressed; she liked whate'er
She looked on, and her looks went everywhere.
Sir, 'twas all one! My favor at her breast,
The dropping of the daylight in the west,
The bough of cherries some officious fool
Broke in the orchard for her, the white mule
She rode with round the terrace—all and each
Would draw from her alike the approving speech,
Or blush, at least. She thanked men—good! but thanked
Somehow—I know not how—as if she ranked
My gift of a nine-hundred-year-old name
With anybody's gift. Who'd stoop to blame
This sort of trifling? Even had you skill
In speech—(which I have not)—to make your will
Quite clear to such an one, and say, "Just this
Or that in you disgusts me; here you miss,
Or there exceed the mark"—and if she let
Herself be lessoned so, nor plainly set
Her wits to yours, forsooth, and made excuse,
—E'en then would be some stooping; and I choose
Never to stoop. Oh, Sir, she smiled, no doubt,
Whene'er I passed her; but who passed without
Much the same smile? This grew; I gave commands;
Then all smiles stopped together. There she stands
As if alive. Will't please you rise? We'll meet
The company below, then. I repeat,
The Count your master's known munificence
Is ample warrant that no just pretense
Of mine for dowry will be disallowed;
Though his fair daughter's self, as I avowed
At starting, is my object. Nay, we'll go
Together down, Sir. Notice Neptune, though,
Taming a sea-horse, thought a rarity,
Which Claus of Innsbruck cast in bronze for me!

The dramatic monologue, like a miniature play, is often specific about place, scene, and time. The subtitle tells us that this poem is set in Ferrara, a town in Italy. The speaker, we gather, is a Duke who is negotiating dowry terms for his upcoming marriage to a count's daughter. His listener is the emissary of the count, sent to negotiate the terms of the dowry. The setting, the Duke's obvious vanity about his art collection, his reference to his nine-hundred-year-old name, and his mention of the dowry system are often used to date the poem in the Renaissance, a period that Browning knew well and wrote extensively about.

The techniques for characterizing in a poem differ little from those used by the novelist, short-story writer, and playwright. If there is a difference, it lies in the greater compression of poetry over other literary forms. Here, for instance, it is hinted in a single line that the Duke was responsible for the disappearance of the Duchess: "I gave commands;/Then all smiles stopped together." This, coupled with the sentence that follows, "There she stands/As if alive," implicates the Duke in her murder. But the reference is so fleeting and quick that an unalert reader might altogether miss it.

The murderous jealousy of the Duke likewise must be inferred from the language of the poem and could easily escape the naive reader. We learn of it early, in lines 7 through 13, when the Duke accuses his listener of having noticed "the depth and passion" in the glance of the Duchess and of wondering—like others who also yearn to ask but dare not—how it came there. At this point, an alert reader might begin to suspect the Duke of projecting a curiosity into his listener that does not actually exist—a suspicion confirmed by the Duke's explanation of his ex-wife's "depth and passion." It was "not her husband's presence only" which called a "spot of joy into the Duchess' cheek," the Duke charges, and he catalogs in an obviously aggrieved tone the objects of his jealousy: her response to the "dropping of the daylight in the west, / The bough of cherries some officious fool / Broke in the orchard for her, the white mule / She rode with round the terrace," all seemingly harmless and innocent diversions. Yet they aroused the Duke to a murderous rage.

It is at this point that we grasp the focus of the poem: it is not on the external world, but on the demented mind of the Duke. Nothing he says can be taken as reliable or truthful; but everything he tells us gives further insight into his twisted personality. When he hints that his Duchess was adulterous—"She thanked men—good! but thanked / Somehow—I know not how—as if she ranked / My gift of a nine-hundred-year-old name / With anybody's gift"—we do not believe him. When he confesses that he seethed in silence with his suspicions because he chose "never to stoop," we get a glimpse into his towering arrogance. And when he tells us, "Oh, Sir, she smiled, no doubt, / Whene'er I passed her; but who passed without / Much the same smile?" we infer that the Duchess was innocently unaware of his mounting rage.

The burden of characterizing the persona in a dramatic monologue depends wholly on the reader's grasp of the normal and reasonable. A reasonable man does not become jealous over harmless courtesies paid to his wife, does not assume that even a stranger can see unchecked passion burning in her portrait, does not murder her over imaginary slights and neglects. When the "I" in a poem is acting, thinking, and behaving in a way that strikes us as singularly different from what we would expect most people to do, then we can assume that we are dealing not merely with a speaker, but with a persona—the poet wearing the mask of a character. And once we grasp this fact about a poem, we must completely alter our way of reading and interpreting it. We must take the poem as a microcosm of a unique mind rather than a factual statement about the real world.

Sample student paper about literature

While the writer of the critical analysis below contradicts traditional evaluations of Dylan Thomas's famous poem, he has the courage to present an unusual view and to support it with evidence from the work itself. Here is the poem:

DO NOT GO GENTLE INTO THAT GOOD NIGHT

Do not go gentle into that good night,
Old age should burn and rave at close of day;
Rage, rage against the dying of the light.

Though wise men at their end know dark is right,
Because their words had forked no lightning they
Do not go gentle into that good night.

Good men, the last wave by, crying how bright
Their frail deeds might have danced in a green bay,
Rage, rage against the dying of the light.

Wild men who caught and sang the sun in flight,
And learn, too late, they grieved it on its way,
Do not go gentle into that good night.

Grave men, near death, who see with blinding sight
Blind eyes could blaze like meteors and be gay,
Rage, rage against the dying of the light.

And you, my father, there on the sad height,
Curse, bless, me now with your fierce tears, I pray.
Do not go gentle into that good night.
Rage, rage against the dying of the light.

—Dylan Thomas (1914–1953)

<u>Critical analysis of "Do Not Go Gentle into That Good Night" by Dylan Thomas</u>

John Ingram

Do not go gentle into that good night, unless you care more about verse than truth. For the verse appears to stand as the primary, if not the only, purpose for this poem. Every painstaking line and carefully developed stanza add to the impression of a meticulously crafted work of superficial and repetitious rhyme and rhythm. Also, considering the subject and the way it is treated, the verse form merely denigrates the theme of the poem.

What is most offensive about this poem is the way it assaults the reader with figurative language that does not give due gravity to the subject of death, but instead treats it with a tasteless whimsicalness. The figures of speech tend toward eccentricity and seem chosen more because they fit the rhythm and the villanelle rhyme scheme or create excitement than because they suit the subject. I refer specifically to such lines as these: "Because their words had forked no lightning;" "Their frail deeds might have danced in a green bay;" "Blind eyes could blaze like meteors and be gay." This is rather absurd language to use to describe man's agonizings about death. In my job as a hospital orderly, I deal with death every day. Night after night I witness the increasingly labored breathing, the waning energy, and the deepening despair of those who are fated to die. It is my job to bag the corpses after the doctors, nurses, and death have done with them. Nothing in this poem corresponds to my experience of death. Not a single line of it rings true. The many patients that I have watched dying show no desire to rage but in fact do in the end "go gently" – and seem relieved to do so.

If the unsatisfying choice of imagery in the poem were not enough to create a false mood, the use of repetitive lines and silly rhymes certainly are. Repetition in a poem can enhance its tone or reinforce a special mood, but here it only annihilates effectiveness. The repetition of "Do not go gentle into that good night," and "Rage, rage against the dying of the light," thuds endlessly in every stanza. The repeated rhymes of "night" with "right," and "light," and "flight," and "height," become wearying, making the poem seem almost like a child's jingle. Both the frivolous rhymes and the silly refrains mock the seriousness of the poem's subject.

There is no merit to be found in this poem because its mood and form simply do not fit the subject. Perhaps if the subject had not been death but, instead, something lighter, then this particular verse might have succeeded. But the subject was death, so the writing is both inappropriate and trivial. The act of dying is made to look like a wild athletic feat instead of the quiet biological end that in reality it is.

12
Writing reports

Report me and my cause aright.

—William Shakespeare

REPORTS ARE THE WORKHORSES of all organizations and much sought after these days. Executives everywhere loudly lament the fact that few of their subordinates can write readable reports. In this chapter we attempt to give you some general guidelines for writing short, narrative, operational reports of the kind most commonly required by business firms or civil service organizations. Because of their highly specialized nature, the following reports are not included in this chapter:

Printed form reports built to a predetermined plan

Professional reports, such as legal briefs, medical case histories, or engineering proposals

Reports based on tables, graphs, or illustrations

Long, formal, analytical reports

The information in this chapter *will* prove particularly useful in writing the following:

Advertising reports
Aeronautics reports
Attitude surveys
Committee reports
Employee appraisals
Employee bulletins
Improvement reports
Interview reports
Market surveys
Police reports
Problem-solving reports
Procedure statements
Product analyses
Progress reports
Sales reports
Proposals
Prospectuses
Technical reports

While we cannot provide examples of each specific report, we have divided the field of short narrative reports into four general types that include most of the above. The four types are:

1. Evaluative reports
2. Problem-solving reports
3. Analytical reports
4. Descriptive reports

Each of these reports follows a general format that is flexible enough to fit various situations. Once you understand the basic framework, you can adapt it to suit a specific circumstance.

Needless to say, all the writing skills you have learned so far can be applied to reports. Principles such as developing an idea coherently, using concrete words, and being yourself are as important in writing a report as they are in writing a creative essay. A good report does not have to be a literary masterpiece, but most busy executives do have certain similar expectations from written reports. These can be summarized in four points:

1. A visible method of organization; that is, a pattern the reader can see
2. A purposeful direction in which the report moves
3. Sparse language to fit the reader's limited time
4. Accurate evidence to support assertions

Determining the purpose of your report

All the writing talent in the world cannot disguise a report that leads nowhere. Unless your reader can tell at first glance what you intend to report, you have not communicated. Therefore, begin your report with a statement of purpose that encapsulates the core of your report. This statement then becomes a peg on which you can hang the rest of your report. Make this statement of purpose clear and concise. Do not waste words building suspense or stating the obvious.

Wrong: Here in the Philadelphia plant of NICON Corporation we have had a problem for a long time that has to do with the rapid expansion of the number of employees and their time computations. We believe we can solve this problem.

Better: This report proposes the installation of time clocks for the Philadelphia NICON Corporation because it will result in greater efficiency in the accounting office, in improved accuracy of time computations, and in less tardiness among employees.

Wrong: Heritage Gardens Convalescent Hospital has a dreadfully high turnover in nurses' aides, the reasons for which are not agreed on by everybody involved.

Better: The turnover in nurses' aides at Heritage Gardens Convalescent Hospital is due to three factors analyzed in this report: 1. the competitive wages paid by the nearby Veterans Hospital, 2. poor personnel relations on the part of the head nurse, 3. lack of variety in patient care.

Wrong: The introduction of a line of Judith Leiber belts would maybe give prestige to our store, but we would lose our shirts because the stock would not move.

Better: The analysis that follows will indicate clearly that introducing a line of Judith Leiber belts is not economically profitable for our business because, although the markup on Judith Leiber fashion items is high, stock would not move since our store caters to a middle-class clientele that will not pay the retail price demanded by the Judith Leiber label.

Wrong: Financial statements presented by corporate enterprises to shareholders are often a broken and winding path.

Better: The objective of this report is threefold: 1. to point up specific areas where there was lack of communication in this year's stockholders report, 2. to analyze the causes for this failure in communication, 3. to suggest some changes that will remedy the problem.

The evaluative report

The evaluative report passes critical judgment on a subject. The most common is the report evaluating a person (also called a personal reference). It is often requested of people in supervisory positions. Evaluative reports must be kept confidential, to be discussed only with those individuals directly involved in the hiring, firing, or promoting of the person evaluated. In writing an evaluation, you have every right to assume complete confidentiality. You also have the responsibility to be honest and objective. An evaluation is no place for undeserved praise nor for disparagement based on personal grudges. Tell the truth the way you actually see it. The person asking for an evaluation is depending on your judgment as a basis for his or her decision. If you provide overblown compliments or sarcastic criticisms, you are of no help.

Your evaluation of a person should include the following information:

1. Statement of purpose summarizing your attitude toward the person being evaluated
2. Name and position of person being evaluated
3. Length of person's association with you, and your relationship
4. Job description
5. Most valuable assets

6. Least valuable assets
7. Personal traits, including the person's public relations, interoffice relations, character integrity, and presentability
8. Final summary statement

Be sure to back up general statements with specific evidence, particularly if the statement is a negative criticism. Avoid hackneyed phrases, such as:

> In the line of duty . . .
> With a character beyond reproach . . .
> My considered opinion of her is . . .
> Above and beyond the normal average . . .

Unless you are filling out a particular personnel form, the following questions will help you in evaluating a person:

1. Does he/she have adequate skills?
2. Does he/she make sound decisions?
3. Does he/she plan ahead?
4. Does he/she work well with others?
5. Does he/she consider the welfare of the organization?
6. Does he/she interfere with the performance of duties by others?
7. Does he/she communicate?
8. Does he/she get jobs done?
9. Does he/she have personal integrity?
10. Does he/she look presentable?

Sample Evaluative Report

STATEMENT OF PURPOSE

JOB DESCRIPTION

It is my pleasure to recommend Karl L. Folger. He worked for me as part of a three-person clerical pool from January 1, 1972, to November 19, 1973. During this time, he was expected to answer my correspondence, handle my appointments and phone calls, and organize the office files. His job was complicated by the fact that he was responsible to two other sales managers besides me. Keeping three employers happy during hectic periods was no small task.

MOST VALUABLE ASSETS

Mr. Folger's most valuable asset is his total commitment. During the two years that he worked for me, he rarely allowed work to pile up, but would prefer working at the office on weekends rather than getting noticeably behind. I could usually count on beginning the week with a clean slate.

Most of Mr. Folger's work involved typing, which he did accurately and efficiently as long as he could copy or transcribe

LEAST VALUABLE ASSETS

from dictation. He was, however, reticent about composing memos or other material on his own. Such original work always had to be checked for precision in form and content. For instance, I could not rely on him to take committee minutes or to write a letter based on a few kernel ideas. In this area Mr. Folger needs further training.

PUBLIC RELATIONS

An important function of our office is serving the public. Nervous, disgruntled clients come in expecting immediate attention. Some of them are occasionally rude. In this area of our business Mr. Folger showed poise and maturity. He was friendly, unflustered, and dignified. During the two years he worked for me, I did not receive any complaints about him from clients, which in itself is a remarkable recommendation.

INTEROFFICE RELATIONS

Mr. Folger worked well with the other clerks in our firm, but he did not waste time talking with them or taking excessively long coffee breaks. He avoided getting entangled with "gripe" factions and he did not court special favors. He was perhaps somewhat of a "loner," but I believe he saw his job as a job and not as a place where he satisfied his social needs.

PERSONAL APPEARANCE

In his personal appearance Mr. Folger was adequate. He was well groomed and dressed appropriately.

INTEGRITY

I do not hesitate to praise Mr. Folger's honesty and discretion. Our transactions involve dossiers that must be handled discreetly. Never have I known Mr. Folger to give out private information or twist the truth. I respect his integrity fully.

FINAL SUMMARY

In brief, except for his inability to write original material, Mr. Folger is a capable, loyal, and efficient secretary.

Signed: ____________________

Title: ____________________

Date: ____________________

The problem-solving report

The problem-solving report provides a workable plan to get an organization out of trouble. Companies such as the Chase Manhattan Bank or Standard Oil rely for their solution to problems on highly sophisticated methods of investigation and prediction. The executives of these huge corporations have at their disposal professional analysts with computers that can process in minutes what ordinarily would take years of painstaking information gathering and classifying. Business problems are translated into symbols, numbers, or mathematical formulas that the computer then processes and reads back.

Most small organizations, however, still have to rely on human investigation unaided by computers. But the steps involved in solving an organizational problem are basically the same, regardless of whether you use a computer or your own resources. No matter how simple or complicated, a problem-solving report proceeds in four steps:

1. Pinpointing the problem
2. Establishing a goal
3. Finding methods to achieve the goal
4. Applying the methods

Your first step is to *pinpoint the problem* for your reader. More than likely your employer will have done this for you when assigning the report. However, if finding the problem is part of your report, then you must locate it by the best means available. Check the company files; interview reliable workers who might know something about the problem; talk to authorities in the problem area. If you need information requiring public reaction, you may want to initiate your own survey by phone, interview, or questionnaire. As a hypothetical case, let us look at the Edwards Brothers Roofing Tile Company, a small manufacturing concern with assets of approximately $200,000. One of the owners is ill, and you have been hired as assistant manager to help solve the company's problem of operating at a $500 per month deficit. When writing the report, first state the problem: The company is losing $500 per month.

Your second step is to *establish the goal* that ultimately must be achieved in order to solve the problem. In the case of the Edwards Brothers Roofing Tile Company, the goal is to convert the malfunctioning company into a profitable business.

The third step, *finding the methods to achieve the goal*, usually involves the most creative part of your report. You must answer the question, What will it take in order to turn the Edwards Brothers Roofing Tile Company into a profit-making business? After careful investigative research, you come up with the following answers:

1. The Company must update their equipment in order to reduce the number of faulty tiles coming off the production line.
2. The company must create a greater demand for the tile by a stepped up sales force and increased advertising.
3. The company must wrest a share of the market from existing competitors by stressing the unique qualities of its tile.

Your report will point out that if the three above-mentioned conditions are met, the goal will be achieved, and the problem will be solved.

Step four, *applying the methods*, is the core of your report because it sets up the mechanisms by which the problem will be solved. At this point it is difficult to separate skillful investigation from skillful reporting. In order for your report to be helpful, the suggestions it contains must be helpful. Bad ideas cannot be masked by elegant language. Likewise, good ideas cannot be recognized if they are reported in fuzzy language. The ideal is to match up good ideas with good reporting. Providing you with good ideas is beyond the scope of this book; however, we can give you some help with the actual reporting.

Suppose that these are your specific proposals for the Edwards Brothers Roofing Tile Company:

1. To borrow $25,000 from the bank, to be used as follows:
   a. $10,000 to convert the present equipment
   b. $ 5,000 for advertising and promotion
   c. $ 5,000 to pay off accumulated debts
   d. $ 5,000 in ready reserves
2. To replace the present sales manager with a new one who knows the market and knows how to train other salespersons.

You might also want to include in your report an alternative solution, which in this case might be to liquidate the company at the going rate and invest the money in some suitable way. Your alternative solution will probably be discounted by the information you supply in support of the solution you are proposing. But your inclusion of an alternative solution indicates that you have studied the problem carefully and considered all possible solutions before advising the company on what course to take.

Your final report should read something like the following.

Sample Problem-solving Report

To: Edwards Brothers Roofing Tile Company

From: ______________________________

STATEMENT OF PURPOSE

The purpose of this report is to propose a bank loan of $25,000 in order to make the company's product competitive, or, as an alternate plan, to liquidate the company at the going rate and invest the money in a suitable way.

PINPOINTING THE PROBLEM

The Edwards Brothers Roofing Tile Company is a family business, which in the last year has experienced a steady slump in profits. The land, building, and equipment are currently appraised at $200,000, although it is doubtful that the company could be liquidated at that figure.

ESTABLISHING A GOAL

If the Edwards Brothers Roofing Tile Company is to survive, it must be converted from its present debt-ridden state into a profitable business.

Research into the company's books and files, conversations

FINDING THE METHODS TO ACHIEVE THE GOAL

with competitors, and interviews with steady customers have convinced me that the main problem lies with the tile itself: too many tiles leak. Everyone I talked with agrees that the tile is beautiful and strong, but that it is not consistently leak-proof. Apparently the problem of leakage has developed recently as the result of obsolete equipment. The problem can be solved by updating the equipment. Numerous builders in the Napa Valley wish to use the tile, but they want a guarantee that it will not leak.

Lack of promotion is another problem, especially since Mr. Daniel Edwards has been ill. Edwards Brothers tile has no significant competitors since the tile is a unique blend of the modern bar tile and the old-fashioned Spanish tile. Many designers are pleased with the striking looks of the tile, but rumors of leakage have reached their ears, and they hesitate to commit themselves. The company needs a salesperson who will allay these fears and push the product. At the same time, the company must put out some effective ads in the form of flyers, newspaper inserts, and write-ups in trade magazines.

The promotion just suggested must stress that Edwards Brothers tile is different from any other tile. It must be pointed out that Edwards Brothers tile is the nearest thing to handmade pottery.

The competition in this location consists only of two building emporiums that stock bar tile imported from Oregon and regular red Spanish tile. No other company in the area offers a product that approaches the individuality and beauty of Edwards Brothers tile. This lack of competition is the key factor in my suggestion that the company should not close down. I am convinced that if it can present a leakproof tile, it can regain a big share of the tile market.

APPLYING THE METHODS

Now I come to two specific proposals on how to solve the Edwards Brothers Roofing Tile Company's financial problems. My first suggestion is to borrow $25,000 from the bank, to be appropriated as follows:

1. $10,000 to update the present equipment in order to decrease the number of faulty tiles
2. $5,000 for immediate advertising and promotion
3. $5,000 to pay off accumulated debts
4. $5,000 in ready reserves

My second suggestion is to replace the present sales manager with one who is successful in persuasive strategy and who knows how to train and inspire other salespeople. According to my findings, this is something the Edwards Brothers Roofing Tile Company has never had, but has an urgent need for.

CONCLUSION

The only other option available is to liquidate the company at the going rate and invest the money in some suitable way. However, I do not see this second option as financially nearly so feasible as the first, which is to keep the company, improve the product, and step up promotion.

Signed: ____________________

Title: ____________________

The analytical report

Any analytical report answers the question, What is the nature of the subject? It investigates by noting how a thing functions or what its characteristics are. It differs from a descriptive report in that its emphasis is on breaking the subject into parts in order to see how these parts function in relation to the whole. In other words, an analytical report can break up a process to scrutinize each stage in it, or it can break up a subject in order to get a better look at the components involved. Analytical reports are of particular value in the area of salesmanship, consumer reaction, and market surveying.

The most important requirement of a good analytical report is logical organization. If, for instance, you are assigned the job of analyzing a certain city to see if direct-mail solicitation of the teenage market would be profitable to your company, your investigation must result in an organized analysis. The following breakdown is a possibility:

1. Actual number of teenagers in the designated market
2. Number of teenagers forecasted for the next ten years
3. A comparison of the size of this market with other market targets in other age brackets
4. The potential spending force the teenage market represents
5. The kinds of merchandise teenagers in the designated area are most likely to buy

But if you were asked to analyze for your firm the advantages of a tax deferred annuities program, your breakdown would be entirely different. You might settle on the following:

1. Advantages as a savings fund
   a. You invest a regular portion of your monthly income in a stable mutual fund at a guaranteed interest
   b. Your annuities can be cashed in at any time

c. You receive a monthly statement that informs you of the separate unit purchase price and of the accumulated value of your investment

2. Advantages as a tax deferment
   a. You pay no tax on the money you invest until you cash in some shares
   b. The assumption is that you will hold on to the investment, letting it accumulate until you have retired and are in a lower tax bracket than you are in now

Regardless of the organization chosen, you must comment appropriately on each entry in your outline in order to give your reader a clear view of the total subject. The kind of assignment will dictate the breakdown you will choose.

Below is a sample analysis of the market for a political science and comparative government college textbook. The publishing company involved has written a letter to one of their field representatives requesting that she survey the market and report her findings in a memorandum. Notice how all the findings are summarized for quick assessment by the reader.

Sample Analytical Report

To: Ken Bancroft
From: Judith King
Subject: Possible market for McFarland manuscript

This is in reply to your memo requesting information on the size of the introduction to political science and comparative government markets at the college level in my territory. An analysis follows. Also included are my recommendations for possible reviewers of the McFarland manuscript.

1. *Market*
   a. *Junior colleges*

      The market at this level is good, but not especially large. I estimate the California junior college market in any given spring semester to be about 3,000 students. This includes both the comparative government and introduction to political science courses, as these course titles tend to be used interchangeably in many college catalogs. The fact is that most, if not all, introduction to political science courses are essentially courses in comparative government. They deal with political science methodology as it exists in theory and as it applies to the study of various governments. The countries selected for study are usually: Great Britain, France, Germany, and Russia.

My estimate of the Arizona junior college market is 1,000 students in any given spring semester. The total junior college market in my area is therefore about 4,000 students.

b. *Four-year colleges*

The four-year college market is difficult to estimate. In California I estimate the enrollment to be about 1,000 in any given spring semester, in Arizona about 300. In my territory junior colleges outnumber four-year colleges about ten to one, which accounts for the difference in enrollment. I am also assuming that the book is pitched strictly for the undergraduate course and will not be used on the graduate level.

c. *To sum up the market:*

1) My estimate of the total market in my area, including both four-year colleges and junior colleges, is 5,300 students in any given spring semester. I emphasize "any given spring semester" because the junior colleges tend to offer this course only in the spring. Some of the larger colleges will offer it in both fall and spring semesters, but these are few when compared to the entire junior college market.
2) At the junior college level comparative government and introduction to political science tend to be the same course. If the junior college offers a course in introduction to political science, it will not offer a course in comparative government; if it has a course in comparative government, it will offer no course in introduction to political science.
3) The course is usually taken by political science majors or by social science majors.
4) I estimate the national market to be about 50,000 students in any given spring semester.

2. *Recommended reviewers for the McFarland book*

The following persons will do a competent review for us:

Rita Specht
Political Science Department
Sierra College

Jeb Janicki
Political Science Department
Sierra College

Prof. Specht has done reviews for Harper & Row and is familiar with what is involved.

3. *To sum up*

There is a fair market that is worth publishing for. The only reservation I have is that the McFarland manuscript does not deal with all the countries usually studied in this course. I think we should pursue this point carefully with the reviewers.

Signed: ____________________

The descriptive report

The descriptive report aims at verbally recreating an object, a person, or an incident so that the reader can portray in his mind's eye what is being described. It is not the aim of such a report to create fictitious or fanciful impressions such as we find in poetry or stories. The aim here is to reproduce faithfully what is being described, without personal coloring or emotive suggestion. Police reports, real estate notices, weather reports, or accidents reports are descriptions of this kind. The following three paragraphs are examples of uncolored, objective reporting:

For Sale

Regency-type house in College Hills, overlooking the Interstate Freeway. 3 bedrooms, living room 15′ x 25′, family room with sunken conversational area near marble fireplace. Modern kitchen with microwave oven and General Electric built-ins. 3 baths and a 2-car garage. Corner lot 150′ x 200′ surrounded by cyprus hedge. Little yard upkeep due to ivy. Radiant heat and central air conditioning. Excellent residence for professional or businessperson. Price: $180,000.

Wanted by the United States Marshal

Harry Foster, alias "Stan Porter." Escaped after committing armed robbery of a house in the Chevy Chase Estates. White, male, aged 26, black hair, brown eyes, 5′11″, weighs 165 lbs. Occasionally wears a beard and mustache. Missing thumb on right hand. Walks with hitching gait due to knee injury. $1,000 reward for information leading to his arrest.

The Weather

Bay Area: Mostly cloudy today with chance of rain in the afternoon. Rain likely at times tonight with snow on the hills. Clearing

> Wednesday, then fair. Not so cold at night. High today and Wednesday in the 40s. Winds becoming westerly 10 to 20 m.p.h. today. Chance of rain 40 percent today and 60 percent tonight.

These descriptions are literal, factual and photographic. They do not go beyond the simple enumeration of parts and characteristics.

Another kind of objective description is found in reports that recreate an incident the way it happened. Police and insurance agents are often required to submit such descriptions. Success in writing them depends on the use of clear, factual language and on careful observation of the event to be reported. Good reporters arrange all the details systematically either according to how they took place chronologically or where they happened geographically. They do not shift from a chronological sequence to a geographic sequence or vice versa. In other words, they maintain a single organizational scheme. The following paragraph stresses chronology:

> The victim stated that at approximately 11:40 P.M., as he was unlocking his vehicle parked behind the Crest Theater on Vachel Avenue, Suspect No. 1 grabbed him from behind, put his right hand over his mouth while keeping him in a wrestling hold with his left arm, and then forced him to the ground. Next, Suspect No. 2 grabbed his briefcase from his hand and rammed his fist in his face. Leaving the victim stunned and bleeding from his nose, both suspects fled down a dark alley next to the theater.

The following paragraph stresses geography:

> My client stated that she was driving her 1970 Camaro south on Barton Road in Springfield. She stopped for the stop sign at the intersection of Barton and Benton, looked to the left and right, then proceeded slowly across the intersection. The next thing she remembers is seeing a two-ton Ford truck bearing down on her from the west. My client says she tried to speed up to avoid a collision, but she was too late. Before she could escape, the truck had rammed into her broadside, crushing the entire right side of her car.

Whether the stress is on chronology or geography, a description is coherent only when the order of events is arranged in a manner that the reader can follow and interpret. Descriptions must never range erratically forward and backward in time, or willy-nilly left, right, up and down in place. Such descriptions confuse.

Below is the description of an arrest as reported by the police. Only the narrative portion of the report is provided here. The person arrested is charged with wife-beating.

Sample Descriptive Report

While working as Desk Man at the Hillhurst Station on the above date, Officer Thomas Bolen observed the defendant standing in front of the station and asked him what business he had in the neighborhood. The defendant stated that his wife was in the station filling out a crime report for wife-beating and that he was waiting to talk with her. He stated: "I don't want to do anything. I just want to talk to her for about five minutes or so. Then I'll leave town. When I broke through the window Friday, I did it because I wanted to talk to her, and she didn't want to open the door for me. Yes, I had a knife that I took from the kitchen, but I wasn't going to kill her. I was just going to scare her. I don't want a divorce. I want to go back to her. I don't want to break up the marriage."

The victim's crime report alleges that on February 24, 1972, between 10:00 and 10:15 P.M. the above defendant, who is the victim's husband, broke into the victim's apartment and attacked her. The victim has been separated from the defendant since January 3, 1972. After breaking into the apartment, the defendant took a butcher knife from the kitchen sink and lunged toward the victim, threatening, "I'm going to kill you." The defendant then attacked the victim, who struggled to protect herself and in the process sustained a slight laceration on the left side of her neck and a deep cut on her left ring finger. The defendant then knocked the victim to the floor and then fled on foot.

Because of the circumstances involving the crime report, Officer Bolen took both the defendant and the victim to the Hillhurst Station detectives for interrogation. Upon the detectives' orders, Officer Bolen booked the defendant on charges of wife-beating.

Photographs have been taken of the left side of the neck, left cheek, and left ring finger of the victim.

The knife used by the defendant to threaten the victim has been booked as evidence and marked "MJG" for identification.

While checking the defendant's record through the City Police Department and Sheriff's record through the City Police Department and Sheriff's Record, the defendant was found to have a traffic warrant (#T95505) from Oakville S.C. for $46.

The abstract

Just as the President of the United States is briefed through condensed versions of longer documents because he is often too busy to read the original, so many other managers rely on abstracts to remain informed about their business operations. An abstract is a reduction that summarizes and highlights the major points of a larger work so that the reader either gets the general gist of the original without actually reading it, or decides that the subject matter is important enough to warrant reading the entire original. Composing abstracts is one of the most important aspects of report writing. Averaging about two hundred words at most, an abstract must make sense independently of the matter it is condensing. It should avoid referring to the original or reproducing charts, illustrations, or bibliographies from it. The best way to think of an abstract is as an expanded table of contents written in paragraph form. Here is a typical example:

Abstract

After thorough analysis of all pertinent factors, Grover-Quimby and Associates concludes that in the next five years Fontana's most likely industrial growth will occur in two areas: 1) diversification of present industries to attract new markets, and 2) introduction of some new high-technology industry. Grover-Quimby predict that at least one new shopping mall will be built near the center of town within the next two years and that as a result of this modest industrial growth, the general economic condition of Fontana will improve. Finally, Grover-Quimby suggests the following steps to be taken immediately by the Fontana Chamber of Commerce: a) Hiring a public relations firm to publicize the growing image of Fontana, 2) Devising a specific five-year plan for attracting new industry and real estate investments.

The following rules must be observed in writing an abstract:

1. Summarize only the most important points of the original report. (These are often found in major headings or in topic sentences.)
2. Retain the basic ideas of the original, but omit all details.
3. Stick to simple language, avoiding technical terms, especially if the reader may not be familiar with the subject matter of the abstract.
4. Do not omit articles *(a, an, the)* or transitional expressions *(however, therefore, for example)*.
5. Avoid direct references to the original report. Remember that an abstract must be able to stand on its own.

Part FOUR Handbook

Basic grammar
Punctuation
Mechanics
Effective sentences

Basic grammar

A COMMAND OF BASIC GRAMMAR is as essential to writers as water is to fish. No matter how clever and creative a writer you are, if you cannot string coherent sentences together, use verbs and nouns properly, and make pronouns agree with their antecedents, your writing will inevitably appear amateurish. Yet the odd thing is that you are likely to receive little, if any, praise for mastering grammar. "Nobody ever admired an orator for using correct grammar." wrote Cicero. "They only laugh at him if his grammar is bad." So it is, too, with writers. They are expected to write grammatically, but get no glory for doing it.

It follows that the explanations of grammar, punctuation, mechanics, and style in this section may not help you to write exceptionally or even well. They will, however, help you to write correctly. To write well, you need to be grammatical and imaginative; to write exceptionally, you need to be grammatical, imaginative, precise, colorful, witty, and inspired. But no matter what level of excellence you hope to achieve in your writing, mastering grammar is an indispensable first step.

1. Parts of speech

Words are the smallest grammatical parts of a sentence. Every word in a sentence performs a particular function by which it can be classified. These functions are carried out by eight parts of speech. Originally devised by Dionysius Thrax, a Greek grammarian, in 100 B.C., these categories have come down to us relatively intact.

The eight parts of speech are *verbs, nouns, adjectives, adverbs, pronouns, prepositions, conjunctions,* and *interjections*. Verbs, nouns, adjectives, and adverbs comprise almost all of the words in the dictionary. But even though the other four account for less than one percent of all words, they are used again and again in sentences.

1a. Verbs

The verb is the most crucial word in the sentence since it expresses an action a process, or a state of being and since without it no sentence is complete. Verbs express commands, make statements about subjects, or link the subject to some idea about the subject.

Sit
Stop! } Verbs express commands. (The subject *you* is understood.)

God loves.
Serpents hiss.
Fish swim. } Verbs make statements about the subjects.

John is hungry.
The children feel tired. } Verbs link the subject to some idea about the subject.

Most verbs express action or process. Linking verbs express a state of being. In addition to all forms of the verb *be*, they include *seem, feel, grow, look, sound, taste*.

Action: The cow *jumped* over the moon.

Process: The clock *ticked*.

State of being: He *is* happy.
We *felt* sick.

The verbs in the examples above are complete in a single word, but others include one or more auxiliary (helping) words, thus forming a verb phrase:

The clouds *had disappeared*. (*had* is an auxiliary word.)
I *should* never *have taken* the money. (*Should* and *have* are auxiliary words.)

NOTE: Neither gerunds nor participles function as complete verbs, but more about them on page 000.

(1) Tense Because actions take place at different times—in the present, past, or future—verbs can be adjusted to reflect this fact. The six tense are:

Present tense expresses actions that happen now or that seem forever true:

I *am eating* breakfast.
John *likes* to eat.
Roses *are* beautiful.

Past tense expresses an action happening sometime in the past:

Nan *ate* all the cherries.
Jack *sent* me these roses.

Future tense expresses an action that will happen sometime in the future.

Will you *buy* some more cherries?
The roses *will die* soon.

NOTE: It has become popular to use *shall* and *will* interchangeably. Nevertheless, purists of the English language make the following distinctions. To express a future action:

I *shall* eat	We *shall* eat
You *will* eat	You *will* eat
He/she/it *will* eat	They *will* eat

To express determination:

I *will* eat	We *will* eat (We are determined to eat)
You *shall* eat	You *shall* eat
He/she/it *shall* eat	They *shall* eat

In the case of questions in the first person, *will* and *shall* are not interchangeable:

Shall we stay till 9:00 or *shall* we leave now?
but
Tomorrow we *will* (or *shall*) stay till 9:00.

Present perfect tense indicates that the action has taken place in the past but lasted until now.

Nan *has eaten* all the cherries.
The roses *have lasted* ten days.

Past perfect tense indicates that an action in the past took place before another past action:

Nan *had eaten* all the cherries before the guests arrived.
The lawyer *had gone* to court before June 15.

The *future perfect tense*, which is not often used, indicates a future action that will take place before another future action:

Nan *will have eaten* all the cherries by lunch time.
The roses *will have died* before the gardner arrives.

NOTE: Most verbs form the past tense and past participle by adding *ed* or *d* to the infinitive: *walk, walked, walked; believe, believed, believed*. Many verbs, however, form their principal parts through an internal vowel change *or* a final consonant change (*drink, drank, drunk; build, built, built*) or by not changing at all (*let, let, let*). If you are in doubt, check the dictionary, where you will find the principal parts of verbs listed. The principal parts of the following verbs are commonly misused:

lie, lay, lain (I *lie* in the sun.)

lay, laid, laid (He *laid* the book on the table.)

sit, sat, sat (The baby *sits* in her crib.)

set, set, set (John *has set* the vase on the shelf.)

rise, rose, risen (We *rise* for prayer.)

raise, raised, raised (Two men *raised* the flag.)

(2) Voice Voice indicates who or what is doing the acting and who or what is receiving the action. Voice is either *active* or *passive*. In the active voice the subject always performs the action:

Helen drank a gallon of water. (*Helen* is the subject.)

In the passive voice the subject always is acted upon:

A gallon of water was drunk by Helen. (*Gallon* is the subject.)

Sometimes the passive voice omits the doer of an action:

A gallon of water was drunk.

NOTE: Only transitive verbs (see next page) have voice.

(3) Forms Verb forms are *transitive* or *intransitive*. A verb is transitive if it requires an object:

> Maria *discovered* an error. (*Error* serves as direct object.)

Occasionally a transitive verb will take a direct, as well as an indirect, object:

> She gave her sister a sandwich. (*Sandwich* is the direct object; *sister* is the indirect object.)

A verb is *intransitive* if it does not need an object to complete its meaning:

> The orchestra *played* beautifully.

NOTE: Some verbs are transitive only *(take, enjoy)*, while others are intransitive only (*frown, giggle*). However, many verbs can function either way:

> He sang loudly; he sang an opera.

1b. Nouns

A noun is the name of a person, place, thing, idea, or event:

Persons: Dr. Wells, girl, Becky
Places: Chicago, heaven, school, world, park
Things: table, rice, chess, history, politics
Ideas: love, fear, humility, patriotism, stinginess
Events: war, trip, Christmas, Monday

Common nouns represent the names of general classes of persons, places, or things:

> boxer, state, writer, cereal

Proper nouns are always capitalized and name a particular person, place, or thing:

> Mohammed Ali, Michigan, the Constitution, Lake Tahoe

Compound nouns are proper nouns or common nouns that consist of more than one word and function as a single unit:

> South Africa, exchange rate, sunset, headache

1c. Pronouns

A pronoun is used in place of a noun. It is clearer and more concise to say "The man took off *his* coat" than "The man took off *the man's* coat." The antecedent of a pronoun is the word it replaces. Every pronoun must be in the same gender (masculine or feminine), case (subject of the sentence or object of the verb), and number (singular or plural) as its antecedent. Thus, "We saw the girl" will become "We saw *her*" because *girl* is feminine, object of the verb, and singular.

Pronouns may be grouped into seven categories:

Personal pronouns stand for someone or something specific: *I, you, he, she, it, we, you, they.*

Demonstrative pronouns point to nouns: *this, that, these, those.* They can be used as pronouns or as adjectives.

Pronoun: I reject *this.*
Adjective: I reject *this* idea.

Indefinite pronouns are unspecific: *anyone, everyone, each, someone.*

Interrogative pronouns ask a question: *who? what? which?* (Who destroyed the tree?)

Relative pronouns relate back to an antecedent (the banker *who,* the table *that,* the story *which*): *who, whom, those, which, that.*

Intensive pronouns emphasize: *myself, yourself, himself, ourselves, yourselves, themselves.* (I drove it *myself.*)

Reflexive pronouns function as objects or complements. They always refer to the person or thing named in the subject:

She drives *herself* to work every day.
The hot-water heater blew *itself* to smithereens.
I shall buy myself a car.

To use personal pronouns correctly, it is necessary to distinguish among their *subjective, objective,* and *possessive* cases. (See also 7. *Pronoun Case*). The following table makes these differences clear:

SUBJECTIVE	OBJECTIVE	POSSESSIVE
I	me	mine
you	you	yours

he, she, it	him, her, it	his, hers, its
we	us	ours
you	you	yours
they	them	theirs

NOTE: A special case is *it* or *there* used as an expletive to postpone the sentence subject:

It is best that John be present.
There will be two books on the shelf.

1d. Adjectives

The adjective describes or limits nouns or pronouns. This describing or limiting is referred to as *modifying*. Generally, adjectives appear next to the nouns they modify:

The *green* sweater cost *twenty-five* dollars.

However, adjectives used with linking verbs (see 1a. *Verbs*) may occur after the noun and verb and are called predicate adjectives:

Dr. Jones is so *competent, thorough,* and *kind*.

Many adjectives are formed by adding suffixes such as *-al, -able, -ible, -ative, -ish, -ous,* or *-ic* to certain verbs or nouns:

VERB	**ADJECTIVE**
digest	digestible
communicate	communicative
NOUN	**ADJECTIVE**
fame	famous
penny	penniless

NOTE:
1. *A, an,* and *the* are special kinds of adjectives called articles.
2. Demonstrative pronouns often function as adjectives:

Pass me *that* napkin.
This book is Mary's.

1e. Adverbs

An adverb can modify verbs, adjectives, or other adverbs. Generally, adverbs are formed by adding the suffix *-ly* to an adjective:

The following examples illustrate how adverbs are used:

ADJECTIVE	ADVERB
normal	normally
quick	quickly
animated	animatedly

She moved *swiftly*. (*Swiftly* modifies the verb *moved*.)

It is an *exceptionally* boring game. (*Exceptionally* modifies the adjective *boring*.)

The queen whispered *very* softly. (*Very* modifies the adverb *softly*.)

The usual function of the adverb is to say *when*, *where*, *how*, and *to what extent* something happened:

She came *soon*. (When did she come?)

He put the book *there*. (Where did he put the book?)

She fought *furiously*. (How did she fight?)

Our love will last *forever*. (To what extent will our love last?)

See also 1g. *Conjunctions, conjunctive adverbs*.

NOTE: Both adjectives and adverbs can be used in three forms: *positive*, *comparative*, and *superlative*. The positive form is the unchanged adjective or adverb; the comparative form indicates *more* or *less*; the superlative form indicates *most* or *least*. Here are some examples:

Positive: He spoke *loudly*. (adverb)
She is a *loud* person. (adjective)

Comparative: He spoke *louder*. (adverb)
She is a *louder* person. (adjective)

Superlative: He spoke *loudest*. (adverb)
She is the *loudest* person. (adjective)

The following forms are irregular:

Adjectives

POSITIVE	COMPARATIVE	SUPERLATIVE
good	better	best
bad	worse	worst

Adverbs

POSITIVE	COMPARATIVE	SUPERLATIVE
well	better	best
badly	worse	worst

Be sure that you distinguish between *good* and *well*, *bad* and *badly*:

Wrong: He plays tennis *good*. (adjective)
Right: He plays tennis *well*. (adverb)

Wrong: Sam burned his finger *bad*. (adjective)
Right: Sam burned his finger *badly*. (adverb)

When discussing health, use *well* and *bad*:

Jack feels *well*.
John feels *bad*.

When discussing feelings, use *good* and *bad*:

I feel *good* about my job.
He feels *bad* about the misunderstanding.

1f. Prepositions

A preposition shows the relationship between nouns, pronouns, verbs, adjectives, and adverbs:

John stood *behind* the doors. (*Behind* indicates relationship between John and the doors.)

A less complicated definition of the preposition is any word that describes what an airplane can do when approaching clouds. The airplane can go *by, across, above, below, into, between, over, through, inside, beyond, from*, *to* the clouds, among other things. However, not all prepositions qualify under this definition. *Concerning*, *regarding*, *of*, *for*, or *during* are examples of prepositions that do not.

A few prepositions consist of more than one word: *in spite of*, *because of*, *on account of*, *instead of*, *together with*, *in regard to*.

NOTE: A preposition and its object make up a *prepositional phrase*:

They strolled *inside the garden*. (prepositional phrase)

1g. Conjunctions

A conjunction connects words, phrases, and clauses. Incoherent or mispunctuated sentences often result from misused conjunctions. There are three kinds of conjunctions: *coordinating*, *subordinating*, and *conjunctive adverbs* (also called *logical connectives*).

Coordinating conjunctions (and, but, nor, for) join words, phrases, and clauses of equal importance:

Words: Silk *and* velvet are my favorite materials.
Phrases: Living in pain *or* dying in peace was his choice.
Clauses: George continued to make money, *but* he was miserable.

NOTE: A special type of coordinating conjunction is the *correlative conjunction*, which also joins elements of equal importance but occurs only in pairs:

not only . . . but also
neither . . . nor
both . . . and

Not only did he buy a Porsche, *but also* he paid cash for it.
Neither she *nor* her husband appeared at the reception.
Both my father *and* my grandfather agree with me.

Subordinating, conjunctions (such as *if*, *because*, *when*, *since*, *where*, *while*, *whereas*, *after*, *before*, *until*, *as if*) are used to join subordinate clauses with independent clauses, as:

Felice studies *because* she is ambitious.
If if rains, we must buy an umbrella.

However, place a subordinating conjunction before an independent clause and you will have a *sentence fragment*—a transformation often overlooked by student writers:

The man stood at the door. (independent clause)

While the man stood at the door. (fragment caused by subordinating conjunction)

Such a fragment can be corrected by attaching it to an independent clause:

While the man stood at the door, the dog barked.
The dog barked *while* the man stood at the door.

See also 3. *Sentence Fragments*, page 368.

NOTE: Relative pronouns can function as subordinating conjunctions to introduce adjective or noun clauses (see 2d):

We blamed the man *who* was driving without a license.

The house *that* she had just finished paying for burned down.

Conjunctive adverbs (such as however, consequently, moreover, besides, on the other hand, that is to say, yet, furthermore, nevertheless, meanwhile, indeed, anyhow, hence, henceforth, then) are adverbs used to connect independent clauses. Always place a semicolon before and a comma after a conjunctive adverb that connects two independent clauses:

The tickets are three dollars apiece; *however,* members of the club pay only two dollars.

The sky was dark and cloudy; *nevertheless,* we pressed onward.

NOTES:

1. A comma should be used before and after the conjunctive adverb when the conjunctive adverb is parenthetical:

   My friend drove her car to the party; I, *however,* took the bus.

   The other half of the restaurant, *meanwhile,* stood empty and forsaken.

2. The use of *yet* and *so* as coordinating conjunctions has been more or less accepted in informal writing. However, careful writers use *yet* only as a logical connective, and seldom use the anemic *so*.

1h. Interjections

An interjection is used to indicate emotion. Usually, interjections have no grammatical connection with other words in the sentence. Interjections may be either mild or forceful. If forceful, they are followed by an exclamation point.

Mild: *Ah,* you kept your promise.
Well, let's move ahead.
Forceful: *Oh!* I lost my wallet!
Phew! That's hard work!

We began this discussion by saying that a part of speech can be classified according to the way it functions in a sentence. It follows that the same word may serve as a different part of speech in different sentences. Here are some examples:

The stairway contains one broken *step*. (noun)
Please do not let her *step* in the mud. (verb)

The man accompanied her *inside*. (adverb)
Her *inside* pocket is torn. (adjective)
The teacher disappeared *inside* the room. (preposition)

Exercise keeps a person limber. (noun)
They *exercise* every day. (verb)
We need an *exercise* room. (adjective)

EXERCISE 1: Parts of speech

In the sentences below, name the part of speech of each italicized word.

MODEL: The plum was *overly* ripe.

Ans: **Adverb**

1. The priest picked up the book and *caressed* it.
2. The English tried to find a *northern* route.
3. The people were poor, *but* they wore fur pelts.
4. I don't care for *this*.
5. *If* he is allowed to dominate her, he will.
6. He had come on deck *without* notice.
7. There was not enough *space* for the food.
8. The breeze *had wafted* a strand of hair into her eyes.

9. In time, he *will explain* himself to all of us.
10. Her name was remembered *because of* her book.
11. My husband has five *living* sisters.
12. Why hurt a human being just to please *someone*?
13. The musket shot was aimed *directly* at the frigate's lower sails.
14. She was asked to stay *exactly* alongside.
15. *Wow!* What a beautiful pair of shoes!
16. *Not only* did he say the word in private, *but* he *also* repeated it in front of the crowd.
17. The *cold* was unbearable to anyone from the south.
18. The ballet dancers made one *final* effort before the curtain went down.
19. Mr. Thornburg swam *for* one hour and felt better.
20. *Proudly* she saluted the flag.
21. He blamed *himself* for all of the year's troubles.
22. The fish was white, slimy, and almost *tasteless*.
23. *Well*, perhaps he should take some Vitamin C.
24. The Japanese lady *had waved* her fan and had smiled encouragingly.
25. You have a terrible temper; *nevertheless*, you will make a good leader.
26. *Perhaps* she would suit another company better than mine.
27. Martha had remained thoughtful and *reserved*.
28. They discussed the *feasibility* of a full-scale war.
29. The old woman looked away *and* scowled.
30. In some countries, *it* is considered polite to sip soup from a bowl.

EXERCISE 1: Parts of speech

Identify the part of speech of each boldface word in the following paragraph.

> It was **evening.** Around the low **fire, inside** the **paramount** chief's hut **sat** the **leading** men of the village, **each** swaying to the **rhythmic** tom-tom of the tribal drum. The wrinkled **witch doctor** squatted **near** the chief, **but** he seemed **totally unafraid as** his cunning, birdlike eyes restlessly **sought** the attention of **each** man. His hands were deftly arranging some tiger teeth **and** chicken bones; **however, he** was obviously **completely aware** of the **solemnity** of the occasion. **"Oh,** witch doctor, **we are listening,"** a voice suddenly murmured. The **wrinkled old** man drew his basket of charms **close to** his crossed legs. He **then** threw some charms on the ground **while** he mumbled a monotonous formula in his untranslatable tribal dialect.

2. Sentences

The parts of speech, when put together in certain ways, constitute a sentence. All sentences have a *subject* and a *predicate*. A working knowledge of these components is useful to both the beginning and the veteran writer.

2a. Subjects and predicates

The subject is what a speaker or writer makes a statement about; the predicate is what is said about the subject. A *noun*, or group of words functioning as a noun, makes up the core of each subject; a *verb*, or group of words functioning as a verb, makes up the core of each predicate. The essence of a sentence may then be said to consist—in its simplest form—of two words, a noun and a verb:

NOUN/SUBJECT	VERB/PREDICATE
People	think.
Bees	sting.
Dogs	bite.

In all three examples, a verb (predicate) makes an assertion about a noun (subject). This basic division applies even if a sentence is written as a question. *Where is my book?* can be divided into subject and predicate just as readily as the sentence *My book is there*. At the heart of both constructions are a noun and a verb—that is, a part about which something is said and a part that either asks or asserts something about a subject.

The three examples given above illustrate sentences in their most rudimentary form: a *simple subject* and a *simple predicate* with a single word functioning in each role. The *complete subject* and *complete predicate* consist of all those words that are a part of the subject and all those that are part of the predicate. Here are some examples:

SIMPLE SUBJECT	SIMPLE PREDICATE
People	think.
COMPLETE SUBJECT	**COMPLETE PREDICATE**
People of all creeds, ages, and nationalities	think about life, love, and death.
People of all creeds, ages, nationalities, no matter what their life-styles or politics,	think about life, love, death, and other eternal questions.

SIMPLE SUBJECT	**SIMPLE PREDICATE**
He	ran.
COMPLETE SUBJECT	**COMPLETE PREDICATE**
Grabbing his overcoat and umbrella, he	ran away from the house as fast as he could.

The ability to recognize the complete subjects and complete predicates of sentences is especially useful in properly punctuating them.

2b. Complements

A complement is a word or group of words that completes the meaning of a verb. Complements are divided into the following categories: direct object, indirect object, subject complement, and object complement.

(1) Direct object A direct object answers the question *What?* or *Whom?* in connection with a verb. In the following sentences, the direct object is italicized:

> The dog chewed the *rug*. (What did the dog chew?)
> He married *Cynthia*. (Whom did he marry?)

(2) Indirect object The indirect object usually precedes the direct object, and tells *to whom* or *for whom* (or *to what* or *for what*) the action of a verb is done. In the following sentences, the indirect objects are italicized:

> The salesperson gave the *man* a blank look. (To whom did the salesperson give a blank look?)
>
> Her parents ordered *her* a Datsun. (For whom did her parents order a Datsun?)

(3) Subject complement The subject complement completes the sense of the verb by further explaining the subject. The following qualify as linking verbs that can be completed by subject complements:

> Forms of the verb *to be: am, are, is, was, were, been*
>
> Verbs having to do with the senses: *smell, look, taste, feel, sound*, and so forth
>
> Certain other verbs: *seem, appear, become, remain, grow, prove*, and so forth

The subject complements are italicized in the following sentences:

Most Spaniards are *Catholics*.
That animal seems to be a *wolf*.

In addition to nouns, adjectives and pronouns can serve as subject complements:

The blanket feels *warm* and *comforting*.
My perfume smells *exotic*.
He will not admit that it was *she*.

(4) Object complement The object complement further explains the direct object. In the following example, the object complements are italicized:

The mob called the criminal a cold-blooded *murderer*.

An adjective can also serve as an object complement:

The thought of going home made her *depressed*. (*Depressed* modifies the direct object *her*.)

2c. Phrases

A phrase is a group of words, usually without subject and verb, that expresses a thought but is not a complete statement. Phrases can be classified as: prepositional, verbal, absolute, and appositive.

(1) Prepositional phrases A prepositional phrase consists of a preposition followed by a noun (or pronoun) and any words that modify that noun (or pronoun). The prepositional phrase usually functions as an *adjective* or *adverb*. In the following sentences, the prepositional phrases are italicized:

Jane left home *without a jacket*. (The prepositional phrase modified the verb *left* by specifying how Jane left home. It therefore functions as an adverb.)

Behind the bush huddled a savage dog. (The prepositional phrase modifies the verb *huddled* by specifying where the dog huddled. It therefore functions as an adverb.)

The slipper *under the bed* was too big. (The prepositional phrase modifies the noun *slipper* by specifying which slipper was too big—the one *under the bed*. It therefore functions as an adjective.)

(2) Verbal phrases A verbal phrase consists of a verbal and all the words immediately related to it. Do not confuse verbals with verbs. Verbals are derived from verbs, but make no statement about a subject. They function as *nouns, adjectives*, or *adverbs*. There are three kinds of verbals: *infinitive, gerund*, and *participle*.

An *infinitive* is used as a noun, an adjective, or an adverb and is usually made up of the construction *to* + the present form of the verb.

> *To study* is smart. (noun)
> This is the way *to study*. (adjective)
> John left *to study*. (adverb)

A *gerund* is used only as a noun and has an *ing* ending:

> *Skiing* is my favorite sport. (noun as subject)
> She hates *gardening*. (noun as direct object)
> Their goal is *making* money. (noun as subject complement)
> Before *stopping* he wants to finish. (noun as object of preposition)

A *participle* is used as an adjective. Participles are either present (ending in *-ing*) or past (commonly ending in *-d, -ed, -n, -en*. In the case of irregular verbs, vowels may change, as in *brought* and *clung*.) Participles and gerunds can be distinguished from one another by their functions in a sentence. The gerund functions as a noun; the participle, as an adjective:

> *Suffering* is a part of life. (gerund)
> The *suffering* child was hospitalized. (participle)

Like verbals, verbal phrases are either infinitive, gerund, or participle:

(a) Infinitive An infinitive phrase consists of an infinitive followed by its modifiers. The infinitive phrase may function as an adjective, adverb, or noun. In the following sentences, the infinitive phrases have been italicized:

ADJECTIVE	INFINITIVE PHRASE AS ADJECTIVE
The comedian used *appropriate* humor.	The comedian used humor *to match the occasion*.
ADVERB	**INFINITIVE PHRASE AS ADVERB**
The lecturer spoke *informatively*.	The lecturer spoke *to inform the audience*.

NOUN	INFINITIVE PHRASE AS NOUN
Larceny tempts many people.	*To steal money* is a common temptation.

(b) Gerund A gerund phrase consists of a gerund and its modifiers. The gerund phrase functions as a noun. (Although a gerund and a participle may share the same *-ing* ending, the gerund always functions as a noun.) In the following sentences, the gerund phrases have been italicized:

> *Chewing gum with her mouth open* was her worst habit. (The gerund phrase functions as a noun and as subject of the verb *was*. Notice that the entire phrase, like all nouns, may be replaced by a pronoun: *It* was her worst habit.)
>
> The reporter praised *the guitarist's loud and regular twanging*. (The gerund phrase functions as the object of the verb *praised*.)

(c) Participial A participial phrase consists of a participle followed by modifiers. It functions as an adjective. In the following sentences, the participial phrases have been italicized:

> *Crying in pain,* the football player limped away. (The participial phrase modifies the compound noun *football player*.)
>
> The windows of the car *parked in the driveway* were shattered to bits. (The participial phrase modifies the noun *car* by specifying which car was meant—the one *parked in the driveway.*)
>
> *Bent by old age,* the man struggled on. (The participial phrase modifies the noun *man*.)

(3) Absolute phrases Absolute phrases stand grammatically independent ("absolutely" alone). They have no identifiable grammatical link to the rest of the sentence. Nor are they linked to an independent clause by a subordinating word. Absolute constructions are therefore difficult to identify and easy to misuse. Here are some examples:

> *The diver having finished his dive,* we left for tea.
>
> *All things being equal,* tomorrow will be our big day.
>
> *Considering the state of the budget,* the hearings should be continued.

An absolute construction should not be confused with a dangling participial phrase. Here are some examples to clarify the difference between them:

The meeting having gone as planned, we broke for lunch. (absolute construction)

Wrong: *Having met for five hours*, lunch was then served. (Dangling participle implies "lunch" had met for five hours.)

Right: *Having met for five hours*, we were then served lunch. (Participial phrase modifies "we.")

See also 26. *Dangling Modifiers*.

(4) Appositive phrases An appositive phrase is a word or phrase placed beside another word whose meaning it expands or explains. The appositive must always be syntactically parallel to the word it stands in apposition to—that is, it must be the same part of speech and must fulfill the same grammatical function:

(a) Appositive as subject: Paul's father, *a wealthy businessman*, was forced into bankruptcy.

(*Father* and *businessman* are both subjects.)

(b) Appositive as object: He rejected his first love, *oil painting*.

(*Love* and *oil painting* are both objects.)

(c) Appositive as adjective: He spoke in a paternalistic, that is, *authoritative*, manner.

(*Paternalistic* and *authoritative* are both adjectives.)

(d) Appositive as adverb: The essay was proofread carefully—*with utmost precision*.

(*Carefully* and *with utmost precision* are both adverbials.)

Think of appositives as abbreviated or reduced clauses because they can be expanded into clauses by using some form of the verb *be*:

His father, *who was a wealthy businessman*, was forced into bankruptcy.

He rejected his first love, *which was oil painting*.

He spoke in a paternalistic manner, *which was an authoritative manner*.

The essay was proofread carefully, *meaning that it was proofread with utmost precision.*

2d. Clauses

A clause is a group of words containing a subject and a predicate. If the words make sense by themselves, they are said to constitute an independent clause. A clause that does not make sense by itself is called a dependent clause.

(1) Independent clauses What makes a clause independent is its ability to stand alone and make complete sense. Here are some examples:

The man had bad breath.
People need to buy health insurance.
Fairy tales are important reading for children.

(2) Dependent clauses A clause that does not make sense by itself is called a dependent clause since it must "depend" on an independent clause to complete its meaning. Here are some examples:

Who was standing next to me
Even though they have Social Security
That fairy tales teach about good and evil

Attached to appropriate independent clauses, however, these dependent clauses become grammatically complete:

The man who was *standing next to me* had bad breath.

Even though they have Social Security, people need health insurance.

That fairy tales teach about good and evil makes them important reading for children.

Dependent clauses can be recognized by the connectives binding them to independent clauses. These connectives are always subordinating words such as the subordinating conjunctions *although, even though, despite, what, that, who, which, when, since, before, after, if, as, because* that introduce adverbial clauses, or the relative pronouns *who, what, that, which* that introduce noun and adjective clauses. (See also 1g. *Conjunctions.*) Dependent clauses can also function as grammatical units in a sentence, playing the equivalent role of a noun, an adjective, or an adverb.

(a) Noun clauses A noun clause is a subordinate clause that acts as a noun.

Noun clause as subject:
What he demanded frightened the pilot. (The noun clause is the subject of the verb *frightened*. As with all nouns, a pronoun—in this case *it*, *this*, or *that* could be substituted for the entire noun clause.)

Noun clause as direct object:
I request *that you clean up your room*.

Noun clause as indirect object:
The government will give *whoever is hungry* food stamps.

Noun clause as object of a preposition:
She longs for *whatever is right*.

Noun clause as subject complement:
Rest is *what he needs*.

Noun clause as appositive:
We suspected the object, *whatever it was*.

(b) Adjective clauses An adjective clause modifies either a noun or a pronoun in a sentence:

He remembered the place *where they had first kissed*. (The italicized adjective clause modifies the noun *place*.)

Look at the flower *she picked yesterday*. (The italicized adjective clause modifies the noun *flower*.)

(c) Adverb clauses An adverb clause modifies a verb, adjective, or adverb in the sentence. It may occur in various positions in a sentence, at the end, the beginning, or in the middle. An adverb clause is usually introduced by a subordinating conjunction:

ADVERB	ADVERB CLAUSE
She blew the trumpet *loudly*.	She blew the trumpet *so that everyone could hear*.
Later he made tea.	*When the water boiled*, he made tea.

ADVERB	ADVERB CLAUSE
Everyone *here* plays the guitar.	Everyone *where I live* plays the guitar.

As you can see from the above examples, the way to identify the function of a clause is to see what part of speech may be substituted for it. A noun clause may be replaced by an equivalent noun or by a pronoun; an adjective clause may be replaced by an adjective; and an adverb clause may be replaced by an adverb.

2e. Kinds of sentences

Sentences are grouped into four types according to the number and kinds of clauses involved: simple, compound, complex, and compound-complex. A knowledge of the different sentence types is useful to anyone who aims for sentence variety and correct punctuation.

(1) Simple sentences A simple sentence has one subject and one predicate:

Jim is getting married.
We will sail tomorrow.

NOTE: A simple sentence may have two or more nouns as subject and two or more verbs as predicate:

The *birds* in the sky and the *fish* in the sea add to life's beauty. (*Birds* and *fish* form a compound subject.)

The entire town *praised* and *thanked* the mayor. (*Praised* and *thanked* form a compound predicate.)

(2) Compound sentences A compound sentence consists of at least two independent clauses.

The houses are tall, but the streets are narrow.

Behind the fence is a garden, and beyond the garden lies a lake.

We sang songs and offered prayers, and we waited for rescue.

(3) Complex sentences A complex sentence consists of one independent clause and one or more dependent clauses. The dependent clauses are italicized in the following examples:

Everyone arrived *when the sun came out.*

If he were to inherit a million dollars, he would give it all to people *who work on farms.*

(4) Compound-complex sentences A compound-complex sentence consists of two or more independent clauses and one or more dependent clauses. The independent clauses are in boldface and the dependent clauses are italicized:

> **He refused to enter the house** *unless I went with him*; yet, *while we were inside,* **he showed no fear.**
>
> *When they pay their gas bill,* **they will he happy** *that they bought the car,* but **they will never thank me for my advice.**

EXERCISE 2a: Complete subjects and complete predicates

In the sentences below, separate the complete subject from the complete predicate by a vertical line.

MODEL: The country road | stretched into the distance.

1. The traveler, a tall man in his late thirties, stood looking up into the branches of the oak tree.
2. Now old and bent, his father had loved to sit beneath the bridge.
3. Wandering about the campus with Francis, he remembered suddenly a particular summer morning.
4. The pattern of the coming year and of his behavior was set.
5. Like most religious fanatics, she had absolutely no sense of humor.
6. Its remarkable beauty did not lie only in its bright glitter.
7. Mrs. McClosky, a guest of the mayor, refused to ride in a car driven by a chauffeur.
8. Facing each other in front of the fire, two red sofas always waited for us every evening.
9. A hint of anger or coldness in his voice would keep her in the depths of despair for weeks on end.
10. The old man arose hurriedly and disappeared into the woods.

EXERCISE 2a: Simple subjects and simple predicates

In the following sentences, underline the simple subject once and the simple predicate twice.

MODEL: Moved almost to tears, I whispered back.

1. Perhaps his answer was an assent of the heart rather than of the mind.
2. Next year, too many people will visit the Vatican.
3. According to the Bible, “A prating fool will come to ruin.”
4. The pilot was landing the plane during wind, rain, and hail.

5. Beside the President stood the Secretary of State.
6. Gentlemen, please take your seats.
7. Did you remember the poem on the wall of the library?
8. John simply could not reject his past.
9. By jumping into the water first, he avoided being pushed by his friends.
10. There are always two sides to a question.

EXERCISE 2b: Complements

In the sentences below, decide whether the italicized words are direct objects, indirect objects, object complements, or subject complements.

MODEL: More and more, he appeared to be *alone*.

Ans: **Subject complement**

1. She had gone to bring the *eggs* from the henhouse.
2. Spring is a *time* of glorious magic.
3. The children considered him *king* of the block.
4. I had learned a great *principle* of the way grief affects people.
5. Because of its timing, the visit was *oppressive*.
6. Without further thought, Joanne labeled the teacher a *Communist*.
7. We could have simply given *him* a pile of money, but he needed attention and love.
8. To me, her thoughts seemed *nuggets* of gold.
9. Being a respectful man, he gave our *flag* a brisk salute.
10. While singing cheerfully, he stirred the *pot* of soup on the fire.

EXERCISE 2c: Phrases

In each of the sentences below, indicate what kind of phrase the italicized words are:

MODEL: *To own one's home in California* is extremely expensive.

Ans: **Infinitive phrase**

1. *Hoping not to be called on duty*, I snuggled up in my blanket.
2. *The club meeting having adjourned*, the students trudged home.
3. He heard the sound *of boots marching down the corridor*.

4. The rain, *little more than a cool mist*, refreshed us immensely.
5. *To say goodbye without hope of seeing one another again* was heart-rending.
6. *Cooking from scratch* is becoming a lost art.
7. More than anything else, we wanted *to know our neighbors across the street*.
8. *Playing poker* did not interest him in the least.
9. We looked at Sylvia, *a radiant young woman in her white gown*.
10. We lived *in the community of Whiting Woods*.

EXERCISE 2d: Independent and dependent clauses

In the sentences below, enclose the dependent clauses in parentheses and underline the independent clauses.

MODEL: (That Carl was not musical) disappointed his parents; however, they bought a piano (because they never lost hope.)

1. He had never doubted that the vessel was westward bound, nor had he ever believed that it would withstand a week of stormy waters.
2. The thought of that wonderful homemade bread conjured up images of a mother who worked day and night so that her family could be well fed.
3. Somehow her parents had instilled in her a clear idea of everything that is honorable.
4. If they wanted to remain allies, they were running a terrible risk.
5. At the same time, we met another friend, Bernard Townsend, witty, intelligent, handsome, who loved the poetry of John Donne.
6. We began, hardly knowing we were doing it, to revise our opinion of the strikers who had suffered so much.
7. Our fundamental assumption, which we had been foolish enough to consider intelligent insight, had been that all Christian church members were rigid and unwilling to think through important issues that affect a citizen's ethical commitments.
8. If they had been asked what they meant when they spoke of life on another planet, they would have answered with pure nonsense.
9. The Benedictine monks built the long, lovely buildings that are still part of one college quadrangle at Oxford University, where John received his degree in 1978.
10. Another reason for not skiing faster was that she was exhausted; however, her companions did not realize her fatigue and kept goading her on until she sat down in the snow and cried with frustration.

EXERCISE 2d: Identifying types of dependent clauses

In the sentences below, underline each dependent clause and indicate if it is an adjective clause, an adverbial clause, or a noun clause.

MODEL: We decided to study the painting that had been shipped from New York.

Ans: **Adjective clause**

1. The truth was that she had heard that tune before.
2. While he loved her desperately, he did not want to give up his job for her.
3. The problem that had been solved yesterday loomed up twice as big today.
4. It has been said that the fourth dimension is time and duration.
5. As a nun, she went where life would be calm and tranquil.
6. The disease, with all of its suffering, would return unless we could find the right specialist.
7. The friend from whom she had received the book never contacted her in the years to come.
8. The job was much more difficult and exhausting than she had expected.
9. The point is to admit candidly what bothers you.
10. Did you spend the entire day looking for the thief who stole your wallet?

EXERCISE 2e: Kinds of sentences

Identify each sentence below as simple, compound, complex, or compound-complex.

MODEL: When the great tree came down, it left an empty space against the sky.

Ans: **Complex sentence**

1. I was conscious of a sort of amazement that a steak could taste so good.
2. They had decided from the beginning to reach out and draw in all of the richness of this great university around them.
3. I did not admit it, but I was beginning to love poetry.
4. She stuck five-dollar bills into the drawer and then she escaped through the front door without leaving a note about where she was going.
5. His grandfather on his mother's side and his grandfather on his father's side were not at all the same, for the former was educated at Princeton whereas the latter had no formal education beyond the fifth grade.
6. When she looked up into those branches filled with rust- and gold-colored autumn leaves, she wanted to stay in New England forever.

7. War was no longer merely a rumor circulated by adventurers and fanatics in an attempt to get some attention.
8. It would seem that a career in the theater requires both an emotional and intellectual commitment.
9. He had not rejected the offer; he merely had not decided yet.
10. Our tacit understanding was that whoever went to the library would pick up the book.

3. Sentence fragments (frag)

A fragment is a phrase or dependent clause capitalized and punctuated as though it were a complete sentence:

> An interesting book from the library.
> Who screamed in a loud voice.

These fragments are incomprehensible by themselves although they are written as if they were complete sentences. The easiest way to correct a fragment in your own writing is to add enough words to make the fragment into an independent clause. In the following examples, words have been added to make each fragment a complete sentence:

> I am reading an interesting book from the library.
>
> The child who screamed in a loud voice was frightened by a nightmare.

Sometimes, the correction can be made by adding the fragment to a preceding or a following independent clause:

Wrong: Ken might get a job. *If he will contact the manager of the store by Monday.* (The italicized phrase is a fragment.)
Right: Ken might get a job if he will contact the manager of the store by Monday.

In order to avoid sentence fragments in your writing, remember that dependent clauses cannot stand by themselves, and that the addition of any subordinating word to a sentence automatically makes it a fragment. Consider these examples:

Complete sentence: I was tired.

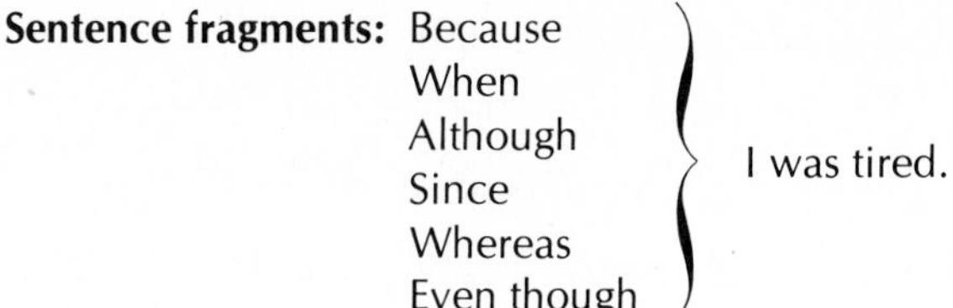

Sentence fragments: Because / When / Although / Since / Whereas / Even though } I was tired.

Be alert to any construction beginning with a subordinating word. Make sure it is properly joined to an independent clause.

Writers sometimes use fragments for a stylistic effect. In the example below the writer used fragments to make a pair of climactic utterances about bones:

> Bones. Two hundred and eight of them. A whole glory turned and tooled.
>
> —Richard Selzer, "Bone"

This sort of writing, however, is not recommended for college students. Leave fragments to professional writers, and frame your own thoughts in complete, coherent sentences.

4. Comma splices (cs)

A comma splice occurs when a comma is used to connect two independent clauses not joined by a coordinating conjunction such as *and, nor, but,* or *for*:

Wrong: The nurse brought in the tray, Mr. Jones began to eat his breakfast.

4a. Correcting comma splices

(1) Comma and coordinating conjunction Use a comma and a coordinating conjunction to connect independent clauses of equal strength:

> The nurse brought in the tray, and Mr. Jones began to eat his breakfast.

(2) Semicolon Use a semicolon to connect two independent clauses that are closely related in thought:

> The nurse brought in the tray; Mr. Jones began to eat his breakfast.

(3) Period Use a period between two independent clauses that require separate emphasis:

> The nurse brought in the tray. Without complaint Mr. Jones began to eat his breakfast.

(4) Subordination Subordinate one idea to another:

> When the nurse brought in the tray, Mr. Jones knew it was time to eat his breakfast.

5. Run-on sentences (ro)

A run-on or fused sentence, as the name implies, consists of two independent clauses improperly connected, with neither link or break between them.

Wrong: Robert stared at the screen he knew he had seen this fellow before.

5a. Correcting run-on sentences

The same methods of correction used on comma splices can be applied to run-on sentences.

(1) Comma and coordinating conjunction Use a comma and a coordinating conjunction between clauses of *equal strength*:

> Robert stared at the screen, and he knew he had seen this fellow before.

(2) Semicolon Use a semicolon between two independent clauses that are closely related in thought.

> Robert stared at the screen; he knew he had seen this fellow before.

(3) Period Use a period between two independent clauses requiring separate emphasis.

> Robert stared at the screen. He knew he had seen this fellow before.

(4) Subordination Subordinate one idea to another.

> As Robert stared at the screen, he suddenly realized that he had seen this fellow before.

EXERCISE 3: Sentence fragments

Rewrite the following passages, correcting sentence fragments. If a passage contains no fragments, leave it alone. Add words if needed.

MODEL: On the surface Jane appears to be a young woman. Struggling between a career and marriage.

Ans: **On the surface, Jane appears to be a young woman struggling between a career and marriage.**

1. Randy is getting more decisive each day. Having promised himself to move in one direction.
2. Among married teenagers, one of the most popular routes out of the locked-in position is divorce. Because it supplies a quick and definite way out.
3. One part of him is searching for freedom. The other part desiring to be rooted and tied down.
4. Whereas the women seemed more mature than the men who entered college.
5. Although some parents offer glamorous opportunities to their children, they usually contaminate these offers with parental rules and values.
6. We each have our own set of ethics. The way we see and interpret right and wrong.
7. The simplest, and what appears to be the safest option, is for Mary to drive the car herself. Then Jack can pick it up from her.
8. On the other hand, if she were to sink all of her money into this publishing company, believing that eventually it would make her rich.
9. To be consigned to a life of boredom just because one wanted to please one's parents.
10. The older we get, the more we become aware of our mortality. Hoping against hope that we shall remain among the lucky few who live to a ripe and contented old age.

EXERCISES 3, 4, 5: Sentence fragments, comma splices, run-on sentences

Indicate whether the following are complete sentences, fragments, comma splices, or run-on sentences.

MODEL: Marvin had a difficult time in life, he took himself too seriously.

Ans: **Comma splice**

1. Three days passed, however, he still did not recognize anyone.

2. While the man was asleep, she had carefully gone through his belongings.
3. Her dresses were made from the most delicate silk her shoes were made from the softest leather.
4. Since the children were playing outside in the blizzard.
5. Of course, it would not pay to make that kind of man angry or jealous.
6. Attempting to make him forget his troublesome past in order to start a new life.
7. He bit his fingernails; his heart was beating rapidly.
8. She wished she could stay with him forever, she could not understand her own feelings about this simple man.
9. Is it possible to calculate the effect of a nuclear attack in our era?
10. Ginger eagerly swallowed her glass of champagne, her face was flushed and hot.
11. I want to be candid, our financial situation does not look good.
12. Jim balanced himself precariously, holding the book high in the air.
13. Confessing to the crowd that he had lied all along.
14. The poor girl is ill; she is not well at all.
15. We listened with great interest after all he was an expert in his field.
16. The message fell on deaf ears, ears that no longer responded to truth.
17. He was not a man to act on the spur of the moment, however, this telegram called for a response.
18. The lawyer called me into his office to explain all of the details involved in signing the papers.
19. While George was completely fascinated by the artist's bizarre use of black polka dots.
20. From now until tomorrow not eating another bite.
21. She felt sick, but the unkind words could not be recalled.
22. Having given directions to the nurse to prepare for the next operation.
23. He had had ten years of pain from the broken bones, ten years of suffering from that spreading ulcer.
24. It was a dark night, the children had walked silently along the dim path.
25. You look healthy you look strong.
26. Then addressing the group of amateur photographers who seemed to need a leader.
27. When he came to our town, he was young and strong.
28. The spots on his body disappeared his skin became healthy again.
29. His raised voice directed to the people who would take the long journey with him.
30. Sylvia Plath wrote depressing poems, she eventually committed suicide.

6. Agreement (agr)

A subject and its verb and a pronoun and its antecedent must agree in number.

6a. Subject-verb agreement

Once you have decided on a subject, it determines what form of verb you will use. For instance, you will write, "A fish swims," not "A fish swim," because *fish* in this instance is third-person singular. On the other hand, you will write, "Most fish swim" because in this instance *fish* is third-person plural. Agreement errors are primarily caused by the unusual word order of a sentence or by words intervening between a verb and its subject.

(1) Unusual word order Unusual word order in a sentence may confuse you. Consider the following examples:

> The one fruit that I love *is* (not *are*) oranges. (The subject is *fruit*.)
>
> *Have* not (not *has*) the warm days of this lovely summer delighted your heart? (The subject is *days*.)
>
> Too many temper tantrums *were* (not *was*) the reason for their divorce. (The subject is *temper tantrums*.)
>
> Wrapped inside five blankets *was* (not *were*) a tiny white kitten. (The subject is *kitten*.)
>
> There *are* (not *is*) numerous ways to make good fudge. (The subject is *ways*.)
>
> There *remain* (not *remains*) many unsolved problems. (The subject is *problems*.)

(2) Intervening words Intervening words may make it difficult to identify the subject. Study the following examples until you recognize the correct subject:

> Several of the students in Professor Smith's course *were* (not *was*) nominated for an award. (The subject is *several*.)
>
> The transportation of diamonds *is* (not *are*) dangerous. (The subject is *transportation*.)
>
> The discussions of that subject *are* (not *is*) necessary. (The subject is *discussions*.)
>
> Hunger, along with inadequate housing, *causes* (not *cause*) riots. (The subject is *hunger*.)

> Inner longings, as well as an outward goal, *drive* (not *drives*) ambitious people. (The subject is *longings*.)

(3) Special words and word connectors To avoid some common agreement errors be alert to certain words and word connectors. Remember the following rules:

(a) A relative pronoun usually refers back to, and agrees with, the nearest noun:

> Rod Laver is one of the greatest tennis players who *live* (not *lives*) in this country. (*Who* refers back to *players*.)
>
> Tokyo is among those cities that *are* (not *is*) filled with smog. (*That* refers back to *cities*.)

Note the following exception:

> This is the only one of the streets that *has* (not *have*) two-way traffic. (*That* refers back to *one*, emphasizing the fact that only one street has two-way traffic; the other streets do not.)

(b) Subjects joined by *and* require a plural verb:

> Both his eyesight and his hearing *have* (not *has*) gone bad.
> The boys and Elsa *were* (not *was*) caught up in the drug cult.
>
> **but**
>
> My best friend and confidante *is* (not *are*) having lunch with me. (*Friend and confidante* refers to the same person.)

(c) Singular subjects joined by *or, either . . . or, neither . . . nor* require a singular verb. However, if one of the subjects is singular and the other is plural, then the verb agrees with the nearer subject:

> A large camera or a small computer lies (not *lie*) under that cover.
>
> Neither the chair nor the couch *feels* (not *feel*) comfortable.
>
> **but**
>
> Neither his money nor his innumerable fans *make* (not *makes*) him happy. (*Make* agrees with the nearer subject, *fans*.)

(d) When used as subjects, indefinite pronouns like *either, neither, everyone, no one, anyone, each, everybody,* and *anybody* require singular verbs:

> Everybody who is anyone *goes* (not *go*) to the ballet.
> Each of the grandmothers *was* (not *were*) given a rose.

NOTE: *All, any, half, none, most,* and *some* are singular or plural, depending on the context:

Singular: Some of the wine *was* (not *were*) sour. (*Wine* is singular.)
Plural: Some of the stairs *were* (not *was*) terribly steep. (*Stairs* is plural.)

(e) Collective nouns (nouns that are singular in form but plural in meaning) require a singular verb unless members are acting individually.

Singular: The crew always *meets* (not *meet*) for a swim at sunrise.
Plural: The crew *are* (not *is*) coming to work in their overalls.

(f) Certain words are plural in form but singular in meaning and require a singular verb:

Physics *is* (not *are*) difficult.
Mumps *keeps* (not *keep*) children in bed for days.
The news today *scares* (not *scare*) us all.

NOTE: If in doubt about whether a noun is singular or plural, check your dictionary.

(g) Words denoting sums of money and measurements take a singular verb when considered as a single unit, but take a plural verb when considered as separate units:

Singular: One hundred dollars *is* (not *are*) too much money for a wool sweater.
Plural: Three silver dollars *were* (not *was*) stacked on the game table.
Singular: Two miles *is* (not *are*) as far as I can jog.
Plural: Those two miles *stretch* (not *stretches*) into the distance like a snake.

NOTE: Problems in arithmetic can be plural or singular:

Three and three *is* (or *are*) six.

(h) Titles of literary works, whether singular or plural, require singular verbs:

The Captains and the King is (not *are*) Taylor Caldwell's best novel.

Myths of the Norsemen tells (not *tell*) about the twilight of the gods.

6b. Pronoun-antecedent agreement

A pronoun always refers back to an antecedent (the word for which it stands) and must agree in person, number, and gender with that antecedent. The following words are singular and require singular pronouns: *person, each, either, neither, everyone, everybody, someone, somebody, one, anyone, anybody, no one, nobody.*

> The teacher asked, "Did anyone leave *his* (not *their*) workbook on my desk?"
>
> Neither of the girls gave *her* (not *their*) correct address to the police officer.
>
> Anyone who loves *his* (not *their*) country must be willing to enlist in the army.

NOTE: Usage and common sense dictate that the masculine pronoun be used for words that include both sexes in order to avoid the stilted use of *he or she, him or her,* and *his or hers*. Recasting the sentence into the plural is often possible:

> Each of the speakers alluded to *his* (not *his or her*) past.
>
> or
>
> All of the speakers alluded to *their* pasts.

Collective nouns acting as a single unit require a singular pronoun; those acting as individuals require a plural pronoun:

Singular: The faculty has posted *its* (not *their*) list of demands. (The faculty is acting as a unit.)

Plural: The faculty gave differing responses to *their* (not *its*) heavier teaching loads. (The members of the faculty are acting individually.)

Antecedents joined by *and* require plural pronouns:

> Charles and Richard passed *their* (not *his*) exams.
> The horse and buggy have had *their* (not *its*) day.

Antecedents joined by *or* or *nor* require a singular pronoun when the antecedents are singular; if one antecedent is singular and the other plural, the pronoun agrees with the nearer antecedent:

Singular: Either the custodian or a guest left *his* (not *their*) coat in the room.

Plural: Neither the guard nor the hostages were happy about *their* (not *his*) situation. (*Their* agrees with the nearer subject, *hostages*.)

but

Singular: Neither the hostages nor the guard was happy about *his* (not *their*) situation. (*His* agrees with the nearer subject, *guard*.)

NOTE: Be sure to use the noun *kind* or *kinds* with the right demonstrative pronoun:

I will not associate with *those kinds* (not *those kind*) of people.
The lecturer suggested *that kind of book* (not *that kind of books*).

EXERCISE 6a: Subject-verb agreement

In the following sentences, choose the correct form of the verb.

MODEL: The guild of carpenters and blacksmiths (*was, were*) important during the Middle Ages.

Ans: **Was**

1. Americans belong to the nation that (*has, have*) always been vigilant about freedom.
2. A sack of gold coins (*is, are*) far more valuable today than a year ago.
3. There (*is, are*) dozens of rats in that old building.
4. The beautiful maple trees growing along Main Street (*keeps, keep*) the houses cool during summer.
5. Gymnastics (*was, were*) Alex's favorite sport.
6. An umbrella or heavy boots (*is, are*) what he needs.
7. The peasants were indebted to the king for one of the loans that (*was, were*) made.
8. War and peace often (*resides, reside*) side by side in a country.
9. The *Los Angeles Times* (*is, are*) news at a high professional level.
10. The Council of Venice (*was, were*) dogmatic about burial laws.
11. Love, along with strong family roots, (*helps, help*) to create a sense of identity.
12. Organized groups of 200 to 300 and possibly more (*is, are*) marching toward the city.
13. (*Does, Do*) everyone have an umbrella?
14. Measles still (*causes, cause*) permanent damage to some children.
15. Deceptive smiles (*was, were*) the weapon he used most often.

EXERCISE 6b: Pronoun-antecedent agreement

In the following sentences, choose the correct words in parentheses.

MODEL: Each of the tenants is complaining about (*his, their*) rent.

Ans: **His**

1. A person can count only on (*himself, themselves*).
2. If any one of the sorority members gets three *C*s, (*she, they*) will have to resign.
3. A person should not have to worry about (*his, their*) health during adolescence.
4. Everyone spoke (*his, their*) mind.
5. Neither the sky nor the clouds revealed (*its, their*) famous silver lining.
6. Neither a German nor a Frenchman finds it easy to get rid of (*his, their*) accent.
7. Every woman on the staff thinks (*she is, they are*) not paid as well as the men.
8. I hate those (*kind, kinds*) of roving eyes.
9. The genuine belief in fairies and ghosts has seen (*its, their*) heyday.
10. No one who has lived alone in the wilderness for a week can consider (*his, their*) life immortal.
11. Through love and understanding the church wooed back (*its, their*) members.
12. The Chicago police made (*its, their*) legal view quite clear.
13. The long list of names spoke for (*itself, themselves*).
14. The Bible states that one should forgive (*his, their*) enemies.

7. Pronoun case (case)

According to their function in a sentence, personal pronouns can appear in three different case forms: subjective, objective, and possessive.

SUBJECTIVE	OBJECTIVE	POSSESSIVE
I	me	my, mine
you	you	your, yours
he, she, it	him, her, it	his, her, hers, its
we	us	our, ours
they	them	their, theirs
who	whom	whose

The *subjective* case is used for pronouns functioning as subjects and as predicate pronouns:

We own this house.
Is that Mike standing there? Yes, it is *he*.

The *objective* case is used for pronouns functioning as direct objects, indirect objects, objects of prepositions, and subjects or complements of an infinitive:

The truck hit *her*.
He gave *them* a package.
The laugh came from *him*.
To see *her* was to love *her*.

The *possessive* case is used for pronouns indicating possession:

Nothing stood in *its* way.
The money is *theirs*.
That watch is *yours*.

Notice that possessive pronouns require no apostrophes.

Wrong: Nothing stood in *it's* way.
The money is *their's*.
That watch is *your's*.

7a. Using the subjective case

Ordinarily we naturally use the correct subjective pronoun. Few of us are tempted to write "Me want to eat" instead of "I want to eat." Nevertheless, some constructions require careful thought.

Treat a clause of comparison introduced by *than* or *as* as if it were written out in full and use the appropriate pronoun case.

Richard is taller than *I* [am].
No one plays as well as *he* [plays].

Pronouns that follow forms of the linking verb *to be* usually are in the subjective case:

I swear it was *she* (not *her*).
We expected that the winners would be *they* (not *them*).

NOTE: An exception is a pronoun functioning as an object complement of the infinitive *to be*. (See 2b(4), *Object Complement*.)

We expected the president to be *her* (not *she*).

Pronouns used in apposition should be in the same case as the nouns or pronouns to which they refer:

Two runners—*you* and *he*—were seen late at night.
We—John and *I*—did our best.

A pronoun functioning as the subject of a subordinate clause must be in the subjective case even when the entire subordinate clause is used as an object:

The flowers will be presented to *whoever* (not *whomever*) serves as choreographer of the dance. (*Whoever* is the subject of the verb *serves*.)

They never forgot *who* (not *whom*) had won the war. (*Who* is the subject of *had won*.)

When parenthetical expressions like *I believe, you think, one supposes*, or *he says* come between the verb and its subject pronoun, the pronoun must be in the subjective case:

Who (not *whom*) does he say repaired the light? (*Does he say* is parenthetical. If you ignore it, you will probably choose the right case.)

The woman *who* (not *whom*) the papers think committed murder has disappeared. (*The papers think* is parenthetical.)

NOTE: A noun in the possessive case cannot function as an antecedent for a pronoun in the subjective case:

Wrong: At the very start of Julie's vacation, she sprained her ankle.
Right: At the very start of her vacation, Julie sprained her ankle.

7b. Using the objective case

An objective pronoun must be used when a pronoun functions as a direct or an indirect object, as the object of a preposition, as the subject or as the object of an infinitive. The following is an example of a pronoun used as a direct object:

Everyone loved *him* (not *he*).

Special care needs to be taken with compound constructions:

> Everyone loved him and *me* (not *I*).

When a pronoun is the object of the verb in a subordinate clause, it requires the objective case:

> He always hurts whomever (not *whoever*) he loves. (*whomever* is the object of the verb *loves*.)
>
> **but**
>
> He always hurts *whoever* loves him. (Now *whoever* is the subject of the verb *loves*.)

HINT: Always treat the *whoever* or *whomever* clause as if it were separate; then you will use the correct case by judging whether the *whoever/whomever* is subject or object.

A pronoun can also be used as an indirect object:

> Throw *them* (not *they*) a pillow.

Errors of this type by native English speakers are rare.

When a pronoun is used as the object of a preposition, some writers have trouble using the correct case:

> The book was given to *him* (not *he*) and *me* (not *I*).

Do not yield to the popular temptation to say "between you and *I*." Although this error is often made by prominent people on television or on the lecture platform, it is ungrammatical. The correct form is "between you and *me*."

Pay special attention to the case of a pronoun combined or in apposition with a noun in the objective case:

> Everyone spoke highly of *us* (not *we*) teachers.
> The mayor invited two of us—Jack and *me* (not *I*)—to speak.

A pronoun serving as subject or as object of an infinitive is in the objective case:

Subject: They expect *him* (not *he*) to be discharged soon.
Object: We expected to see *him* (not *he*).

Avoid the common confusion of *who* and *whom*. *Who* is always a subject whereas *whom* is always an object:

Who has seen Jim? (subject)
Whom did Jim see? (object)
The girl *who* sold you the ticket is here. (subject)
The man *whom* you recognized has the ticket. (object)
To *whom* are you speaking? (object of preposition)

7c. Using the possessive case

The possessive case should be used before a noun or a gerund:

He will pay *his* son's tuition.

My parents denounce *our* (not *us*) seeing that violent movie.

I appreciate *your* (not *you*) lending me the money.

However, note this exception:

We noticed *him* (not *his*) playing the piano. (The emphasis here is on *him*, not on *playing*, which is a participle.)

NOTES:
1. *My, our, your, her, his, its* and *their* are classified as adjectives when they modify nouns.
2. By all means learn the difference between:

it's (for *it is*) and *its* (the pronoun)
Who's (for *who is*) and *whose* (the pronoun)

EXERCISE 7: Pronoun case

Underline each pronoun used incorrectly and replace it with the correct form. If the entry is correct, leave it alone.

MODEL: Give the money to the preacher and I.

Ans: **Me**

1. The fence was taller than him.
2. Does the novel reveal who they killed?
3. The barons built their castles for whoever was within their vassalage.
4. My father gave us boys two dollars in addition to board and room.
5. Tom is certainly far stronger than they.
6. They—the landscaper and him—planted ten rose bushes.
7. Between you and I, the entire project isn't worth a dime.
8. The party was in honor of he and she.

9. The psychologists consider him to be a sociopath.
10. We hoped beyond hope that the victims would not be them.
11. Why doesn't the captain order either Luke or he to play center field?
12. I have just reread the story about them crossing the Rhine River.
13. The accident was caused by him, not I.
14. It was evident that whoever the mob controlled would become the next victim.
15. His father opened the door, expecting that the visitor would be me.
16. The table is ugly because two of it's legs are missing.
17. Regardless of who's wallet this is, the money is gone.
18. Most of the jury members found she to be mentally ill.
19. The community admired both he and she.
20. Whom do they say is the best candidate for the job?

8. Adjectives and adverbs (ad)

Although adjectives and adverbs are both modifiers, they cannot be used interchangeably. Adjectives modify nouns whereas adverbs modify verbs (or adjectives or other adverbs).

Adjective: The pork chop is *good*.
Adverb: I dance *well*.

Exceptions to this rule are certain linking verbs that require adjectives rather than adverbs because the modifiers following these verbs describe the subject rather than the verb. The most common of these linking verbs are *seem, be, appear, become, look, smell, sound, feel,* and *taste*:

The fish smells *bad* (not *badly*).
The patient feels *terrible* (not *terribly*).

8a. Adjectives and adverbs after sense verbs

Verbs of the sense (*look, smell, sound, feel,* and *taste*) are particularly tricky since they require either an adverb or an adjective, depending on their meaning in the sentence:

The young man looked *eager*. (He is an eager man so an adjective is the appropriate modifier.)

The young man looked *eagerly* into his lover's eyes. (The act of looking is described so an adverb is the appropriate modifier.)

8b. Don't confuse adjectives and adverbs

Don't use *sure, real,* and *good* when you should use *surely, really,* and *well*:

> The climb was *really* (not *real*) steep.
> I *surely* (not *sure*) enjoyed the concert.

8c. Comparative and superlative forms

See 1e. Parts of speech. Also, use the comparative degree when comparing two items and the superlative degree when comparing three or more items:

> Japan is the *stronger* of the two countries.
> Japan is the *strongest* of the Asian countries.
>
> Today I got the *highest* score of anyone in class.
>
> Is this your *best* effort?

Be sure to complete your comparisons:

Wrong: Marie is much healthier.
Right: Marie is much healthier than she used to be.

8d. Don't convert nouns to adjectives

Don't make awkward conversions of nouns to adjectives. Nouns frequently function as adjectives, as in *torpedo boat, hospital care,* or *fur coat,* but avoid these forms if the resulting words sound confusing, ambiguous, or awkward:

Wrong: president bearing
Right: presidential bearing

Wrong: jealousy results
Right: results of jealousy

EXERCISE 8: Adjectives and adverbs

Underline the correct modifier and identify it as an adjective or an adverb.

MODEL: The moon shone (bright, brightly) through the clouds.

Ans: **Adverb**

1. Before a large crowd she was told that she had done (well, good).

2. The apple tasted so (sour, sourly) that I threw it away.
3. The teacher looked (disapproving, disapprovingly) at her.
4. Speaking as (honest, honestly) as ever, he refused to be translated.
5. "He (sure, surely) was betrayed by you," they insisted.
6. "Did you do (well, good) on the final exam?" she asked him.
7. Of the three contestants, she was the (prettiest, prettier).
8. Offer him the (largest, larger) of the two rooms.
9. Most of us consider ourselves (real, really) fortunate if we haven't had surgery by the time we reach middle age.
10. The war continued (steady, steadily) for five years.
11. Drive (slow, slowly); someone is crossing the street.
12. That time he took an (awful, awfully) big chance.
13. She played the violin extremely (soft, softly).
14. I found it difficult to determine which was the (worse, worst) pain of all.
15. At home he felt (capabler, more capable) than at school.

Punctuation

PUNCTUATION MARKS help to clarify the meaning of sentences. Without punctuation, sentences and paragraphs would not be intelligible to the reader. Some punctuation marks tell when a statement ends, whether it states a fact or asks a question; others form groups of words and ideas for emphasis, or set off material written by someone else. Punctuation marks are not decorative symbols to be used at random. In order to write effectively, you must be familiar with punctuation conventions.

9. The comma (,)

The comma is the most difficult punctuation mark to use. It has so many uses that writers tend to add it everywhere on a page, often incorrectly. Commas are correctly used under the following circumstances.

9a. Commas before coordinating conjunctions

Use a comma before a coordinating conjunction (*and, but, or, nor, for, so, yet*) that links two independent clauses:

> The trees had delicate foliage, but no birds nested in the branches.
>
> I grew up among these people, and their language was familiar to me.
>
> The weather was warm, yet the crops failed.

NOTES: 1. Do not use a comma to separate a compound predicate:

Wrong: We put on our hats, and opened our umbrellas.
Right: We put on our hats and opened our umbrellas.

2. The comma may be omitted between short independent clauses:

Wrong: It rained, and I wept.
Right: It rained and I wept.

9b. After introductory elements

Use a comma after an introductory subordinate clause and an introductory phrase.

(1) Introductory clause

Before I received my diploma, my father gave me a car.

No comma is needed if the dependent clause *follows* the independent clause:

My father gave me a car before I received my diploma.

(2) Introductory phrase

In the exquisite house of his dreams, all colors of the rainbow would be represented.

Speaking of the Devil, there she comes.

To understand the French sense of humor, one needs to be sophisticated.

After paying all of his bills, he invested in an old Chevrolet.

No comma is necessary after short prepositional phrases:

From surgery he was taken to intensive care.

9c. Series

Use a comma after each item in a series except the last.

(1) Words in a series

We shall need ribbons, flowers, and balloons.

NOTE: Careful writers use a comma in front of the final *and* in a series; otherwise, the last two items tend to be taken as a pair:

Confusing: He used different types of conveyances: train, camel, bicycle, horse and cart. (Is the horse separate from the cart?)

(2) Phrases in a series

We looked under the table, behind the desk, and above the fireplace.

(3) Clauses in a series

He arrived, he moved in, and he took over.

9d. Nonrestrictive clauses or phrases

Use commas to set off a nonrestrictive clause or phrase.

(1) Nonrestrictive clause A nonrestrictive clause adds descriptive information but is not essential to the meaning of the sentence.

Harvard, which is one of the most prestigious universities in the United States, has an excellent law school.

In the sentence above, the clause *which is one of the most prestigious universities in the United States* could be deleted without changing the meaning of the rest of the sentence. Consider, however, the following italicized restrictive clause:

Sarah wants to attend the law school *that her father attended.*

The restrictive clause is essential to the rest of the sentence because it identifies which law school Sarah wants to attend. Therefore, the clause is *not* set off by commas. To decide whether a clause is nonrestrictive or restrictive, leave it out of the sentence. If the meaning of the sentence changes, the clause is restrictive; if the meaning does not change, the clause is nonrestrictive.

Nonrestrictive: The three couples, who all lived on Coldwater Canyon, sued the contractor.
Restrictive: Only the three couples who lived on Coldwater Canyon sued the contractor.

(2) Nonrestrictive phrase Like the nonrestrictive clause, the nonrestrictive phrase adds descriptive but nonessential information to the sentence, as in the following example:

Eldon Rogers, dying of cancer, still attends work regularly.

Nonrestrictive: My cousin, employed by the May Company, refuses to buy an insurance policy.
Restrictive: Every person employed by the May Company must buy an insurance policy.

9e. Apposition

Use commas to set off appositives:

Albert Einstein, one of the most brilliant men of the twentieth century, permitted his brain to be dissected after his death.

Charles Benjamin Witt, Ph.D., will give a piano recital in March.

Lone Pine, home of Mt. Whitney, is a popular fisherman's resort.

Appositives are almost always nonrestrictive, but in the following examples they are restrictive and therefore require no commas. The appositives are italicized:

The movie actor *John Wayne* was on the cover of a magazine.
I was counting on my cousin *Harry*.
Edward *the Confessor* died before the Battle of Hastings.

9f. Parenthetical expressions

Use commas to set off parenthetical expressions, which are words or phrases that supply supplementary information and interrupt the flow of the sentence.

Rembrandt, I suppose, loved his work more than he loved his wife.

Walking under a ladder, for example, is said to bring bad luck.

Quite often, conjunctive adverbs serve as parenthetical expressions that help make a smooth transition from one sentence to the next. (See 1g. *Conjunctions, conjunctive adverbs*.

She did, nevertheless, graduate from nursing school.

We wondered, furthermore, whether or not he would admit the truth.

9g. Miscellaneous elements

Commas are used to set off a variety of other elements in a sentence.

Use commas after *yes* and *no* when they begin a sentence:

Yes, he did return the sweater.

Use commas to set off words of direct address:

My dear, he warned you not to touch the water pipe.

Use commas after mild interjections:

Well, why didn't you say so?

Use commas to set off absolute phrases. (See 2c[5]. *Absolute phrases*.)

Their prayers recited, they left the mosque to go back to work.

Use commas to set off expressions of contrast:

The pillow was embroidered by my aunt, not my sister.

Use commas to introduce brief quotations and to set off quoted material from the rest of the text:

"Then God or Nature calmed the elements," wrote Ovid. The Bible tells us, "Judge not lest you be judged."

NOTE: When a quotation is interrupted by explanatory words, use a comma before and after the interruption. Always place commas inside the quotation marks:

"When you have been driven out of your homeland," said Jake, "you feel like a piece of drifting seaweed."

See also 16. *Quotation Marks*.

Follow convention in the use of commas for dates, addresses, and places:

Dates: Today is February 25, 1980.
On July 4, 1776, our nation was born.
The company will be solvent by June, 1985.

A comma goes between the day (or month) and the year and after the year if the sentence continues.

Addresses: 1500 North Verdugo Road, Glendale, California 91208 (Do not place a comma between the state and the zip code.)

A comma goes between the city and the state and after the state if the sentence continues.

Use a comma before examples introduced by *such as* or *especially*:

> A writer should avoid using trite figures of speech, such as "big as a bear" or "white as a ghost."
>
> Americans love spectator sports, especially football.

Use a comma when it will prevent misreading a sentence:

Confusing: As soon as the airplane lifted the gauges began to fluctuate.
Clear: As soon as the airplane lifted, the gauges began to fluctuate.

Confusing: After Friday afternoon classes will be filled.
Clear: After Friday, afternoon classes will be filled.

NOTE: For fear of omitting commas, many students overuse them. There are a number of places commas are not needed.

1. Don't separate a subject from its verb with a comma:

Wrong: All of the elderly people, expected the tax vote to fail.
Right: All of the elderly people expected the tax vote to fail.

2. Don't separate a verb and its object with a comma:

Wrong: He loudly demanded, all of the money.
Right: He loudly demanded all of the money.

3. Don't use a comma before the first or after the last item in a series:

Wrong: St. Paul gave Christianity, a theology, a church organization, and a sense of purpose.
Right: St. Paul gave Christianity a theology, a church organization, and a sense of purpose.

10. The semicolon (;)

The semicolon is a weak period and cannot be replaced by a comma. Use the semicolon between independent clauses to replace the coordinate conjunction:

> The days were dreary; the nights were unbearable.
>
> The people gathered in the streets and in the market places; they seemed to crawl out of nowhere.

Use the semicolon between independent clauses joined by a conjunctive adverb (*however, consequently, moreover, besides, on the other hand*):

> Everyone demands more and more services from the government; *consequently*, taxes are sky high. (It is customary, although not technically necessary, to place a comma after the conjunctive adverb.)

NOTE: A conjunctive adverb, used parenthetically, is enclosed by commas:

> My sister sings beautifully; my brother, *however*, sounds like a fog horn.

Use semicolons between items in a series when the items contain commas, and between independent clauses joined by a coordinate conjunction if the clauses contain commas:

> For our clothing we wore bathing suits, shorts, and overalls; for our shelter we had tents, caves, and sleeping bags; for our food we ate nuts, dates, and bananas.
>
> During the Middle Ages the average person believed in ghosts, magic spells, and omens; but today he believes in television, computers, and stock-market reports.

11. The colon(:)

A colon is used to indicate that something is about to follow. It can be used to introduce a list preceded by *as follows, following, follows*:

> The following officers were elected: president, secretary, and treasurer.

NOTE: Use the colon only at the end of an independent clause. Do *not* use it between a verb or preposition and its object:

Wrong: England has produced: Chaucer, Shakespeare, and Milton.
Right: England has produced Chaucer, Shakespeare, and Milton.

Wrong: My three favorite cities are: Paris, London, and Rome.
Right: The following are my three favorite cities: Paris, London, and Rome.

Wrong: Pam had a passion for: reading, writing, and traveling.
Right: Pam had a passion for reading, writing, and traveling.

Use a main clause followed by a colon to introduce quotations of more than three lines:

> This is how Sidney J. Harris defines a *jerk*:
>
> > A jerk, then, is a man (or woman) who is utterly unable to see himself as he appears to others. He has no grace; he is tactless without meaning to be; he is a bore even to his best friends; he is an egotist without charm.

Use a colon to direct attention to a summary, explanation, or appositive:

> The entire problem can be summarized in one word: *poverty.*
>
> Two passions have a powerful influence on men: *ambition* and *avarice*.
>
> One thing he always remained: a *gentleman*.

Use a colon to separate the greeting in a letter from the body of the letter:

> Dear Sir:

Use a colon to separate a title from a subtitle:

> *The Masks of God: Oriental Mythology*

Use a colon between Bible chapter and verse:

> Genesis 3:15

Use a colon between hours and minutes:

> 4:15 P.M.

Use a colon to separate the name of the speaker in a play from words spoken:

> Hamlet: To be or not to be . . .

12. The dash (—)

The dash should not be used for mere visual effect or as a substitute for a comma. Use the dash to show a sudden break in thought:

> She was certain that he was dead and she—but no, his body moved.

Use the dash to signal an interrupted or unfinished dialogue:

> "I want to be a farmer," he enunciated slowly.
> "A farmer? But your father—"
> "Don't ever mention my father again. For me, he no longer exists."

Use the dash after a statement, to explain or amplify it:

> Barbara began to despise everything associated with the modern world—inflation, revolution, pollution.

Use the dash to emphasize parenthetical elements, particularly when they also contain commas:

> She believes that there is nothing—no hell or paradise—after a person dies.
>
> Four planets—Mars, Saturn, Jupiter, and Pluto—were embroidered on silk tapestries.

NOTE: The dash is typed as two hyphens with no space before or after; it is written as an unbroken line the length of two hyphens.

13. The period (.)

The period is the first punctuation mark an elementary school student learns. It is most basic because it signals the end of a sentence.

Use a period to end a declarative statement:

> The dinner was excellent.

Use a period to end a command:

Don't do that.

Use a period to end an indirect question:

We wondered when the truck would arrive.

Use a period to indicate an abbreviation or a contraction:

Dr.	Fed.	assn.
Mrs.	Co.	secy.
Ms.	M.D.	etc.
Mass.	Inc.	hwy.

NOTE: It is becoming increasingly popular to abbreviate well-known names without periods:

TWA, TV, NATO, HEW, CBS, YMCA

Use a period to indicate decimals:

$60.50 2.5%

A group of three spaced periods is used as an ellipsis to indicate that some words have been omitted from a quotation:

Original passage: "These gods, who do not die, cannot be tragic."
With ellipsis: "These gods . . . cannot be tragic."

NOTE: If the omitted portion of the quotation follows a period, the period is retained, followed by the ellipsis:

Original passage: "The narrative is incomplete. And it may remain so. Nevertheless, it is one of the finest epics from any age."
With ellipsis: "The narrative is incomplete. . . . Nevertheless, it is one of the finest epics from any age."

Ellipsis are also used to indicate a pause:

"Listen to me," she said, trembling with fury. "Don't you ever . . . touch my brother again. If you do . . . I'll shoot you."

14. The question mark (?)

Use a question mark to end a direct question:

Do you love rain? Why?

The food was really good? (The question mark cues the reader that what would have been a declarative sentence is functioning as a question.)

NOTE: Do not follow a question mark with a comma or a period:

Wrong: "Do you like red hair?," she asked.
Right: "Do you like red hair?" she asked.

Question marks can indicate uncertainty, especially in historical dating:

The clay tablets date back to 1750(?) B.C.
Antiochus II, king of Syria (261?–247 B.C.)

15. The exclamation point (!)

Use an exclamation point to indicate a strong emotion or an emphatic command:

Whew! You stink!
What a surprise!
Quick! Bring me some bandages!

Do *not* use an exclamation point to indicate a mild feeling or to emphasize an idea:

Wrong: I was surprised!
Right: I was surprised.

Wrong: Milton is a better writer than Shakespeare!
Right: Milton is a better writer than Shakespeare.

NOTE: Do not follow an exclamation point with a comma or period:

Wrong: "My God!," screamed the woman.
Right: "My God!" screamed the woman.

16. Quotation marks (" ")

The primary use of quotation marks is to set off the exact words of a speaker or writer. Quotation marks are always used in pairs to indicate the beginning and the end of a quotation. Do not enclose any introductory words within the quotation marks:

> He answered sarcastically, "You may be rich, but you're stupid."

Do not use quotation marks for indirect address:

Indirect: He told him that Thursday would be soon enough.
Direct: He told him, "Thursday will be soon enough."

NOTE: Use commas to set off interruptions such as "he said" or "she observed":

> "As far as I am concerned," he said, "she is right."

When the quotation contains a question mark or an exclamation point, the question mark or exclamation point replaces the commas:

> "What does the master wish?" she asked.
> "A kiss at least!" he demanded.

Long quotations (four lines or more) are indented. They do not require quotation marks:

> Alan Simpson offers the following insight into our society:
>
> > The health of society depends on simple virtues like honesty, decency, courage, and public spirit. There are forces in human nature which constantly tend to corrupt them, and every age has its own vices. The worst feature of ours is probably the obsession with violence.

Quoted dialog requires a separate paragraph for each speaker to stress the change from one speaker to another:

> After a long silence, Kevin muttered, "What's the use? Tomorrow I must leave."
> "But why must you leave?" Rosie asked.
> "Because I need money."

Quoted lines of poetry require no quotation marks since their stanza format already sets them off from the regular text. Quoted poetry should be double-spaced and centered between the left and right margins:

> One equal temper of heroic hearts,
> Made weak by time and fate but strong in will
> To strive, to seek, to find, and not to yield.
>
> —Alfred Lord Tennyson, "Ulysses"

Quotation marks are used to indicate the title of any subdivision in a printed publication: a chapter, an essay, a short story, a poem, a song, a lecture, a newspaper headline.

> "Pharaoh and His Subjects" is the title of Chapter 3 in *The Dwellers on the Nile*.
>
> "A New Year's Warning" is a *Time* magazine article on terrorism in Turkey.
>
> "The Flowering Judas" is a short story by Katherine Anne Porter.
>
> Robert Frost's poem "Design" questions God's providence.
>
> "A Mighty Fortress Is Our God" is a marvelous hymn of confidence.
>
> Professor Lang's lecture was entitled, "How to Sell Yourself."
>
> The headline in Part II of the *Los Angeles Times* reads as follows: "FBI May Intervene in Athlete's Fraud Case."

Quotation marks can set off words used in a special sense:

> Whenever my grandmother became schizophrenic, Grandpa said she was "exhausted."
>
> What he called "art" had no more merit than did the scribblings of a child.

Quotation marks are used to enclose definitions:

> The word *dulcet* means "gently melodious."

Definitions may also appear in italics:

> *Kinetics* is *the study of motion*.

For a quotation within a quotation, use single quotation marks:

Thoreau once said, "I heartily accept the motto, 'That government is best which governs least.'"

17. The apostrophe (')

Generally speaking, the apostrophe replaces *of* to indicate possession: "the people's choice" rather than "the choice *of* the people." It is also used to form contractions and certain plurals.

To indicate possession, add an apostrophe plus *s* to singular nouns:

Mabel's dress
someone's house

NOTE: Add only an apostrophe to singular words ending in an *s* sound:

Keats' "Ode to a Nightingale"
Jesus' words

Add an apostrophe plus *s* to plural nouns to form the possessive:

the children's hour
women's clothes

NOTE: Add only an apostrophe to plurals already ending in *s*:

three tigers' teeth
several teachers' lectures

Place an apostrophe plus *s* after the last word in a hyphenated word to form the possessive:

mother-in-law's hat (not mother's-in-law)

sisters-in-law's hats (not sisters'-in-law)

Informal English allows writers to shorten words by omitting certain letters. Such shortened words are called contractions:

can't (cannot)	we're (we are)	In January of '55 (1955)
won't (will not)	there's (there is)	o'clock (of the clock)
who's (who is)	it's (it is)	ma'am (madam)

An apostrophe is used to indicate the plural of letters, numbers, symbols, and words referred to as words:

> His *f*'s look like *t*'s.
>
> Then they were hit by the Depression of the 1930's. (An acceptable alternative is 1930s.)
>
> +'s and −'s often add nothing to a grade.
>
> Delete all those innocuous *very*'s.

NOTE: Avoid the possessive apostrophe with inanimate objects:

> **Awkward:** the chair's paint
> **Better:** the paint on the chair

18. The hyphen (-)

Use a hyphen to form certain compound words:

> mother-in-law
> cave-in
> paste-up
> red-handed
> court-martial

Writers frequently construct their own compound words:

> All of us need to get rid of our I-don't-give-a-damn attitudes.

Rules for hyphenating compound words are varied. Check your dictionary to be sure you are following convention.

Use a hyphen to join two or more words used as an adjective before a noun:

> a home-grown tomato
> a well-known song

However, when the compound adjective follows the noun, no hyphen is necessary:

> The tomato is home grown.
> The song is well known.

Do not use a hyphen when the first word of a compound is an adverb ending in *-ly*:

a dangerously long tunnel
two badly hurt victims

Suspension hyphens are used in series:

They ran two-, three-, and four-mile distances.

Use a hyphen after the prefixes *ex, self, cross, all, great*; before the suffix *elect*; between the prefix and a proper name:

ex-football player
self-educated
cross-ventilation
all-purpose glue
great-uncle
president-elect
pro-Irish

The hyphen is used to avoid ambiguity:

He *recovered* from the shock of losing $10,000.
Mrs. Jones *re-covered* her sofa.

Aerobic dancing is good *recreation*.
The novel was a *re-creation* of his own childhood.

Use a hyphen with compound numbers from twenty-one to ninety-nine and with fractions:

twenty-two
three-fifths

A compound adjective that contains numbers is also hyphenated:

a thirteen-year-old boy

19. Parentheses ( )

Parentheses are used to enclose incidental information:

His home town (Bern, Switzerland) sent flowers to the funeral.

Brigham Young (1801–1877) was once territorial governor of Utah.

NOTE: 1. No capital letter or period is used when a sentence in parentheses is part of a larger sentence:

He believed in the efficacy of yoga (the term means *union*) as a way of uniting the body and the mind.

But a period is placed at the end of a sentence used independently within parentheses:

Earl Kemp Long was the brother of Huey Long and an important political figure in America. (See his biography by A. J. Liebling.)

The comma follows the closing parenthesis in sentences such as the one below:

Despite the emperor's warning (ten days prior to the festival), the soldiers continued the siege.

2. A question mark or exclamation point is placed inside the parentheses if it belongs to the parenthetical material, and outside if it does not:

Inside: She arrived (had she grown older?) once again to captivate him with her beauty.
Outside: Have you read Baker's *Practical Stylist* (latest edition)?

Use parentheses to enclose numerals or letters in enumerations:

The babysitter was expected to (1) care for the children, (2) cook meals, and (3) wash the dishes.

Parentheses are used around a question mark to indicate uncertainty or doubt:

In this frieze, the god Osiris (Re?) is seen seated on a throne.

20. Brackets ([ ])

Use brackets to insert editorial comments in quoted material:

According to Campbell, "the Bull of Heaven seems to be the storm god [scholars do not clarify his exact identity] controlling the sky."

Use brackets to set off parenthetical material within parentheses:

> (See *The New Columbia Encyclopedia* [New York: Columbia University Press, 1975].)

EXERCISE 9: Punctuation: The comma

Insert commas wherever they are needed. If the sentence is correct, leave it alone.

MODEL: Try reading the poetry of Chaucer of Donne and of Dryden.

Ans: **Try reading the poetry of Chaucer, of Donne, and of Dryden.**

1. As the proverb says "He that would bring home the wealth of the Indies must carry out the wealth of the Indies."
2. Were those teachers as all teachers before them preoccupied with trivial facts?
3. As Bill saw the case he had simply missed class.
4. There was obviously something missing in me.
5. I wanted to confront that ill-bred woman who hated Germans so much.
6. Yes we did have some moments of delight.
7. She was as efficient as a machine as friendly as a Dalmation puppy and as beautiful as a movie star.
8. Doctors surgeons in particular have a god complex.
9. I promptly boarded the airplane that he had pointed out.
10. He would stand before us rejoicing in his sinewy body every inch an open air man.
11. We shall reside at 1344 Woodland Drive Detroit Michigan.
12. On March 13, 1950 her first child was born.
13. "But you are prejudiced" she insisted "because you hate him although you don't even know the person."
14. "Take a deep breath" he exhorted us.
15. Man is a gregarious animal but he does not always enjoy harmony with his fellow humans.
16. Hemingway's poignant war novel *A Farewell to Arms* reflects a pessimistic world view.
17. The judge having entered and the audience having risen, the trial began.
18. Because these boys were adolescents, they considered all adults brainless and stultifying.
19. If you set out to climb a mountain no matter how high you climb you have failed if you do not reach the top.

20. He had been on the quest so to speak from the beginning.
21. John Barrymore a member of the famous family of stage actors once played the role of Hamlet while he was drunk.
22. Many infirm lonely people prefer living in a convalescent hospital.
23. Before dying had been an irrelevant mystery to her but now it was a reality.
24. George Orwell said that political writing was often the defense of the indefensible.
25. The great enemy of concise writing one might say is a lack of politeness.
26. Before delving into his personal life let us study his doctrine.
27. Magnificent stately mansions leaned against the hillside.
28. Furthermore the word *science* has the ring of truth and authority.
29. An understanding of art requires that art be evaluated on more than just Aristotelian principles.
30. My little sportscar which has given me nothing but trouble was sold for twice as much as I paid for it.

EXERCISE 9, 10: Punctuation: The comma and the semicolon

In the following sentences, place a semicolon or a comma or no punctuation within the brackets.

MODEL: The minister asked the audience to rise [ ] everyone stood immediately.

Ans: **The minister asked the audience to rise [;] everyone stood immediately.**

1. I hated him for making so much money [ ] and keeping it all to himself.
2. By sunset the hunters retired [ ] however [ ] at dawn they continued with renewed vigor.
3. Because initiative and trust were sorely lacking [ ] the business went bankrupt within a year.
4. Here are the key people in this venture: Jack Jennings, chairman of the board [ ] Milton Le Cuyer, president of the overseas operation [ ] Dorothy Nibley, marketing supervisor.
5. The nights [ ] however [ ] seem long and cold.
6. Please give her the directions [ ] as soon as she asks for them.
7. As late as 1835 [ ] human sacrifices were performed in India.
8. The community college system in California [ ] without tuition and with open access [ ] is succeeding beyond the wildest and most hopeful dreams of its supporters.

9. All this was unsettling [ ] since I believed in democracy.
10. He had always been short of stature [ ] consequently [ ] he decided to make a success of himself.
11. The stars sparkled [ ] it was a lovely night.
12. Everything was finally in our hands [ ] we were completely in charge.
13. Either these few are considered to be innately superior [ ] or they are selected for special assistance.
14. Give her a telephone call [ ] as soon as you have received the grant money.
15. "It is fortunate that you live in a house [ ]" he stated [ ] "otherwise you might be paying an exorbitant rent."
16. She was a calm woman [ ] not one to be scandalized easily.
17. Ask any of the officials [ ] if you can catch them on duty.
18. The mad elephant had destroyed one of the bamboo huts [ ] it had also turned over the rubbish truck.
19. They stood in line clear around the block [ ] the news having reached the neighborhood that free tickets were being supplied.
20. In the rough [ ] the amethyst was worth $20 [ ] honed and polished [ ] it was worth $200.

EXERCISE 9–20: All punctuation marks

In the following sentences, supply any missing marks of punctuation. If the sentence is correct, leave it alone.

MODEL: The peoples choice is what counts thats how democracy works

Ans: **The people's choice is what counts; that's how democracy works.**

1. They were asked to supply the following items towels, sheets, and soap
2. He demanded to know when she was going to pay the rent.
3. Do you live in a politically active community he asked.
4. What remains but to spare him all of the unpleasant aspects of keeping house
5. Caroline yelled Fire Get out
6. His cat weighed so much that he called her tons of fun
7. Everybodys a damnable liar he shouted with fury
8. She is a well dressed beautifully groomed woman
9. Our campus bookstore is student owned.
10. Have him read "The Last Ditch," an essay by Robert Coles.
11. Don't write your 7s and 9s so much alike.

12. Albert Schweitzer 1875–1965 was awarded the Nobel Peace Prize
13. He called me a let's see what did he call me
14. The question is this Where do we go from here
15. Poets philosophers hermits all are idealists
16. Jackies bloodstained suit now displayed in the Smithsonian Institution is a horrifying symbol of the vanished Camelot
17. My father-in-law is a loving grandfather
18. Will you come soon perhaps tomorrow
19. Boston, Massachusetts is his hometown
20. "The Lord is my shepherd. . . . He maketh me to lie down in green pastures."

Mechanics

STUDENTS OFTEN WONDER whether mechanics will count as much toward their grade as content. The answer is that the mechanics of writing are often inseparable from content and therefore must exert a nearly equal influence on the grade. A manuscript that abides by the rules is like a city whose traffic flow is controlled by lights, signs, and regulations; a manuscript that ignores the rules is like a city whose traffic has run amok. You will increase the readability of your writing and make your reader immeasurably happier if you observe proper mechanics.

21. Capitalization (cap)

Capitalization is a way of drawing attention to certain words. Observe the following conventions of capitalization in your writing. Whenever you are in doubt about whether or not a word should be capitalized, consult your dictionary.

21a. First words

Use capitals for the first word in a sentence:

> Above all else, we want peace.
> How did life on our planet begin?

Use capitals for the first word in a line of traditional poetry:

> The sun does arise,
> And make happy the skies;
> The merry bells ring
> To welcome the spring.
>
> —William Blake

Much modern poetry is in free verse, and the first words in a line are not always capitalized.

NOTE: If the quotation fits grammatically into a sentence, the first word need *not* be capitalized:

> William Faulkner once said (in a *Paris Review* interview) that "if a writer has to rob his mother, he will not hesitate; the 'Ode on a Grecian Urn' is worth any number of old ladies."

21b. Proper nouns

Capitalize proper nouns, words that are part of proper nouns, and adjectives derived from proper nouns, as well as names of specific people, races, nationalities, languages:

Abraham Lincoln	French
Levite	Asian
Russian	Latin

21c. Names

Capitalize names of continents, countries, states, cities, neighborhoods, streets, buildings, parks, monuments, oceans, lakes, rivers:

Africa	Union Oil Building
Sweden	Central Park
Michigan	Statue of Liberty
London	Atlantic Ocean
Morningside Heights	Lake Louise
Brand Boulevard	Tigris River

21d. Other capitalization rules

The following rules are to be used as guidelines for the use of capitals in your writing.

(1) Specific organizations and institutions

the Lakers
Daughters of the American Revolution
Smithsonian Institution
Federal Reserve
Democratic Party (or Republican)

(2) Historical periods, events, or documents

Middle Ages
Renaissance
Battle of Hastings
Bill of Rights

(3) Members of national, political, or religious groups

Rotarian
Democrat
Methodist

(4) Religions and sacred religious works or terms

Islam	the Virgin
Hinduism	Allah
Catholicism	the Bible
God	the Torah

Some people capitalize pronouns referring to the deity: His, He, Him, Thee, Thou

(5) Names of days, months, and holidays

Wednesday
August
Thanksgiving
Valentine's Day

(6) Names of academic degrees and specific courses

Ph.D.
Doctor of Jurisprudence
English 135
Advanced Typing

Usually if the course is a general course, it is not capitalized: psychology, biology, mathematics.

(7) Names of stars, planets, constellations

Pluto
Mars
North Star
Milky Way

Unless they are personified, *earth*, *sun*, and *moon* are not capitalized.

(8) Names of ships, trains, and aircraft

the Queen Elizabeth II
the Lark
Air Force One

(9) Personifications

Father Time
Mother Nature

(10) Abbreviations indicating time, government divisions, or media stations

A.M., P.M. (also a.m., p.m.)
HEW
FHA
NBC
KNXT

(11) Titles preceding names

Dean Katz
Reverend D. L. Smith
Mr. Eric Reese
President June Willard
Governor Mario Cuomo
Chief Justice Burger

NOTES: 1. Do not capitalize a title when it is not part of the name:

a former senator, Harold Berman
Gail French, director of personnel

2. An abbreviated title, used before or after a name, is capitalized:

Dr. Sigmund Freud
Fernando Garcia, Esq.
Richard Bauer, M.D.

3. Titles of distinction are capitalized when they take the place of the person's name:

The President spoke on TV.
The Archbishop offered the prayer.

(12) First word of each outline entry

I. Advantages of credit cards
  A. Instant money
  B. Delayed payment

(13) Titles of literary works Capitalize all words except articles, conjunctions, and prepositions unless they are the first word in the title.

For Whom the Bell Tolls
"Ode on a Grecian Urn"
The Taming of the Shrew

NOTE Conjunctions and prepositions of five letters or more are sometimes capitalized:

War Against the King
"Comin' Through the Rye"

(14) Points of the compass Capitalize when they refer to a specific area, but not when they refer to direction:

My aunt lives in the East.

but

Turn west on Broadway.

(15) Titles of relatives Capitalize when they are not preceded by an article or a pronoun, when they are followed by a name, and in direct address:

Give the rose to Grandmother, my dear.
I owe Aunt Margaret twenty dollars.
Please, Mother, pay no attention.

but

My mother has arrived.
They told us that the aunt was wealthy.

(16) The pronoun *I* and the interjection *O*:

As far as I am concerned, he might as well go home.

How many crimes, O Liberty, have been committed in your name?

NOTE: *Oh* is not capitalized unless it appears at the beginning of a sentence.

EXERCISE 21: Capitalization

In the sentences below correct all capitalization. Underline small letters that should be capitalized and strike through capital letters that should be in lower case. If the sentence is correct, leave it alone.

MODEL: Many Ancient sumerian myths, such as the *epic of gilgamesh*, were found in ashurbanipal's Library at nineveh.

1. If we need money for the First Mortgage, I can always borrow some from uncle charlie.
2. Because dr. Lewis, my English professor, lived in the south for many years, he has remained a baptist.
3. The Monarch butterfly has wings that resemble dead autumn leaves.
4. Anton Chekhov's short story "the new villa" portrays a clash between two cultures, the Aristocracy and the Serfs.
5. When we take our cruise to alaska, we shall go on the olav, a scandinavian Vessel.
6. I am sending grandmother some Violets for her Birthday.
7. The tiv, an african tribe, began their stories, "not yesterday, not yesterday."
8. During the Middle Ages, London had no sewers; consequently, the plague broke out from time to time.
9. After Adam and Eve had eaten of the tree of the knowledge of good and evil, they were expelled from eden.
10. Helen likes to be addressed as "ms. Griffith" rather than "miss Griffith."
11. My grandfather watched Charles Lindbergh land the spirit of St. Louis at orly airport in paris.
12. He will be made a fellow of the royal academy of surgeons next Spring.
13. How many more American Embassies will be attacked by Foreign countries who want to be our enemies?
14. We sat down and listened to the president's state of the union address on tv.
15. The Lincoln Memorial in Washington, D.C. will always remind us that civil war is possible.

22. Italics (ital)

In handwritten or typewritten manuscripts, italics are indicated by underlining. In printing, *italic* type is used.

Use italics for the titles of books, magazines, and newspapers:

> One of the most thoroughly American books is *Tom Sawyer* by Mark Twain.
>
> Occasionally I don't understand *Time* magazine's choice for "Man of the Year."
>
> He relies on *The Wall Street Journal* for news about economic trends.

NOTES: 1. Copy the title of a newspaper as it appears on the masthead:

> *Los Angeles Times* (not *The Times* or *Times*)

Use italics for the titles of pamphlets or bulletins, musical compositions, plays, films, television programs, and long poems:

> *MacDowell Musical Society News Bulletin*
> *Rock Climbing in the Sierras*
> Verdi's *La Traviata* (opera)
> Beethoven's *Concerto No. 2*
> *My Fair Lady* (musical comedy)
> Neil Simon's *Chapter Two* (play)
> *All That Jazz* (film)
> *60 Minutes* (TV broadcast)
> Byron's *Don Juan* (long poem)

NOTES: 1. Titles of brief musical pieces or songs are usually placed within quotation marks:

> "Scaramouche" by Milhaud
> "I Could Have Danced All Night" (from *My Fair Lady*)

2. Titles of short poems are placed within quotation marks:

> "Journey of the Magi" by T. S. Eliot

Use italics for the names of ships, aircraft, spacecraft, and trains:

> *USS Missouri* (ship)
> *Spirit of St. Louis* (aircraft)
> *Apollo 17* (spacecraft)
> *Orient Express* (train)

Use italics for titles of visual works of art:

Discus Thrower by Myron (ancient Roman sculpture)

Girl Pouring Perfume (detail from a wall painting)

Alexander at Issus (second century Greek mosaic)

Leonardo da Vinci's *Mona Lisa* (painting on canvas)

Use italics for foreign words not yet absorbed into the English vocabulary:

Schopenhauer had a gloomy *Weltanschauung*. (world view)

When I entered the room, I had a feeling of *déjà vu*. (already seen)

This day is certainly *bellissimo*. (most beautiful)

Latin abbreviations are not italicized:

etc., i.e., viz., et al., e.g.

Use italics for words, letters, figures, or symbols referred to as such:

Words like *superannuated* instead of *old* sound overblown.
The French have a way of gargling their *r*'s.
Move those *10*'s over to the next column.
Students should avoid using the *&* sign in formal essays.

NOTE: Quotation marks are sometimes used for cases such as those listed above, but we recommend italics.

Use italics for emphasis when it cannot be achieved by choice or placement of words:

Which of the following is *not* a fairytale:

a. "The Descent of Ishtar into the Netherworld"
b. "Snow White and the Seven Dwarfs"
c. "The Frog and the Prince"
d. "Sleeping Beauty"

(To draw attention to the direction in a multiple-choice examination)

I said that she should comp*li*ment, not comp*le*ment him. (To emphasize the distinction in meaning between the two words)

EXERCISE 22: Italics

In the following sentences underline all words that should be in italics. If the sentence is correct, leave it alone.

MODEL: On my flight to New York, I read Belva Plain's *Evergreen*, a charming novel.

1. If I had the money, I would subscribe to The New Yorker.
2. When you say you saw Gerald Ford, do you mean the Gerald Ford?
3. My history professor is constantly using the phrase coup d'état.
4. Does it bother you when someone misuses the word disinterested?
5. One television commentator gave the movie The Last Married Couple in America a bad review.
6. My favorite hors d'oeuvre is stuffed mushrooms.
7. The Dome of the Rock in Jerusalem is a holy shrine for both Jews and Moslems.
8. I have Van Gogh's Sunflowers hanging on my office wall.
9. Some of Toulouse-Lautrec's best paintings feature La Goulue, a cabaret dancer whom the artist befriended.
10. Numerous tourists each year take a Mediterranean cruise aboard the Royal Viking Sea, a luxury ship.

EXERCISE 16, 22: Quotation marks and italics

In the following sentences, underline words that should be in italics and use quotation marks where needed.

MODEL: Although poetry has never been my favorite literary genre, I am deeply touched by Edwin Markham's "Man and the Hoe."

1. The chapter entitled China: War and Resistance in Theodore H. White's book In Search of History is informative.
2. Although it has almost become commercialized, Michelangelo's famous David never fails to impress me with its youthful courage and zeal.
3. Ain't Misbehavin' is a zesty, jazzy musical.
4. The literary term used to describe stories that begin in the middle of the action is in medias res.
5. No television show has surpassed the Show of Shows in pure comic effect.
6. The Catbird Seat by James Thurber is a short story about a meek little office clerk who gets even with an overbearing female coworker.
7. In his article Why I Am an Agnostic Clarence Darrow tries to make some Christian beliefs look absurd.
8. John Ciardi's translation of Dante's Inferno keeps the complex gestalt of the original twenty-seven cantos.
9. A tragic loss of lives and property took place when the Titanic sank on April 10, 1912.
10. You Ain't Nothin' But a Hound Dog was one of Elvis Presley's earliest successes.

23. Numbers (nu)

In the following circumstances numbers are usually written out.

Numbers that can be spelled out in two words or less:

seventy thousand years ago
forty-five senators
three fourths of the country

A hyphenated number is considered as one word:

thirty-five thousand voters

Numbers used as compound adjectives:

a ten-year-old refrigerator
a three-wheel electric car

In the following circumstances numbers must be written as figures.

Numbers expressed in more than two words:

Much had changed in 225 years.
a list of 3,250 people
not more than 56¼ inches

Dates:

November 19, 1929
19 Nov. 1929
11/19/29
55 B.C.
A.D. 105

"B.C." follows the year, but "A.D." precedes the year. The day of the month may be written out when the year does not follow:

On the sixth of October

Decades may be written out or expressed as figures:

In the nineteen sixties
In the sixties
In the 1960's (or 1960s)

Centuries are expressed in lower-case letters:

Following the seventeenth century

Addresses:

245 Earlham St.
Apt. 15
Pasadena, California 91106

Time of day:

4:14 P.M.

If the expression "o'clock" follows, then the hour should be written out:

three-thirty o'clock

Exact amounts of money:

$15.98
$1,350
$2.5 million (or $2,500,000)

Mathematical scores and statistics:

20¼
⅝
3.5% (or 3.5 percent)
a median score of 48

Numbers of books, volumes, pages, acts, scenes, verses, and lines:

Book 3 (or Book III)
Volume 4 (or Volume IV)
page 23 (or p. 23)
Act 3, Scene 2, lines 15–18 (or Act III, Scene 2, lines 15–18)
Verse 3

NOTES:

1. The documentation for research papers follows a special format, as explained in Chapter 10 "The Research Paper."
2. Never begin a sentence with a figure. If necessary, rewrite the sentence:

Wrong: 36 was the score.
Right: The score was 36.

3. If you are writing a paper that contains many numbers, use figures throughout for consistency.

EXERCISE 23: Numbers

Correct all numbers used incorrectly. If the sentence is correct, leave it alone.

$5.23.
MODEL: That pound of chocolates costs ~~five dollars and twenty-three cents.~~

1. She swam 3 full miles.
2. Louis XIV was born in 1638.
3. Flapper girls were a product of the nineteen twenties.
4. 1980 was a year of strained relations between the U.S. and Iran.
5. Our flight leaves at three-thirty A.M.
6. The score was 30 to 1.
7. If 48% of the product sells, we shall profit.
8. The bridge cost three million and a half dollars.
9. Volume Three is the most difficult of all.
10. A foot has twelve inches.

24. Abbreviations (abb)

In general, avoid abbreviations. Under the following circumstances abbreviations are correct:

Titles preceding proper names:

Dr. Strangelove
Mr. Sebastian Peters
Mrs. Reinbolt
Ms. Balucci
St. Theresa

The following titles are written out:

President Harding
Senator Baker
Professor Fiedler
The Honorable George Lundquist
The Reverend Jesse Jackson

Titles following proper names:

Marcel Ford, Jr.
Christopher J. Marsh, Esq.
Frances Moore, M.D.
Henry A. Look, Ph.D.
Gilbert Blaine, LL.D.

Names of well-known organizations and a few countries:

FBI	YMCA
CIA	OPEC
HEW	USA
IBM	USSR
CBS	NBC

Words used with dates or figures:

23 B.C. (or A.D. 23)
8:00 A.M. (or 8:00 P.M.)
I answered No. 4 wrong.
See Fig. 17.

Incorporated, *Company*, *Brothers*, and the ampersand when they are part of the official name of a business:

Doubleday & Co., Inc.
Cotton Bros., Inc.

Abbreviations used in footnotes, endnotes, or bibliographies (See pages 242–43):

e.g.	for example
i.e.	that is
etc.	and so forth
et al.	and others
ed.	edited by, editor, edition
trans.	translated by, translator
p., pp.	page, pages

The English versions of the first four abbreviations above are preferred for writing not related to formal research.

NOTE: Do not abbreviate the following:

1. Names of geographical areas, months, days:

Wrong: The cruise left for the Med. last Wed.
Right: The cruise left for the Mediterranean last Wednesday.

2. Names of people:

Will Matthew (not *Matth.*) pay the bill?

3. The words *volume, chapter, page* unless used in research-paper documentation or technical writing:

He fell asleep after reading three pages (not *pp.*) of the first volume (not *vol.*).

4. Names of courses of study:

She failed chemistry (not *chem.*).

5. The word *Christmas*:

Christmas (not *Xmas*) will be here soon.

6. The words *street, avenue, road, park, mount, drive, lane, river*, and similar words when they are used as essential parts of proper names:

Maiden Lane is filled with charming shops.
The club climbed Mount Whitney.
Their summer home is on the Colorado River.

EXERCISE 24: Abbreviations

Strike out the version that would be incorrect in formal writing:

MODEL: ~~Give Geo. a call.~~ / Give George a call.

1. Please consult Doctor Smith. / Please consult Dr. Smith.
2. Senator Cranston was interviewed. / Sen. Cranston was interviewed.
3. In the year 55 before Christ's birth, Rome controlled Palestine. / In 55 B.C. Rome controlled Palestine.
4. Terrence Belford, Junior, was in town. / Terrence Belford, Jr., was in town.

5. They returned $3.58. / They returned three dollars and fifty-eight cents.
6. His largest class was Eng. lit. / His largest class was English literature.
7. The Federal Bureau of Investigation was forced to investigate. / The FBI was forced to investigate.
8. Park Ave. is beautiful at Xmas. / Park Avenue is beautiful at Christmas.
9. The first payment is due in Nov. / The first payment is due in November.
10. The men are stationed in Switz. / The men are stationed in Switzerland.

Effective sentences

NOW THAT YOU have studied basic grammar, punctuation, and mechanics, you are ready to use your knowledge of all these elements to write effective sentences. A study of the principles in this section will help you to write an essay, a research paper, or a report that is made up of clear, concise sentences.

25. Subordination (sub)

Subordination is the use of dependent elements to give focus to a main clause or a kernel sentence. Subordination is one way of combining short, choppy sentences into a longer, smoothly integrated one—a technique that requires an understanding of the different types of phrases and clauses explained at the beginning of this handbook. Consider, for example, the following sentences:

> Caedmon was an ignorant herdsman.
> He believed that his poetic powers came from God.

These two sentences may be combined:

> Caedmon was an ignorant English herdsman who believed that his poetic powers came from God.

The second sentence (or independent clause) has been turned into a dependent clause and subordinated to the first. The result is a sentence that is smoother and longer yet still includes all the original information found in its constituent parts.

Many sentences can be subordinated without changing their original sense. Others, however, cannot be subordinated because they express ideas that are equal in value:

> Today, schools provide an education.
> Today, schools do not guarantee jobs.

To subordinate one of these sentences to the other would be to change the original meaning of both:

> Today, schools provide an education because they do not guarantee jobs.

A causal connection, not originally intended, has been established. Sentences such as these should be combined by placing a coordinate conjunction between them:

> Today, schools provide an education, but they do not guarantee jobs.

Subordination can be used only between ideas of unequal importance. Learn to assign the correct value to each sentence and reflect it through a subordinated structure. Consider the following independent clauses:

1. Lake Como is a tourist resort.
2. It is situated in the foothills of the Alps.
3. It is one of the most beautiful spots in Europe.

Through the process of subordination, these three independent clauses can be integrated into one clear and logical sentence:

> Lake Como, a tourist resort situated in the foothills of the Alps, is one of the most beautiful spots in Europe.

The most important independent clauses are 1 and 3, while 2 acquires a less prominent position by becoming a participial phrase and being squeezed into the middle as a parenthetical statement. If we had decided that 1 and 2 were the more important, then the subordinated sentence would have read as follows:

> Lake Como, one of the most beautiful spots in Europe, is a tourist resort situated in the foothills of the Alps.

To subordinate logically as well as coherently, you must decide which ideas are more important and which less, and construct your new subordinated sentence to mirror this decision.

Here are some further examples of subordination. Examine them carefully to see how the combining process works:

Choppy: 1. English architecture evolved in the twelfth century.
2. It began with the Norman style.
3. It was especially noticeable in the Norman churches.
4. These Norman churches have long naves.
5. They also have rectangular east ends.

Better: English architecture evolved in the twelfth century with the Norman style, which was especially noticeable in the Norman churches with their long naves and rectangular east ends.

Here, sentences 2, 3, 4, and 5 are subordinated to sentence 1. Notice, however, that 4 and 5 are combined with the coordinate conjunction *and* because they express ideas of equal value.

Choppy: 1. In ancient Greece, fire was considered one of the four basic elements.
2. It was considered a substance from which the other elements were composed.
3. The other elements were earth, water, and air.

Better: In ancient Greece, fire was considered one of the four basic elements, a substance from which all other elements—earth, air, and water—were composed.

In this combination, 2 is subordinated to 1, while 3 is inserted parenthetically into 2.

Choppy: 1. The speaker raised his hands to silence the audience.
2. The applause continued.
3. It was punctuated by boos.
4. The boos were isolated.

Better: Although the speaker raised his hands to silence the audience, the applause continued, punctuated by isolated boos.

Here, 1 is subordinated to 2; 4 is merged into 3 as an adjective and then attached to 2 as a participial phrase.

In sum, subordination can be achieved in three ways:

Subordinating a clause:

The beggar played his guitar.
He was hungry.

The beggar played his guitar because he was hungry.

or

The beggar, who was hungry, played his guitar.

Subordinating a phrase:

The mountains reach into the sky.
Their peaks are covered with snow.

Their peaks covered with snow, the mountains reach into the sky.

Subordinating a word:

The atmosphere was damp.
It was marked by darkness.

The atmosphere was damp and dark.

NOTE: Beware of the reverse subordination that results when the less important of two ideas is expressed as an independent clause:

Reverse subordination: Although Alex was accepted into Harvard, her entrance examination showed some weakness in vocabulary. (The fact that Alex was accepted into Harvard is the more important fact and should be expressed in the independent clause.)

Correct subordination: Although her entrance examination showed some weakness in vocabulary, Alex was accepted into Harvard.

Reverse subordination: His legs paralyzed for life, he was stricken with polio when he was twelve. (The fact that his legs are paralyzed for life is the more important idea and should be placed in the independent clause.)

Correct subordination: Stricken with polio when he was twelve, he suffered paralysis of the legs for life.

EXERCISE 25: Subordination

By careful subordination, combine the ideas in each of the following sets of sentences into one effective sentence.

MODEL: Marcia was highly intelligent.
Nevertheless she suffered from extreme timidity.
She never learned to hide this timidity.

Ans: **Although Marcia was highly intelligent, she suffered from extreme timidity, which she never learned to hide.**

1. My father died.
   We moved into a small town.
   It was outside of Boston.
   It was called Reading.
   There was almost no intellectual life there.
2. Mary Todd Lincoln longed desperately for Willie's presence.
   She longed for him so desperately that one night she awoke.
   It was midnight.
   She had the impression that Willie was standing at the foot of her bed.
3. He was lying on the bare earth.
   He was shoeless, bearded, and half-naked.
   He looked like a beggar or a lunatic.
4. The frightened hawk lay there for a long minute.
   He had no hope.
   He did not move.
   His eyes were still fixed on that blue vault above him.
5. Ulysses S. Grant and Robert E. Lee met on April 9, 1865.
   They met in the parlor of a modest Virginia house.
   They met to work out the terms for the surrender of Lee's Army of Northern Virginia.
   At this meeting a great chapter in American life came to a close and a great chapter began.
6. The mockingbird took a single step into the air.
   His wings were still folded against his sides.
   He accelerated thirty-two feet per second.
   Just a breath before he would have been dashed to the ground, he unfurled his wings.
   He then gracefully floated onto the grass.
7. Cleopatra worked diligently to learn coquettishness and flattery.
   She was the most famous courtesan of the ancient world.
   She reportedly practiced on slaves.
8. It was a cold, bright December morning.
   It was far out in the country.
   An old Negro woman came along a path through the pinewood.
   Her name was Phoenix Jackson.
   A red tag was tied around her head.
9. The priest nodded.
   Then I surprised the audience.
   I recited a sixteenth century poem about love and commitment.

The poem caused my bride to burst into tears.
I was amazed.

10. I refused many prestigious jobs.
One job I refused was clerking for a judge.
Another job I refused was joining a wealthy law firm.
I favored the public service sector.
11. Most primitive mythologies contain a flood story.
In each of these stories the gods decide to destroy all human beings.
However, they make an exception for one favored family.
This family survives the catastrophe.
Such a family was Noah and his brood.
12. My brother's face remains scarred for life.
When he was a mere baby, he was bitten and scratched by a Siamese cat.
13. There are thousands of marvelous summer resorts in the world.
There is Monte Carlo.
There is Bermuda.
There is Hawaii.
However, I prefer Miami Beach.
14. The highland wind blows steadily from north to northeast.
It is the same wind that blows down on the coasts of Africa and Arabia.
Down there they call it the "monsoon."
"Moonsoon" was the name of King Solomon's favorite horse.
15. I have a vivid picture in mind.
It is a picture of Dr. Albert Schweitzer.
I see him at the age of eighty-four spending most of his time answering his correspondence.
It often consisted of silly questions.

26. Dangling modifiers (dm)

A dangling modifier is a word or a group of words that does not modify anything in the sentence:

> Jogging along the beach, the sun set in a blaze of crimson glory.

A reader who took this sentence literally would think that the setting sun was jogging along the beach. The dangling participle, "jogging along the beach," appears to modify "the sun." Here is one way to correct the sentence:

As I was jogging along the beach, the sun set in a blaze of crimson glory.

Now *I* is the subject of *jogging* and the phrase becomes a dependent clause. Here are some more examples of dangling modifiers:

Dangling: After our fight, she walked toward me while sitting on a bench. (How can she simultaneously walk and sit?)
Better: After our fight, she walked toward me while I was sitting on a bench.

Dangling: Crying her heart out, I was deeply moved by the sound. (How can the speaker cry another person's heart out?)
Better: I was deeply moved when I heard her crying her heart out.

Dangling: Looking to the far end of the football field, there he was. (The participle *looking* has no logical subject at all.)
Better: Looking to the far end of the football field, they saw him.

Dangling modifiers are usually corrected in two ways: by leaving the dangler as is but recasting the remainder of the sentence; or by expanding the dangling part into a complete dependent clause.

NOTE: Certain absolute constructions are exceptions to these rules: (see page 359).

Generally speaking, men are taller than women.
To sum up, cocktail parties are boring.

EXERCISE 26: Dangling modifiers

Indicate which sentences are correct and which contain dangling modifiers. Rewrite the sentences that contain dangling modifiers.

MODEL: While sneaking into our house through the back door, my father confronted me.

Ans: **While I was sneaking into our house through the back door, my father confronted me.**

1. When looking toward the sky, the enormous white clouds sailing across the deep blue are a breathtaking sight.
2. After complaining in two letters, the client finally received his rebate.
3. By showing respect for my teachers, they respected me in return.
4. After gaining her employer's confidence, doors began to open, and opportunities came her way.

5. Coming from a Persian background, her complexion is a lovely deep olive.
6. To be successful, a person must be willing to persevere despite failures.
7. Barking and snarling, the guests were scared by our big German shepherd dog.
8. Having pimples and lacking self-confidence, my grandmother reassured me that someday I would be beautiful.
9. Realizing that a course in western civilization would broaden his political views, Jack enrolled at UCLA.
10. Grease-stained and covered with dust, Margie rediscovered her diary.
11. The wind began to blow immediately after opening the windows.
12. Never having met the instructor, it seemed foolish of her to be so nervous.
13. Truthfully speaking, Miami, Florida, has a *nouveau riche* atmosphere.
14. Before entering the water, the scuba diving equipment should be checked.
15. Sitting in a sidewalk cafe listening to lovely violin music, San Marco Square seemed utterly romantic.

27. Misplaced parts (mp)

A well-constructed sentence raises no uncertainty about which words belong where. Modifiers should stand as close as possible to the words they modify. Notice how each sentence below takes on a different meaning, depending on where the word *only* is placed:

> *Only* I loved her. (No one else did.)
>
> I *only* loved her. (I didn't hate, pity, or envy her.)
>
> I loved *only* her. (I loved no one else.)

A writer must be careful to place modifiers in positions that most clearly convey the meaning intended. The following is an example of a misplaced part:

> The United States has seen its President burned in effigy *on the living room TV.*

The writer has created an absurdity by having the phrase *on the living room TV* modify the verb *burned*. The following version makes clear the writer's intentions:

On the living room TV the United States has seen its President burned in effigy.

Some modifiers, if ambiguously placed between two elements, will seem to modify both:

The waiter who had served them *swiftly* disappeared.

The meaning of the sentence is unclear because it is impossible to know whether the waiter served swiftly or disappeared swiftly. Here are two clearer versions:

The waiter who had served them disappeared *swiftly*.

or

The waiter who had *swiftly* served them disappeared.

Diligent proofreading is a good defense against misplaced parts.

EXERCISE 27: Misplaced parts

Indicate which sentences are correct and which contain misplaced parts. Rewrite the sentences that contain misplaced parts.

MODEL: It only takes Wally ten minutes to clean his room whereas it takes me one full hour.

Ans: **It takes Wally only ten minutes to clean his room whereas it takes me one full hour.**

1. Self-esteem is someone's own sense of his value and strength.
2. I almost love everyone of my neighbors.
3. Those men who had snored loudly greeted the morning.
4. Darwin wrote his famous book on the origin of the species in England.
5. All of the old people may be exposed on this trip to diseased water.
6. Because Marie believed in complete abstinence, she ordered merely a bottle of Perrier water.
7. To our amazement, the man almost spent half of his time collecting buttons from all over the world.
8. Some threadbare woman's underwear lay in the middle of the alley.
9. I discovered a sweater knit by my sister under the snow on the roof of our mountain cabin.
10. Last year, our publishing business grossed nearly a million dollars.
11. No one was allowed to use the condominium tennis courts except people living in the Northridge development.

12. A life of luxury was the only kind of life she knew.
13. All students will not be required to register for the draft.
14. One pedestrian got struck down by a truck emerging from the bus.
15. The carpet was laid on the parquet floor, which was made of silk and tied by hand.

28. Parallelism (//)

Parallelism enables a writer to express equal thoughts by using equal grammatical structures. In a parallel sentence, the writer balances noun against noun, adjective against adjective, infinitive against infinitive to emphasize the equality of ideas. Faulty parallelism upsets this balance of ideas in a sentence:

Awkward: My plan was to fish, hunt, and hiking.
Parallel: My plan was to fish, hunt, and hike.

In short sentences such as the one above the preposition need not be repeated, but in longer sentences it should be.

Parallel prepositional phrases:

He talked to us about devotion ‖ to our family,
to our neighborhood, and
to our country.

Parallel subordinate clauses:

All of us knew ‖ that he was petty,
that he was jealous, and
that he was vain.

Parallel gerunds:

What I despised about him was his ‖ drinking,
gambling, and
cursing.

Parallel independent clauses:

‖ We counted our losses;
we cared for the wounded;
we advanced once again.

28a. Basic rules

There are some basic rules to follow when using parallelism. Do not use *and who* or *and which* unless preceded by another *who* or *which* clause.

Awkward: Pope John Paul II is a man with charisma *and who* is admired throughout the world.
Parallel: Pope John Paul II is a man || who has charisma and
who is admired throughout the world.

When using correlative conjunctions (*either . . . or, neither . . . nor, not only . . . but also, both . . . and*), use parallel constructions to complete the sentence.

Awkward: Either you pay the fine or jail is where you will go. (*Either* is followed by a pronoun, whereas *or* is followed by a noun.)
Parallel: Either || you pay the fine
or || you go to jail.

Awkward: They not only invaded our privacy, but also our time was taken by them. (The *but also* part is in the passive.)
Parallel: They || not only invaded our privacy,
but also wasted our time.

To emphasize parallelism in a sentence, it is sometimes necessary to repeat a preposition, an article, or words in a phrase.

Awkward: She rummaged about in the kitchen, in the basement, and the attic.
Parallel: She rummaged about || *in* the kitchen,
in the basement, and
in the attic.
(The preposition *in* is repeated.)

Awkward: Love is a gift as well as responsibility.
Parallel: Love is || *a* gift as well as
a responsibility.
(The article *a* is repeated.)

Awkward: Where he works and the place he lives are two completely different places.
Parallel: || *Where he* works and
where he lives
are two completely different places.
(*Where he* is repeated.)

EXERCISE 28: Parallelism

Indicate which sentences are correct and which have faulty parallelism. Rewrite the sentences with faulty parallelism.

MODEL: Most of the students in my art class are youths of talent and who want to make a living from their art.

Ans: **Most of the students in my art class are youths who have talent and who want to make a living from their art.**

1. The pleasure of snow skiing comes from the thrill of speeding downhill and that it is out in nature.
2. She told Marie either to clean her fingernails or cut them shorter.
3. His rise had been predicted by astrology, prophecy, and dreams.
4. The crowds at the Olympic games seemed relaxed and enjoying themselves.
5. The father wanted to work rather than have free handouts.
6. He underwrote the cost of the journey, guaranteed revenue to the workers, and promising decent shelter for families with children.
7. My two favorite sports are fishing and to hike.
8. After attending the literature class, Leonard did not feel so much informed on issues as that he had increased his sensitivity to human needs.
9. The assignment was to create a myth about the edges of the universe and read it in class.
10. The bird flew above the tree, beyond the horizon, and into the blue yonder.
11. My salary is not as big as my sister.
12. The king demanded expulsion of the bishops, annihilation of all taxes, and burials.
13. All six of us agreed that we would ride the gondola to the top of the mountain but to hike back.
14. He came; he saw; he conquered.
15. The buildings of our city are black from soot and old age has cracked them.

29. Illogical constructions (ill)

The illogical construction is inexact, confusing, or vague, and may be so for a variety of reasons, a few of which are cataloged below.

29a. Illogical comparisons

Comparisons require that the items being compared be similar and that the comparison be complete. Study the following sentences:

> The rose is prettier than any flower in the world.

Since the *rose* is included in the classification of flower, the sentence is really saying that the rose is prettier than the rose. Here is the comparison logically stated:

> The rose is prettier than any *other* flower in the world.

Another common error is ambiguity resulting from a badly stated comparison:

> He loves me more than his son.

Does he love me more than he loves his son? Or does he love me more than his son loves me? The comparison must be reworded to specify the intended meaning.

Perhaps the most common error in comparisons is incompleteness. Here is a typical example:

> Anacin gives more relief.

More relief than what? Copy writing is replete with this sort of carelessness. Here is an improvement:

> Anacin gives more pain relief than does any other analgesic sold over the counter.

If not marketable, this comparison is at least logically complete. Here are some more examples of comparisons that are illogical and vague because of incompleteness:

Illogical: Women are more aggressive today.
Better: Women are more aggressive today than they were twenty years ago.

Illogical: French chefs cook better meat sauces.
Better: French chefs cook better meat sauces than do American chefs.

or

French chefs cook better meat sauces than they do cream pies.

29b. Mixed constructions

A mixed construction is a sentence that begins in one grammatical pattern but ends in another. Here is an example:

> It was because all members of the firm stood by time-honored moral values that enabled them to survive.

The sentence develops logically until it reaches the word *enabled*, when it takes a sudden lurch into another pattern for which the reader is entirely unprepared. Confusion and misreading will inevitably result. The correct version starts with and ends on the same grammatical pattern thus fulfilling reader anticipation:

> It was because all members of the firm stood by time-honored moral values that they were able to survive.

Here are additional examples of mixed constructions followed by corrected versions. Some of the shifts are subtle variations on the grammatical pattern one would ordinarily anticipate.

Mixed: When the stock market crashed and Sully couldn't get help from anyone, not even Joseph, therefore he committed suicide.
Better: When the stock market crashed and Sully could not get help from anyone, not even Joseph, he committed suicide.

Mixed: As for the effects the large city had on Nancy were typical of what happened to many young people abroad.
Better: As for the effects the large city had on Nancy, they were typical of what happened to many young people abroad.

Mixed: His free will is limited to the circumstances by which his destiny has forced upon him.
Better: His free will is limited by the circumstances his destiny has forced upon him.

EXERCISE 29: Illogical constructions

Indicate which sentences are correct and which contain illogical constructions. Rewrite the sentences that have illogical constructions.

MODEL: The weather in California is far better than New York.

Ans: **The weather in California is far better than the weather in New York.**

1. The first play concerns the blacks and how they maintained their dignity and facing difficulties caused by the whites.
2. It was in my ability to look past the bad in people to the good that helped me to like my classmates.
3. His mother's judgment of financial investments and real estate values is much sharper than his father.
4. Edmund's job pays better than Mark's.
5. A tragic hero is when a tragic flaw causes his downfall.
6. The reason for the decline of Rome was because the Romans had become morally flabby.
7. Mt. Everest is higher than any mountain in the world.
8. It was not until Antony died before Cleopatra realized how much she loved him.
9. The reason education in the United States seems to have become mediocre is that our schools have been asked to educate more illiterate people than ever before.
10. The emphasis on human rights makes America more democratic.
11. When he dissected a frog in biology lab was the experience he remembered years later.
12. We bought an old cabin which by repairing the roof we could use it for camping in during the summers.

30. Shifts (shift)

It is very important to be consistent in your use of tense, mood, person, voice, and discourse. If you shift your point of view, you will confuse your reader.

30a. Tense (shift/t)

Tense is the form of a verb that expresses the time of its action. The correct tense for a verb is normally dictated by the chronology of the situation being written about. Most of us use the proper tense out of habit. However, here are a few general rules:

Use the present tense to express timeless, general truths or prevailing customs:

> Copernicus pointed out that the world *is* (not *was*) not the center of our universe. (Copernicus' discovery was in the past, but the truth of it still applies today.)

The rabbi reminded everyone that the Sabbath *begins* (not *began*) Friday at sunset. (The rabbi's warning was given in the past, but the Jewish sabbath still begins on Friday.)

Indicate differences in time by using different tenses:

Wrong: Eric admitted that he *used* all of the wood.
Right: Eric admitted that he *had* used all of the wood. (Eric must have used up the wood before making the admission.)

Wrong: *Getting* permission from my boss, I will take a day of vacation next week.
Right: *Having gotten* permission from my boss, I will take a day's vacation next week. (The permission has to be granted before the vacation can be taken.)

Indicate simultaneous happenings by using the same tense:

Wrong: Mark waxed his skis while George *gazes* at the mountains.
Right: Mark waxed his skis while George *gazed* at the mountains. (Both the waxing and the gazing happen simultaneously and must therefore be expressed in the same tense.)

Wrong: Because my girlfriend remained at home alone, she *writes* me this melancholy letter.
Right: Because my girlfriend remained home alone, she *wrote* me this melancholy letter. (Both the remaining and the writing took place in the past and therefore require the same past tense.)

Wrong: We had packed our suitcases as well as *ate* our lunch before the train arrived.
Right: We had packed our suitcases as well as *eaten* our lunch before the train arrived. (The packing and eating both took place before the arrival of the train; they therefore require the same past tense.)

30b. Mood (shift/m)

Mood (or mode) indicates under what conditions a statement is being made. In English we have three moods: *indicative*, *subjunctive*, and *imperative*. The indicative mood is used for the majority of declarations ("The fields are blossoming.") or questions ("Do you feel any better?"). The subjunctive mood is used to express a wish ("I wish I *were* wealthy."), a necessity ("It is necessary that he *see* his children."), or a condition contrary to fact ("If she had taken the medicine, she *would be* alive today."). It is also used for a request or an indirect command ("He insisted that the suitcase *be* checked for drugs."). The imperative mood is used for direct commands ("*Give* me liberty or *give* me death!").

When you are writing, make sure you don't shift from one mood to another:

Wrong: They insisted that the money *be* collected and that a receipt *is* given in return. (shift from the subjunctive to the indicative)

Right: They insisted that the money *be* collected and that a receipt *be* given in return.

Wrong: *Pay* your taxes and you *should* also *support* your representatives in Congress. (shift from the imperative to the indicative mood)

Right: *Pay* your taxes and *support* your representatives in Congress.

Don't use *would have* when *had* is sufficient:

Wrong: If I *would have* been born in this country, I *would have* to enlist in the army.

Right: If I *had* been born in this country, I *would have* to enlist in the army. (The *if* clause requires only *had*, not *would have*.)

The subjunctive mood should be used in certain idiomatic expressions:

Come (not *comes*) hell or high water, we'll be there.

NOTES: 1. Study the following rules on how to form the subjunctive.

The present subjunctive of *to be* is invariably *be*:

I demand that he *be* on time.

In all other forms, the subjunctive differs from the indicative only in that in the third person the third-person ending is dropped:

I suggest that she *listen* (not *listens*).

2. *Should* or *would* are often used to indicate suppositions as well as contrary-to-fact conditions:

Should an enemy attack, we *would* go to war.

3. You may prefer to avoid the subjunctive altogether by rewording the sentence:

Subjunctive: Suppose she *were to resign*.

Rewrite: Suppose she *resigns*.

Subjunctive: Let's require *that he sign*.
Rewrite: Let's require *him to sign*.

Subjunctive: It is necessary *that we be* kind.
Rewrite: We *must be* kind.

30c. Person (shift/p)

A writer who doesn't write from a consistent point of view will bewilder the reader. Consider the following:

> Basically each individual creates your own psychological self-portrait; however, others do contribute factors we use in evaluating oneself.

Like surprise flashes of lightning, the writer has struck from four different points of view: *each, your, we, oneself.* This fractured sentence is easily corrected if a single, consistent point of view is established:

> Basically we each create our own psychological self-portrait; however, others do contribute factors we use in evaluating ourselves.

Most point of view errors occur when a writer attempts to speak about people in general. Here is a typical example:

Wrong: *Their* first thought is that *you* can't get the job. (The writer has shifted from *they* to *you*.)
Better: *Their* first thought is that *they* can't get the job.

See also 31. *Pronoun Reference*, for the use of *one* and *you*.

30d. Voice (shift/v)

The voice of a verb tells you whether or not the subject acts or is acted upon:

> The boy ate the doughnut. (Here the subject *boy* is acting; he is eating the doughnut. Therefore, the voice is *active*.)

Now consider this version of the sentence:

> The doughnut was eaten by the boy. (In this case, *doughnut* is the subject and it is being acted on by the boy. Therefore, the voice is *passive*.)

The choice between active or passive voice depends on whether you wish to emphasize the actor or the receiver of an action. As a general rule, the active voice is preferable because it is stronger and more direct than the passive. But whichever you use, don't shift unnecessarily from one voice to another:

Wrong: Although the Black Plague killed thousands of anonymous poor, the rich were attacked by it also.

Better: Although the Black Plague killed thousands of anonymous poor, it also attacked the rich.

Wrong: Jerry devoured a steak, and an entire half gallon of ice cream was eaten by him.

Better: Jerry devoured a steak and ate an entire half gallon of ice cream.

30e. Discourse (shift/d)

Discourse means conversation. Discourse can be direct, as:

> The flight attendant told the passengers, "Fasten your seat belts."

Or it can be indirect, as:

> The flight attendant requested that all passengers fasten their seat belts.

In the first example, the exact words of the speaker are used and enclosed in quotation marks. In the second example, the speaker's exact remarks are paraphrased. You may use either direct or indirect discourse, but you must not shift from one to the other:

Wrong: All of us wondered how the highjacker had boarded the plane and why didn't the security guards catch him? (shift from indirect to direct)

Better: All of us wondered how the highjacker had boarded the plane and why the security guards had not caught him.

Wrong: The salesperson informed me that she was collecting money for the blind and would I buy a broom.

Better: The salesperson informed me that she was collecting money for the blind and asked me if I would buy a broom.

or

The salesperson said, "I am collecting money for the blind. Would you buy a broom?"

EXERCISE 30: Shifts in tense, mood, person, voice, discourse

Identify the kind of needless shift in each of the sentences below and then rewrite the sentences from a single point of view.

MODEL: Their first thought is that we will never learn the dance step.

Ans: **Shift in person**
Their first thought is that they will never learn the dance step.

1. In those early days the primary reason for my happiness lay in the ability I possess to take people for what they are.
2. Henry asked if he could accompany us and would we reserve an airline ticket for him?
3. She swayed back and forth and her body was swung from side to side.
4. When one feels accepted by a peer group, you become a stronger individual.
5. Look for some yeast and you should also pick up a newspaper.
6. His leg was fractured, his face was cut, and he looks like an inflated beach ball.
7. Fine athletes function as role models. If one can measure up, fine; if you can't, you are consigned to the uglies.
8. She held her trophy high, and her medal was worn with pride.
9. As the motorcycle hit the wall, the crowd screams in fear and delight.
10. The crusaders exposed themselves to every peril, and their bodies were given up to the adventure of life in death.
11. The treasurer testified that she just finished her report when the phone rang.
12. Years later she wondered why her youth had been so miserable and how could it have been improved.
13. If he wasn't such a monster of conceit, I would admire him for his talent.
14. The young man declared that he was in love and would she please marry him.
15. The corpses are dragged to the courtyard of the palace and were left there for all to see.

31. Pronoun reference (ref)

Every pronoun must have an antecedent. To avoid faulty pronoun reference, make sure that the antecedents of your pronouns are clear.

Do not use a pronoun that could refer to more than one antecedent:

Wrong: The bartender yelled at Harry that *he* could lose his job. (Is it the bartender or Harry who could lose his job?)

Better: The bartender yelled at Harry, "You could lose your job!" (Recasting the sentence is better than creating an awkward repetition, such as "The bartender yelled at Harry that Harry could lose his job.")

Avoid pronouns that refer to entire clauses or sentences:

Wrong: His room is cluttered; his clothes are wrinkled; and even the pages of his books bear stains of grease. *This* really bothers me. (Three full clauses form the antecedent of *this*; the reference is too broad.)

Better: His room is cluttered; his clothes are wrinkled; and even the pages of his books bear stains of grease. *This sloppiness of his* really bothers me.

Avoid pronouns that have no antecedent:

Wrong: In *Oedipus Rex* there is no free will; *it* was predestined by Apollo. (*It* has no antecedent.)

Better: In *Oedipus Rex* there is no free will; *all of the tragic events* were predestined by Apollo.

Avoid pronouns whose antecedents are only implied by context:

Wrong: John lived in Italy during the first eight years of his life; consequently, he speaks *it* fluently. (The antecedent *Italian* is only implied.)

Better: John lived in Italy during the first eight years of his life; consequently, he speaks *Italian* fluently.

Avoid using *it* or *they* without a clear antecedent:

Wrong: In the *Los Angeles Times it* expressed the opposite point of view. (*It* has no antecedent.)

Better: The *Los Angeles Times* expressed the opposite point of view.

Wrong: *They* say that migraine headaches are often caused by repressed anger. (Who are *they*?)

Better: *Some neurologists* say that migraine headaches are caused by repressed anger.

Notice the following correct uses of the impersonal *it* when referring to weather, time, or distance:

It is foggy today. (weather)
It is precisely two o'clock. (time)
Is it much farther to your house? (distance)

Avoid using *you* and *your* except when addressing the reader specifically.

Wrong: If *you* want to be happily married, *you* have to be willing to sacrifice *your* own pleasure.

Better: People who want to be happily married must be willing to sacrifice their own pleasure.

NOTE: To refer to all human beings or people in general, use general terms like *we, one, a person,* or *people*. Notice, however, that throughout this book we often use the pronoun *you* because we are addressing you, our reader, specifically.

EXERCISE 31: Pronoun reference

Indicate which sentences contain a faulty pronoun reference. Then rewrite those sentences to correct the error.

MODEL: She seemed so young and innocent, which made Helene jealous.

Ans: **Her apparent youth and innocence made Helene jealous.**

1. As serious as our differences may seem, it is a common case of dissimilarities.
2. At midnight the doctor came out and told us that he had survived the surgery.
3. Deprecating comments are made all of the time, and it makes the victim have a low opinion of himself.
4. The nurse's aide lied by writing on the chart that she had been given a bath.
5. She had a house which survived her only three years.
6. The senator squirmed in his seat and avoided the question, which amused the reporters.
7. His best friend warned him that he might get an F.
8. Many youths feel that their environment is prejudiced against them, and this increases their hostility.
9. If I'm having a boring time, it shows on my face.
10. If a person wants to make money, he must learn how to take risks.
11. Although my brother is taking pre-med courses, I doubt if he will ever be one.
12. How far is it to the main library?
13. In Islam they believe that Jesus was a prophet.
14. I was stood up on two separate occasions, which embarrassed me.
15. Since the children want to make some animals out of apple cores, I need to buy some at the store.

Copyrights and Acknowledgments

For permission to use copyrighted material, the authors are grateful to the following publishers and copyright holders:

The Atlanta Constitution for "Series May Be Key to Presidential Race" by Rep. Wyche Fowler. © 1980 *The Atlanta Constitution*.

George MacKay Brown for "Unlucky Boat." Reprinted by permission of the author.

Neeli Cherry for "Every Jew Is a Poet." Reprinted by permission of the author.

Harper & Row, Publishers, Inc. for an excerpt from "Daddy" from *Ariel* by Sylvia Plath. Copyright © 1963 by Ted Hughes. For the excerpt from "Motor Cars" from *One Man's Meat* by E. B. White. Copyright 1940, 1968 by E. B. White.

Holt, Rinehart and Winston, Inc. for "Design" from *The Poetry of Robert Frost*, edited by Edward Connery Lathem. Copyright © 1964 by Lesley Frost Ballantine. Copyright © 1969 by Holt, Rinehart and Winston. Reprinted by permission of Holt, Rinehart and Winston. Reprinted also by permission of the Estate of Robert Frost and Jonathan Cape Ltd.

Olwyn Hughes for an excerpt from "Daddy" by Sylvia Plath, published by Faber and Faber Limited. Copyright Ted Hughes, 1965. Reprinted by permission of Olwyn Hughes.

Alfred A. Knopf for an excerpt from *The Uses of Enchantment: The Meaning and Importance of Fairy Tales* by Bruno Bettelheim. Copyright © 1967 by Bruno Bettelheim. Reprinted by permission of Alfred A. Knopf, Inc.

Little, Brown and Company for an excerpt from "The Waltzer in the House" from *The Poems of Stanley Kunitz: 1928–1978* by Stanley Kunitz. Copyright © 1958 by Stanley Kunitz. Reprinted by permission of Little, Brown and Company in association with Atlantic Monthly Press.

New Directions Publishing Corporation for "This Is Just to Say" from *Collected Earlier Poems* by William Carlos Williams. Copyright 1938 by New Directions Publishing Corporation. Reprinted by permission of New Directions Publishing Corporation.

Virginia Parra for "Psychological Interpretation of 'Every Jew Is a Poet.'" Reprinted by permission of the author.

Michael Swift and the *Los Angeles Times* for "Age Sneaks Up, Leaves You with Compromises." Originally published in the *Los Angeles Times*, February 1, 1982.

Universal Press Syndicate for "Dear Abby," November 7, 1979. Copyright 1979, Universal Press Syndicate. All rights reserved. Reprinted by permission of Universal Press Syndicate.

Index

5
6
D 7
E 8
F 9
G 0
H 1
I 2
J 3

DETAILED CORRECTION CHART FOR HANDBOOK

BASIC GRAMMAR

1 Parts of Speech

- a Verbs
  - (1) Tense
  - (2) Voice
  - (3) Forms
- b Nouns
- c Pronouns
- d Adjectives
- e Adverbs
- f Prepositions
- g Conjunctions
- h Interjections

2 Sentences

- a Subjects and predicates
- b Complements
  - (1) Direct object
  - (2) Indirect object
  - (3) Subject complement
  - (4) Object complement
- c Phrases
  - (1) Prepositional phrases
  - (2) Participial phrases
  - (3) Gerund phrases
  - (4) Infinitive phrases
  - (5) Absolute phrases
  - (6) Appositive phrases
  - (7) Verbals
- d Clauses
  - (1) Independent clauses
  - (2) Dependent clauses
  - (3) Noun clauses
  - (4) Adjective clauses
  - (5) Adverb clauses
- e Kinds of sentences
  - (1) Simple sentences
  - (2) Compound sentences
  - (3) Complex sentences
  - (4) Compound-complex sentences

3 Sentence Fragments

4 Comma Splices

- a Correcting comma splices
  - (1) Comma and coordinating conjunction
  - (2) Semicolon
  - (3) Period
  - (4) Subordination

5 Run-on Sentences

- a Correcting run-on sentences
  - (1) Comma and coordinating conjunction
  - (2) Semicolon
  - (3) Period
  - (4) Subordination

6 Agreement

- a Subject-verb agreement
  - (1) Unusual word order
  - (2) Intervening words
  - (3) Special words and word connectors
- b Pronoun-antecedent agreement

7 Pronoun Case

- a Using the subjective case
- b Using the objective case
- c Using the possessive case

8 Adjectives and Adverbs

- a Adjectives and adverbs after sense verbs
- b Confusing adjectives and adverbs
- c Comparative and superlative forms
- d Don't convert nouns to adjectives